Major Leagues

To
Patty,
who changed my life
and
who I thank for putting up with
my passion for baseball

MAJOR LEAGUES

The Formation, Sometimes Absorption
and Mostly Inevitable Demise of
18 Professional Baseball Organizations,
1871 to Present

by
David Pietrusza

with a Foreword by
LEE MACPHAIL

McFarland & Company, Inc., Publishers
Jefferson, North Carolina, and London

Acknowledgments

In any endeavor of this nature one depends on a number of friends – both old and new. To all who aided me I offer heartfelt thanks for their selfless assistance.

First, gratitude to the staffs of the National Baseball Library at Cooperstown, New York (Tom Heitz, Bill Deane and company), the Newark, New Jersey, Public Library, the Albany, New York, Public Library, the Schenectady, New York, Public Library and the New York State Library. For his invaluable assistance on the United States League, thanks to Frank Phelps of King of Prussia, Pennsylvania, the foremost expert on the topic. For the generous use of his unpublished research on the Colonial League, thanks to Jack Kavanagh of North Kingston, Rhode Island. For data on Henry Lucas' Union Association thanks to Ralph Horton of St. Louis, Missouri, who through his reprinting of the old Reach and Spalding Guides has invaluably aided so many baseball researchers.

Gracias for help on the Mexican League to Bill Williamson of Glendale, California; Jim McCurdy, San Benito, Texas; John Holway of Alexandria, Virginia; and especially Jim Overmyer of Pittsfield, Massachusetts, who has unearthed new material on its relationship to the Negro leagues. For information on the always-amusing Global League my gratitude to Tom Tuley and Dave Johnson of the Evansville *Courier* and to Hall of Famer Enos Slaughter. Gratitude goes out to Chuck Hershberger of Pleasant Ridge, Michigan, not only for info on the Western League and for more-recent defunct entities, but for his constant encouragement.

Special kudos to veteran researcher Joseph M. Overfield of Buffalo, New York, for his assistance on Buffalo's role in the International Association, the Players' League, the Federal League and the Continental League. For use of the photographs seen here, thanks go out to Joe Overfield, W. Lloyd Johnson, the National Baseball Library and Edward J. Kennedy. A special note of appreciation for David Walsh of Glenville, New York, who had the unenviable job – somebody had to do it – of proofing and offering critical – and invariably helpful – comments on this manuscript.

And most of all thanks and love to my wife Patty, who never once discouraged my curiosity about such topics as the Union Association or Walter J. Dilbeck, and cheerfully helped once again in the truly gruesome task of indexing and proofing, and has made my life an absolute joy.

British Library Cataloguing-in-Publication data are available

Library of Congress Cataloguing-in-Publication Data

Pietrusza, David, 1949–
    Major leagues : the formation, sometimes absorption and mostly
    inevitable demise of 18 professional baseball organizations, 1871 to
    present / by David Pietrusza.
        p. cm.
    Includes bibliographical references (p. 343) and index. ∞
    ISBN 0-89950-590-2 (lib. bdg. : 50# alk. paper)
    1. Baseball – History – 19th century. 2. Baseball – History – 20th
    century. 3. Baseball – United States – History – 19th century.
    4. Baseball – United States – History – 20th century. I. Title.
    GV875.A1P54 1991
    796.357'64'0973 – dc20   90-53521
                                                       CIP

Manufactured in the United States of America

McFarland & Company, Inc., Publishers
  Box 611, Jefferson, North Carolina 28640

Contents

Foreword

by Lee Macphail

As a former American League president, I can tell you how a major league is run. I can inform you about scheduling, assigning umpires, discipline and fines and about the 101 mundane details that go into operating a big league.

What I cannot so effortlessly tell you is how a major league is formed. I came to the American League presidency three-quarters of a century after Ban Johnson and Connie Mack and John McGraw turned a fairly successful minor league into one of the two great majors. The struggle of these historic figures is well documented here, as are those of William Hulbert, Albert Spalding and Morgan Bulkeley in establishing the senior circuit, the National League.

These are success stories, but most often the attempt has ended fruitlessly. So here, too, are such erstwhile circuits as the National Association, the American Association, the Mexican League and the Federal League. Those leagues lasted for a few seasons, but their longevity topped such flops as the Union Association, the Players' League, and the United States and Global leagues.

What David Pietrusza has done is to recount the story—for the first time—of how such enterprises are formed, how they succeed, why they failed, the men who made them, and the playing talent they showcased. But there's more; it's how the game developed from a loose consortium of teams in the National Association of the 1870s to the million—billion—dollar business of today.

It's all here: the initiation of the reserve clause, the weeding out of gambling by the National League, the building of Wrigley Field for the Federal League, the plight of the Mexican League jumpers, the expansion efforts of the 1960s, and the story of Branch Rickey's and Bill Shea's Continental League.

Right now, there is even talk of forming a third major league; it is probably idle chatter, but someday there could be a genuine challenge to the organized structure of the game. If its organizers wish to learn the triumphs and tragedies, the victories and blunders, of those who have gone before, I recommend this volume to them. And the same goes for any serious scholar of the game. The various major leagues have formed the structure by which our great game has thrived. Their history is an integral part of our national game.

Prologue

Baseball is a game of inches, but it is also a game of leagues. It wasn't until the founding of the first professional league, the National Association in 1871, that baseball truly put itself in the position of being the "National Pastime."

Thousands may play the game professionally and millions may take to amateur diamonds, but it is the major leagues that dictate to the game its structure and its rules, which serve as the primary vehicle for the continuing popularity — and profitability — of the game.

What this book attempts to do is to fix a careful eye on what goes into a major league's success or failure.

To accomplish this, we must go beyond looking at the American and National leagues. Of course, we will peruse them, and in some detail, because they are prime examples of how to succeed. But we shall also put the microscope to such circuits as the National Association and the American Association, leagues that established themselves as full-fledged major leagues but ultimately fizzled. And we shall go beyond even that to such entities as the Players' League, the Federal League and the Union Association, circuits which collapsed after just a season or two.

But there is territory to explore even beyond that, in the domain of the Global League, the United States League and various circuits which threatened to operate but never did.

From all of these cases we can determine four criteria for the survival or demise of a projected major league:

1. *Money.* This may seem pretty basic, but you'd be surprised how often someone starting a new enterprise of any sort forgets that sufficient capital is necessary to surmount the red ink of those rough early years. The Union League and Mexican League, for example, each had one strong source of funds but little overall strength. Both failed.

2. *Leadership.* The National League had William Hulbert and the American League possessed Ban Johnson (or was it the other way around?). The Feds were blessed with "Fighting Jim" Gilmore, but other loops were not as lucky. The American Association had a lot of advantages, but it ultimately collapsed due to lack of leadership, as did the National Association. The

Players' League had a lot going for it, but despite the talents of John Montgomery Ward, it had no dictatorial figure at the top. Someone is needed to keep the boys in line when things get tough.

3. *Player dissatisfaction.* The National and American leagues attracted large numbers of the very best players in the game. So did the Players' League, but the Union Association and the Federal League signed only marginal talent, and the United States and Global leagues attracted no talent whatsoever. (Who says players are dumb?) Without the big stars the public will be wary of any new circuit.

4. *Necessity.* This point consists of the basic question, "Is this league *really* necessary?" The National Association, National League, American Association, American League and Continental League filled real voids. Did the Union Association or Federal League? Was there a crying need for three major league teams in St. Louis in 1914? Or for a big league club in Altoona in 1884?

It may be fairly asked why the Negro leagues are not included in this book. Certainly, their playing talent, organization and longevity compare favorably with many of the circuits examined here. But the Negro leagues did not see themselves as rivals to the white leagues. They inhabited different financial and social universes, and while their talent may have been awesome, their goals were more modest than the often-grandiose purposes stated by such entities as the United States League or Daniel Fletcher's League. For those wishing to learn more about the Negro leagues I recommend the invaluable works of Robert Peterson and John Holway.

A study of the formation—and demise—of projected major leagues sheds a unique perspective on the history of baseball. I hope you enjoy it.

David Pietrusza
Scotia, New York
February 1991

Chapter 1

The National Association

Baseball didn't start out in leagues; it began as a child's game, in fields and in vacant lots, taking a good while to evolve even to rounders and townball, let alone into the prestigious amateur teams like the Knickerbockers and Atlantics that flourished in the New York City area just prior to the Civil War.

Those first organized teams were the banding together of gentlemen, their clubs composed of merchants and lawyers and clerks. Commercialized sports seemed an oxymoron, but as baseball's popularity burgeoned in mid-century, it was inevitable in capitalist America that the national game would be played for profit.

The first money involved was on bets. Each side would put up an often-sizable amount, with the money to be divided among winning club members.

As early as 1858 admissions were charged (50 cents on July 20, 1858, for a game between Brooklyn and New York players; 4,000 fans attended). Then came the paying of players. At first, compensation was under the table, and baseball, as historian Harold Seymour has noted, "entered a twilight zone between amateurism and professionalism, a semi-professional period in which hypocrisy reigned."

"Rounders" or "revolvers" shifted from club to club depending on who bid the highest, often by lucrative no-show jobs. The Mutuals of New York, for example, were controlled by the infamous William Marcy "Boss" Tweed, and team members could all be found on the city payroll, usually in the street-sweeping or coroner's departments. Tweed's patronage cost taxpayers $30,000 annually.

The Mutuals were not alone. The Athletics, the Atlantics and the Unions of Morrisania employed these tactics. The federal Treasury Department was the haunt of many of Washington's "amateur" players. In Troy, New York, political employment, as well as jobs in local private industry, were benefits accruing to the Haymaker Club.

Conflicting accounts exist of the nature and extent of professionalism at the close of the 1860s. One version reports players' salaries were paid openly in upstate New York, Columbus, Baltimore, Fort Wayne, Pittsburgh, Chicago and Cincinnati.

Another contends that by 1869 there were as many as seven "professional" clubs: the New York Mutuals, the Brooklyn Atlantics, the Washington Nationals, the Unions of Lansingburgh, the Excelsiors of Chicago, the Athletics of Philadelphia and the club which history remembers as the "first" of the professionals—the Red Stockings of Cincinnati.

The First Professional Team

The first fully—and openly—salaried squad was the renowned 1869 Cincinnati Red Stockings. Their situation was made possible by an 1868 action of the National Association of Baseball Players, the governing amateur body. It repealed the prohibition against National Association clubs playing against teams employing professionals. With this simple act, history was set in motion.

Cincinnati's Aaron B. Champion, a 26-year-old lawyer, boldly organized this new venture, initially raising $11,000 to beautify the team's existing field and to recruit players. Shortly thereafter he floated another stock issue of $15,000 to further strengthen personnel.

Even for the Red Stockings the move to full professionalism was gradual. In 1868 only four members drew salaries, but the remainder were all compensated via shares of the gate receipts. Such schemes were not uncommon (the Athletics, the Mutuals and the Atlantics were all doing it as well), and the practice would continue after 1869.

The '69 Red Stockings salary structure, as found in *Baseball: Diamond in the Rough* by Irving Leitner, was as follows:

Harry Wright	$1,800
George Wright	1,800
Asa Brainard	800
Charles Gould	800
Fred Waterman	800
Charles J. Sweasy	700
Douglas Allison	700
Andrew J. Leonard	700
Cal McVey	700
Richard Hurley	600
	$9,400 TOTAL

Not all of Harry Wright's players could be described as gentlemen. Ace hurler Asa "Count" Brainard was a hypochondriac and a carouser. In one game Brainard was distracted by a rabbit on the field. As he held onto the ball and drew a bead on the varmint, two runs scored. Brainard had married Mary Truman (sister of Margaret Truman, knitter of the original footwear which gave the team its name) but deserted her after the 1870 season.

The 1868 Cincinnati Red Stockings. Members of the famed 1869 Reds pic-
tured are Harry Wright (seated at left), Charlie Gould (seated third from left)
and Asa Brainard (standing at right). (Courtesy of National Baseball Library,
Cooperstown, New York.)

The Red Stockings undertook a remarkable 12,000-mile tour in which they
went undefeated, with 56 victories and one tie (resulting from the Haymakers'
walking off the field in the sixth inning so that gamblers would not have to pay
off an estimated $17,000). Eventually, the winning streak reached an amazing
80 games. In their first fully professional season, the Red Stockings played
before 200,000 paying fans. When their streak was snapped in 1870 by the
Brooklyn Atlantics, to see the historic game 9,000 persons had each laid down
50 cents, and every Atlantic took home $364.

Professionalism was here to stay, although the actual profit by the Red
Stockings for the season was a mere $1.39!

By the start of the 1870 season, the New York *Times* was able to report
on the status of 18 professional clubs and their method of compensation via the
following chart:

CLUB	LOCATION	SYSTEM
Atlantic	Brooklyn, N.Y.	Share gate money
Athletics	Philadelphia, Pa.	Pay by salary
Cincinnati	Cincinnati, Ohio	Pay by salary

The 1870 New York Mutuals, claimants to the unofficial title of champions of professional baseball. (Courtesy of National Baseball Library, Cooperstown, New York.)

CLUB	LOCATION	SYSTEM
Chicago	Chicago, Ill.	Pay by salary
Eckford	Brooklyn, N.Y.	Share gate money
Forest City	Rockford, Ill.	Share gate money
Irvington	Irvington, N.Y.	Share gate money
Keystone	Philadelphia, Pa.	Share gate money
Kentucky	Louisville, Ky.	Pay by salary
Mutuals	New York, N.Y.	Pay by salary
Maryland	Baltimore, Md.	Pay by salary
Nationals	Washington, D.C.	Appointed to office
Olympic	Washington, D.C.	Appointed to office
Olympic	Baltimore, Md.	Share gate money
Olympic	Philadelphia, Pa.	Share gate money
Tri-Mountain	Boston, Mass.	Pay by salary
Union	Lansingburgh, N.Y.	Share gate money
Union	Morrisania, N.Y.	Share gate money

As no league existed, differences of opinion could exist over who the actual champion of the professional world was. For 1870 both the White Stockings of Chicago and the Mutuals of New York laid claim to the title and both had "whip-flags" sewed up and displayed. Chicago's was exhibited in business manager Tom Foley's saloon.

Such confusion would be another impetus to institution of the first defined league.

Formation of the National Association

Many more clubs began openly paying their players, and by late 1870 the National Association of Baseball Players proposed restrictions against the tide of professionalism. In November in New York a resolution condemning the practice was defeated 17–9.

At first the professionals failed to respond to the threat of a crackdown by the amateurs. As each month passed in the winter of 1870–71 their chances of success seemed to grow slowly dimmer.

Then in March 1871 a fully professional league was advanced: the National Association of Professional Base Ball Players.

Among its advocates were sportswriters Henry Chadwick of the New York *Clipper* and Al Wright of the Philadelphia *Mercury*—but so too were many of the players.

Aaron Champion had been forced out as Red Stockings president by cost-conscious stockholders, and Harry Wright switched allegiance to a new Boston club, headed by Iver Adams. Wright's new salary was to be $2,500. The trend to professionalism, though, did not seem inevitable to Wright, who felt that there remained considerable Eastern opposition to outright commercialism. On a player-recruiting trip to Rockford, Illinois, he sought out a 19-year-old, hard-throwing pitcher named Albert Goodwill Spalding. Wright proposed Spalding "join a club [Boston] ostensibly amateur but really professional."

Spalding would have none of that.

"I had determined to enter Baseball as a professional," he later wrote. "I was neither ashamed of the game nor of my attachment to it. Mr. Wright was there to offer . . . cash. . . . Why then go before the public under false pretenses? The assumption of non-professionalism would not deceive anyone. It was not possible that any could be found so simple as to believe that [we] were in the game merely for healthful and philanthropic reasons. We went over the whole subject, thrashed it out in all its bearings, and finally agreed to come out openly and above-board as a professional organization."

On March 4, 1871, ten clubs attended a preliminary session of the National Association of Professional Base Ball Players. Then, on St. Patrick's Day at Collier's Rooms, a rather tony Broadway barroom run by a well-known New York City actor of the day, representatives of the professional clubs met to form this new league. Time was running out; the new season was about to begin, and they had only that single evening to lay the groundwork.

Boston Red Stockings recruit Al Spalding campaigned against the pretense of amateurism for the National Association. (Courtesy of National Baseball Library, Cooperstown, New York.)

Officers were quickly chosen: James N. Kearns, a United States Marshall and a representative of the Philadelphia Athletics, as president; J. S. Evans of the Forest City club as vice president; Nicholas E. Young of the Olympic club as secretary; J. W. Schofield of the Haymakers as treasurer; and Harry Wright as head of the Steering Committee.

Nick Young is an interesting example of the individuals involved in the new enterprise.

Born in 1840 in the small New York village of Fort Johnson, Young was one of 15 children born to Almarin Young, a prosperous New York City importer of Swiss watches who had come upstate for health reasons. In fact, Nick was born in the former home of baronial English Indian-trader Sir William Johnson. As the senior Young's fortunes waned due to the Panic of 1857, he moved his family to nearby Amsterdam, where he was appointed postmaster by newly elected President Lincoln. There Nick played not baseball, but cricket. He volunteered for service in the Civil War and became proficient in the new game of baseball, helping organize the Olympic Club of Washington, for whom he played right field in 1867. For regular employment he held an accounting position with the United States Treasury Department.

The new National Association was organized partially on Young's suggestion, and in it he would manage teams in Washington and Baltimore and would even umpire.

In their haste, the first organizers adopted the rules of the old amateur group wholesale, even though they did not have a copy at hand; Nick Young was instructed to write to the old Association for a copy.

The New York *Clipper* was gratified by the unanimity displayed: "The moment the association had been permanently organized everything went on as harmoniously as a club meeting. In fact, we have never attended any convention of the fraternity which reflected so much credit on the delegates and the clubs they so ably represented."

A partial reason for such smooth sailing was that important issues were simply swept under the rug. Membership was open to any entity producing the $10 franchise fee, opening the door to any number of weak clubs that would eventually cripple the Association. Even for this small amount, some delegates apologized, noting it was necessary for the purchase of the championship pennant.

Critical issues were left to individual clubs. No staff of Association umpires existed (or would ever exist). Umpires were chosen by the home clubs, and were unpaid. Ironically, in this new consortium of professional players, compensation for umpires was still considered demeaning. Even Henry Chadwick still held to this archaic notion. Each volunteer arbiter had his own style—of balls and strikes, of dress, where he took his position on the field. It was chaos.

And then there was scheduling. The Association prescribed that each club play its rivals five times annually and that no game would occur later than November 1 so the pennant could be awarded on November 15. It did not even bother to draw up a schedule, leaving individual clubs to arrange such details. This was a big portion of the organizational meeting, as teams scurried about to garner the choicest dates.

Nor did the Association dictate on the issue of ticket prices. Most clubs eventually settled on a 50 cent admission charge, of which two-thirds reverted to the home club. But there was no fixed rule, and this issue proved to be a bone of contention for the life of the circuit.

The National Association's original roster consisted of the Philadelphia Athletics; Forest City of Rockford, Illinois; the Chicago White Stockings; Forest City of Cleveland; the Boston Red Stockings; the Troy Haymakers; the New York Mutuals; the Washington Olympics; the Washington Nationals; and the Kekiongas of Fort Wayne, Indiana.

The Brooklyn Eckfords, who were to have joined, ducked out at the last minute, not wanting to risk $10 on a venture they feared would not succeed. They did enroll in midseason as a replacement for the ill-fated Kekiongas. Joining as they did, they were barred by initial agreement from any chance at the pennant.

Also noticeably absent were the Cincinnati Red Stockings, who after two seasons of artistic but not financial success, reverted to amateur status in consideration of Harry Wright's jumping ship to Boston.

The First Professional Season: 1871

Even before Opening Day the National Association saw history made. In March, 11 White Stockings, headed by captain Jimmy Wood, embarked on the first southern spring training trip, heading for New Orleans, a city they had visited the previous year but not for training purposes.

The very first National Association contest was Cleveland at Fort Wayne on May 4, 1871. Before approximately 200 fans, Cleveland's James "Deacon" White was the first batter. (Oddly enough, the first leadoff hitter was a catcher.) He achieved a number of other "firsts" during that contest: first hit, first extra-base hit (a double) and first time hitting into a double play. White went 3 for 4 as his team lost to the Kekiongas 2–0.

It was to be the lowest-scoring game in the first four years of the Association.

For the record, here is the box score of the first major league game:

Cleveland	AB	R	H	O	A	Fort Wayne	AB	R	H	O	A
J. White, c	4	0	3	9	0	Williams, rf	4	0	0	4	0
Kimball, 2b	4	0	0	3	4	Mathews, p	4	0	0	1	0
Pabor, cf	4	0	0	0	0	Foran, 3b	3	0	1	2	0
Allison, rf	4	0	1	2	0	Goldsmith, 2b	3	0	0	3	1
E. White, lf	3	0	0	1	0	Lennon, c	3	1	1	9	1
Pratt, p	3	0	0	1	0	Carey, ss	3	0	0	3	1
Sutton, 3b	3	0	1	0	0	Mincher, lf	3	0	0	2	0
Carleton, 1b	3	0	0	6	0	McDermott, cf	3	0	1	0	1
Bass, ss	3	0	0	2	3	Kelley, 1b	3	1	1	3	0
	31	0	5	24	7		29	2	4	27	4

```
Cleveland     0 0 0  0 0 0  0 0 0 – 0
Fort Wayne    0 1 0  0 1 0  0 0 x – 2
```

Opposite left: Nick Young, a founding father of the National Association; right: Al Reach, called by some baseball's first paid player.

First base by errors—Cleveland 4, Fort Wayne 0. Two-base hits—J. White, Lennon. Double play—Carey (Unassisted). Walks, by—Mathews 1, Pratt 1. Strikeouts, by—Mathews 6. Passed balls—J. White 2, Lennon 1. Umpire—J. L. Boake. Time—2 hours.

The White Stockings of Chicago faced a unique problem in 1871. In early October, the Great Chicago Fire destroyed the club's new 7,000-seat Union Base-Ball Grounds. The Pale Hose, aided by free railroad passes, concluded their campaign on the road in borrowed uniforms. ("Not one of the nine were dressed alike," noted one report, "all the uniforms having been consumed at the fire. They presented a most extraordinary appearance from the parti-colored nature of their dress. All who could get White Stockings did so, but they were not many.") They lost their last three contests (two to the Haymakers and one to the Athletics) and saw their chance at the pennant fade.

Despite being paid off by their insurance policy at only ten cents on the dollar for the $4,000 Union Grounds, the club showed a net $2,000 profit. The financial report was given from memory by Secretary Ed Thatcher, whose records had perished in the flames.

Not everyone was in a rush to restore baseball to the Windy City. "Chicago," observed the New York *Clipper,* "will want all her means to supply the necessities of life, and in re-building her homes for their suffering people for a year at least, . . . therefore, . . . dealing in such a recreative luxury as a professional base ball club" was clearly not possible. Others such as Chicago *Tribune* publisher Joseph Medill shared such sentiments.

The club determined to go on, but not right away. One faction dubbing itself the "Phoenix Base Ball Club" tried to recruit amateurs to fill its now-empty roster (most had moved onto a new Philadelphia club dubbed the "White Stockings" in their honor). The majority was more conservative. It first secured a new park on the South Side and rented it out to raise funds to recruit a respectable professional nine. The White Stockings would have to wait until 1874 to rejoin the Association.

The 1871 pennant was not finally decided until a November 3 National Association meeting in Philadelphia. Because the fatality rate for clubs was high in those days—and would remain so for quite some time—rules existed as to which games against defunct clubs would be counted in the official standings.

Going into the session the margin separating Chicago, Boston and the Athletics was razor-thin. The White Stockings and Athletics had 21 victories each, the Red Stockings 20. When games versus Rockford (the Forest Cities had used an ineligible player, Scott Hastings) and Brooklyn were reversed, the Athletics emerged as champions.

It was all very confusing, but every decision (including one concerning the Washington Olympics and their use of an ineligible player) favored the

Philadelphians. Neither Chicago (which was not represented at the session) nor Boston was pleased, but the Athletics were Association champions.

After that first National Association season the champion Athletics under Hicks Hayhurst saw fit to display their pennant in a local saloon. Harry Wright was enraged. "To elevate the National Game we must earn the respect of all; and now the Athletics are Champions—first legal and recognized champion of the United States—they will be looked up to as exponents of what is right and wrong in baseball, and will have it in their power, in a great measure, to make the game a success—financially and otherwise. . . ."

Wright had a point, but may also have been expressing sour grapes over the circumstances regarding awarding of the championship to the Athletics.

Financially, the Athletics were a modest success in their pennant-winning year, earning a $200 profit after expenses, which included salaries of $22,457.14. Diminutive English-born Al Reach served as an interesting contrast to George Wright on the Philadelphia club. He earned pennies as a Brooklyn newsboy and iron molder, but like Wright became a multimillionaire sporting goods dealer. Starting with the Eckfords in 1861, he switched to the Athletics in 1865 for $25 in "expense money." Some say he was the first paid player. In 1871, his career year, he was named by the New York *Clipper* as the first All-Star second baseman as he hit a robust .353.

Ball Yards

Ballparks were rudimentary affairs, roughly hewn stands meant to last only a few years. In 1870 Chicago had played at Dexter Park, a racetrack that featured two significant disadvantages: a five-mile distance from downtown and a grandstand too far from the diamond. The White Stockings' new park, the Union Grounds, had been a dump situated on Michigan Avenue near Lake Michigan. It featured a two-tiered grandstand as well as bleachers, and was surrounded by a cheaply built six-foot-high white wooden fence. Distances from home plate averaged 375 feet. Men and women were seated separately, with gentlemen having preference; a separate section accommodated city officials. Season tickets cost $15 and holders were promised their seats would not be given out in their absence.

As noted earlier, the Union Grounds burned in the Great Chicago Fire of 1871. The Chicago Base Ball Club replaced it with a park (The 23rd Street Grounds) at 23rd and State, but on July 15, 1874, it also burned. This time not so much of Chicago was destroyed (a relatively small 19 blocks) and the White Stockings salvaged their equipment. Games were relocated to Ogden Park for the remainder of the season.

Brooklyn's Union Grounds served as home for the Mutuals, the Eckfords and the Brooklyn Atlantics, as well as for two contests of the 1873 Elizabeth (N.J.) Resolutes. Built near the East River by William Cammeyer in 1862, it was the first enclosed park and featured a horseshoe-shaped single-decked grandstand.

But this was not Brooklyn's only park. The Atlantics played at the Capitoline Grounds at the beginning of the 1872 season before moving over to the Union Grounds in mid-campaign. In centerfield of the Capitoline Grounds stood a little round brick house. Anyone hitting a ball over it received a bottle of champagne.

In Washington, the Olympic club also played at a variety of sites: the Olympic Grounds, shared with the Nationals in 1872–73, with a seating capacity of just 500; the White Lot, just across from the White House, where President Andrew Johnson viewed amateur contests in the 1860s; and occasionally at the Maryland Avenue Park.

Fort Wayne went all-out to welcome its short-lived N.A. franchise with a new ballpark. Commented *The Old Fort News:* "The local citizenry, visualizing a possible championship for their fine team, jumped into the project with a vengeance and raised funds to erect a beautiful ornamented grandstand. . . . The grandstand was finished and christened 'The Old Duchess,' so lavish was its construction."

Boston's South End Grounds was a portrait in extremes. The dimensions were 250 to left, 445 to left-center, 440 feet to center, 440 to right-center and 155 to right. Its infield was totally bereft of grass.

Philadelphia's Athletics Park housed both the Athletics and the less-talented White Stockings. In 1871 a scribe commended it for its press facilities: "The reporters' stand will be placed directly back of the catcher and will be sufficiently elevated to be out of reach of strong foul balls that may chance their way."

The Troy Haymakers played at three parks: Rensselaer Park, the Bull's Head Tavern Grounds and Green Island Park, which was located on an island in the Hudson River.

Rockford's home field for its lone National Association season, Fairgrounds Park, was described thus: "A poorer field, to my mind, has never been known. There was a cluster of five trees around third base. The catcher was hemmed in by trees with the exception of a space about 30 by 50 feet. The umpire could not see a foul unless it was hit back of the plate or a few feet on either side of the base lines.

"Between the plate and second base the terrain was fairly level, but approaching third base there was a notable rise. From third to the plate there was a depression. The baserunner had to dig for life.

"At the edge of the outfield was a deep gutter that drained a nearby quarter-mile track. Only Providence's protection kept more players from breaking legs in that trap. Bad as the playing field was, all the stars of the day came there to do [their] stuff."

At these new parks crowds could be partisan. In Chicago, noted actress

Lotta Crabtree became so agitated she broke her parasol over the head of an unsuspecting stranger. In Cincinnati, a game against Boston was called after the fifth inning when the crowd surged onto the field making it "impossible to proceed with the game." In prim and proper Boston in 1874 the umpire had to be spirited off the grounds to avoid injury following a game against the Athletics. "The whole affair," noted the Boston *Journal* with some embarrassment, "was an unusual one for Boston."

Boston and the Wright Brothers

It was these Red Stockings who dominated the new circuit, and it was baseball's Wright brothers, George and Harry, who had a major impact upon the game.

Brought from Sheffield, England, as an infant by his father, a celebrated cricket player, Harry first excelled in that sport for Staten Island's St. George Cricket Club. He later earned $1,200 per season with Cincinnati's Union Cricket Club. In 1858 he switched to baseball, joining the Knickerbocker Club. In 1868 he had put together the Cincinnati Red Stockings and by 1869 converted them into the first all-openly professional team, revolutionizing the game. He also caused a fashion revolution when Cincinnati became the first club to wear knickers instead of long pants.

By the 1870s Harry was already being called "The Father of the Game." (Oddly enough, George Wright was elected to the Hall of Fame in 1937, while his brother had to wait until 1953.) His Red Stockings would take the pennant in 1872, 1873, 1874 and 1875.

Wright's presence dominated the Association; some dubbed it "Harry Wright's League." He drilled his players endlessly on fundamentals, developed new strategies such as backing up plays, and made stars of players previously regarded as discipline problems, like former Hartford pitcher Tommy Bond. "It shall be our endeavor to develop all the good there is in him," wrote Wright, "and restrain all the bad. In fact to make a man of him, if it is in him. . . . A pitcher we know he is."

Wright was the product of his era, with an emphasis on professionalism and gentlemanly conduct. "In regard to diet," he advised, "roast beef rare will aid, live regularly, keep good hours, and abstain from intoxicating drinks and tobacco."

Overall, he managed professionally for 23 seasons, and though burdened late in his career by mediocre Philadelphia teams, his lifetime percentage was still an amazing .581.

Star of the team was his brother, slick-fielding George Wright, widely credited with being the first shortstop to play beyond the baselines. Henry Chadwick wrote of his "sure catching of high balls" and his "swift accurate throwing." His .917 lifetime fielding average was remarkable in an age when

gloves were unknown; no other contemporary shortstop maintained a .900 average. Wright's hitting was nothing to be ashamed of either. In one pre–Association season he hit 59 homers in 66 games. His National Association averages ranged from .336 to .409.

Following his playing days, George became a prominent sporting goods dealer with the firm of Wright & Ditson. He is credited with playing the first game of golf in New England, and possibly the United States, and with importing and manufacturing the first tennis equipment in the nation. In 1903 he served on the blue-ribbon Mills Commission, which settled upon Cooperstown as the birthplace of the game.

It is ironic that the Red Stockings barely survived beyond the 1872 season. A fire ravaged Boston that year, and financially the club was in poor shape. Albert Spalding was owed $800 in salary and took a job with the New York *Graphic* to make ends meet. A club meeting held at Brackett's Hall in December 1872 to salvage Red Stockings finances had an attendance of 150, 50 of whom pledged financial support.

The Red Stockings were saved, and when their first pennant, 36 feet long, was unfurled on January 2, 1873, it mistakenly—but prophetically—read "CHAMPIONS 1873."

Spreading the Gospel Overseas

Scheduling games in the National Association was still a joke. The Association, drawing up no itinerary whatsoever, saw clubs fail to fulfill their meager obligation to play each rival five times annually. Some Eastern clubs declined to go west at all.

Yet while some neglected to fulfill their Association touring obligations, others were eager to embark on arduous missionary work for the new sport.

In 1872 the Boston Red Stockings diverted from their regular schedule to promote baseball in Canada, visiting London, Guelph, Toronto, Dundas, Ottawa and Montreal.

In 1874 the Red Stockings, along with James Ferguson's Philadelphia Athletics, took time off from their Association schedule in late July and the entire month of August and headed for England. Although Harry Wright had long yearned to introduce the game to his homeland, there were other less-sentimental reasons for the junket, and these he revealed in a letter to Ferguson, contending the trip would play for itself and that its "notoriety" would boost attendance once they returned home.

As an advance man, Wright deputized Albert Spalding, who some say

Opposite: Brothers Harry (left) and George Wright were the dominant figures on the dominant team of the National Association, the Boston Red Stockings. (Courtesy of National Baseball Library, Cooperstown, New York.)

thought up the trip. In any case, Spalding needed no urging, as he was possessed of an "intense yearning to cross the Atlantic." Once there he arranged exhibitions with cricket clubs, such as the distinguished Marylebone club, in both England and Ireland. One catch: besides playing baseball, the Americans would have to contest the locals in their native sport. During his advance journey, on February 27, 1874, at the Cricket Oval at Lords' Field, Spalding participated in the very first baseball game on English soil.

It was a tour of decidedly mixed results. The party left Philadelphia aboard the steamship *Ohio* on July 17, 1874. President Grant, who had met the Red Stockings during their 1869 tour, was invited to help send them off, but failed to attend. That did not stop the champagne corks from popping as tugs accompanied the ballplayers out to the open sea.

Altogether 14 baseball games were played: two each in Liverpool, Manchester, Sheffield and Dublin, and six in London. Boston took the series eight to six.

The St. Louis *Democrat* described one day's action:

> A large number of the spectators seemed immensely pleased with the game, and expressed their pleasure in good, hearty, English applause. There were those, however, . . . who could not be made to hide their contempt for it. . . . These persons were for the most part active cricketers.

Catcher Calvin Alexander McVey was one of the Red Stockings taking part in the tour. He had joined the Red Stockings on the founding of the National Association, but in 1873 became manager—at age 22—of the Lord Baltimores, before returning to Boston the following year. An amateur boxer and a real crowd pleaser, he hit .419, .306, .369, .382 and .352 in the N.A.

"It was in England," noted McVey, "that I played the most scientific game of baseball ever produced up to that time. The game was played at the Edgehill Grounds in Liverpool, between the Bostons and the Athletics on July 30, 1874, the score being 14 to 11 in favor of the Athletics. It was the finest exhibition of skill, mettle and clean playing that I ever participated in.

"While in England the American nines played cricket on several occasions with picked British teams . . . made up of crack cricket players from among the British nobility. We sprang several surprises on our English cousins. For instance, instead of batting, or guarding the wicket with the ordinary-shaped cricket bat, I entered the fray armed with a baseball stick, at which our opponents poked good-natured fun. . . .

"At bowling, with my record as a thrower, I gave them another surprise, as did also others of the Americans. We were far better fielders than the Englishmen, but they had us on guarding the wickets, for at that we were very green and quite as poor, unless it be George Wright, Harry Wright and Dick McBride, who were really expert cricketers."

With such an unorthodox style, the Americans won every match (as indeed they should; they were allowed 18 or 22 to their side against the customary 11 their hosts were employing). And although crowds in the United Kingdom were small, two well-attended "Welcome Home" games back in the States allowed for a profitable conclusion for the tour.

The League Stumbles and Falls

In 1875, the Red Stockings continued their National Association dominance, with their strongest season yet (71–8, an .899 percentage). They went undefeated at home. The team's closest rival, the Athletics, finished 15 games back. With such a shambles made of the pennant race, 7 of 13 teams folded in mid-campaign. The Brooklyn Atlantics were particularly woeful, going 2–42, an .045 mark.

Albert Spalding won 57 games. Ross Barnes led the league in runs, hits, and average. Red Stockings players finished in the top five in both runs and hits. Boston's Barnes (.372), Deacon White (.355) and Cal McVey (.352) had the three best averages in the circuit, and George Wright was fifth at .337.

In a league whose composite batting average was .250, the Red Stockings team mark was .326.

A record of the Red Stockings' finances for their greatest year, the National Association's last:

Balance from former account	833.13
Gate receipts	34,987.74
Members' tickets	1,946.19
	37,767.06

Expenses

Players' salaries	20,685.00
Advertising & Printing	1,410.88
Rent of Grounds	617.50
Care of Grounds & Wages	888.82
Repair of Grounds	689.27
Sundry Expenses	304.00
Uniforms, bases, bats, etc.	223.94
Old Accounts	470.33
Rent of rooms and sundry accounts	1,955.37
Travelling expenses	6,808.56
Telegrams, postage, etc.	750.82
	34,505.99
Balance on Hand	3,261.07

Though the club's math was off by nearly $300, it was still a profitable year.

But all was not rosy in the National Association. A wide variety of problems haunted the circuit.

Dissension wracked the New York Mutuals as they pursued a policy of paying some players salaries and others a percentage of the gate. Bickering ensued as the "percentage" players carped at the salaried players for poor performance, which lowered attendance and hence receipts and paychecks. The New York *Clipper* noted that until the club was based on a sound salary structure, "those who invest in the business of engaging the club players cannot expect to run the machine successfully."

Ugly rumors of gambling and fixed games — "hippodroming" — haunted the Association from the beginning. In 1871, the Fort Wayne Kekiongas were mobbed by enraged local bettors after a hard-fought victory at Troy's Bull's Head Tavern Grounds. Thereupon they seemed incapable of winning on the road, and attendance dried up at home. Manager Harry Deane was fired after just five games and was replaced by catcher Bill Lennon. With a 7-21 record by July, the franchise folded.

Beadle's Base Ball Player for 1873 (an official Association publication) charged that "since the introduction of pool-selling at Base Ball matches, pools amounting to over $20,000 have been known to be sold on a single match." *Beadle's* describes a game in Philadelphia in July 1873 where an umpire "had to be protected from the assaults of the crowd." In another contest, umpire Bob Ferguson accused a lazy New York Mutual of being in league with gamblers. The player retorted with a stream of invective that led to a mob scene, and Ferguson was escorted by police from the field for his own protection.

Spalding's Base Ball Guide for 1888 cryptically notes that Philadelphia would have taken the 1873 championship "but for crookedness in its ranks."

Even the champion Red Stockings were not immune from accusations of "hippodroming." In one midsummer contest in 1873, after leading 14–4 over Baltimore, they were shockingly defeated 17–14. An outraged fan took pen in hand and wrote the Boston *Herald:*

> We paid our money last year to see base ball played, but we are not so green as to imagine we see square games this year. Like a hundred or more we have spent our last half dollar on the Boston ground. As the land is in the market for sale, I presume we will not have to be humbugged more than this season. We don't believe the club exists that can fairly beat Boston in three innings, when the score stands 14–4. We don't know, but we think, and are sorry that we must, that the Boston club is on the make; but they cannot make fools of the public any longer. The club of '72 is not the club of '73, and we hope they will disband before they go backward any farther.

> /*signed*/Fair Play

To which the ballclub responded:

> Fair Play seems afraid to say the Boston Club sells games, but if that is what he means, I will pay him $50 for every game he will prove was sold either by the club as a club or by individual players. I have heard that kind of talk in Philadelphia and New York from purchasers of pools, etc., but not from honest men.
>
> B.B.C.

An odd incident occurred in 1874 when the re-born Chicago White Stockings visited New York. Pitcher George "The Charmer" Zettlein and outfielder Ned Cuthbert were accused of throwing contests and were forced to sit out the games there. With both on the bench the White Stockings lost every game in New York. With the series over, both were immediately exonerated. Cynical observers suspected the accusations were a mere ploy to temporarily cripple the Chicago team.

In August the Mutuals visited Chicago and this time the accusations were on the other foot. Pitcher Bobby Mathews left after the first inning, claiming illness, and eventually the White Stockings pulled out a 5–4 victory. At the contest's conclusion Mutual catcher Doug Allison charged that Mathews had feigned sickness and had been in league with gamblers to throw the match.

Mathews was found to have been consorting with a New York gambler named McDonald; McDonald and a friend had placed bets in the amount of $50 with Tom Foley, a prominent gambler and the former Chicago business manager.

It turned out that Mathews' illness was real, but such continuing incidents did little to encourage confidence in the emerging national game.

That same month, five Philadelphia club players—pitcher William "Candy" Cummings, outfielder John J. Radcliff, first baseman Denny Mack, catcher Nathaniel Hicks and second baseman Bill Craver—were charged with "hippodroming." Craver had been banned for "life" for gambling back in 1870 by the old amateur Association. He, Hicks, Cummings and Mack were cleared, but Radcliff was found to have attempted to bribe umpire William B. McLean. Radcliff was expelled from the club, but showed up in the Association next year playing for the Philadelphia Centennials.

During the off-season, newly appointed White Stockings manager Jimmy Wood gave an interview to the Chicago *Tribune* implying that the Mutuals, Philadelphias, Athletics and Atlantics each contained a core of crooked personnel. He exonerated the Red Stockings from any corruption, but his words fueled public dissatisfaction.

During the 1875 season, the Chicago *Times* printed a report that Wood had accused pitcher George Zettlein of throwing games. Wood denied all in an interview given to the rival *Tribune*, but Zettlein (who was annoyed anyway that White Stockings management was signing better pitching for 1876) demanded his outright release. Zettlein then signed with Philadelphia, where more accusations of "hippodroming" awaited him.

At the same time his teammate, catcher and team captain Dick Higham, was expelled for throwing games. Nonetheless, he was signed by the New York Mutuals. Unbelievably, he was hired as a National League umpire in 1881. The following year he was fired for tipping off gamblers as to who would win games he was officiating.

Clearly the National Association was tumbling into chaos.

Henry Chadwick in the New York *Clipper* cautioned against the evils of gambling: "When the system of professional ball playing . . . shall be among the things that were, on its tombstone—if it have any—will be found the inscription, 'Died of Pool-Selling.'"

Other Controversies

"Revolving," or free agency, was also an issue. Players moved at will from one club to another at season's end, causing salaries to escalate. Were it not for the Great Fire, Chicago's 1872 payroll would have set a record, with three players at $2,500, four at $2,000 and a total outlay of $24,100. Even such a minor franchise as New Haven boasted in 1875 that its men were being paid $1,600 each.

The 1875 Red Stockings, with a $20,685 payroll, set a mark that would not be equaled until the next decade.

Although Chicago and Philadelphia were relatively profitable in 1871, baseball was not a lucrative endeavor under the Association. Even the artistically successful Red Stockings, with a schedule heavily augmented by exhibitions, returned only modest profits. In winning their first pennant in 1872 they lost $3,000. The next year they cleared $4,020.38 but put the great majority of it back into the team, leaving a balance of only $767.93. A modest $833.13 was returned in 1874, and even in the great year of 1875 only $2,962.57 was made—and that was plowed back into the club.

Alcohol could also be a problem, as informal bars sprang up along the sidelines and led to displays of wanton drunkenness and violence by fans and players alike.

The Association's weak standard for admission (a ten dollar bill) and continued dominance by the Red Stockings led to an alarming dropout rate. The Kekiongas departed in July 1871 ("thrown out owing to illegal games," noted *Spalding's Guide*), being replaced in August by the Brooklyn Eckfords.

The 1872 season saw such abortive franchises as the Washington Olympics (2-7), the Washington Nationals (0-11), the Middletown Mansfields (5-19), the Forest City Club of Cleveland (6-15) and the Eckfords (3-26). Every team lost money that season, even pennant-winning Boston.

The 1873 campaign included such failures as the Elizabeth Resolutes (2-21) and the Baltimore Marylands (0-5). Despite the fact most clubs stuck the course, the season was still a money loser due to player salaries which were more than this feeble structure could support.

During 1874 just one team, the Lord Baltimores (9-38) dropped out, but only champion Boston completed its schedule. The Association continued to hover near financial ruin.

In 1875, with the Red Stockings running away with the flag, six teams folded: The Keokuk Westerns (1-12), the Brooklyn Atlantics (2-42), the New Haven Elm Cities (7-40), the St. Louis Red Stockings (4-14), the Washington Nationals (4-23) and the Philadelphia Centennials (2-12).

The pathetic outfits often failed to make any attempt at playing out their road schedules. The St. Louis Red Stockings never played east of Chicago. New Haven, Washington and the Brooklyn Atlantics (whose 38 players never received a salary, merely a share of whatever gate there was) never went west.

In fact, so weak was the Association's structure, only five clubs even bothered to turn in their statistics to Association Secretary Nick Young.

Nevertheless, there were some interesting innovations during the National Association's short existence.

In 1872 the Association adopted the rule that, as it was the National Association of Professional Base Ball *Players*, only a player could serve as president. They elected Bob Ferguson of the Atlantics as their chief. He would serve until the league's dissolution.

In 1873, on Henry Chadwick's suggestion, a tenth man was added to the lineup. As the second baseman was still playing very close to the bag, a new "right shortstop" was to play roughly where the second baseman would play today. A reason for this proposal not readily apparent today was the existence of "fair-foul" hits: any ball that hit fair ground was fair, whether past the infield or not. "There is not a reasonable objection that can be brought against it," maintained Henry Chadwick. At the same time the game became one of ten innings (metric baseball?). Both experiments were unpopular, and were abandoned after just a few exhibitions.

In 1875 the first player "sale" occurred when Bill Craver and outfielder George Bechtel were sold by the woeful Centennials to the contending Athletics.

"The National Association," summed up Bill James, "is to the National League precisely as the American states under the Articles of Confederation are to the United States. There were agreements but no provisions for enforcing them, no strong central authority. . . ." In some cases with the National Association, there weren't even agreements.

Like the framers of our Constitution meeting in Philadelphia, the baseball power brokers of 1876 were determined to correct these fatal flaws.

Chapter 2

The National League

The National League resulted from a coup. How easily it succeeded indicated just how rickety a structure the National Association was.

The individual behind this revolt was William Ambrose Hulbert, a White Stockings stockholder since 1872, club secretary since August 1874, and by October 10, 1875, their president.

Born on October 23, 1832, in tiny Burlington Flats, not far from Cooperstown, he was brought to Chicago at age two. A Beloit College graduate, he married the boss' daughter and prospered as a groceries wholesaler and a coal dealer, becoming a prominent member of Chicago's Board of Trade. "I'd rather be a lamp post in Chicago than a millionaire elsewhere," the large-framed Hulbert boasted of his adopted city.

"Mr. Hulbert," observed *Spalding's Guide,* "was a man to command attention; . . . of magnificent physique, commanding presence, and strong personality, endowed with a commanding intellect, keen logic, and impressive directness of speech, he was essentially a leader among men. . . ."

Hulbert was also determined to build a team that could beat the seemingly unstoppable Red Stockings. And he had visions of a league that would be financially viable.

To form a stronger Chicago team, Hulbert secretly and illegally signed players from other teams before the conclusion of the 1875 National Association season.

Illegal—or highly dubious—contract practices were commonplace during the period. Hulbert felt Chicago had had several star players snatched from it by Eastern clubs that back-dated contracts with players who had originally signed with the White Stockings. He was particularly bitter about the loss of diminutive (5'4") but excellent shortstop Davy Force to the Athletics.

Force signed a contract with Chicago in September 1874 for the upcoming season. Because the season was still taking place, his contract was invalid. In November he signed again with Chicago, but for some reason back-dated that contract to September. Technically, it too was invalid. By December, Force realized he wished to play for the Athletics and signed with them.

The issue went to the Association Judicial Committee, which was headed

William A. Hulbert, founder of the National League.

by a Philadelphian, Charles Spering, and stacked with representatives of Eastern clubs. It ruled 4–0 that Force belonged to Philadelphia.

Hulbert moved into action. The first player he approached was the Association's star pitcher, Albert Spalding. "Spalding," Hulbert argued, "you've no business playing in Boston; you're a Western boy and you belong right here. If you come to Chicago, I'll accept the presidency of the club and we'll give those Easterners the fight of their lives. You can be captain and manager at four thousand dollars a year."

The ever-ambitious Spalding needed no further urging: "When I come, I'll bring a team of pennant winners with me. I'll get Ross Barnes, Cal McVey, and Deacon White. The people call us 'the Big Four,' but the owners won't pay us very well. A championship team should be paid like champions."

Spalding's allegations of poverty were somewhat overblown. The salaries that Harry Wright paid the Red Stockings were actually generous, but what irked Spalding was that in an era when clubs presented certain "gifts" to a player to supplement his salary, Wright demurred, feeling it some sort of subterfuge. In any case the "Big Four" were signed by Hulbert in June 1875.

Additionally, Hulbert took two more prizes from the Philadelphia Athletics: Adrian C. "Cap" Anson, four-year veteran first baseman and a future

Hall of Famer, and Ezra B. Sutton, who has been termed the outstanding third baseman of the nineteenth century.

The financial terms of this raiding were most interesting. Spalding cut a deal for $2,000 salary plus 25 percent of the club's net profits. McVey signed for $2,000 each year for two seasons. White signed for a $2,400 salary plus $100 "Additional provided [the] club proves financial success." Anson was signed for $2,000, with $50 in cash immediately and another $150 to be handed over when the contract actually took force. Sutton signed for the same overall amount, but wanted $50 up front and $350 more to be paid over the winter of 1875–76. Barnes signed for a straight $1,500.

All of this was quite risky business. Chicago's press soon heard the rumors. The Chicago *Times* printed a false report that it was George and Harry Wright who were coming to Chicago. Within a few days the Chicago *Tribune* had the real story and was trumpeting Hulbert's triumph. The cat was out of the bag, and Boston's press was livid. The "Big Four" were to be jeered for the rest of the season by irate Boston "cranks," who used such repartee as "You seceders, your White Stockings will get soiled in Chicago."

One reason the Association banned such advance signings was quite logical: there was a fear that players still with one club but engaged to play with another would "lie down" against their future teammates. The "Big Four" did their best to squelch any such accusations, as the superb record of both Spalding (57-5) and the 1875 Red Stockings (71-8) will attest.

Despite the signings, in the confused atmosphere of the National Association, it was not at all certain these six players would report to their new club. The "Big Four" had strong emotional ties to Boston. Even Spalding admitted they had been treated "magnificently" there. Anson had just married a Philadelphia girl who had no great desire to leave home, and Spalding himself was about to take a Massachusetts bride. Both cities were making valiant efforts to retain their stars, offering as much as it would take. Ezra Sutton did in fact stay with the Athletics. Anson had an $1,800 contract with Chicago, but was offered $2,500 to stay with the Athletics. At one point Anson even offered the White Stockings $1,000 to buy out his contract.

Red Stockings President Nathaniel T. Appolonio responded calmly to the Chicago juggernaut, saying he would meet and probably better any White Stockings offer.

It was all to no avail. At a postseason Red Stockings club dinner, Spalding made a toast: "To the Boston club, its officers, members and stockholders— may they fly the pennant in 'seventy-six'—if the Chicagos don't."

National Association rules prohibited the in-season signings that Hulbert had engaged in, and he theoretically faced either the loss of these players or outright expulsion from the circuit, although in the N.A.'s loose atmosphere nothing was certain. In part to forestall any possible penalties, he mulled founding a new league.

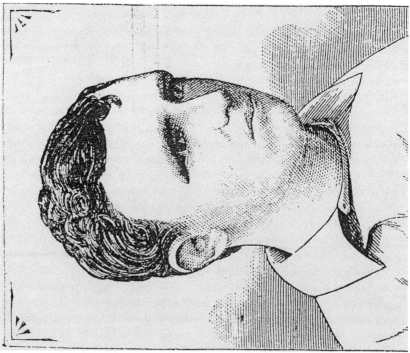

Spalding and Hulbert were genuinely worried. "Mr. Hulbert and I were in a serious discussion," Spalding wrote in his memoirs. "For a few moments I noticed that he was engrossed in deep thought, when suddenly he arose from his chair and said, 'Spalding, I have a new scheme. Let us anticipate the Eastern cusses and organize a new association before the March [1876] meeting, and then we shall see who does the expelling.'"

Genesis of a New League

Forestalling expulsion was only part of his rationale. The National Association was tottering—and worse, unprofitable. With its $10 entrance fee and few other qualifications, it was always filled with deadwood franchises such as Fort Wayne, Middletown and Keokuk, not to mention three separate Philadelphia franchises in 1875.

In fact, the situation was growing worse. By October 1875 17 clubs had announced their intentions of competing for the upcoming championship.

Hulbert was not alone in his musings. On October 24, 1875, Lewis Meacham, sports editor of the Chicago *Tribune*, ran a piece entitled "The Professional Base Ball Association—what it must do to be saved." It argued for a league made up of stronger clubs, a monopoly of one club in each city, and that no city of less than 100,000 persons should be represented. It was remarkably similar to Hulbert's later plan, and at least two modern scholars (Harold Seymour and Larry Names) feel Meacham acted as Hulbert's "mouthpiece."

The Eastern press reacted with hostility and ridicule. Meacham struck again in November, suggesting a Western Union of clubs augmented by Harry Wright's moving the Red Stockings to Indianapolis!

And then there was Spalding. On his honeymoon he visited his home of Rockford, Illinois, and was tracked down by a reporter for the *Tribune*. Spalding, now the new secretary of the White Stockings, was concerned about the weak sisters of the Association: "It is the intention of the larger clubs to make some rules about contending for the championship [i.e. being a league member] so that clubs that have no earthly chance to win will not be allowed to play with first-rate clubs." He also advocated clear demarcation between "the control of the executive management . . . and the playing of the game."

Players should, of course, receive "commensurate pay," but Spalding contended they should no longer have any responsibility to "secure grounds, erect grandstands, lease and own property, make schedules, fix dates, pay salaries,

Opposite: Two of William Hulbert's prize recruits for his Chicago White Stockings, Adrian C. "Cap" Anson (left) and Ezra B. Sutton. Sutton later reneged, staying with the Philadelphia Athletics.

assess fines, discipline players, make contracts, control the sport in all its relations to the public. . . ." These were all the proper concerns of "management."
And this newest member of the White Stockings front office saw that this
transfer of power was all part of "the irrepressible conflict between Labor and
Capital."

In any case, Hulbert swung into action. First, he approached Charles
Fowle, owner of the National Association's St. Louis Brown Stockings, and
Campbell Orrick Bishop, a St. Louis attorney and former player with the
amateur St. Louis Unions. Next, two strong "Western" independent teams, the
reborn Cincinnati Red Stockings and the Louisville Grays, were secretly contacted on December 17, 1875. Even before this session, Hulbert emanated
confidence. He wrote to Fowle: "You and I can carry the day for everything
we want. Then, firmly established with four powerful clubs welded together,
we can easily influence such of the remainder that we desire to join us."

Cincinnati and Louisville readily agreed, giving Hulbert and Fowle power
of attorney for a meeting being arranged with the more stable Eastern franchises, Boston, Hartford, the Philadelphia Athletics and the New York
Mutuals.

Hulbert's every move was deft. First, he conferred separately with each
club. Then at New York's Grand Central Hotel on Wednesday, February 2,
1876, he met with the heads of the four Eastern clubs—G. W. Thompson of
the Athletics, Nathaniel T. Appolonio of the Red Stockings, William H. Cammeyer of the Mutuals and Morgan G. Bulkeley of the Hartford Dark Blues.

For Hulbert to face—let alone expect the cooperation of—these Eastern
clubs showed remarkable courage, for he had stolen away four of Boston's
greatest lights and two from Philadelphia. In his written invitation, though, he
played upon a concern for "matters of interest to the game at large" and the
necessity for "reforms of existing abuses." He urged that "all past troubles and
differences be ignored and forgotten and that the conference we propose shall
be a calm, friendly, and deliberate discussion, looking solely to the general good
of the clubs . . . calculated to give character and permanence to the game."

A 70-mile-an-hour gale was whipping the entire East Coast and New York
City in particular as the meeting began. "Do not be alarmed, gentlemen,"
Hulbert grandly stated as he turned and locked the group into the hotel's second floor meeting room and then placed the key in his coat pocket. "I merely
took the precaution that there will not be any intrusion from the outside, and
there is some business that has to be finished and no one will leave the room
until I have explained everything.

"Inflated salaries, players jumping from team to team during the season,
gambling scandals, team imbalance, incomplete schedules—all these can and
will be wiped away," Hulbert promised, finally arriving at his central point:
"Why should we be losing money when we represent a game that people love?"
This made sense to everyone in the room.

The group adopted a constitution for a new "National *League* of Professional Base Ball *Clubs*," [emphasis mine] a document largely the work of the crafty Spalding ("I spent thirty days in Mr. Hulbert's house with him, writing the first constitution. . . ."), but with major input from Campbell Orrick Bishop.

The change in title was no mere semantic exercise. The substitution of "Clubs" for "Players" was deliberate and foretold a major shift in emphasis. As Albert Spalding had informed the Chicago *Tribune,* baseball was now about to see "the irrepressible conflict between Labor and Capital."

Major tenets of this new league were as follows:

1. The franchise fee was increased from $10 to $100.

2. No city would be represented which had a population of less than 75,000, except by "unanimous vote of the League." This would eliminate such mistakes as Fort Wayne (pop. 25,000).

3. Each club's territorial sanctity was to be respected; there would be no more than one club from each member city, thus eliminating dual-member situations that had existed for the National Association in Washington, Philadelphia and St. Louis.

4. Although there was no expressed limit to the number of clubs that could join, a *de facto* "black ball" vote by two club members would be sufficient to block a prospective member.

5. Clubs were to play out their schedules.

6. No club would "employ any player who has been dismissed or expelled by the League or any club members thereof."—Thus, a blacklist could be created.

7. The League would develop its own playing schedule (this actually had to wait until 1877). A club would play its rivals ten times each between March 15 and November 15.

8. Umpires would finally be remunerated—at the rate of $5 per game—and would be chosen from an approved list.

Those were the major rules regarding organization and membership. Additionally, there were major reforms regarding drinking and gambling designed to elevate the sport's rapidly sinking image; both were banned on League grounds.

"Any player," stated the new rules, "who shall, in any way, be interested in any bet or wager on the game in which he takes part, either as umpire, player, or scorer, or who shall purchase or have purchased for him any 'pool' or chance—sold or given away—on the game he plays in, shall be dishonorably expelled both from the club of which he is a member and from the League.

"A player who shall be similarly interested in any regular match game between two clubs of the League, shall be suspended from legal service as a member for the season during which he shall have violated this rule."

Commented a pleased Spalding, "Mr. Hulbert magnificently dominated the whole situation."

Nonetheless, Hulbert was not the first president of his creation. On his suggestion, the first five club presidents whose names were picked from a hat would constitute the League Board of Directors, and the name drawn first would be president. The honor went to 39-year-old Morgan G. Bulkeley of Hartford.

Bulkeley's father had founded the Aetna Life Insurance Company, where 14-year-old Morgan started as a $1-per-week sweeper. A year later he left Hartford for Brooklyn, where he worked at his uncle's dry goods store, rising from errand boy to partner. Bulkeley enlisted during the Civil War and fought in the Virginia campaigns of General George McClellan as a private.

On his father's death in 1872, he returned home and became a member of Aetna's Board of Directors as well as an organizer of the United States Bank of Hartford. It was through this bank that Bulkeley became involved in the Hartford Dark Blues.

Bulkeley announced he would serve but one term as league president. He honored that pledge, and did not even bother to attend the December 1876 session in which Hulbert became his successor (although Hulbert had nominated an indifferent Nick Appolonio for the post). He went on to become president of Aetna, eventually the nation's largest insurance company, and he took an active role in Republican politics. In 1876 he became a Hartford alderman; in 1880, mayor; and in 1888, governor of Connecticut.

He did not seek re-election to that office, but a deadlock developed in choosing his successor. Bulkeley, citing a section in the state constitution that a governor would remain in power until a successor was inaugurated, stayed on for another two years, although not without controversy. New York's Governor David B. "I am a Democrat" Hill refused to recognize Bulkeley as a legitimate chief executive, and the Democratic state comptroller ordered Bulkeley's offices padlocked. Bulkeley personally pried open the door with a crowbar, and henceforth was tagged as the "Crow-Bar Governor."

In 1904 he was elected a member of the United States Senate, where he championed the rights of the black troops stationed at Brownsville, Texas, dishonorably discharged by President Roosevelt.

For his rather negligible contribution to the national pastime, the distinguished Bulkeley was ultimately elected to the Hall of Fame, while Hulbert, the League's real founder and its president from 1877 until his death in 1882, has never been so honored.

The League's new Board of Directors (consisting of Bulkeley, Apollonio, Cammeyer, Fowle and Louisville President Charles E. Chase) was empowered to chose a league secretary, to be paid $400 annually (increased to $500 in 1877), who would be "a gentleman of intelligence, honesty and good repute, versed in Base-Ball but not connected with the press and not a member of any professional club." The post would go to Nick Young, who would hold the office until becoming league president in 1885.

Oddly enough, the new League was not greeted by hosannas. In the Eastern press, no notice appeared for three days, and even then it was buried in one morning paper along with items on horse racing and pigeon shooting (pigeon shooting received more space, by the way). The Chicago *Union* sniffed, "The whole thing is a monopoly." Other epithets flung about were "star chamber" and even "anti–American." Henry Chadwick, who was excluded from the League's formation, termed it "a startling coup d'etat" and "a sad blunder." "Reform should not fear the light of day," he complained in the *Clipper.*

The First Season

So the inaugural season of 1876 began, running from April 22 until October 21, with games played each Tuesday, Thursday and Saturday. Each contest would start in late afternoon; as the season progressed it was not uncommon for games to be called on account of darkness.

The National Association expired rapidly, however. It had met on March 1, but none of the major clubs had shown up, merely a handful of nonentities from Pennsylvania, Ohio and Maryland. They met again in April in Philadelphia, but the intervening founding of the National League knocked out the little wind remaining in them.

It was all over for baseball's first professional league.

The very first National League game was at Philadelphia's Athletics Park at Twenty-fifth and Jefferson streets, on Saturday afternoon, April 22, 1876.

Fittingly, the Boston Red Stockings were the first team to come to bat, with George Wright batting leadoff. It was not planned this way; all other league games that day were rained out. Wright grounded to Davy Force, the shortstop whose presence on the Athletics did more than anything to set William Hulbert in motion.

Wes Fisler, one of the shortest (5'6") of all first basemen, made the first putout; Jim O'Rourke had the first hit; Tim McGinley scored the first N.L. run; Tim Murnane stole the first base. On the debit side, Ezra Sutton made the first error, and Tim McGinley was the first to strike out.

Boston triumphed 6–5 as "Josephus the Phenomenal" Borden outpitched Alonzo Knight before an estimated 3,000, and 26 errors were made by the bare-handed fielders. That first National League box score is on the next page.

As one would guess, Chicago's strengthened roster delivered the 1876 pennant to William Hulbert, as the White Stockings outhit the rest of their infant league with a .337 team average, coasting to a 52-14 record. The White Stockings were simply overwhelming. Ross Barnes led the league in runs (126), hits (138), average (.429), triples (14), total bases (190), slugging percentage (.590) and on-base percentage (.462). Three other White Stockings finished in the top

Influential journalist Henry Chadwick termed the founding of the National League "a sad blunder." (Courtesy of National Baseball Library, Cooperstown, New York.)

BOSTON	TB	R	1B	PO	A	E	ATHLETICS	TB	R	1B	PO	A	E
Wright, ss	4	2	1	2	2	0	Force, ss	5	0	1	0	4	1
Leonard, 2b	4	0	2	0	4	1	Eggler, cf	5	0	0	4	1	1
O'Rourke, cf	5	1	2	0	0	0	Fisler, 1b	5	1	3	13	0	1
Murnane, 1b	6	1	2	8	0	0	Meyerle, 2b	5	1	1	3	2	0
Schafer, 3b	5	1	1	1	0	1	Sutton, 3b	5	0	0	1	0	2
McGinley, c	5	1	0	8	0	3	Coons, c	4	2	2	1	2	3
Manning, rf	4	0	0	4	0	0	Hall lf	4	0	2	1	0	0
Parks, lf	4	0	0	3	0	1	Fouser, rf	4	0	0	3	1	1
Borden, p	3	0	0	1	1	1	Knight, p	4	1	1	1	3	2
TOTALS	40	6	8	27	7	7	TOTALS	41	5	10	27	13	11

Boston   0   1   2   0   1   0   0   0   2–6
Athletic   0   1   0   0   0   3   0   0   1–5
   Runs earned—Boston, 1; Athletics, 2.
   Total bases on hits—Boston 9; Athletics, 12. First base by errors—Boston, 6; Athletics, 3. Total left on bases—Boston, 7; Athletics, 9. Double-plays—Eggler and Coons, 1; Force, Fouser and Fisler, 1. Umpire, Wm. McLean. Time, 2h. 5m.

five in batting—Anson (.356), John Peters (.351) and Cal McVey (.347). Spalding paced the circuit in wins (47) and won-lost percentage (.797).

1877: The Spectre of Gambling

Gambling unfortunately continued, for despite the new league's pious hopes, human nature was not to be transformed overnight. At the advent of the National League one *Clipper* correspondent charged, "Any professional base ball club will 'throw' a game if there is money in it. A horse race is a pretty safe thing to speculate on, in comparison with an average ball match." Public opinion on the issue would not immediately change—and with good reason.

"Pool-selling" particularly afflicted the game. "Pools" were not direct bets between two parties; one might welsh on those bets. Instead, "pools" involved a third party who held the cash, and were formed in "pool rooms" usually near the local park.

The system was relatively complicated. Prior to a game (actually days in advance), an auction was held, with bidding on the right to bet on favorite clubs. Then bids were made on the opposing nine. If the odds were not favorable, bets could be withdrawn. The pool seller kept records of these transactions, paid the winners, tried to maintain a reputation for honesty and received a percentage of each bet.

Although by 1877 "pools" were being challenged by the new English practice of "bookmaking," they were still exceedingly popular. Straitlaced Boston alone had eight such rooms, and pools on a single game in larger New York establishments could reach as high as $70,000.

Rumors particularly swirled around the New York Mutuals in that first N.L. season. The Chicago *Tribune* reported that a few of the Mutuals had plotted to go into the tank on a given date, but when their manager, William Cammeyer, became aware of the conspiracy, it collapsed and the team won the game in question. The New York *Herald* published an account of a gamblers' plot to bribe Mutuals pitcher Bobby Mathews (21-34) to throw a game. Mathews declined, however, and nothing more came of the matter in regard to him. But investigations of several pool-sellers revealed crookedness, and some were put out of business.

William D. Perrin of the Providence *Journal* wrote that when the Grays

Philadelphia first baseman Wes Fisler recorded the National League's first put out.

joined the League in 1879, two "professional men" of the city got together a pool of $2,000 on the team. Five hundred dollars was wagered at even odds that Providence would finish above Cincinnati; the same money at the same odds that they would best Boston; and $1,000 against $4,000 that Providence would win the pennant. How much of this money was ever placed is unknown.

But the greatest infamy was that of the 1877 Louisville Grays. On August 13 the Grays had a 27-13 record and a large lead in the pennant race. With 15 contests remaining, Louisville needed to win roughly half. Instead, they played wretchedly, at one time dropping eight in a row, and lost to Boston by seven games.

Louisville's troubles began when third baseman Bill Hague was disabled

The 1876 National League champion Chicago White Stockings.

by a boil under his throwing arm. To replace him, Grays outfielder George Hall suggested signing utility infielder Alfred H. Nichols, a former Mutual now with an independent Pittsburgh club.

Suspicion centered on four key Grays, who were ostentatiously sporting diamond stickpins and rings: pitcher James Alexander Devlin, who pitched particularly poorly in the stretch (and who like Hague was also afflicted with boils that season); shortstop and catcher William H. Craver, who in 1870 had been expelled from the Chicago White Stockings for insubordination and gambling and in November of that year banned for life by the National Association of Base Ball Players; Hall, around whom rumors of corruption had also circulated back in his days in the National Association; and Nichols, allegedly involved with prominent New York City gamblers.

But there were more than rumors. As Louisville headed east to play Hartford in Brooklyn (Hartford played home games there due to lack of support in Connecticut) during the Grays' final road trip, club president Charles E. Chase received an anonymous telegram charging that gamblers were laying down serious money against the Grays. At first Chase dismissed the cable as a hoax.

Nonetheless, Louisville lost 5–1 as Nichols, Hall and Craver committed errors. Chase was surprised to learn Nichols was still in the lineup, since Hague had fully recovered. Manager Jack Chapman responded that he had penciled Nichols in on suggestion from Hall, who argued that the Brooklyn native would bear down harder in front of his hometown crowd.

Chase received another mysterious cable prior to the second game in the series, and once again Brooklyn lost (7–0) to the Dark Blues. Devlin, Nichols and Hall made damaging errors. Chase ordered Chapman to bench Nichols.

But the nose dive continued. The Louisville *Courier-Journal* was incredulous, running headlines such as "!!! – ??? – !!!" and "What's the Matter?" The paper even made the rumors public when Devlin mysteriously regained his form in postseason exhibitions ("The Celt has completely given himself away"). Particularly interesting was that the *Courier-Journal* story was by John Haldeman, son of Louisville owner Walter N. Haldeman.

Chase confronted the suspect players, starting with Devlin. The hurler admitted he may have been careless in some exhibitions, but that was all. Chase wasn't buying it. "I want a full confession," he barked. "I'll give you until 8 p.m. to tell me the full story."

Returning to his hotel, Chase found Hall waiting for him. Hall wrongly surmised that Devlin had cracked. Chase did nothing to dissuade him, and soon Hall was spilling his guts, freely admitting throwing games. He also implicated Nichols, claiming Nichols was the contact with the gamblers.

Chase returned to Devlin, telling him Hall had confessed. Devlin admitted his guilt.

The next evening, Chase called a team meeting. He requested permission to obtain each Western Union telegram sent from or received by each Gray during the season. Only team captain Bill Craver refused, and he was summarily suspended.

The contents of these telegrams revealed that Hall, Devlin and Nichols had been in virtually open communication with the gamblers, particularly a New Yorker named McLeod. Fixes occurred in both exhibition and League contests; the code word in the telegrams for a fix was "sash." No other Grays were proven to be involved.

Nobody owned up to instigating the plot, and each man's degree of guilt is still a matter of confusion. Hall blamed Nichols, but many believed it was Hall himself (whose brother-in-law, Frank Powell, had been after him for a year and a half to throw games), as he had originally recruited Nichols for the team. Some said it was Hall and Nichols who approached Devlin, offering him $100 to throw a meaningless exhibition game at Lowell, Massachusetts. Others said it was Devlin himself who had been the first of the players to contact McLeod.

In any case, Devlin saw no harm in going into the tank for a non-championship contest, but once involved he was virtually blackmailed into throwing the pennant race. He claimed he never received another cent from the gamblers, but again that contention is disputed. Some sources indicate he received another $300 for hippodroming three exhibitions at Indianapolis.

The League expelled all four in December 1877 "for conduct in contravention of the objects of this League."

Devlin had been an outstanding pitcher, winning 30 games in 1876 and 35 in 1877, leading the league in games and innings pitched both seasons, and being among the best in ERA. In 1877 he hurled every single inning for his team — the only pitcher ever to do so. He begged the authorities repeatedly for mercy, contending his family needed the money, and further pleading that since expulsion his wife and child had been in penury. He implored Harry Wright to grant him a second chance, to give him any sort of position at all, even as Boston's groundskeeper.

"I Can asure [sic] you Harry," wrote the semiliterate Devlin, "that I was not Treated right and if Ever I Can see you to tell you the Case you will say I am not to Blame I am living from hand to mouth all winter I have not got a Stich of Clothing or has my wife and Child. . . . the Louisville People have made me what I am today a Begger [sic]."

On one occasion Devlin visited League President Hulbert in his Chicago offices, again pleading for reinstatement. The scene was recorded in melodramatic fashion by Albert Spalding, nonetheless portraying a very real human tragedy:

> I was sitting in the reception room and Mr. Hulbert was . . . in the inner apartment, when the outer door opened and a sorry-looking specimen of humanity entered. It was midwinter and very cold, but the poor fellow had no overcoat. His dust-covered garments were threadbare and seedy. His shoes were worn through with much tramping, while the red flesh showing in places indicated that if stockings were present they afforded not much protection to the feet. Everything about the man's appearance betokened weariness and woe. His face was a picture of abject misery. The visitor passed me without a glance in my direction. His eyes were fixed upon the occupant of the farther room. He walked straight to the chair where Mr. Hulbert sat, and dropping his knees at the big man's feet, lifted his eyes in prayerful entreaty, while his frame shook with the emotion so long restrained. Then his lips gave utterance to such a plea for mercy as might come from one condemned to the gallows.
>   . . . How Devlin reached Chicago I never knew. There was everything in

his condition to indicate he might have walked all the way from Louisville. The situation as he kneeled there in abject humiliation, was beyond the realms of pathos. It was a scene of heartrending tragedy. Devlin was in tears, Hulbert was in tears, and if the mists of a tearful sympathy filled my eyes I have no excuse to offer here.

I heard Devlin's plea to have the stigma removed from his name. I heard him entreat, not on his own account — he acknowledged himself unworthy of consideration — but for the sake of his wife and child. I beheld the agony of humiliation depicted on his features as he confessed his guilt and begged for mercy. I saw the great bulk of Hulbert's frame tremble with the emotion he vainly sought to stifle. I saw the President's hand steal into his pocket as if to conceal his intended act from the other hand. I saw him take a $50 bill and press it into the palm of the prostrate player. And then I heard him say, as he fairly writhed with the pain his words caused him, "Devlin, that is what I think of you personally; but damn you, you have sold a game, and I can't trust you. Now go and let me never see your face again; for your act will never be condoned as I live."

Oddly enough, Devlin was able to find work as a Philadelphia policeman (and odder still, Craver became a highly respected policeman in Troy, New York) before dying of consumption on October 10, 1883. Before Devlin died, a benefit game raised over $1,000 for him.

Adding to public disgust over baseball's gambling was an allegation by National League umpire Dan Devinney that St. Louis Brown Stockings manager George McManus had offered him a $250 bribe to throw an August 1, 1877, Louisville game to St. Louis. Louisville won that game 3–1, however, and no further investigation took place. Devinney did not officiate in the League the following season.

DeWitt's Base-Ball Guide was particularly harsh on the subject of gambling. The *Guide*, pointing out that New York State had legislated against pool-selling in 1877, hoped that the evil had peaked; but the publication despaired of the gambling mania in the Western states. In Chicago even the respected Board of Trade had sold pools on the White Stockings.

"Why the base-ball press of the West support the pool-selling curse as they do, . . . is a mystery," the *Guide* editor wrote. "Of course while reporters and club directors and managers countenance pool-selling, as they did in so many instances in 1877, any hope of reforming players, even by expulsion, is illusory. While the pool-box is countenanced there will be rascality among tempted players, despite the most stringent League laws. . . ."

The St. Louis *Globe-Democrat* offered a gloomier picture. "The days of professional baseball are numbered," it opined, "and the hundreds of young men who have depended on the pastime as their means of earning a livelihood will be obliged to change their plans of operation."

Revolving Franchises

Gambling was not the sole problem vexing League officials. Not all clubs were serious about the new rule regarding playing out their official itineraries. In 1876 neither Philadelphia nor New York finished its schedule.

G. W. Thompson, Philadelphia's president, pled with Hulbert not to his team, arguing that he could not afford a Western trip due to player injuries, a grinding burden of debt, and low gates (in one contest the visitors' gate share was only $3.75) resulting from free entertainments in Philadelphia that Centennial year. He even offered the White Stockings and the Brown Stockings 80 percent of the gate if they would come east for extra games. Hulbert was unmoved, sniffing that Thompson should have made his offer before Chicago's last trip east.

As for the Mutuals, both Hulbert and Fowle offered New York President William H. Cammeyer a sizable $400 guarantee to travel west. When Cammeyer refused, he was out. Even though the fledging circuit would be minus teams in the nation's two most-populous cities, reducing the League to six franchises, Hulbert's ruling stuck.

Financially, the National League was no instant success, starting as it did in years of economic down-turn. In 1876 it is likely only pennant-winning Chicago returned a profit. The formerly solvent Red Stockings showed a loss each year from 1876 to 1880:

$$1876 - \$777.22$$
$$1877 - \$2,230.85$$
$$1878 - \$1,433.31$$
$$1879 - \$3,346.90$$
$$1888 - \$3,315.90$$

In 1877, estimated losses were: St. Louis, $8,000; Chicago, $6,000; Hartford, $2,230.85; Louisville, $2,000; and Boston, $1,500. No figures are available for Cincinnati, but its season was a disaster. The team folded after just five games, jeopardizing the whole league. It was hastily put back together to finish the season, but so great was the confusion that some newspapers printed League standings featuring the rebuilt team, but others did not.

At the 1877 annual League meeting at Cleveland's Kennard House, certain economic moves were instituted. Players were expected to buy their own uniforms (cost: $30) and bear the cost of their maintenance. Players were also assessed 50 cents for each day they were on the road. In the days of the National Association, clubs had borne this expense; Harry Wright, for example, had spent $1 per diem on each player's road expenses.

St. Louis, Louisville and Hartford could no longer take the losses and dropped out of the League. Both St. Louis and Louisville were casualties of the latter city's gambling scandal, as St. Louis had planned on signing Devlin, Hall, Nichols and Craver for the 1878 season. Without this core of talent, management felt it unwise to continue. Clubs in Providence (the "Grays"), Milwaukee (the "Grays" or "Cream Citys") and Indianapolis (the "Blues") replaced them for 1878.

Franchises placed a heavy emphasis on colors in the formation of team nicknames, particularly in 1878. This became so ingrained that by December 1881 the League actually legislated that teams would wear certain colors: Chicago, white; Boston, red; Providence, light blue; Detroit, old gold; Worcester, brown; Troy, green; and Buffalo, gray. These applied to the total uniform. The following year this applied to just the hose. The regulation stocking colors adopted were: Boston, red; Buffalo, gray; Chicago, white; Cleveland, blue; Providence, light blue; Detroit, brown; Philadelphia, white and blue check; and black and crimson for New York.

Albert Spalding outfitted his White Stockings so that each position player wore a different color cap. Some observers thought the idea rather festive, and noted that the players looked like jockies. But most found it a bit excessive, and the practice was quickly discontinued.

The League's game of revolving franchises continued after 1878. Milwaukee was ousted from membership for non-payment of obligations. Indianapolis went broke. Joining for 1879 were the Cleveland Blues and three upstate New York teams—the Buffalo Bisons, the Troy Trojans, and the Syracuse Stars. Syracuse was history by 1880, replaced by the Worcester Ruby Legs.

How Worcester, a losing International Association team, joined the League revolves around the Troy franchise. Albany attempted to join along with Troy in 1878, but this would have resulted in an unwieldy (in terms of scheduling) nine-team League, and Albany was refused.

Albany continued playing other League members in local exhibitions. The Trojans protested, contending that Albany was within Troy's five-mile territorial limit; they even cajoled the local city engineer to swear that the two cities were only four and three-quarters miles apart.

Troy was upheld, but it had not counted on one ramification of its victory: cancellation of its own exhibitions against Albany. In those days of short league schedules, tight budgets and many non-league exhibitions, this was a powerful setback. Troy changed strategy and successfully petitioned for a rule change; the territorial limit was now reduced to four miles instead of five.

In 1880 Syracuse abandoned ship, and both Albany and Worcester applied for League membership. Troy wished to have its nearby rival in the circuit. League sentiment was for Worcester, but Troy announced it would veto Worcester unless Albany was also admitted. As Worcester contained fewer than 75,000 persons, an unanimous vote was required. Ironically, neither Troy nor Syracuse had the minimum population. (The National League also declined

Lake Front Park, home of the Chicago White Stockings, as it appeared in 1878. (Courtesy of National Baseball Library, Cooperstown, New York.)

an early move into Canada when the Tecumsehs of London, Ontario, population 25,000, were denied membership.)

Because of the persistent debate over the Troy-Albany issue, territorial boundaries were still on the League's mind. It was proposed that everyone within the four-mile radius be counted to determine population. Worcester now had over 75,000 souls and became a League member—for all of three seasons, before becoming the Philadelphia Phillies in 1883.

Membership was so volatile that when Abraham G. Mills became League president, replacing interim Arthur H. Soden in 1882, he did not want franchises listed on his stationery. Between 1876 and the turn of the century, when stability finally arrived, 21 American cities were members of the fledgling circuit.

Resolving Major Issues

Yet slowly the League was advancing toward its goals—and dealing with such major issues as equipment, Sunday baseball, "revolving," alcohol and discipline.

A. G. Mills, fourth president of the National League.

An issue dealt with almost immediately was a rather basic one, the uniformity of baseballs. Under the old Association, the only criterion was that balls be nine and one-quarter inches in circumference and five and one-quarter ounces in weight. Until 1875, when the Ryan ball was made standard, several different manufacturers supplied them, with results varying from firm to firm. Red as well as white baseballs were employed. The National League went one step further, giving A. G. Spalding the concession and mandating much stricter standards. Part of the reason for choosing Spalding's product was that he offered it free to the League—not out of the goodness of his heart but rather for the public-relations value of supplying the official League ball. Ironically, this former pitcher was accused of supplying too "lively" a product.

From its inception, the National League had frowned on Sunday baseball. The reservation of the Sabbath exclusively for the Lord was a particularly nineteenth century American predilection, partly based on traditional piety and partly as a means of declaring sovereignty over the largely Catholic hordes of immigrants who were flooding the nation.

As the League endeavored to secure the approval of the "better" elements of society, it embraced a prohibition on Sabbath ball, even though it meant that most workmen (who then worked a six-day week) would be unable to patronize the contests.

In 1878 the League institutionalized the ban on Sunday ball, going so far as to threaten expulsion of any club that harbored on its roster anyone who had taken part in such contests – not only as a player but as a scorer or umpire as well.

In 1879 came a revolutionary innovation. High player salaries, caused by the competition for players, gnawed at the magnates' collective consciousness – and worse, at their profits. Players were free to sign contracts with any club for any amount of time. Clubs bid against one another, driving prices up. Aggravating the situation were unscrupulous practices by players and management alike. A particularly ugly case involved the Binghamton Crickets and the Utica Utes of the rival International Association with Binghamton unsuccessfully attempting to hijack several players from Utica's 1877 squad. (The matter was settled by the Association Judicial Committee.)

In the 1870s player salaries accounted for roughly two-thirds of all club expenses. "It is ridiculous to pay ballplayers $2,000 a year," fumed William Hulbert, "when the $800 boys often do just as well."

Finally, on a motion from Boston owner Arthur Soden at the annual League meeting at Buffalo's Palace Hotel on September 29, 1879, a secret "reserve list" was created. Each club could "reserve" the services of five players; other owners solemnly agreed not to "contract with, employ, engage or negotiate" with these reserved players. Nor would any League member play against any club – in the League or not – which employed "a player reserved to another League Club."

The Buffalo *Express* broke the news to the public three days later:

> It was revealed that each club should have five of their present team who would be inviolate, that is that no club would have the right to approach them without consent of the club that had reserved him. Each delegate selected five men. The names were all put in writing and the representatives attached their names to the pact, binding them to adhere to the agreement.

Oddly enough, the first "reserved" players took a certain pride in their status. In some sense this tangibly indicated what the owners' felt of their value. It also guaranteed them a job for the next season. William A. Hulbert even argued, "They [the players] are all anxious to be reserved, and their only fear is they won't be."

The heavily German populations of St. Louis and Cincinnati favored a good time once off work, as opposed to their old-line American Protestant neighbors. Specifically, they wanted to go to a ball game on a Sunday and imbibe a few suds before going home. William Hulbert would have none of this.

There was already bad blood between Hulbert and the Queen City. After the 1879 season Hulbert had grabbed rookie outfielder Mike "King" Kelly and pitcher Fred Goldsmith from the disintegrating Cincinnati roster for his White Stockings.

Ballplayer-turned-businessman A. G. Spalding, whose sporting goods company provided the official baseball of the National League.

When late in the 1880 season Hulbert began to move against Cincinnati beer sales, Cincinnati *Enquirer* sports editor O. P. Caylor blasted him, threatening among other things to oust Hulbert or to form an entirely new league.

Hulbert soon had his say. At October's League meeting, on a motion by Henry T. Root of Providence, "a pledge was made to add a forfeiture of membership for selling malt or spiritous liquors on League grounds, or in any building owned or occupied by a League club." This was a motion specifically aimed at the Cincinnati club, which took in $3,000 a year from the beer concession. The Red Stockings' W. C. Kennett protested, but that did not prevent the League's declaring his franchise vacant, in effect expelling the club for behavior which until that instant had been perfectly legal.

But drinking among the fans in the stands was not baseball's only encounter with demon rum. The players also showed up plastered at the ball yard. *Beadle's Dime Centennial Base-Ball Player* editorialized:

> Any man now desirous of using his physical and mental powers to the utmost advantage, must . . . refuse to allow a drop of alcoholic liquor, whether in the form of spirits, wine or beer, to pass down his throat. We are not preaching "temperance" to the fraternity, but telling them facts, hard incontrovertible facts, which experience is gradually proving to those who have charge of the training of athletes. . . . How many ball-players . . . at match after match, are deluded into the notion that by drinking whiskey in the midst of their game, they thereby impart new vigor to their bodies, clear their judgement and sight, and inspirit them to greater endurance, when the undeniable fact is, that the liquor they drink does the very reverse of all these things, as it neither nourishes the system nor clears the sight; on the contrary, inflames the stomach, clouds the brain, and actually weakens the whole man.

As late as 1884 *Spalding's Base Ball Guide* was noting the seriousness of the problem (reporting that it was worse in 1883 than 1882, actually) and calling for wholesale blacklisting of drunken players and the enactment of rules insisting upon "total abstinence during the championship season."

The price of tickets continued to be a thorny issue. Henry Chadwick was among those unsuccessfully urging lower admission prices, tying his plea to a topic he knew owners would be interested in, lower salaries. "Say what you will, gentlemen of the league, you must come down . . . to the twenty-five-cent admission fee, and you must proportionately lower your salaries. . . . Catchers and pitchers deserve more than players at other positions, but $1,000 is good pay even for them, and a hundred dollars a month (for six months) is sufficient for the other positions."

There was no set rule on admission prices (although in 1877 the League mandated 15 cents per head as a visitors' share), only a gentlemen's agreement that 50 cents would be the minimum. Harry Wright had long been an advocate of that figure, stating, "A good game is worth 50cts, a poor one is dear at 25cts."

Clubs such as Buffalo, Syracuse and Worcester were all initially skeptical about the 50-cent amount, but all relented in order to gain League membership. Buffalo and Syracuse continued to carp over the 50-cent figure, but in May 1880 the Worcester *Spy* indicated a change of heart on the issue:

> It is a success thus far, the local patrons of the game taking kindly to the new arrangement. The receipts of the three games with the Troys were equal to an amount that would have required an average attendance of 1,200 to a game at the 25 cent tariff, and it would have required 3,040 persons at 25 cents to have equaled the amount received by Worcester Saturday. As

the average attendance at [National Base Ball Association] championship games last year was only 600, and the money was divided with visitors, or else they received a guarantee of $75, it will not take a mathematician to see that the old heads in the league understand the financial management of the game much better than outsiders, and that Worcester did a wise thing in joining the League.

Both Wright and *Spalding's Guide* argued that a 50-cent tariff was necessary to maintain the league and that fans would be more than willing to pay such a rate to see first-class ball. In point of fact, this amount was in line with other amusements and entertainments of the day. In 1880, the League formally mandated the 50-cent admission.

At Saratoga's fashionable Adelphi Hotel on September 29, 1881, to combat the still-vexing problem of player disorderliness, the National League created a blacklist. Players affected would be those "against whom the charges of general dissipation and insubordination have been repeatedly made." They included outfielders Michael C. Dorgan, "Sadie" Houck, William Crowley and Lewis Pessano "Buttercup" Dickerson; catcher Emil M. Gross; second baseman-outfielder and former manager Lipman Pike; pitchers Edward Sylvester "The Only" Nolan and John J. Fox; and utility man Lewis J. "Blower" Brown.

Not every instance could be called "dissipation." In many cases the magnates were simply lording it over their employees as any nineteenth century captain of industry would. Houck was blacklisted for failing to tip his cap to Boston owner Arthur Soden. Nolan was deprived of employment for asking for a day off to visit his brother William. Unfortunately, "William Nolan" did not exist, and management discovered this fact. Outfielder Charles Wesley Jones was later banned for having the temerity to ask Soden how much salary the owner still owed him.

Players could be reinstated only by unanimous League vote. The original blacklisted players were reinstated in December 1882, along with catcher-shortstop Edward J. Caskin and catcher John Clapp, who had been subsequently banned. The magnates were moved less by a sense of mercy than by the threat of American Association competition.

So while the League was by no means a settled institution, each year it had forcefully dealt with the issues at hand: scheduling (1876), gambling (1877), Sabbath baseball (1878), the reserve clause (1879), the 50-cent admission and sale of liquor on club grounds (1880) and blacklisting of personnel (1881) – and so had strengthened its hand.

The proof was not only that the League survived, but that others were soon willing to form new leagues in competition with it.

Chapter 3
The International Association

While the National Association and the National League had changed the face of professional baseball, they had not totally transformed it.

Many independent teams remained in operation. In fact, the great majority of professional clubs were independent, organizing their own ad-hoc schedules and operating as they desired.

Not everyone *wanted* to compete in the new league system. Being an association or league member translated into onerous and expensive travel obligations, as well as pressure to compete with much larger entities in terms of salaries. It was not immediately apparent to professionals of the 1870s that this was the only way for a club to operate.

Beadle's Dime Base-Ball Player listed the following professional non–League clubs (and their communities when possible) in operation in 1876:

> New York: Cornell (of Ithaca), Star (of Syracuse), Chelsea, Auburn, Rochester, Enterprise, Cricket (of Binghamton)
> Pennsylvania: Allegheny (of Pittsburgh), Philadelphia, Kleinz, Neshannock
> Connecticut: New Haven, Bridgeport
> Massachusetts: Fall River, Live Oak (of Lynn), Lowell, Taunton
> Rhode Island: Rhode Island (of Providence)
> Canada: Tecumseh (of London), Maple Leaf (of Guelph)
> New Jersey: Olympic, Resolute
> Michigan: Aetna (of Detroit)
> Ohio: Buckeye (of Columbus)
> Missouri: St. Louis Reds
> West Virginia: Standard (of Wheeling)
> Tennessee: Memphis
> Indiana: Indianapolis
> Kentucky: Star (of Covington)
> California: San Francisco
> Illinois: Franklin (of Chicago)

Aside from playing each other and amateur clubs, these clubs also took the field against the National League. It was not at all odd for non–League clubs

47

to triumph. In 1876 National League teams usually won, but in 1877, the tables
turned, and the N.L. was defeated by non–League rivals 72 times. Only Hartford had a winning record against independents.

Beadle's Dime Base-Ball Player noted sarcastically that "games won by
non–League clubs over League nines were not so numerous in 1878 as in
1877, one reason being that not half as many inter-association games were
played."

In any case, considerable resentment greeted the birth of the National
League, particularly from such former Association members as New Haven.
Rumors sprung up of competing federations, but only one soon came to
fruition.

A Loose Confederation

On February 20, 1877, an "International Association of Professional Base
Ball Players" formed in Pittsburgh. The conference had been called by L. C.
Waite, secretary of the St. Louis Red Stockings, who in November 1876 wrote
to the 50-odd remaining independent professional clubs. He urged the creation
of a rival group to set its own admission rates, and even recommended a boycott
of the National League as opponents.

Ten delegates representing 17 clubs answered Waite's invitation and convened in Pittsburgh. William A. "Candy" Cummings of the Live Oaks was
chosen president; Harry Gorman of the Tecumsehs was vice president; and
James A. Williams of the Buckeyes was chosen secretary-treasurer and also as
chief administrative officer, posts he would hold for the life of the Association.

Membership was but $10 yearly, the old National Association level. If a
club wished to compete for the championship an extra $15 was required. Seven
did: Lynn; London; Columbus; Pittsburgh; Guelph, Ontario; Manchester, New
Hampshire; and Rochester, New York. Sixteen clubs signed up as non-
contending members. No vote was ever taken on Waite's suggestion of a ban
on play against National League nines.

From a modern perspective, it would be tempting to term the Association
a "minor league." Yet at the time, it could not be so easily pigeonholed. Despite
a rather miserable form of organization, a good caliber of ball was played by
these nines. International Association and National League players were
equally named to nationally recognized all-star teams. Additionally, of course,
the very idea of a minor league simply did not yet exist.

In October 1878 the Philadelphia *Times* charged, "The League has not sustained the reputation it had three or four years ago. There are clubs in the International Association fully as strong as League clubs."

Association President Cummings, reputed inventor of the curve ball and
a National Association veteran, hurled the first International Association game

ever played. He lost to Manchester 14–3, beginning a 1-7 season as Lynn soon dropped out of the Association. Cummings went on to a 5-14 mark for Cincinnati in the National League. The Tecumseh club took the flag with a 14-4 record and featured outfielder Joe Hornung and pitcher Fred Goldsmith. Others on the roster were Phil "Grandmother" Powers, catcher; G. H. Bradley, Dinnin and Herman Doescher, "basemen"; Ed Somerville, shortstop; Mager and Jake Knowdell, outfielders; and Reid and Spencer, substitutes.

Other noteworthy players in the Association that season were Mike "King" Kelly for Columbus and Jim "Pud" Galvin at Allegheny.

The National League Retaliates

More important to the Association than its first pennant race were actions taken by the National League in regard to exhibitions. The National League decided to play hardball with its poor cousins. No game with a non–League club would take place on League grounds. The League ball would be used, and only a League umpire could be arbiter. The League reserved the right to cancel in order to make up rained-out League games, but demanded a $50 payment if the non–League club did not play for whatever reason.

"The truth is, gentlemen of the smaller cities," sniffed the Chicago *Tribune*, "the League . . . finds it doesn't want you on their grounds. . . . The League can make more money off thirty first-class games than they can off sixty . . . and they are going to play the thirty with the clubs they think most likely to interest their patrons."

The non–League clubs (mostly Association members) were incensed. Auburn urged fellow clubs to "stick together and kick together." The Stars of Syracuse were ready to "act promptly, and with firmness, against any attempt at monopoly from whencever [sic] it comes."

A. B. Rankin of Brooklyn, a member of the Association's Judiciary Committee, fired off the following white-hot epistle to International Association clubs:

1118 Fulton Avenue, Brooklyn
New York, January 7th, 1878

Gentlemen:

The high hand with which the League undertakes to control the baseball fraternity, for 1878, is so unreasonably absurd that it behooves us to arouse ourselves to a realization of the situation. Are we to submit to the caprice of a clique or ring? Or, are we to assert our own independence? Their assurance in daring to dictate to organizations that have shown equality in playing, and in some cases, superiority, is the height of presumption. What club, I ask, will give the League a 100% guarantee, or half the gate receipts if that should be preferred by the League; with 50% forfeit for a rainy day—without reciprocation?

The International Association was formed, about a year since, for no other purpose than to protect non–League clubs from being imposed upon; and for that object it will continue to strive. Its motto is "Right, and equal justice to all alike."

The inducements offered by the League to non–League clubs to get them to join a League-Alliance (which they hope will take the place of and destroy the International Association) are, in reality, no inducements at all. It is, mainly the old "pitch and toss" game over again—with the motto "heads I win, tails you lose." The clubs invited to this "feast of empty dishes" are not allowed a voice in the legislation that is to govern them; nor are they to be allowed to play with clubs belonging to any other association; actually requiring men—adult men, not boys—to accept such arbitrary terms or disband. For this sacrifice of manhood what benefit do they offer? Echo answers: What benefit do they offer?

If the non–League clubs, throughout the country, will only stand firmly, by each other they will have no favors to ask. They have the material for building up a grand organization outside the League—which is in successful progress, and has been since February last. In the International Association (which meets in convention, at Buffalo, N.Y., next month, to which you are expected to send a delegate) each club is the equal of each other club. When guarantees are required, they are given in return. The guarantees between clubs not contesting for the championship are matters of business with such clubs and are settled among themselves.

I am a member of the Judiciary Committee of the International Association, but have not consulted with any other person about this letter.

Respectfully,

A. B. Rankin

Association clubs had little leverage, and less inclination to stand together. The League made the small concession of allowing preseason non–League games at its home fields, but that was it. Non-League clubs scrambled to get the best deals they could.

Another League move was the formation in 1877 of the so-called "League Alliance," a plan conceived by A. G. Mills, an associate of William Hulbert and a future president of the National League. This Alliance tied various independent clubs to the National League by common respect for contracts and by mutual agreement to ban "ineligible" players. It was not to be confused with any attempt at creating a farm club, but was aimed at disciplining and controlling personnel. At first, 13 clubs joined (the Red Caps of St. Paul, Indianapolis, Minneapolis, Milwaukee, Janesville and Memphis in the West; and the Star of Syracuse, the Crickets of Binghamtom, Lowell, Fall River, Philadelphia Athletics and the Rhode Island Club of Providence in the East). St. Paul and Syracuse won their respective informal "divisions."

The full text of this historic agreement read:

IT IS HEREBY AGREED, BY THE PARTIES HERETO, AS FOLLOWS:

First. No club that is a party hereto shall employ or play in its nine any player to whose services any other club that is a party hereto may be entitled by contract.

Second. Any player under contract with any club that is a party hereto, who shall, without the written consent of such club, leave its service, or fail to perform his contract, or who shall be proven guilty of disreputable conduct, shall be at once expelled by such club.

Third. No club that is a party hereto shall play any game of ball with any base-ball club whatever that shall employ or present in its nine any player that shall have been expelled from any club that is a party hereto for breach of contract or dispreputable conduct.

Fourth. Each club that is a party hereto shall, upon making a contract with a player, *immediately* notify the Secretary of the National League of Professional Base Ball Clubs, such notice to be in writing, signed by the contracting club and the player, and *in the absence of such notice to such officer, any player shall be deemed to be free from contract obligation.*

Fifth. Each club that is a party hereto shall *upon expelling a player from membership, or releasing him from contract,* notify the Secretary of the National League of Professional Base Ball Clubs, such notice to be in writing, and in the absence of such notice such player shall be deemed to be a member in good standing of the club whose notice of contract with such player had previously been transmitted to such officer, until the expiration of such contract.

Sixth. The notices provided for in the last two preceding stipulations are required to be sent to the Secretary of the League, upon the understanding that such officer will, immediately upon their receipt, communicate the same to all league clubs, as well as to all parties to this agreement; and in the event of the failure or refusal of such officer to perform such service, or his discontinuance thereof, then the parties hereto shall devise other means for the performance of such service.

Seventh. All games played by the clubs that are parties hereto shall be played in accordance with the playing rules of the National League.

Eighth. All disputes that may arise between the clubs that are parties hereto shall be submitted to the Board of Directors of the National League for adjudication, in the manner provided by Sec. 2, Art. XII, of its Constitution, and the finding of such tribunal shall be final and binding upon the clubs that are parties hereto.

Ninth. This agreement shall go into effect and be binding upon each club upon the date of its signature by such club.

Tenth. Each club that is a party hereto shall retain a copy of this agreement and the original shall be deposited with the Secretary of the National League.

Hidden in the legal verbiage of the agreement were provisions giving leadership of the national game to the National League, particularly in terms of setting playing rules and in resolving disputes among signatories. That clubs would meekly submit to rule by boards on which they had no representation revealed dramatically what dominion Hulbert's circuit was already exercising.

Eventually other features were added. Only one Alliance club per city was allowed (in 1879 this rule would be ignored in Albany, New York), and each club's territory was respected in terms of exhibitions.

The National League thus institutionalized its own primacy and achieved a modicum of success in playing off some independent clubs against each other. It also laid the groundwork for the wider frameworks of Organized Baseball that were to come.

In 1878 13 clubs competed for the Association's championship: Rochester; London (captained by Ross Barnes, whose career had rapidly gone downhill); Pittsburgh; Manchester; Lynn; Buffalo (the Bisons); Utica (the Utes); Syracuse (the Stars); Hornellsville, New York (the Hornells); Binghamton (the Crickets); New Bedford, Massachusetts; Lowell, Massachusetts; and Springfield, Massachusetts. In February 1878 an organizational session was held at Buffalo. The season ran from April 15 to October 15, with the entrance fee having been raised to $30 (regular membership had been increased to $20). Each visiting team was now guaranteed $75; the numbers of "deadheads" or those admitted free to each contest was increased from ten to twelve.

A baseball manufacturer from Holyoke named L. H. Mahn attended this session and convinced the circuit to purchase balls from him for $10 per dozen. Shortly thereafter, the Association learned Mahn was selling the same product to the National League for $7.50. They were so outraged they turned to Albert Spalding for equipment. The unused Mahn balls can today be seen at Cooperstown.

1878: Bisons Versus Stars

Membership in any sort of league or association was not valued highly by these professionals. Immediately following the 1878 annual meeting teams huddled together to form a "New York State Association," with an entrance fee of $10. Ten clubs were represented: Auburn, the Alaskas of New York City, Buffalo, Brooklyn, the Crickets of Binghamton, Hornell, the Haymakers of Lansingburg (Troy), Rochester, the Stars of Syracuse and Utica.

The Stars had formed as a club on June 9, 1866. By 1876 they were a professional club under former Live Oaks player, George W. Brackett, and featured many fine players, such as Billy Geer, Jack Farrell, Alex McKinnon, John Dunn, Patrick Henry "Harry" McCormick and Mike Dorgan. Dorgan, who would go on to play for Jim Mutrie's Giants, and four others had all been recruited from the Live Oaks. That year the Syracuse nine bested both the St. Louis Browns and the Chicago White Stockings of the infant National League. Their record stood at 46-13, with pitcher McCormick winning 33 games. The Stars were numbered among the best seven or eight clubs in the nation.

When the Stars entered the championship campaign of the International Association in 1878, they had already established a formidable reputation. The pennant race between them and the highly talented Buffalo club was so close that it was decided on the validity of an August 23 forfeit by the disbanded Rochester club to Syracuse. Not until the Association met in March 1879 at Utica's Baggs Hotel was the pennant decided. Even aside from that, Buffalo's championship was marred by allegations that the Bisons had won it largely on the calls of local umpire C. W. Nichols, who was known throughout the league for his bias. Late in the season Buffalo won 13 straight at home, allegedly aided by Nichols.

The attrition rate was high for 1878, the circuit's first championship season. New Bedford dropped out before it even began and was replaced by New Haven in early May; on the 20th of that month, the franchise transferred again, to Hartford. On June 4, the Lynn nine moved to Worcester. Pittsburgh expired on June 8. On June 20, Hartford was expelled for stiffing the Buffalo club of its share of the gate receipts. The carnage continued: Binghamton quit on July 19; on August 21, Hornell, Rochester and London disbanded. Allegations of gambling haunted the Tecumsehs. In October, Worcester fell apart.

So despite three midseason franchise shifts, only six of the original 13 franchises were able to stumble through to season's end.

Failing franchises were not the only problem. Forfeits were common. The Live Oaks walked away from a game at New Haven even though leading 3–2. In the midst of a scoreless tie at Lynn, the Tecumsehs, unhappy with the umpire, forfeited. Utica forfeited under similar circumstances (a 2–2 tie) at Springfield.

The Manchester management took the action of suspending pitcher Leary for drunkenness on the playing field. A few days later he was nonetheless reinstated by the club, which gave as a reason the fact that it had "not reported the expulsion to the national authorities."

The season was not without its humorous moments. On August 26, the Manchesters played a non–Association contest against a reformatory. During the game, a thief using a skeleton key gained entrance to Manchester's locker room and stole various jewelry and $48. Center fielder John O'Rourke's inscribed watch, a gift from admiring fans, was left behind, however. "Sentimental fellow!" exclaimed the astonished O'Rourke.

While there was chaos in the circuit, a good caliber of ball was being played. Preston D. Orem, a little-known but quite invaluable scholar of the game's early history, wrote of 1878 that "the association included many players who could have played in the National League if they had wished to do so but

The 1878 Buffalo Bisons. Back row, from left: Tom Dolan, Jack Allen, Bill McGunnigle, Jim Galvin; middle row: Bill Crowley, Dave Eggler, Steve Libby, Charles Fulmer, Denny Mack; front: Davy Force, John McSorley. (Courtesy of Joseph M. Overfield.)

who preferred the more relaxed and easy atmosphere of the International."

"Several of the better clubs," Orem contended, "were superior to Indianapolis and Milwaukee, at least, in the National League."

"I hear we was going to join the League I hope & pray not for if we do we are gone financially . . . for there is nothing in it," Davy Force wrote to his Buffalo club in 1878.

Despite any controversy, the champion 1878 Buffalo Bisons were very good indeed, featuring future Hall of Famer Pud Galvin (who pitched between 895 and 905 innings that season), Davy Force, Dave Eggler, John "Trick" McSorley, Cyrus "Jack" Allen, Charley Fulmer (a seven-year major league veteran) and Joe Hornung. Every member of the Bisons went on to play in the big leagues. When the New York *Clipper* chose an all-star team that year, five Buffalo Bisons were on it: Galvin, Force, Hornung, Steve Libby, and Bill McGunnigle. Their overall record (including exhibitions) was 81 victories, 32 losses and 3 ties. Against National League competition that season they were 10-7.

International League star John Montgomery Ward.

The Buffalo roster for 1878:

PLAYER	POS.	HR	AVG.
Jack Allen	3b	0	.139
Bill Crowley	lf	0	.289
Tom Dolan	c	0	.226
David Eggler	cf	0	.191
David Force	ss	0	.302
Charles Fulmer	2b	0	.214
Jim Galvin	p	1	.198
Joe Hornung	of	0	.254
Steve Libby	1b	1	.184
Denny Mack	2b	0	.280
Bill McGunnigle	p/of	0	.214
John McSorley	util.	0	.162

The Bison payroll matched its talent. Salaries ranged from $700 for McSorley to $1,000 for Eggler to $1,200 for Force. The club even constructed a new playing field on the city's West Side, Riverside Park. Despite all this expense (including $11,068.23 in salaries for players and staff), the club turned a modest profit of $248.94.

Like so many other successful International Association clubs (Tecumseh, the Haymakers, Albany, the Stars, Worcester), the Bisons were eager to join the National League. Buffalo became a member (along with Syracuse) in 1878 and finished in a respectable tie for third.

Other Association players who went on to big league careers included Lou Say, John Montgomery Ward, Ned Williamson and "Pebbly Jack" Glasscock.

1879: Treachery and Success in Albany

In 1879 the International Association became the National Base-Ball Association, as all Canadian teams dropped out. Nine clubs competed for the flag: Utica, Manchester, New Bedford, the Nationals of Washington, Holyoke, Worcester, Springfield and two clubs from Albany—Albany and Capital City.

Capital City dropped out on May 9, many of its players transferring over to the new Hop Bitters of Rochester. The circumstances regarding this shift were highly irregular. A gentleman named Cummings (not league President Candy Cummings) was engaged as manager for $1,200, and although he had the backing of the majority of the directors, some "despised" him.

The Capital City club had started with high hopes. Part of the reason that the club formed was civic pride; another was convenience and safety. The already-existing Albany club played at Riverside Park across the Hudson River in Rensselaer County. Boosterism demanded that a field and a team actually be secured in the capital city itself. Beyond that, getting across the Hudson was no easy task. Some feared the "danger of crossing the river in small skiffs," although a ferry, the "George Marks," carried less-adventurous passengers to the park.

A field for the new team was secured on Lark Street for $4,000, with $1,000 paid in cash up front. Three hundred dollars was expended on uniforms, shoes and bats. Salaries ran as follows:

Leonard	$1,500
Manning	1,500
Schaffer	1,500
Murnane	1,350
McClure	1,050
Allison	1,200
McKinnon	1,200
Smiley	1,200
Higham	1,200
Corey	1,200

The club was soon behaving shabbily as reported in an Albany newspaper: "Their playing was entirely different from what it was represented to be; the most insignificant club walked away with them. The number of errors committed, and those too, by the men who were receiving the highest salaries, led to but one conclusion, that something was rotten in Denmark."

Individual actions were particularly objectionable: "One or more of them were addicted to the drinking of whisky, and that too, immediately prior to a game; one or more partook quite freely of large quantities of lager; one or more spent as much spare time as other indulgences would permit, in the fascinating pastime of draw-poker; none of them practiced as they should, and some of them practiced hardly any."

Cummings had allegedly been in communication for two months with interests in Rochester, the goal being to transfer his team to that city. He supposedly reasoned that the way to gain their release from Capital City was for them to play badly; in this they succeeded admirably, being unable to win a single game on their Lark Street grounds.

In early May the club directors were introduced to a gentleman from Rochester who informed them of the scheme. Although some directors wished to take "stringent measures" against their players to prevent them from ever playing again, the sickened majority merely desired to wash their hands of the venture. The whole team was released and promptly signed with Rochester. "Without consideration," the directors handed over all their expensive equipment to the Hop Bitters.

Ironically, Cummings was not signed by the Hop Bitters and remained behind in Albany. On May 12 he was used in a game as "change pitcher" at Albany by Worcester. His talent for losing was still evident: he gave up three runs in the ninth inning to lose 7–5.

Albany citizens weren't the only people upset over the incident. The Utica *Herald* observed: "An associated press dispatch . . . says the team will hereafter be known as 'Hop Bitters.' This looks as though the club is to be used as an advertising dodge. Although there is no national rule prescribing the name under which a club shall play, it is doubtful whether Rochester can get a club into the championship contest under the name announced. In any event the Albanys have a clean field which they are abundantly able to fill."

But Rochester continued to play under the "Hop Bitters" name, although in at least one dispatch the Albany *Daily Evening Times* referred to the team as the "Quack Bitters."

Late in May, Albany Alderman Thomas Cavanaugh indicated how deep feelings against the Capital Citys remained, as he brought charges before the judicial committee of the National Base-Ball Association of "crooked" playing by five of the current Hop Bitters.

Further evidence of confusion in this circuit abounded. At about the same time that Cavanaugh made his accusations, the local Troy independent club expelled an ex–Capital City player named McKinnon because he had signed with them, accepted a $75 advance, and then signed with the Hop Bitters.

In mid–June a club from Hudson, New York, endeavored to rename itself the "Capital Citys" and play Utica at the Capital City's old Lark Street grounds. The Albany club protested, saying it would be a "reflection" on their game that same day at their Riverside Park home against the Manchesters. The Uticas left for home without the contest taking place.

During the season a large number of clubs besides Capital City folded. The Manchester club, suspected of being in league with gamblers, was so un- popular at home (one game against Albany drew fewer than 100 customers) it was forced to play entirely on the road before collapsing entirely. Utica was a casualty on July 11. The Hop Bitters soon followed. Springfield disbanded in early September.

Games continued to feature turbulent behavior. On June 7 Albany forfeited to Springfield after the fourth inning, "owing to the unsatisfactory deci- sion" of umpire C. P. Field of Springfield. A May 20 contest in Washington was marked by "boisterous and abusive treatment of the visiting club" by the crowd of 1,800 "cranks." Two days later Albany indicated in the second inning that it was playing under protest, alleging the umpire "was bulldozed by the crowd in attendance to decide against the Albanys continually."

Back home in upstate New York, fans were avidly following events thanks to a fairly new technology. A Pearl Street saloon posted a sign indicating that the play-by-play would be telegraphed back to Albany and posted inside.

> Between four and five o'clock in the afternoon the returns began to come in and were announced not only in the place alluded to but also in two cigar stores on the other side of the street. Between six and seven in the evening the score stood Nationals 6, Albanys 6. Then the excitement was at fever heat, and large crowds assembled at the corner, of State and Pearl and Beaver streets, where the blackboards were situated showing how the game stood. Bets of lager ale, cigars, cigarettes, and money, were freely offered and taken that the Albanys, would beat this time. The crowd was increasing all the time and any one not knowing what was the cause of such an assemblage would have thought it was election day. The arrival of the telegraph boy, bearing the important message, was looked for with great anx- iety, and when he did come it was almost impossible for him to get through the crowd to deliver the result, so anxious were they to know. Before he got to Pearl Street he was beseiged with the question "How has it gone?" but he did not know any more about it than any one else, and told them so. When the young man came out to mark the score, the crowd pressed up around him, and it was with difficulty that he made the figures as they were reported, viz:
> Nationals 8; Albanys 7.

As Ernest Thayer wrote, there was no joy in Mudville.

At season's end Albany was declared the pennant winner. The club featured some real talent, including Tommy Burns (.262 in 49 games and a sparkling defense, although the Albany *Daily Evening Times* complained of his "slouchy ways," Ned Hanlon (.316 in 47 games), Lipman Pike (.356 overall for the year; he also played with Holyoke and Springfield) and Fred Dunlap (.259 in 51 games).

Albany's regular lineup was as follows: Keenan, catcher; Critchley, pitcher; Tobin, first base; Dunlap, second base; Burns, third base; Say, shortstop; Hanlon, Thomas and Rocap, outfielders.

However, not all of Albany's players were major league material. Their reserve center fielder, a fellow named Quinton, no longer with the club in 1880, met with a noteworthy accident in April of that year. Sound asleep on a pool table in Gillespie's saloon on Albany's Hudson Street, he became restless and rolled off his makeshift bed. Trying to catch himself he smashed his hands through a plate glass window, "cutting his wrists terribly, completely severing some of the arteries." The blood "flowed in torrents," and it was thought the wounds would be fatal. Quinton was rushed to a doctor, though, and "in a very few hours he was reported as being very comfortable."

1880: The End of the National Base-Ball Association

Only four clubs showed up for the International Association annual meeting on February 18–19, 1880, in New York—Albany, Washington's National club, Baltimore and Jersey City. Only the first three enrolled for the pennant, while 17 others affiliated with the Association. "Thanks," noted one account, "were voted to the members of the New York press—reporters were admitted to the National Convention, as there was nothing to hide from the public."

Association teams were still playing heavy exhibition schedules against League clubs. The Nationals played 12 such contests before Opening Day of the championship season:

April 8—Providence 6, Nationals 3
April 9—Providence 4, Nationals 4
April 10—Nationals 3, Providence 2
April 14—Cincinnati 6, Nationals 3
April 17—Nationals 10, Cincinnati 3
April 20—Chicago 6, Nationals 1
April 21—Nationals 4, Chicago 3
April 22—Chicago 7, Nationals 2
April 24—Nationals 3, Chicago 1
April 26—Cleveland 1, Nationals 0 (five innings)
April 27—Cleveland 8, Nationals 4
April 28—Cleveland 5, Nationals 0

Albany also took on League teams, defeating Troy 8–7 on May 17, Worcester 7–3 on May 19, Boston 4–1 in a rain-shortened seven innings on May 26 and Buffalo 5–4 on June 1, but losing to Worcester 5–0 on April 28, Cincinnati 7–5 on June 7 and Cleveland 3–2 on June 15.

Despite creditable outings against the League, and despite having such players as Lipman Pike, Mike Dorgan and Jimmy Say, Albany was not up to repeating its 1879 performance. As early as April 29, the Albany *Daily Evening Times* griped that the team "should either win a game once in awhile or disband. They are laughed at on all sides as it is now." The call was repeated after a June 26 16–3 drubbing by the Nationals in which Albany committed 19 errors.

The *Daily Evening Times* did make a historic suggestion on April 19, 1880. Noting that the Cincinnati *Enquirer* was urging that batters' names be posted on the scoreboard, the local paper went one step further: "Or, why not have each man outnumbered, and the number put opposite his name on the scorecard!"

We have no record of whether Albany acted on this thought.

For all intents and purposes, 1880 was the end of the line for the Association. Baltimore fell apart in June; Albany gave up in July, Rochester in early September. The Nationals were awarded a hollow championship. Their lineup consisted of Trott and Snyder, catchers and outfielders; Lynch, pitcher; Gerhardt, second base; Warner, third base; Powell, first base; Meyerle, Booth and Ellick, "basemen"; McClellan, shortstop; Holly, left field; Baker, center field; Bielaski, right field; and Derby, right field and change pitcher.

A caustic obituary was written by the 1883 *Spalding's Guide:* "The old International Association was organized by a special class of club backers in order that its clubs might be governed in the interests of an unscrupulous minority of club officials, without the restrictions on their 'little games' to which they were subjected under League government; thereby opening the door to a season's experience of the old evil of 'crooked play,' 'revolving,' and other like abuses. The National Association which followed the International, was an organization intended by the majority of the clubs composing it, simply to be a step-ladder to gain admittance to the League."

Basically, the International Association and the National Base-Ball Association were ultimately unsuited to competition with the more-aggressive, better-organized, larger-population-based National League. Yet they proved life could exist outside the National League. It would not be long before others were willing to take up the cudgel against William Hulbert's powerful combine.

Chapter 4

The American Association

Several key issues—including ticket prices, Sunday baseball, alcohol on the grounds—continued to plague the National League throughout its formative years. The League took decisive steps to deal with them, but that did not mean everyone was pleased with the result.

Despite the League's existence, many independent professional clubs continued to be quite viable.

Given these two facts, the League faced renewed competition.

After the 1880 season many large metropolitan areas were left without League ball. New York and Philadelphia were expelled following the 1876 season. Louisville and St. Louis collapsed in the wake of the Grays scandal of 1877. Cincinnati was expelled in late 1880.

At the same time the burgeoning national population could easily support a second major league. To replace these franchises, though, the League reached further and further down to establish clubs in smaller cities like Syracuse, Troy, Worcester and Providence.

Viable baseball still existed in the League's jilted cities. In Cincinnati, Oliver Hazard Perry Caylor, sports editor of the Cincinnati *Enquirer* (ordinarily "a sedate, dignified sort of chap") was incensed by the "outrageous proceedings" of the Red Stockings' expulsion in October 1880. He scheduled a December 4 meeting to start up a new circuit, but nothing came of his scheme.

In St. Louis, teams continued in the League Alliance (1877) and the International Association (1878). Louisville, as well, maintained a professional team, which in 1881 included Pete Browning, Fred Pfeffer and William "Chicken" Wolf. In Philadelphia, fans could continue to follow either the still-functioning Athletics or "Philadelphias."

The Founding of the Metropolitans

But it was in New York, the game's actual birthplace and the nation's largest city, that feeling remained strongest.

In September 1880, a new club, the "Metropolitans," was organized.

61

Manhattan businessman and amateur player John B. Day had been pitching that summer and at one game was not doing particularly well. Watching was former Fall River shortstop James Mutrie. After a while an exasperated Mutrie declared to Day: "If you will furnish the money, I'll get you a team that can beat the other nine." Mutrie's Metropolitans, drawing talent mostly from the Unions of Brooklyn and the disbanded Rochester Hop Bitters, did well that autumn. Playing 26 games, they took 11 of 12 from local competition and split 14 contests with professionals, including three wins versus the Washington Nationals, champions of the rapidly expiring National Base-Ball Association.

In 1881 the Mets entered the new Eastern Championship Association. Other teams were New Boston (which dropped out almost instantly and was replaced by the Philadelphia club), the New York and Quicksteps clubs of New York, the Brooklyn Atlantics, the Philadelphia Athletics and the Washington Nationals.

Day leased the Polo Grounds and had a success on his hands. On May 30 an overflow crowd of 15,000 (including 5,000 standees) watched the Mets defeat the Atlantics 6–4. The Metropolitans took the Eastern Association pennant, playing before crowds averaging over 3,000 for the season. They played 151 games, the largest number to date in a single season. Sixty were versus the League; the Mets won 18.

Clubs from these larger cities were being irresistibly drawn together. A Cincinnati team using the old "Red Stockings" name and the Athletics made highly successful trips to St. Louis in 1881.

Birth of a New Challenger

The time was clearly ripe for a new league.

Philadelphia's Manager Horace B. Phillips, in conjunction with Justus Thorner, ex-president of Cincinnati, actually was responsible for calling a meeting to form a new league. Unfortunately, soon after he sent out postcards announcing an October 10, 1881, session in Pittsburgh, he was fired as manager, and promptly forgot about the enterprise.

Cincinnati was the only club taking the matter seriously enough to go to Pittsburgh. Thorner, sports editor Caylor and an *Enquirer* reporter named Frank Wright arrived, but there was absolutely no one to meet with. As fate would have it, as they trudged about the darkened town wondering what sort of fools they had been, they met with a local fan, bartender Al Pratt, a former pitcher for the Forest City club of Cleveland in the old National Association. Pratt advised them to contact a fellow "crank," Pittsburgh iron manufacturer Harmer Denny McKnight, who had headed the old Alleghenys of the International Association.

O. P. Caylor, a Cincinnati sports editor influential in the founding of the American Association.

The meeting proved congenial. This new combine, operating on pure bluff, wired the other clubs and skillfully implied to each that it was the only one missing at Pittsburgh. In the interim, McKnight reorganized the Allegheny Club on October 15, with himself as president and Edward C. Hetzel as secretary. A fund of $5,000 was raised as capital.

This rather transparent scheme actually worked. Its first effect was that Hulbert was so upset by developments he suffered a heart attack. As events would later show, his health would be permanently damaged by the incidents.

A second conference, utilizing the slogan "Liberty for All," was scheduled for November 1–2 in Cincinnati, with Thorner, Caylor and Victor H. Long of that city; McKnight of Pittsburgh; J. H. Pank and John Reccius (with his brother Philip the first twins to play in the majors) of the Eclipse Club of Louisville; Chris Von der Ahe and David H. Reid of St. Louis; William Barnie of the Brooklyn Atlantics; and Charley Fulmer of the Philadelphia club present.

St. Louis, Louisville, Cincinnati, Brooklyn and Pittsburgh were admitted immediately. The Philadelphia issue was a thorny one. "Philadelphia" and the "Athletics" both expressed an interest, but as neither was willing to consolidate, a choice had to be made. The Athletics were finally admitted.

JAMES MUTRIE,

James Mutrie, manager of the New York Metropolitans.

Also present was Jim Mutrie of the Metropolitans, who cautiously refused to commit himself; with his heavy schedule of games against the League he was not about to alienate Hulbert. In fact, Mutrie immediately went to Chicago to confer with him. Still hesitant, Mutrie declined to join, but did attend the next meeting on March 13, 1882.

In the interim before the March session, the various Association clubs were more than busy. On November 16 the Cincinnati franchise organized, with Thorner as president, Long as vice president and George Herancourt as secretary-treasurer.

On November 19 the Browns signed former N.A. and N.L. outfielder Ned Cuthbert as playing-manager. David Reid was engaged as business manager.

On December 3 Philadelphia was "reorganizing" under former Centennial first baseman-outfielder Charlie Mason, theatrical manager Billy Sharsig and shortstop Charley Fulmer. When Fulmer, who was spending the off-season managing a Long Island touring company of "Uncle Tom's Cabin," found out a $200 investment was required, he dropped out as an investor and was replaced by Lew Simmons, who later became the manager. The club then refurbished its home grounds, the rather run-down Oakdale Park, which had been abandoned for the past six years.

Lew Simmons managed the Philadelphia Athletics to the 1883 American Association championship.

At a March session at Philadelphia's Continental Hotel, the following representatives from members and other interested clubs attended: Thorner and Caylor of Cincinnati; McKnight of Pittsburgh; Pank of Louisville; Von der Ahe and Reid of St. Louis; Barnie and A. B. Rankin of the Atlantics; Fulmer and Simmons of Philadelphia; James Mutrie of the Metropolitans; manager-shortstop Henry C. Myers and outfielder Charles C. Waitt of Baltimore; Fergy Malone of Atlantic City; and a J. Sheldon of the Alfred Merrills Club of Camden, New Jersey.

The Atlantics dropped out but were replaced by the Baltimore club owned by brewer Harry Vonderhorst. Basically, the National League's constitution was adopted by this new "American Association," but there were several significant distinctions "affording more significant conditions to cities and players." Clubs were free to charge a 25-cent admission. Both Sunday ball and sale of alcohol on the grounds were allowed. At the Association's first meeting, alcohol had been banned, but on March 13 the St. Louis and Cincinnati franchises objected, noting that such trade meant between four and five thousand dollars worth of business annually. The change was made without objection.

A permanent paid staff of umpires was retained, a significant improvement

**Chris Von der Ahe, St. Louis saloon keeper and owner of the American
Association Brown Stockings.**

over the hit-and-miss tactics previously employed. Steps leading to this had
been slow. Umpires were first paid in 1876, and then only at the rate of $5
per contest. In 1879 William Hulbert created the first League-approved list,
20 men from whom home clubs could choose an arbiter. Obviously, this did
little to free umpires from the suspicion of favoritism toward the home nine.

The four men the Association hired were S. M. Decker of Bradford, Pennsylvania; Frank Law of Norwalk, Ohio; A. F. Odlin of Lancaster, New Hampshire; and W. E. Furlong of Kansas City, Missouri. They were guaranteed a
$140 monthly salary and $3 per day in expenses and were mandated to wear
blue flannel jackets and caps while officiating. They were still not fully
autonomous and could be removed on the complaint of four clubs.

Dues for the Association were set at $50 annually (raised to $100 in 1883),
the Association secretary was to be salaried, and any Association director
broaching the content of a closed-door meeting was to be expelled. Each
visiting club was guaranteed $65 per game (the Atlantics dropped out over this
issue; they preferred a percentage of the take, as then practiced in the National
League). On major holidays, however, the gate was to be split 50-50.

In a measure which would eventually come back to haunt the Association,
each member club was free to leave the circuit at will.

McKnight was elected president; J. H. Pank of Louisville, vice president; and James A. Williams of Columbus, Ohio, former International Association chief administrative officer, secretary-treasurer.

Nonetheless, the establishment scoffed. The Chicago *Tribune* jeered: "By all means form an anti–League Association, with Cincinnati, St. Louis, and a few other villages as members. The League would be glad to be rid of some of its dead wood."

The "Beer and Whiskey" League

The Association soon became known as the "Beer and Whiskey" League. First, it owed its very existence to a Pittsburgh bartender. Secondly, it tolerated alcohol in its parks. And third, several prominent backers were connected to the industry: Justus Thorner (with J. G. Sohn & Company, a Cincinnati brewer), J. H. Pank (secretary and treasurer of the Kentucky Malting Co.), Vonderhorst of Baltimore and Chris Von der Ahe of St. Louis.

Von der Ahe is the figure most prominently linked by history with the American Association. Born in Hille, Germany, on November 7, 1851, Chris came to New York City around 1864. By the 1870s he was in St. Louis and earning his keep as a grocer and saloon keeper. Slightly east of his establishment was a jerrybuilt ballpark called Sportsman's Park, originally built as a *schutzpark* or shooting club for the area's German immigrants. Von der Ahe became interested in baseball as a means to sell more beer. In 1880, with Canadian-born Alfred H. Spink (later the founder of the *Sporting News*), he became an active participant in the city's sporting scene.

Spink, then sports editor of the St. Louis *Chronicle*, and a close friend scraped together $500 to purchase long-idle Sportsman's Park from owner Gus Solari.

On their way to close the deal, they stopped at Von den Ahe's Golden Lion Saloon. Von der Ahe, known throughout St. Louis as "The Lucky Dutchman," was grilling the two about their plans and posed the question: "Suppose you give Solari your last $500. What will you do then?"

This hadn't been a particular concern until then. "The thing to do," Von der Ahe explained, "is to form a regular corporation. I'll join you and get others to join." Chris took the original 180 shares at $10 apiece.

The Sportsman's Park and Club Association was the result – with Von der Ahe as president and Al Spink as secretary. In Von der Ahe, Spink "found a plump angel who, knowing next to nothing about baseball, was still ready to finance any outdoor recreation that promised to bring crowds of people into one place on Sunday, where he might sell them beer."

Chris really did know virtually nothing about baseball. After the first game with Cincinnati, Von der Ahe marveled to Al Spink over the size of the throng.

The St. Louis Browns, winners of four consecutive American Association championships. (Courtesy of National Baseball Library, Cooperstown, New York.)

"Vot a fine pig crowd," he exclaimed, "but the game, Al, how was the game? You know, Al, I know nawthing."

"He was pudgy," wrote the great sportswriter Fred Lieb, "and had a nose on which Jimmy Durante and W. C. Fields would have looked with envy; as Chris seldom passed when drinks were on the house his proboscis usually was lit up like a red bulb on a Christmas tree. . . . He was one of St. Louis' best known citizens. He wore a stovepipe hat, gaudy waistcoats and in his flush days almost as many diamonds as Jim Brady, who dazzled New York around the same time."

Many are the stories told of Chris Von der Ahe, and they are usually narrated in some form of German dialect. There was a time he harangued his Association colleagues for scheduling so many rained-out games in St. Louis.

"I don't want to be greedy," he maintained in all seriousness, "but next year I vant ze goot games in St. Louie when it doesn't rain. Let it rain in Zinzinnatti or on that dumkopf Vonderhorst for ze goot games. Not in St. Louie."

When told of a player who'd been released by three clubs, Chris responded, "Dot is right, a rolling moss never catches a stone."

The enterprise was a grand success. On an initial $5,000 investment the club returned a $25,000 profit in 1881. With such prosperity, Von der Ahe's initial modesty soon disappeared ("I am the smartest fellar in baseball"), even if his ignorance remained. After a long hit to right won a game for the Browns, Von der Ahe ordered his manager to have all batters hit to right. As he led his fellow club owners to the Sportsman's Park mound for Opening Day festivities in 1882 he bragged, "Look around, chentlemen, because this is the largest dimundt in the welt ist." The team captain diplomatically reminded his boss that all diamonds were equal in size. "Vot I meant to say," harrumphed Chris, "vas this is the largest infield in the welt ist."

In 1885 a World Series (since 1882 the League and Association champions had squared off in postseason competition) matched the Browns and Al Spalding's White Stockings. The Series broke up without a decision ("very unsatisfactory to all parties concerned," said *Spalding's Guide*), and the $1,000 prize offered by the *Mirror of American Sports* was split equally.

The next season, both clubs again captured their respective championships. Spalding and Cap Anson challenged Von der Ahe to a high-stakes series ("We will play you under only one condition, and that is winner take all, and by all, I mean every penny that is taken at the gate"), hoping the Teuton would decline. Von der Ahe did no such thing: "Sure, we will take them up and teach those fellars a lesson. No club is goot enough to beat the Browns."

With a reputed $15,000 at stake (actually closer to $13,000), this event caught the imagination of the nineteenth century public as few sporting exhibitions did, radically increasing baseball's already substantial popularity. The Browns won in six games.

Von der Ahe built a row of apartment houses in St. Louis and named them for his players, with a saloon at each corner. He treated his personnel well and even paid for a trainload of reporters and fans (hotel accommodations included) to accompany the team to New York for the 1888 World Series. When they got there he bought everyone a new suit of clothes. Total cost for the trip: $30,000. When the Browns beat the White Stockings for the 1886 championship of the world, Chris had a life-size statue of himself erected in front of Sportsman's Park. It was later moved to his grave.

In those days players would often dress at their hotels and parade to the park. There were two good reasons: publicity and lack of locker rooms. Many of Von der Ahe's squads lived at his apartment houses, and dressed in his gaudy finery and accompanied by his two greyhounds, Chris would lead the march. Behind "Der Boss President" was third baseman Arlie Latham, aping his employer's lurching gait and wearing a false red nose to mimic his most prominent facial feature.

Von der Ahe's ego grew so large he briefly took the reins of the Browns twice himself. Altogether in 17 seasons he made 32 managerial changes, and a number of matrimonial ones as well. In 1896 his wife charged he was carrying on an affair with their maid, Anne Kaiser, and sued for divorce. When the divorce came through he failed to marry the servant—even though he had promised to—and she sued for breach of promise. Chris married avaricious Della Welles, whom he divorced in December 1897 for a variety of reasons, including running up "large bills for things she does not need."

Christian Frederick Wilhelm Von der Ahe died in virtual poverty on June 7, 1913, of dropsy and cirrhosis of the liver. Charles Comiskey eulogized him as "the grandest figure baseball has ever known."

Von der Ahe and Spink were a team. In order to generate events at Sportsman's Park, it was Spink who wrote to Cincinnati's O. P. Caylor to revive the moribund Red Stockings and bring them to St. Louis (even if it were just for expenses and nothing more). This was just the beginning. Soon teams from as far as Brooklyn were appearing, and on one woeful team from Dubuque (the "Rabbits") Spink discovered a 17-year-old prospect named Charles Comiskey.

Now largely remembered as the tightfisted owner of the Black Sox, Chicago-born Comiskey began as a semipro in Milwaukee and Elgin. He was earning $50 a month with the Rabbits when Spink paid him $90 to join St. Louis. Comiskey became manager of the Browns in 1883, leading them to four straight pennants from 1885 through 1888. He had a lifetime A.A. average of only .273 and a major league mark of .264, but he pioneered a method of play at first base by positioning himself away from the bag. (Some credit Joe "Old Reliable" Start with the practice.) Further, the "Old Roman" positioned his fielders to take advantage of hitters' weaknesses as few had done before.

So St. Louis was clearly a dynamic entity to have in this new association.

Fashions in the New Circuit

Each new club would be colorfully attired. Louisville would wear light gray, red trim upon gray caps and red stockings; the Athletics wore drab knickers, shirts and caps, but with red stockings and neckties; the Browns were basically in white, with brown caps and stockings.

Cincinnati was a veritable rainbow. All players started with relatively sedate white knickers and red stockings, but each wore a different-colored cap and silk blouse depending on position. On Opening Day the team captain, catcher Charles "Pop" Snyder, wore scarlet; pitcher Will White, sky blue; first baseman Bill Tierney, red and white; second baseman "Bid" McPhee, black and yellow; shortstop Charley Fulmer, maroon; third baseman "Hick" Carpenter, gray and white; left fielder Joseph Sommer, white; center fielder Rudolph Kemmler, red and black; right fielder Daniel Stearns, gray; utilityman James "Little Mac" Macullar, brown; and "change pitcher" Harry McCormick, green.

Reaction to this fashion show is not known, although one can imagine. One

Portrait of the "Old Roman" as a young first baseman: Charles Comiskey of the St. Louis Brown Stockings.

press account ran as follows: "Will White's sky blue suit makes him look like a dizzy blonde. The new parti-colored uniforms are all a novelty worth seeing. Carpenter's uniform of gray and white is not as pretty as some of the rest, but then Hickory looks well in any color."

The Cincinnati *Commercial* alleged that red-shirted Pop Snyder's favorite song was "When I First Put This Uniform On" from Gilbert and Sullivan's "Patience," with suitably amended lyrics:

> When I first put on the uniform
> I said as I tucked in the shirt
> It's one out of ten

That all the wo—men
With me now will want to flirt
For red has a charm for the fair
And I've plenty of that to spare

The National League Reacts to Its Rival

At first, it appeared that relations between the National League and its new rival would be, if not cordial, at least civilized. William Hulbert observed he could not understand how "one association of baseball clubs could hurt another," although in November of 1881 he also gave some rather strong advice to his new counterpart, Mr. McKnight. "Departure" from the National League way of doing things, chided Hulbert, "would cause havoc in the game. You cannot afford to bid for the patronage of the degraded; if you are to be successful you must secure recognition by the respectable." Shortly thereafter he reminded McKnight: "the sole purpose of the League, outside of the business aspect, is to make it worthy of the patronage, support, and respect of the best class of people."

However, relations were still correct enough in the spring of 1882 for 21 exhibitions to be played between the two leagues, with the Nationals taking all contests and outscoring the Association 225-80 in the process. And while the Nationals took measures to augment and solidify the "League Alliance," there was no indication warfare was about to erupt.

Touching off the battle were two rookie infielders, Samuel Washington Wise and John "Dasher" Troy, both under contract to the 1881 Detroit Wolverines of the N.L. Wise played in but one game; Troy in 11. In 1882 both signed with Association clubs—Wise with Cincinnati and Troy with Philadelphia.

The League chose them as the pretext for war with the Association. Even though both had signed valid Association contracts, the League proceeded to sign them to new pacts—Wise with Boston and Troy back to Detroit.

When Philadelphia complained to Detroit, an insolent communication was dispatched by the Wolverines to Athletics co-owner Simmons:

Sir:

I am in receipt of your favor of the 18th inst. and would say that Mr. Troy has very correctly informed you that he will so play the forthcoming season. I do not know anything about your association, or your claim that Mr. Troy has previously signed with you; if he wronged you in any respect, of course, as you say, you may expel him, and have the courts open to you for redress.

I request that in any proceedings you may take against him, you will make this club party to the proceedings.

Very truly yours,

W. G. Thompson

"The League," remarked William Hulbert, "does not recognize the existence of any Association of ball clubs excepting itself and the League Alliance. . . ." Troy claimed he did not find it "proper to play ball on the Sabbath" and that he did not realize he would have to when he signed with Philadelphia.

The Association retaliated. In May 1882 it adopted a policy of "non–Intercourse" with League clubs: no more exhibitions were to be played, and League reserve lists were no longer to be respected. An American Association version of the "League Alliance" was even instituted.

Originally, the Association steadfastly maintained it would not employ players banned by League authorities. It now determined that suspended or blacklisted players could apply to the Association Board of Directors for reinstatement.

The contract-jumping of Wise and Troy was challenged in the legal system; the entire circuit eventually shared in the expense. Cincinnati sued Boston over the Wise issue and applied to the Massachusetts judiciary for an injunction barring Wise from playing for Boston. The courts refused Cincinnati any relief; this marked the first instance in which the courts became involved in baseball.

Spalding's Guide not surprisingly supported the League line: ". . . some very low grade opponents have even threatened to organize clubs whose teams include not only the recently 'black listed' players of the League, but actually the expelled 'crooks' of past seasons. These wild-talking organizers of 'new Leagues' forget that their efforts only result in showing up in a stronger light the strong foundations the League Association is built upon.

"The League has never opposed . . . any new Association, the objects of which have been plainly to improve the status of professional ball playing, to foster honest play and temperate habits in its ranks, and to add still further to the popularity of our national game; for to do so would be to run in direct opposition to the spirit of our constitutional laws. But the League always has and always will oppose associations whose real object is to serve some special interest at the cost of the welfare of the majority class of the professional fraternity."

The Association went further, signing 13 National Leaguers during 1882 to options for the coming year. Almost all eventually re-signed with N.L. clubs, but such tactics made the cost of labor dearer to the Senior Circuit.

Most notable was the case of Detroit's Charlie Bennett, perhaps his era's outstanding catcher. Bennett, praised one manager, "was the best backstop that ever lived. He went after everything, he knew no fear and he kept his pitcher from going in the air."

For $100 the Pittsburgh Alleghenys signed Bennett to an option to play for them for a $1,700 salary in 1883. He nonetheless jumped back to the Wolverines. Pittsburgh went to court, grieving not only his loss but charging he influenced two other valuable players, pitcher Pud Galvin and power-hitting, slick-fielding third baseman Ned Williamson, to violate their options and return to the National League. The Alleghenys were not sustained, as the bench ruled that the agreement Bennett signed was just a preliminary one, a mere "option," and not at all binding.

Oddly enough, in 1890 Bennett turned in a similar performance on the advent of the Players' League, signing with the Brotherhood, but returning to the Boston Beaneaters before playing a single contest. As a further postscript it might be noted how his distinguished career finally and tragically ended. In 1894 Bennett slipped off a station platform in Wellsville, Kansas. An oncoming train crushed him. His left foot was amputated and his right leg was removed at the knee.

The National League's war against this new combine was hindered by the death of William Hulbert from a heart attack on April 22, 1882. Hulbert was succeeded by an interim executive, Boston's Arthur Soden. Soden was the prototypical tightwad. Despite his many business successes, he always brought his lunch from home. Not surprisingly, he was the type of owner who would demolish the South End Grounds' press box to make room for more paying customers and who would make players' wives pay to get in.

Nevertheless, the frugal Soden was also a baseball fan, making the 1874 trip to England and actually playing center field at Kensington Oval. "Baseball is a game I love," he once said, "whether it represents business with me or not. Keep it from the gamblers, and keep it from the speculators who would jockey with it and destroy its standing as was done in the '70s." Despite such sentiments, he was no Hulbert, and peace would have to await election of a new president.

The First Season Begins

The Association began play on May 2, 1884. Fifteen hundred fans saw Allegheny of Pittsburgh defeat the home Cincinnati club 10–9 behind the pitching of William Henry "Whoop-La" White, who had once studied for the ministry and had even been a circuit rider for five Kentucky congregations. He had given that up to pitch for a team in Lynn in 1875, although he remained a devout Christian and an abstainer from Sabbath ball. White, the first player to wear glasses, was coming back from arm trouble and enjoyed a remarkable season.

At Philadelphia, the Athletics triumphed 10–7 as Baltimore catcher Edward Whiting committed eight passed balls. Twenty-two errors or passed balls were made by the two teams.

Two thousand at St. Louis saw the home Browns nip the Eclipse Club of Louisville 9–7. Louisville third baseman Pete "The Gladiator" Browning, who had predicted he'd have four hits, instead went 0-for-4, committing four errors. Nonetheless, Browning was the greatest hitter in A.A. history (.341 lifetime) and the original "Louisville Slugger" (it was for him in 1884 the first such bat was made).

A chronic drunk and a virtual illiterate, Browning often remarked, "I can't hit the ball until I hit the bottle." His wild lifestyle was reflected in such nicknames as "Distillery Pete," "Old Red Eye" and "The Inspector of Red Lights."

The Yogi Berra of his time, Pete was the butt of such anecdotes as this one involving the assassination of President James Garfield:

> Player: Pete, the game has been called off on account of Garfield's death.
> Browning: How come, I did not know he was playing in the Association. What team was he with?

Also with Louisville was outfielder William V. "Chicken" Wolf, the only player to appear in all ten A.A. seasons, each with Louisville. Known as "Chicken" because that was the only meat he would eat, Wolf was released in 1891 because he had "gotten so fat he could not hit or field, but was so upset by the development that he quickly lost weight and regained his position."

The Reds easily outclassed the rest of the league, pacing it in runs scored, fewest runs allowed, batting average, fielding average (the only club over .900) and ERA (a remarkable 1.67).

Aiding this new Association were the simple dynamics of demographics. The combined population of its six franchise cities (2,370,000) was half a million greater than that of the eight-team Nationals (1,156,000). Five of the six A.A. clubs outdrew all their N.L. rivals except for the champion White Stockings.

All six A.A. clubs showed a profit (despite Cincinnati and Pittsburgh's being flooded out of their home fields in the spring), with the champion Reds clearing an estimated $15,000. Buoyed by such success, the Association added two new franchises – John B. Day's New York Metropolitans and the Columbus (Ohio) "Colts" or "Senators."

The National League retaliated by dropping its weak Troy and Worcester franchises (both were given "honorary" memberships), replacing them with New York and Philadelphia. The "Philadelphians" operated in 1882 in the League Alliance and were headed by former player Alfred J. Reach. The New York Club (called for now just that, "The New York Base Ball Club," only later

St. George Cricket Ground, home of the New York Metropolitans. (Courtesy of National Baseball Library, Cooperstown, New York.)

the "Gothams," and later still the "Giants") was owned, oddly enough, by John B. Day.

Augmenting both clubs' rosters were players formerly on the League blacklist. As a war measure all restricted personnel (save for the Louisville Gray four) had been declared eligible by the League and pressed into service.

With head-to-head competition between the League and the Association in New York and Philadelphia, the nation's two largest cities, the action could only heat up in 1883.

Spalding's Guide's opinion changed markedly after that first season. The Association, it noted, had "gone through its inaugural season without a break in its programme and attended by a degree of financial success unprecedented in the history of non–League professional clubs." Further, the A.A. presented "a series of the most attractive professional contests which ever took place outside the League arena."

Part of this, noted the still partisan *Guide*, could be traced to the League—the Association had profited "by the revival of the public confidence induced by the gradual establishment of honest play under the auspices of the National League. . . .

"The League can have no just cause for opposing any new professional association the objects of which are plainly shown to be similar to its own constitution...."

The First World Series

In fact, by season's end, Albert Spalding was more than willing to do business with the Association. His League champion White Stockings (this was their third straight pennant) were ready to take on the American Association winners, the Cincinnati Reds.

Cincinnati fielded a powerful nine; its 1882 won-lost percentage of .688 remains the franchise record. Seven Reds enjoyed career years and rookie second baseman "Bid" McPhee proved himself not only with the bat, but with one of the slickest gloves around. Pacing the pitching was Will White, who led the Association with 40 victories, 52 complete games, 8 shutouts, 480 innings pitched and a .769 won-lost percentage.

The American Association had banned play with the League when hostilities began. To get around this, the Reds "disbanded" and then masqueraded, somewhat transparently, as an independent barnstorming team. A wealthy local businessman came up with the scheme, which was to work in the following manner. Player contracts ran until October 15. He persuaded the Reds management to release all its players on October 1 (this appealed to the Reds as it was a money-saving proposition). This entrepreneur would then "resign" them and be their technical employer. The newly reconstituted squad started a series against the National League's Cleveland Blues (losing two of three) and then began a sort of "World Series" with the White Stockings.

The first game ended with the Pale Hose shut out 2–0 before 2,700 fans on Friday, October 6. The next day, the tables were turned as the White Stockings' Larry Corcoran whitewashed the Reds 2–0 before 4,500. At this point Association President McKnight stepped in, ordering a halt to the proceedings and threatening to expel the Reds if they continued. The Association's Board of Directors was convened to hear charges against the club, but "after a few hours' friendly chat" they were shelved. It is unlikely, however, that the Series would have continued in any case, as the Reds were scheduled to head for St. Louis for an exhibition and the White Stockings were due in Providence to begin nine games with the second-place Grays.

The Tripartite Agreement

For some while after the American Association's successful initial season ended, there was no movement toward peace. Then an opportunity arose from an unexpected direction. The Northwestern League was reviving itself. Delegates from eight cities gathering at Fort Wayne, Indiana, were concerned their timing was not quite right, that they would be caught amidst the League-Association struggle and find all their better players snapped away.

The Northwestern League wired the National League (coincidentally meeting in Providence), requesting that an alliance be worked out which would mutually guarantee the sanctity of contracts and territories. The League immediately responded, appointing its newly elected president, Colonel Abraham G. Mills, John B. Day and Arthur Soden to confer on these issues with the Northwestern League and, significantly, "with any other association of baseball clubs."

Couched in these seemingly innocent words were the League's first peace feelers. Mills himself was more than willing to negotiate with the Association, as he feared the League's hard-won gains were about to be destroyed in a senseless trade war. American Association leadership, however, was less enthusiastic, and Mills was forced to write to Elias Matter, the Northwestern League's president, that perhaps the two leagues should join together even without the Association.

The Association countered that it would meet with just the National League. Mills then fired off a series of letters, the upshot being a three-way conference at New York's Hotel Victoria on February 17, 1883.

Mills had not been idle. Nor was he content with merely patching up this latest baseball feud; he aimed at creating a lasting framework for baseball government and what many would term a monopoly.

Attending this "Harmony Conference" were Mills, Day and Soden for the National League; Matter for the Northwest League; and O. P. Caylor (sitting in for Association Vice President J. H. Pank, who had refused to leave Louisville), the Athletics' Lew Simmons and Baltimore's Billie Barnie for the Association.

Mills brought with him a draft of what would become known as the "Tripartite Agreement." It was adopted almost verbatim as the basis for peace.

Each league would control its own internal affairs, but leagues would stand united on such issues as player control, territoriality and outside rivals.

Increased rein over players was vital. Competition among clubs or leagues for playing talent invariably inflated salaries.

One section of the new agreement read:

> When a player under contract by any club . . . is expelled, blacklisted, or suspended, . . . notice of such disqualification shall be served upon the Secretaries of the other associations . . . and upon the receipt of such notice, all . . . parties hereto shall be debarred from employing or playing with or against such disqualified player, until the period of disqualification shall have

terminated, or the disqualification be revoked by the association from which the player was disqualified.

Beyond tightening the screws via re-institution of the blacklist, the Tripartite Agreement radically increased the range of the reserve clause — jumping its scope from five to eleven players per club to be reserved at a minimum salary of $1,000 each. Not all the American Association clubs were supportive of this move, but no real steps were ever taken to loosen the bonds on players that this represented.

All seemed to be at peace, but it was a tranquility soon shattered.

Chapter 5

The Union Association

The Tripartite Agreement ushered in an exceedingly prosperous 1883. Both the National League and the American Association saw attendance blossom. *Spalding's Guide* pronounced the 1883 League campaign "beyond question, the most successful one in the history of that class of the fraternity." The *Guide* further contended that while the American Association's 1882 season "was exceptionally successful for an inaugural campaign, . . . it did not approach that of . . . 1883, the financial prosperity of which was very remarkable."

Reports in January 1884 indicated major profits for the American Association, the less-flush of the two major circuits. Profits were reported thus: Philadelphia, $75,000; St. Louis, $50,000; Cincinnati, $25,000; Baltimore, $10,000. Louisville and Columbus had break-even years, and Pittsburgh lost $3,000. No figures were reported for New York. Other sources indicated even higher profits. Von der Ahe boasted he had made some $70,000, and the second-division Baltimore club reported a $30,000 balance.

New York, which in 1882 possessed no major league teams, now had two, both owned by John B. Day and managed by James Mutrie. It was a highly unusual circumstance, to say the least, with both playing in the huge Polo Grounds, which was large enough for two games at once. A canvas curtain was strung between the two diamonds when both clubs were in town, the Mets on the western diamond, the Gothams on the eastern one.

The majors were not the only ones prospering. Other leagues thrived: the Northwestern had clubs in Toledo, Grand Rapids, Peoria, Fort Wayne, Saginaw, Bay City, Springfield and Quincy, Illinois. The Inter-State Association was represented by Brooklyn; Harrisburg; the Actives of Reading; the Quicksteps of Wilmington, Delaware; the Merritt Club of Camden, New Jersey; and the Anthracite Club of Pottsville, Pennsylvania.

Inspired by the success of these circuits, new minors formed. On November 13, 1883, at the Tremont House in Quincy, Illinois, the Western League formed. Representatives met again in January 1884, admitting Rock Island, Kansas City, Omaha, Quincy, Chillicothe, St. Joseph, Keokuk, Springfield and Atchison.

On December 6, 1883, at Pittsburgh's St. Charles Hotel, an Iron and Oil Association formed, with clubs in Oil City, Franklin, East Liberty, New Brighton and New Castle, all in Pennsylvania, along with Youngstown, Ohio. All seemed rosy on the baseball map.

The Idea for a Third League

But trouble was brewing. The game's very prosperity caused jealous eyes. Not everyone desiring a franchise could be granted one.

This prompted a major problem in St. Louis particularly. Some say the original idea for a third league came from St. Louis promoter James "Projector" Jackson, who was seeking a New York franchise. Although taking part in the initial discussions, he was soon frozen out of the endeavor.

The first public mention of the idea came in August 1883. Albert Pratt of Pittsburgh, who had both managed and umpired in the American Association, was reputed to be the organizer. Minor league player Chris Fulmer was also said to be involved. Reports said this new circuit would be called the "American League of Professional Base Ball Clubs" and that the reserve rule was to be abolished for this circuit.

The person most associated with the idea was another St. Louis resident, 26-year-old Henry V. Lucas. Lucas was certainly connected with society in the Western metropolis. His grandfather was one of the city's first settlers, and his family possessed extreme wealth. As president of the Mound City Transportation Company, he also had large holdings in shipping and real estate. His brother, John C. B. Lucas, was a president of the St. Louis Base Ball Association of the preceding decade and in 1877 president of the city's National League entry. His uncle, John R. Lucas, had similarly served as club president in 1876.

Lucas himself was a dedicated baseball "crank," going so far as to construct a ballpark on his estate "Normandy." Guests were often expected to play before dinner. In 1883 Lucas, who had inherited a million dollars on the death of his father, bankrolled the "Lucas Amateurs," for whom he played third base, as well as a local semipro team. In 1884, after the founding of the Union Association, he suited up again and advertised the fact: "Henry V. Lucas, in person, now will play ball with the St. Louis Blues. The only Baseball League President actually playing Baseball."

Lucas dearly wanted a major league franchise, but the American Association already had Chris Von der Ahe in St. Louis. While the National League might put a team there, its 50-cent admission policy and its restrictions on Sunday ball and liquor sales would make competition with the Browns difficult, if not impossible.

After conferring with many professional players (usually after a game, at a local tavern), the portly Lucas became convinced that the reserve clause was simply wrong and should be abolished.

Some thought Lucas' position on the reserve clause mere strategy. The established magnates mocked him as "St. Lucas." One historian, H. L. Dellinger, charges that the U.A. attacked the reserve clause only after a secret request to be recognized as a third major league — with an offer to honor the controversial clause — was turned down. But Ted Sullivan, who would manage for him, spoke of Lucas' "honesty of purpose" and termed him "one of the squarest little men that has been connected with the game."

In partnership with Ellis Wainwright and Adolphus Busch (grandfather of long-time Cardinals owner August A. Busch), Lucas launched the Union Association franchise in St. Louis. Both partners were substantial members of St. Louis' large brewing industry, Wainwright with the Wainwright Brewing Company and Busch with Anheuser-Busch. Four of the eight Union Association franchises were, in fact, connected with brewers. Among the rest, Baltimore mattress manufacturer A. H. Henderson lent support to the Baltimore and Chicago clubs. Officials of the Pennsylvania Railroad were supposedly connected with a club in Altoona, Pennsylvania. George Wright lent prestige to a Boston franchise (perhaps in return, the lively Wright & Ditson ball was adopted as official by the Union Association).

On September 12, 1883, at the Monongahela House in Pittsburgh, the "Union Association of Professional Base Ball Clubs" was formed, with H. B. Bennett of Washington as president (baseball historian Lee Allen claims Bennett formed the U.A. as a minor league in the summer of that year, and that may be the case as well), Thomas J. Pratt of Philadelphia as vice president and William Warren White of Washington as secretary. Chosen for the Association's Board of Directors were A. H. Henderson of Baltimore, Michael B. Scanlon of Washington, Albert G. Pratt of Pittsburgh and Thomas J. Pratt of Philadelphia.

Franchises were awarded to Chicago, St. Louis, Baltimore, Boston, Philadelphia, Cincinnati, Washington and Altoona. Cities which had expressed an interest in joining but were rejected included Brooklyn; New York; Richmond; Kansas City; Columbus, Ohio; Johnstown, Pennsylvania; Evansville, Indiana; and Rock Island, Illinois. A 128-game schedule was adopted. Visiting teams were guaranteed $75 per game except for holidays, when receipts were to be divided 50-50.

The constitutions of the existing leagues were adopted but with a key difference: "Resolved, that while we recognize the validity of all contracts made by the League and the American Association, we cannot recognize any agreement whereby any number of ballplayers may be reserved for any club for any time beyond the terms of their contract for such club."

"We are certain to succeed," brashly stated Secretary White that evening. "We commence with a cash capital of $100,000 and there will be no difficulty in securing more money if necessary.... Our refusal to be bound by the eleven-man reserve rule secures us the goodwill of every player in the country, for [our] stand . . . is directly in their interest. It will enable every man to obtain just as much salary as his services are worth, which is more than the old associations are willing to concede. We do not intend to declare war, . . . but if either of the old associations declares war on us we will not sit idly by. I do not anticipate any trouble, however. I recently received what I consider as good as an official declaration from a League officer that at the League meeting . . . it will be decided to abandon the eleven-man rule."

This was soon to prove wishful thinking.

The Ballparks

Soon the Unions were lining up ballparks: in Chicago at South Side Park, the stamping ground of the Chicago Cricket Club (the Unions even held a few games at Lake Front Park, home of the White Stockings); in Altoona at Columbia Park; in Boston at Dartmouth Street Park in the Back Bay area; in Washington at the Capitol Grounds, literally in the shadow of the Capitol Building; in Philadelphia at Keystone Park at Broad and Moore streets; and in Baltimore at East Baltimore's Belair Lot ("a beautiful greensward," its grandstand "complete in all departments and beautiful architecture").

In Cincinnati the Union forces scored a major coup by gaining control of the American Association's home field, the Bank Street Grounds. The Red Stockings moved three blocks away to an abandoned brickyard, naming it League Park (eventually the site of Crosley Field), where on Opening Day 1884 the hastily constructed stands collapsed. One fan was killed and numerous others were injured.

In St. Louis, Lucas constructed an elaborate 10,000 seat "Palace Park of America." Its stands featured cages full of live canaries. It also contained facilities for such uplifting activities as lectures and receptions.

Organized Baseball Retaliates

The National League was not about to take the Union Association (which it sarcastically dubbed the "Onion Association") lying down, nor was it about to abandon the reserve clause. In November, New York's John B. Day introduced a resolution for League approval, blacklisting any player who jumped to the Union Association and wished to return. Its purpose was twofold: first, to deter jumping in the first place; secondly, to keep League owners from luring back players at higher salaries. Day reasoned, with some logic, that such actions only rewarded jumpers. No immediate action was taken on his motion, but in December the N.L. threatened to blacklist any player not returning his signed contract within the next 30 days.

On December 12, 1883, in Cincinnati the American Association, in a move to tie up territory and personnel for the upcoming war, voted to expand to 12 clubs, adding Washington, Brooklyn (a team soon known as the "Trolley Dodgers"), Indianapolis (the "Blues") and Toledo (the "Maumees").

One newspaper report contended this was at the National League's instigation. "The newspaper idiot you refer to is a greater discoverer than Columbus," wrote A. G. Mills to his A.A. counterpart Denny McKnight. "The idea . . . was certainly never suggested by any one in the League, and the fact that you contemplated taking such a step was news to us all."

Nonetheless, Mills was not taking the U.A. threat lightly. "We should exert the utmost vigilance," he warned McKnight. "I have no doubt that if we can nip this piratical enterprise in the bud, and thus prevent them from gaining a foothold during the present season, that we will be able to indefinitely maintain on a secure basis the future of professional base-ball in this country."

Although noticeably absent from the first list of Union Association officers, Henry Lucas was soon to become highly visible. On December 18, 1883, he succeeded Bennett as U.A. president.

The National League this same month formed "reserve clubs," hoping to tie players to contracts and keep them from augmenting Union rosters. These teams would in some cases play at their parent club's home grounds "when such club is absent," in the fashion of a junior varsity team. In a sense, it was a crude beginning of the farm system.

In January, controversy swirled around Cleveland reserve second baseman Fred "Sure Shot" Dunlap (a .326 hitter in 1883), who signed with the U.A.'s St. Louis Maroons for a reported $2,500. League President A. G. Mills urged Cleveland (which had offered Dunlap $1,500) to recover the player, dismissing any threat of a Lucas countersuit. Complicating the matter was Dunlap's expressed desire to remain in the National League—but in New York, not in Cleveland. He wanted $4,000 in the bargain. Mills considered this "out of the question."

Eventually Dunlap did go to the Maroons, where he was the Union Association's dominant player, leading it in runs (160), hits (185), home runs (13), batting average (.412), slugging percentage (.621), and on-base percentage (.448).

As early as February 1884 Mills was preparing for a long siege, penning some hard-edged advice to Albert Spalding:

> Would it not be a good plan for you to arrange to secure for 1885, a lease of the ground now occupied by the Union Association club, in Chicago, and next year place upon it a nine of your own, to be entered under a different name, and ostensibly under a different management, to enter a Northwestern League; somewhat on the same plan as Day and Appleton run the New York

and Metropolitan clubs. Sooner or later there will doubtless be a second club in Chicago, and in the way proposed you might not only secure the advantage of having both clubs, but at the same time freeze out the Union Association, and, possibly, also provide against the contingency of losing your Lake Front grounds.

That same month, Mills contacted the Washington *Sunday Herald*, providing their readers with a five-page, single-spaced apologia for Organized Baseball's hostility to the Union scheme. Starting with references to the reserve clause, he pointed out that while he did not intend to "impeach the motives" of his opposition, he was "justified in saying some of them have earnestly sought admission to Associations within the 'National Agreement,' and were ready to give a hearty support, if admitted, to this very rule." Further he had no doubt that if the Unions were to "continue in base ball" they would "inevitably" impose the reserve rule on their players.

Next, Mills examined the issue of territoriality. Somewhat lamely, he compared Lucas' league unfavorably to the minor Eastern League which contained a club, the Monumentals, in Baltimore in conflict with the American Association. For this reason, "and this alone," it was not admitted to Organized Baseball, but the Easterns nonetheless "manfully resisted urgent appeals from the Union Association to join forces with it." When the A.A.'s Baltimore club allowed an Eastern club to operate in that city, the E.L. was allowed into full communion with the League-Association structure.

Then Mills dissected the greatest issue, salary inflation caused by Union blandishments. Particularly noxious was their practice of offering "advances" to a player it wishes to sign. "In no case," fumed Mills, "where a player of a League club has been captured by this Association has the amount of such advance money been less than what a few years ago would have been regarded as a high salary to an average ball player for a season's services."

The Union's threat of lawsuits and injunctions against players who had jumped from it filled the National League president with rage. "If I were managing a League club, I would not for a moment be deterred from contracting with any of my reserved players by any such threat.

"A Union club with nine injunctions instead of nine ball players would probably not contribute materially to the exhibition of the National Game," concluded Mills.

In March 1884 the National League finally enacted the Day resolution, the "Order in Relation to Ineligible Reserved Players." Mills, who had formerly supported efforts to win back "secessionists," now was foursquare opposed to ever letting any back into the National League, noting he was "never more earnest . . . that these players should never play with any club connected with the National Agreement."

The glut of clubs made many observers wary from the start. The Cincinnati

Enquirer, a journal favorably inclined to the U.A., warned, "Three professional clubs cannot live in Baltimore; . . . Washington in the past barely sustained one club, two clubs would starve."

The Season of 1884

Opening Day for the Unions' 128-game schedule was April 17, 1884 – two full weeks ahead of their rivals – featuring contests in Baltimore, Cincinnati and Philadelphia. The greatest festivities were reserved for April 20, when St. Louis triumphed at home versus the Chicago Unions 7–2.

A St. Louis newspaper advertisement read, "Reserved, 50 cents; Upper part of Grand Stand, 25 cents; Open seats, 25 cents; Boys, 10 cents; Vehicles, free. 10,000 Union Association Guides are to be given away, Corner, Cass & Jefferson."

The Union League war wreaked havoc upon the minor leagues. Particularly hard-hit was the Eastern League. In the city of Baltimore three clubs took the field. The American Association franchise, owned by Vonderhorst and managed by former catcher Billie Barnie, played at Oriole Park at York Road and Huntingdon Avenue. The Union Association team, owned by I. W. Lowe and B. F. Matthews and managed by William C. Henderson, played at the "Belair Lot." The Monumentals of the Eastern League, owned by dentist George W. Massamore, never collected a salary check and disbanded in May with a 3-10 record. The Union club took over the Monumentals' park, as the crowds they drew could not be held at their old field. Baltimore's position in the Eastern League was taken by the Ironside club of Lancaster, Pennsylvania.

Harrisburg folded in July; its slot was taken by York. The Actives of Reading died that same month and were replaced by the Atlantics of Long Island City. Soon the Atlantics were expelled. Then the Richmond team (the Virginia Club) moved up to the American Association to replace the defunct Washington team, which had expired in early August. The Eastern League's Wilmington Quicksteps had been asked originally to replace the Nationals, but instead graduated to the Union Association.

The 12-club Northwestern League met with similar difficulties. The season, noted *Spalding's Guide,* "was a decided failure . . . not more than half over before symptoms of financial failure arose, and in August [the league] virtually disbanded. An effort was made to carry it through on a smaller basis of representation, but that also proved a failure."

Not aiding the Northwestern cause were the activities of its secretary, Samuel G. Morton, who was funneling players to the Union Association. Bizarrely, Morton was a sales clerk for and reputedly the "right-hand man" of Albert Spalding. Mills held Spalding personally responsible of his lieutenant's actions and threatened to give him "a piece of my mind somewhat more emphatic than I have sent to Morton." Spalding meekly admitted blame and promised to sin no more.

The League and the Association faced major difficulties as well. The A.A.'s expansion to 12 clubs had been a blunder. All four additions played and drew poorly. Faced with direct Union Association competition, the new Washington franchise collapsed in early August, owing $1,500 in player salaries, and finished out the season in Richmond. For the 1885 campaign, the Association returned to an eight-team format, dropping Columbus, Washington/Richmond, Indianapolis and Toledo.

The N.L. faced similar woes. The Cleveland Blues were hit particularly hard by player defections and finished a poor seventh (35-77). Blues owner C. H. Bulkley threatened to throw in the towel. Cleveland's demise would mean the loss of further players to the Unions, besides setting off a possible panic in the ranks. A. G. Mills responded with an indirect subsidy. Via a special division of gate receipts, the Blues would receive half of all road receipts instead of the normal 30 percent. Additionally, Cleveland was given preference in signing player talent made available by disintegration of the Northwest League.

Detroit was not in much better shape, and in July Cleveland Vice President George W. Howe suggested to Mills that the two weak franchises consolidate, playing half their home games in each city.

Defections to the Union Association

The Providence Grays had similarly been shaky, starting with an Opening Day turnout of 2,395 ("a bitter disappointment to the stockholders"). Events were not helped by rumors concerning personnel. "Hints at dissipation are rife," charged the Providence *Journal*, "and one or two of the players are not keeping the terms of their contracts. Suspensions will be in order if the fault is not corrected."

Mills received reports that both of the Grays' pitchers, Charlie Sweeney and Charles "Old Hoss" Radbourn, were jumping to the Unions. He dashed off the following to Providence President Henry T. Root:

> I confidently rely on yourself and associates to hold Providence in the League. Disbandment would be crowning triumph of scoundrels who corrupted your players. Morning newspaper reports indicating disbandment will induce bidding for players, and thus aggravate your situation.
>
> I advise immediate conference with players. I believe they are honorable men, but if any more have been corrupted they should be expelled, and thus forever debarred from playing in any respectable club.
>
> To win championship is laudable object, but more important objects of League will be promoted and your courage vindicated, by carrying the Club successfully through this difficulty.

Crossing the wires was this cable from Grays Secretary Ned Allen: "The Unions at work and seeking to break up our nine. Have you anything to advise? If not shall call a meeting to consider feasibility of disbanding."

Mills responded with Victorian resolve: "Telegram received. See my dispatch to Root this morning. Don't give up the ship."

Allen's spine was stiffened by Mills and by assurances from pitcher Radbourn (then under suspension for insubordination) that he would pitch every game if he had to (he did). Allen responded, "Will run a nine if we put amateurs on the field."

The team's fortunes changed. The Grays ran away with the N.L. flag, triumphing over second-place Boston by 10½ games and remaining highly solvent.

The Union Association faced a severe talent imbalance. Henry Lucas' St. Louis Maroons had been staffed with experienced major leaguers, and it showed, as the team won its first 20 games. "Sure Shot" Dunlap (from Cleveland), outfielder David Rowe (from Baltimore), outfielder George "Orator" Shaffer (from Buffalo), pitcher "Bollicky Bill" Taylor and outfielder Lew "Buttercup" Dickerson (both from Pittsburgh) all gave the Maroons a decidedly big league character.

During the season they even added pitcher Charlie Sweeney, who had begun the year with Providence and struck out 19 batters for the Grays versus Boston on June 7 (a feat matched by Chicago Unions pitcher Hugh "One Arm" Daily just one month later).

According to published reports, "a mischief-maker . . . in the person of an agent of the St. Louis Union team" began working on Sweeney in early July to jump. Compounding the situation was increased drunkenness on the pitcher's part. At a game in Woonsocket, Rhode Island, Sweeney "was stealing into the dressing-room between each inning and getting whiskey . . . ." Following the game he and catcher Vincent "Sandy" Nava did not take the train back to Boston with the rest of the team, but "instead stopped at a well-known hotel," presumably for more libations.

No action was taken until July 22, when Sweeney reported for duty, not only late, but badly hung over. In the seventh inning, with Providence ahead 6–2, Manager Frank Bancroft ordered him to right field, so that "Cyclone" Miller could get some much-needed work. Sweeney responded, "Will I? Well, I guess not. I'll give you a tip, I finish all the games I start or I don't play ball." Whereupon he retreated to the dressing-room, changed and pointedly informed Bancroft "in the vilest language" that he could make a living elsewhere.

"He was just drunk enough to be stupid," reported *Sporting Life*'s Providence correspondent. Providence lost, finishing the game with only eight men. That night the League expelled Sweeney. (He "is still about town, and wherever he goes the women whom he escorted to the ball game . . . are still with him. The conduct of the fellow is shameful. . . ." Sweeney was 17–8 on leaving Providence and went 24-7 with the Maroons.

George "Orator" Shaffer jumped the National League's Buffalo club to join the St. Louis Maroons and led the Union Association with 40 doubles.

Nava was also approached by Lucas to jump, being offered $600 for the rest of the season. "Sweeney says come," wired Lucas.

"No come," responded Nava.

Managing the Maroons at the season's start was Irish-born Ted Sullivan. Never much of player, his talents lay in organizing and promoting. He put together the Dubuque Rabbits, as well as serving as a founder of the Northwestern League, and was the first manager of the St. Louis Browns. He would not finish the season with the Maroons, however, as he chafed at Lucas' interference and was either fired or quit on June 13. He explained he "did not want to manage the team unless he could manage himself." He ended up that season piloting Kansas City, a franchise in which he had a financial interest.

But what of the remainder of this association? Pitcher Hugh Daily and catcher Emil Gross on the Chicago roster and pitcher Tommy Bond with Boston were other Union "name" players, but the Baltimore, Boston, Chicago, Cincinnati and Philadelphia rosters were stocked mostly with mediocrities. The Altoona and Washington clubs could not even say that.

During the season Cincinnati scored a coup in luring shortstop "Pebbly Jack" Glasscock ("I have played long enough for glory, now it is a time for

dollars and cents"), catcher Charlie "Fatty" Briody and pitcher Jim McCormick from Cleveland. McCormick got $2,500 for the last nine weeks of the season, Glasscock and Briody $1,500 each.

Not every player contacted by the Unions signed. The Cleveland *Herald* reported that outfielder Pete Hotaling "was approached at Grand Rapids and offered the same terms as the traitors [Glasscock and Briody] to jump, but he told the wreckers that Cleveland had used him 'white' and he would not break his contract with the club for $5,000. Such rugged honesty is rare, and Pete will not be forgotten for it."

Moreover, the traffic was not all one-way. The established circuits were more than willing to rescue players from Union clutches, scoring several notable successes. The most famous cases involved pitchers Tony "Count" Mullane and Larry Corcoran. Born in County Cork, Mullane was one of the premier hurlers of his time, with 285 lifetime victories. Under contract to the Browns in 1883, in November he signed with Lucas for $2,500. But fearful of the blacklist, Mullane soon developed cold feet and signed with Toledo of the American Association for the same salary—which rumor held was raised in cooperation with other A.A. members. The Unions retaliated with injunctions barring Mullane from appearing in St. Louis and Cincinnati; these later were thrown out on appeal by the Toledo club to the United States Circuit Court.

The White Stockings' Larry Corcoran had won 34 games in 1883 and had little intention of re-signing. He asked for a $4,000 salary, little hoping his demand would be met. Not only would Spalding not meet that figure, but he refused Corcoran's next demand of $2,500, offering $2,100. Corcoran returned the letter unopened, and instead signed with the Union Club of Chicago. "Let the public judge my action," he told the press on December 15, 1883.

He had committed a fatal error, however. On December 7 he had wired Spalding asking for a new contract and a $400 advance. Spalding asked A. G. Mills whether this constituted a contract "in the eyes of the League." Mills responded affirmatively, and Spalding went to work.

"If it [your 'contract'] is not performed," Spalding chided Corcoran, "you will be expelled. Mills will show you the new rules if you want to see them."

Next, Spalding instructed Cap Anson, vacationing in Philadelphia, to hand-deliver a new contract to Corcoran at his home in Camden and to order it returned by January 6, 1884. Corcoran signed for a reputed $2,100 on January 4.

"Whoop-la!" Spalding jubilantly wired Mills. "Corcoran has signed and the back of the Union Association is broken. . . . I look upon this as a great blow to [the U.A.] . . . and a big victory for the League."

Opposite: Two Cleveland Nationals stars lured to the Union Association by Cincinnati, pitcher Jim McCormick (left) and shortstop John Wesley "Pebbly Jack" Glasscock.

Pitcher Larry Corcoran signed with the Union Association club of Chicago, but was coerced by Al Spalding into returning to the White Stockings.

"I thought [Corcoran] was made of more reliable material," sighed a disappointed Lucas. "Still it may be thought I ought not to blame him for I have been informed that Mills, Anson and Spalding threatened him with everything but death."

Also eventually returning were Tommy Bond, who ended the season with Indianapolis; Bill Taylor, who moved over to the Athletics; and "Cyclone" Miller, who jumped to Providence. Young Tommy "Oyster" Burns was lured by the American Association's Baltimore club from a contract with the Wilmington Quicksteps just two games after joining the Unions.

Lucas vowed retaliation. Livid at the breaking of "legal and valid" contracts, he announced plans "to go into the contract-breaking business too."

When queried whether he'd have U.A. support, he shot back, "I am the Union Association. Whatever I do is right. . . . The Association will be with me."

This "L'association c'est moi" pronunciamento was too much for Lucas' opponents to ignore. They immediately christened him "I-am-the-Union-Association-Lucas," but soon he would have his revenge by stealing McCormick, Glasscock and Briody from the faltering Cleveland Blues.

U.A. Disciplinary Problems

Many Union Association clubs suffered from severe disciplinary problems. When the Chicago club transferred to Pittsburgh, one paper noted: "Emil Gross, Gid Gardner and John Leary will certainly help the saloon business in Pittsburgh." Lew Dickerson simply vanished during a Maroons road trip and was expelled for drunkenness. Baltimore suspended Lou Say on July 9. The Boston Unions fined Tommy Bond and catcher Lew Brown each $100 for insubordinate behavior.

Cincinnati Outlaw Reds infielder Francis McLaughlin went out and got drunk after a sweep by Boston. He was expelled by the club but that didn't stop him from playing for two other U.A. teams—Chicago and Kansas City—before season's end.

Managers, too, had a powerful thirst. Cincinnati's "Hustling Dan" O'Leary found himself embarrassed following one hard-fought game, when he dispatched a lad for a growler of beer. Unfortunately, when the boy returned, Cincinnati President Justus Thorner had decided to visit. "Take that bucket back," the manager ordered. "I ordered milk and this isn't milk. I sent you out for milk and I don't want beer."

Thorner stood there silent but extremely skeptical.

Umpires also were less than perfect. Ump David F. Sullivan, not feeling well, took a nap in Baltimore, overslept, and arrived at Belair Lot 15 minutes late for the contest. In the meantime play had begun, with Cincinnati's Dick Burns behind the plate to ump what was termed an "exhibition." Sullivan ordered that ended and the official contest to begin. Baltimore was willing but the visitors were not, so the exhibition resumed with Sullivan behind the plate. Outraged fans demanded their money back, and the constabulary had to be called out to restore order.

By the way, Baltimore won 13.3.

The First Franchise Shift

The first franchise to founder was that of the Altoona Unions (sometimes called the "Ottawas"). They dropped out on Saturday, May 31. While the franchise transferred to Kansas City, most of the team remained behind, as only two players "consented to be transferred."

The 16 Altoona stockholders reorganized the club into a new independent nine, re-signed eight players and solicited dates with N.L., A.A. and Eastern League teams. The team's first game away from the U.A. was versus Johnstown, which won 7–3. "The attendance was small," sadly noted one paper.

Bankrolling the new Kansas City club was 44-year-old malt and grain dealer Americus V. McKim. Assisting him as secretary was former U.A. umpire Alexander Crawford. Crawford was only too happy to leave the umpiring ranks. "Every city supporting a nine," he charged with some understatement, "were prejudiced to such an extent that a decision adverse to the home club would always be greeted with derisive catcalls and such other remarks that were not calculated to inspire the umpire with the agreeableness of the position."

McKim headed to St. Louis to reinforce his depleted roster, and also quickly moved to secure a playing field. His choice was Athletics Park on Southern Boulevard. The price was $500 for a lease till season's end. He also increased capacity from 2,000 to 4,000 seats.

The team did not have a lot of time to prepare itself. Reporting on its first game, the Kansas City *Times* noted, "Quite a number of the players had never seen each other, and several positions assigned to them were entirely new to them."

Veteran outfielder Harry Wheeler was Kansas City's first manager, but he lasted but four games. He was replaced by a local druggist, Matthew S. Porter, who inserted himself in center field, but was gone after just three contests. Finally, Ted Sullivan came over from St. Louis and gave the team stability until season's end.

Disintegration of the Union Association

In August the Chicago Unions shifted over to Pittsburgh and became the "Stogies," but even then could not finish the season, collapsing in September. They were replaced by the St. Paul White Caps of the virtually disintegrated Northwestern League. The White Caps played nine road games, never saw their home Fort Street grounds, and went 3-6.

An October 6 White Caps loss to Kansas city was attributed in part to poor umpiring. "Both sides played well," the Minneapolis . St. Paul *Pioneer Press* noted, "but the umpire [D. McManaway] was absolutely without knowledge of the game. He could not tell a foul tip from a two-base hit and was unmercifully guyed by the crowd and laughed at by the players."

The Keystones of Philadelphia, a horrible team — they once made 20 errors in a single contest—reported losses of $10,000 and dropped out in early August. They were replaced by the Quicksteps of Wilmington, Delaware, which despite leading the Interstate League were operating $4,000 in the red. ("The fine contests with the Allentown Club during the past week were so slimly attended that the management of the home club was almost disheartened," lamented the Wilmington *News*.)

Lucas offered the Quicksteps a deal "unparalleled in baseball history"— road expenses and salaries paid and 50 percent of gross receipts for certain road games. The *Sporting Life*, hardly a supporter of the Unions at this point, said the club's management could "hardly be blamed" for trying to recoup its losses in this fashion.

As most of the Quicksteps refused to join this sinking ship, the team did poorly (2-16) and collapsed in September (aided, some said, by Lucas' failure to come through with promised subsidies).

They were replaced by the Milwaukee Grays of the Northwestern League. Grays Manager Tom Loftus travelled to St. Louis on September 9 to negotiate with Lucas for league entry. A deal was made, and Milwaukee was scheduled for 16 contests, starting on September 27, 1884, all of which were to be played at home.

The Grays drew 1,500 fans to their first game at the Wright Street Grounds, shutting out Washington 3-0. But it was the next day that history was made, as Grays left-hander Ed Cushman no-hit Washington 5-0. "We'll catch fits when we get back to Washington," said embarrassed Nationals pilot Mike Scanlon. "They have no idea what a strong club you have here."

In his next start on October 4, Cushman struck again, one-hitting Boston. One hit allowed over two starts was the major league record until Johnny Vander Meer's 1938 double no-hitter.

With a lopsided pennant race—St. Louis finishing 21 games ahead of second-place Cincinnati—and so many shifting franchises, the season was a financial disaster. Estimates of losses ranged from $50,000 to $250,000. Lucas himself owned up to a $17,000 deficit, mostly from subsidizing the weak links of the U.A. Altoona dropped $12,000 before collapsing. Cincinnati and Chicago lost perhaps $15,000 each. "Only one club paid its expenses," *Spalding's Guide* noted, "even during the season, and that was the National of Washington," which turned a profit of between $7,500 and $10,000. This statement did not take into account the $6,000 profit announced by McKim's Kansas City club.

Union Association competition had little effect on the fortunes of National League clubs. Boston's attendance increased from 138,000 to 146,777 and the club turned a handsome profit. New York, Chicago and Providence also made money. Buffalo most likely broke even financially, and Philadelphia, Cleveland and Detroit—the tail-enders of the circuit—not surprisingly lost money.

Only four Union clubs sent delegates (one was represented by proxy) to a conference at St. Louis on December 18, 1884. Still they professed they would enter the lists for 1885, with St. Louis, Cincinnati, Milwaukee and Kansas City remaining and with new clubs in Indianapolis, Columbus and perhaps Detroit and Cleveland. Player signings went ahead, and very quickly Milwaukee and Kansas City compiled full rosters. Kansas City was planning a new ballpark near McGee Park.

Then came what could only be termed treachery on Lucas' part. (He had just been re-elected Union Association president.) St. Louis, Cincinnati and the old Washington franchise were all said to be jockeying for N.L. or A.A. franchises; Lucas in the National League and the latter two in the American Association.

In Milwaukee on January 15, 1885, the Union Association met for one last time. With only Kansas City and Milwaukee represented, the league formally disbanded.

Noting the Union Association's demise, the Cleveland *Herald* (its bitterness resulting from the wreckage of the local Blues) editorialized: "It has enacted no new laws, brought out no valuable players, and leaves not one piece of healthy legislation on its annals. It has caused players to be cast out of the ranks of reputable professionals and has given a few others a chance to show the treachery that was in them. Thus, accidentally, it may have rendered the National group of clubs a service, but no credit is to be given for the service. The result has been predicted in these columns and its coming so soon is gratifying. All reputable players and managers are to be congratulated on it."

Despite the *Herald*'s judgment a number of players with no prior big league experience did successfully make the jump from the Union Association to the established major leagues. Most notable were pitcher Charles "Lady" Baldwin of Milwaukee; infielder "Chippy" McGarr of Chicago; pitcher "Smiling Al" Maul, catcher John T. Clements and shortstop "Buster" Hoover of Philadelphia; pitcher Ed "Cannonball" Crane of Boston; shortstop George "Germany" Smith of Altoona; outfielder Emmett Seery of Kansas City; catcher Charlie Ganzel and outfielder Billy O'Brien of St. Paul; first baseman Perry Werden, Australian-born infielder Joe Quinn and pitcher "Handsome Harry" Boyle of the St. Louis Maroons; and shortstop Tommy "Oyster" Burns of Wilmington (who would go on to lead the National League in homers and RBIs in 1890).

On the other hand, certain star U.A. players, like Baltimore's dominating hurler Bill Sweeney or Washington's hard-hitting (.336) left fielder Harry Moore (who had a weakness for "strong drink"), disappeared forever from the major league scene.

Of the Union Association's owners, only Lucas—on January 10, 1885—was admitted to the ranks of Organized Baseball, and soon he was to feel cheated. He purchased the Cleveland Blues for $2,500 ($500 in cash; the rest payable later) in order to move the team to St. Louis, thinking part of the transaction included receiving its players. In a somewhat underhanded move, seven of the best men (Bill Phillips, Pete Hotaling, Doc Bushong, Bill Krieg, John Harkins, George Pinkney and Germany Smith) were signed by former Blues manager Charlie Hackett for Brooklyn of the American Association. Lucas, it was noted, "considered himself badly used as he paid that club's officers solid cash . . . solely for the purpose of securing their assistance in obtaining the most desirable reserved players." Lucas sued and refused to pay the $2,000 he still owed. He was taken to court and lost once again.

As would be expected, allowing Lucas to operate in St. Louis raised American Association ire in general ("no little uneasiness was felt") and the hackles of Chris Von der Ahe in particular. He demanded Lucas pay him what his club had lost during the season (which Von der Ahe estimated at $10,000). Lucas was in no mind to pay anything to Von der Ahe and never did. "He says," reported the correspondent of the *Sporting Life*, "if the League will give him 12 hours he will crush Von der Ahe."

His proud Maroons, who had walked over the Union Association, dragged home to a last-place finish in the League of 1885.

Several other Union Association clubs would find themselves in the short-lived Western League of 1885. Kansas City, Cleveland, Omaha, Milwaukee, Toledo and Indianapolis would make up this circuit. Kansas City's A. V. McKim would have a part in operating Kansas City's National League franchise of 1886.

The players A. G. Mills vowed would never be allowed back in Organized Ball in fact returned almost immediately via a League vote on April 15, 1885. True, they had to crawl (contact-jumpers Glasscock, Briody, McCormick and others paid $1,000 fines to be reinstated; mere violators of the reserve clause such as Dunlap, Sweeney and Shaffer, $500), but they were back nonetheless.

A casualty of the settlement was A. G. Mills, unalterably opposed to the return of these deserters. Let them "realize the enormity of their offense," he argued. "This is supine weakness, we are losing the respect of our players." (This was "sheer hypocrisy" on his part, contended Hall of Fame historian Lee Allen years later, remembering Mills' attempts to persuade Larry Corcoran to jump a valid U.A. pact.) Mills resigned as League president in November 1884. He was replaced by the more agreeable "Uncle Nick" Young.

In January 1885 A.A. President McKnight continued to argue against reinstatement of former Union players. "Ability to field and bat and run bases is not everything," he warned. "We want players who are honest and loyal to their clubs and to the general welfare of the profession." At the close of the 1885 season, however, the American Association also ended its blacklist of U.A. players, in part to forestall a lawsuit by Davy Rowe against Von der Ahe.

Henry V. Lucas himself came to a bad end. *Sporting Life* noted: "Lucas retired from base ball after 1886. About the same time a fleet of river barges which he owned was sunk in a storm, and he could not replace the boats because of his heavy base ball losses [estimated at $100,000]. From that time, he always said, everything he touched went wrong." In November 1910 the one-time millionaire died at age 53 as a $75-a-month employee of the St. Louis Street Department.

The Union Association failed for a number of very fundamental reasons. Aside from Lucas it did not contain sufficient financial backing. The players it lured from the established major leagues were not enough to excite the baseball public. Most basically, there was no real need for a third league. The cities capable of supporting big league ball in 1884 already had either National League or American Association franchises.

There was no real cause for this league to have arisen and so there was no great reason for it to survive.

Chapter 6

The Players' League

With the Union Association crushed, the triumvirate of the National League, the American Association and their minor league allies could be well-pleased. The major leagues functioned profitably once more, and even the minors were on the rise, with the Eastern (the old Interstate), the Eastern New England, the Southern New England, the New York State, the Canadian and the Colorado leagues in the ranks.

And with prosperity came arrogance. Players were now more than ever mere chattels and were treated as such. The blacklist was freely employed. Fines and arbitrary treatment increased. Substitute players were forced to do work around the ballpark, including watching turnstiles. Discontent grew.

Chattanooga Manager William H. Voltz, a former sportswriter, took the initial step in forming a players' benevolent association. Accounts vary regarding Voltz's effectiveness. Harold Seymour contends that players were suspicious, and nothing came of the scheme. Lee Allen, on the other hand, records that by mid-1885 over 200 players had joined Voltz's ranks, paying a hefty $5 per month in dues, to be used in creating a fund to benefit sick and indigent members.

Following the 1885 campaign both the League and the Association once again turned the screws on players, instituting a $2,000 salary cap and prohibiting the payment of salary advances.

While neither measure was strictly enforced, both added to already simmering discontent. The seeds of unionism had been planted. On October 22, 1885, nine New York Giants—pitchers Tim Keefe and "Smiling Mickey" Welch; second baseman J. J. "Move-Up" Gerhardt; shortstop John Montgomery Ward; outfielders Mike Dorgan, "Orator Jim" O'Rourke and Daniel Richardson; first baseman Roger Connor; and catcher "Buck" Ewing—banded together to form the Brotherhood of Professional Base Ball Players. The Brotherhood promised "to protect and benefit its members collectively and individually, to promote a high standard of professional conduct, and to advance the interests of the 'National Game.'"

The Brotherhood's Mastermind

Key figure in the Brotherhood and in the subsequent "Players' National League" was founding President John Montgomery Ward. One of the truly imposing figures in baseball history, Ward was the indispensable man in this struggle for players' rights.

Born in Bellefonte, Pennsylvania, on March 3, 1860, Ward attended Pennsylvania State College. Beginning in 1877 he excelled as a pitcher with the Athletics in the League Alliance and with Providence in the League from 1878 to 1882. With the Grays he led the League in ERA in 1878 and twice won as many as 40 games, leading the League with 47 wins in 1879 and nine shutouts in 1880.

On June 17, 1880, he hurled a perfect game against the Buffalo Bisons' Pud Galvin. Oddly enough, this was just five days after Worcester's Lee Richmond hurled the first perfect game ever. The feat would not be repeated for 24 years.

Ward's arm deadened, however, and he was dispatched to the Giants in 1883. He began a new career as a slick-fielding, hard-hitting infielder, stealing 111 bases (in just 129 games) and hitting .338 in 1887.

But as great a player as he was, it was Ward's mind and character which have secured his place in the game. As early as February 1885 Ward eloquently defended the rights of former Union Association players in a letter to the New York *Clipper.* He challenged the validity of the reserve clause, terming it "*ex post facto* law . . . depending for its binding force upon the players solely on its intimidating effect."

There was more to the man than just baseball. In 1885, Ward graduated from Columbia University Law School with honors, having attended on a part-time basis. In 1886, he won an award from Columbia for outstanding work in political science. In 1887 he went on to another sort of triumph, winning the hand of the famed and beautiful actress, Helen Dauvray. In 1888 he wrote "Base Ball: How to Become a Player," a highly praised guidebook of the time.

The Brotherhood idea spread to other League teams as the Giants played each rival city. On May 11, 1886, a chapter consisting of seven Wolverines formed at Detroit. On May 15 three White Stockings joined in Chicago. On May 19 six Kansas City Cowboys put together a chapter. On May 29 nine St. Louis Browns joined. In Boston on June 12, 16 players enrolled. On July 12 in Philadelphia, eight men formed a chapter; in Washington on July 15, three Senators instituted yet another branch. When Kansas City dropped out of the League, a chapter was formed at replacement Indianapolis. Within a year of its founding the Brotherhood contained 107 members, including such figures as Hoss Radbourn, Connie Mack, Ed Delahanty, Ned Hanlon, King Kelly and Dan Brouthers.

Adopting the trappings of the typical fraternal organization, Article VI,

Catcher William "Buck" Ewing, one of nine New York Giants who organized the Brotherhood of Professional Base Ball Players in 1885.

Section I of the Brotherhood Constitution required each member to swear the following oath:

> I do solemnly swear:
>
> To strive to promote the objects and aims of this Brotherhood, in accordance with the Constitution and By-laws;
> Never to take advantage of a brother in good standing;
> Never to permit an unjust injury to be done to, or continued against, a brother in good standing, while it is in my power to prevent the same;
> To assist a brother in distress;

>   To render faithful obedience to the will of the Brotherhood, as expressed
> by the decree of the council, or by a vote of my chapter.
>   To all this I make my solemn oath to Almighty God, and in my presence
> of these witnesses.

Originally a secret organization, in the fall of 1886 the Brotherhood's existence became public knowledge. Ward broke the story to Francis Richter's new weekly, *Sporting Life,* which extolled its "intelligent and reputable" leadership. Other leading journals, such as Al Spink's *Sporting News* ("Only the most intelligent and best-behaved members of the profession are eligible for membership, and there is no place in the ranks for chronic disturbers and lushers") and the New York *Clipper,* also treated the new organization with respect.

In August 1887, Ward published a trenchant essay entitled "Is the Base Ball Player a Chattel?" in *Lippincott's Magazine,* dealing with the sale of King Kelly for the then-record price of $10,000. "Like a fugitive slave law, the reserve rule denies him a harbor or a livelihood, and carries him back, bound and shackled, to the club from which he attempted to escape," Ward argued. "He goes where he is sent, takes what is given him, and thanks the Lord for life."

Instructive, noted Ward, was the case of Buffalo pitcher-outfielder Charley Foley, who, when he became injured in 1883, went unpaid. He started off the next season still unable to play and still without any pay. He recovered by midseason and was offered contracts by three minor league clubs. Still the Bisons refused to pay or release him; in fact, he was reserved by them for 1885!

Ward, from either caution or conviction, was still not attacking the reserve clause. In fact, he defended it: "In order to get men to invest capital in baseball, it is necessary to have a reserve rule. Some say that it could be modified, but I am not of that opinion. How could it be modified? . . . The reserve rule, on the whole, is a bad one; but it cannot be rectified save by injuring the interest of men who invest their money, and that is not the object of the Brotherhood."

Limitation and Classification

The Brotherhood first obtained League recognition on November 18, 1887. Nick Young originally said he would not deal with a "secret society," and the circuit said the players' grievances would be dealt with by the "old and usual means." To which a perplexed Ward responded, "What ones?"

Nonetheless, the League, partially at Albert Spalding's insistence, instructed Young to meet with the Brotherhood, which sent a committee of Ward, Dan Brouthers and Ned Hanlon to negotiate.

Surprisingly, the League met many of the Brotherhood's demands for a

"Model Contract," most notably in specifically writing in the reserve rule, rather than merely referring to its existence in the National Agreement. A request that full salary figures also be included was not acceded to, as this would have amounted to an admission by owners that the Limitation Rule was actually a dead letter. Nevertheless, the League did promise to repeal that salary-limiting measure in spring 1888 if the American Association would go along.

Soon, however, the League announced that no rescission of the Limitation Rule was possible. Following this, salary cuts were promulgated during the season. "It was even whispered," wrote John Montgomery Ward, "and afterwards openly charged that the League committee actually assisted in the failure to secure the repeal, though this was denied."

The match that set off this powder keg was John T. Brush's "Classification Rule." Brush, owner of the Indianapolis club, propounded that players be grouped into five classifications according to "Habits, earnestness, and special qualifications." These would determine their salaries:

CLASS	SALARY
A	$2,500
B	2,250
C	2,000
D	1,750
E	1,500

Players weren't the only ones wary of this scheme. A. G. Mills, long retired from baseball, thought it "wrong in principle" and "technically illegal."

The timing of the "Classification Rule" was either particularly unfortunate or underhanded. Ward and Hanlon were away on Albert Spalding's six-month-long world tour and unable to rally their troops, who in any case were scattered far afield for the off-season.

There was strike sentiment when Ward returned in April 1889, but as many players had signed for the upcoming season, it seemed unfeasible. So on May 19, 1889, the Brotherhood appointed a grievance committee to deal with the League.

Matters dragged on. In June Nick Young was notified of the organization's desire to abolish both the "Classification Rule" and the practice of player sales. The response was a League committee chaired by Spalding. On June 25 Ward and Spalding met without any other committee members present, and Ward was told that neither issue was important enough to warrant the League's taking any immediate measures and that both could wait until the League's regular postseason session.

Strike talk resumed, with some desiring a work stoppage as soon as Independence Day. Still others, like Jack Rowe and Deacon White, were considering going to court to challenge the hated reserve clause. "The League will

**Brotherhood leader John Montgomery Ward, left, on Albert Spalding's 1889
world baseball tour. (Courtesy of National Baseball Library, Cooperstown,
New York.)**

not classify as many as they think," mused Ward's brother-in-law, Tim Keefe
(Keefe was married to Helen Dauvray's sister Clara), secretary of the
Brotherhood.

Exacerbating the situation were the circumstances of Pittsburgh's White
and Rowe. Both purchased shares in Buffalo of the International League and
wished to play for it. Detroit President Fred Stearns, however, adamantly insisted: "White may have been elected president of the Buffalo club or president
of the United States, but that won't enable him to play ball in Buffalo. He'll play
ball in Pittsburgh or get off the earth." White and Rowe made noises about
challenging the reserve rule ("The laws of this country will stop people from
preventing me from making an honest living," White told the Buffalo *Express*),
but perhaps because of the upcoming Players' plot, did nothing.

Secession

On July 14, 1889, at New York's Fifth Avenue Hotel, delegates from the
various Brotherhood chapters met to institute a new league. Ward found

conditions "encouraging," with many financial supporters wishing to advance funds for the new circuit, many of whom, such as young Charles A. Prince of Boston, "were even willing to put in the capital without any return whatever, out of love for the sport. . . ."

The "Players' National League" would usher forth many wide reforms, including the abolition of the reserve clause and the termination of involuntary player sales.

Entering the picture was Albert L. Johnson, brother of the progressive mayor of Cleveland, Tom L. Johnson. Albert was a noted baseball "crank" who socialized and played poker with ballplayers. Both Johnsons were heavily involved in the streetcar business.

Ned Hanlon, representative of the Pittsburgh chapter, sought out Al Johnson at Cleveland's Hollenden Hotel regarding involvement in the Brotherhood. Johnson was instantly receptive, for he had seen opposition streetcars "loaded down with people going to games [both streetcars and the team were owned by one Frank de Haas Robison] and it occurred to me here was a chance for a good investment as I could get grounds on a street car line owned by my brother and myself."

Hanlon put Johnson in touch with Cleveland outfielder Larry Twitchell. Soon Johnson was busy lining up even more support for the P.L. Ward praised him as an "organizing genius" whose services were of "inestimable value."

"He spent time and money for the benefit of the cause he espoused," noted Ward, "travelled long distances to attend meetings, and gave form and encouragement to the various groups out of which the Players' National League was formed."

There was more to Johnson's involvement than mere pecuniary interest. "If the League can hold a man on a contract for any or all time that it may desire," he expounded, "when it simply guarantees him ten days' pay (for that is everything in the world it does for the players), why, then the laws of our land are worse than those of any other nation on earth, and instead of progressing, as we suppose that every civilized country is struggling to do, the sooner we turn back the better."

This activity remained clandestine until early September, when the *Sporting News* broke the story of a "widespread plot." When Boston infielder Joe Quinn spilled the beans, the *Sporting News* headlined, "The Brotherhood/ Every Man But Anson Pledged to Jump/ The Greatest Move in the History of the National Game."

In October events really heated up. Players refused to return contracts. John Montgomery Ward dropped all pretenses with Giants owner John B. Day.

On November 4, 1889, between 30 and 40 players met at New York's Fifth Avenue Hotel, making known their intentions to secede from the National League and stating their grievances in an eloquent "Manifesto":

TO THE PUBLIC: At last, the Brotherhood of Baseball Players feels at liberty to make known its intentions and defend itself against the aspersions and misrepresentations which for weeks it has been forced to suffer in silence. It is no longer a secret that the players of the league have determined to play next season under different management, but for reasons which will, we think, be understood, it was deemed advisable to make no announcement of this intention until the close of the present season; but now that the struggles of the various pennants are over, and the terms of the contracts expired, there is no longer any reason for withholding it.

In taking this step we feel that we owe it to the public and to ourselves to explain briefly some of the reasons by which we have been moved. There was a time when the league stood for integrity and fair dealing; to-day it stands for dollars and cents. Once it looked to the elevation of the game and an honest exhibition of the sport; to-day its eyes are on the turnstile. Men have come into the business for no other motive than to exploit it for every dollar in sight. Measures originally intended for the good of the game have been perverted into instruments for wrong. The reserve rule and the provisions gave the managers unlimited power, and they have not hesitated to use this in the most arbitrary and mercenary way.

Players have been bought, sold, and exchanged as though they were sheep instead of American citizens. "Reservation" became with them another name for property right in the player. By a combination among themselves, stronger than the strongest trust, they were able to enforce the most arbitrary measures, and the player had either to submit or get out of the profession in which he had spent years in attaining proficiency. Even the disbandment and retirement of a club did not free the players from the octopus clutch, for they were then peddled around to the highest bidder.

That the player sometimes profited by the sale has nothing to do with the case, but only proves the injustice of his previous restraint. Two years ago we met the league and attempted to remedy some of the evils, but through what has politely been called "league diplomacy" we completely failed. Unwilling longer to submit to such treatment, we made a strong effort last spring to reach an understanding with the league. To our application for a hearing they replied "that the matter was not of sufficient importance to warrant a hearing," and suggested that it be put off until fall. Our committee replied that the players felt that the league had broken faith with them; that while the results might be of little importance to the managers, they were of great importance to the players; that if the league would not concede what was fair we would adopt other means to protect ourselves; that if postponed until fall we would be separated and at the mercy of the league, and that, as the only course left us required time and labor to develop, we must therefore insist upon an immediate conference.

Then, upon the final refusal to meet us, we began organizing for ourselves, and are in shape to go ahead next year under new management and new auspices. We believe that it is possible to conduct our national game upon lines which will not infringe upon individual and natural rights. We ask to be solely judged by our work, and, believing that the game can be played more fairly and its business conducted more intelligently under a plan which excludes everything arbitrary and un–American, we look forward with confidence to the support of the public, and the future of the national game.

THE NATIONAL BROTHERHOOD OF BALL PLAYERS

Original plans called for franchises in Boston, New York, Washington, Philadelphia, Indianapolis, Pittsburgh, Cleveland and Chicago—in their words, in every League city except Cincinnati. Ultimately, Buffalo and Brooklyn replaced Washington and Indianapolis, both of which had also been dropped by the N.L.

The Players' League was to be governed by a 16-player senate, two from each club. One player from each club was to be chosen by his peers, the other by the financial angels of each franchise. This group would elect a president and vice president from among its membership, but would chose a non-"senator" at $4,000 for the post of secretary-treasurer.

A semi-utopian profit-sharing scheme was established. Originally, all non-salary expenses were to be paid first. Only then would salaries be paid. The players were wary of this arrangement, and a $40,000 fund guaranteeing payrolls was established. Once these obligations (plus a $2,500-per-club payment to support the Pennant Fund) were made, the next $10,000 per club was to go to the owners, the next $10,000 to be divided among all P.L. players, and anything beyond that divided between all players and clubs. Only gate receipts were to be counted in this formula, not program and concession sales.

Gate receipts would be split evenly between home and visiting clubs. All contracts were for three years, and players could be released only at season's end by the vote of a majority of the club's board of directors, which would include players.

The mood was confident. "Gentlemen, we have the players and the fans with us," claimed Ward, "and those National League owners will learn to their sorrow that the public is interested only in the players, not who backs the clubs."

"That's right, John," added Dan Brouthers. "No one would pay a nickel to see [Boston co-owners] Arthur Soden play first, William Conant at second and [J.L.] Billings at third."

"I'm one of the bosses now," crowed King Kelly, "and the triumvirate [Soden, Conant and Billings]—well, to be frank, they are my understudies. . . . Next year [we] will be in command and the former presidents will have to drive horse cars for a living and borrow rain checks to see a game."

Many players were willing to put their money where their mouths were. Ward held stock in both the New York and Brooklyn clubs. Rowe and White brought their Buffalo club into the league, each subscribing $1,000. Former Washington catcher Connie Mack bought $500 worth of stock. ("I was a strong

Brotherhood man and invested all the money I had saved out of my baseball pay in the Buffalo Players' League team.") Ned Hanlon owned part of Pittsburgh.

One observer of these developments was Henry V. Lucas. Just after the Players had issued their proclamation, he chanced upon Cincinnati Reds owner Aaron S. Stern on the streets of Chicago. Stern queried him as to his opinion of events. "It will fail,. . ." Lucas stated bitterly, "simply because the players will not stick together. The average ballplayer cannot be relied on to remain with such an organization if he can see more money somewhere else. They will not take chances of sharing visionary profits when they can work for sure money with a regular club."

The National League responded to the rebellion with the creation of a "War Committee" of Spalding, John B. Day, and Colonel John I. Rogers of Philadelphia. To influence public opinion they issued their own apologia, featuring a lengthy history of the League's battles and of the reserve clause, but eventually getting to the heart of the matter:

> At the annual meeting of the League in November, 1887, the Brotherhood asked and received recognition upon the statement of its representatives, that it was organized for benevolent purposes and desired to go hand in hand with the League, in perpetuating the game, increasing its popularity, and elevating the moral standards of its players. They disavowed any intention to interfere with the business affairs of the League, the salaries of players or the "reserve rule," simply asking that the contract be so revised, that it, in itself would indicate every relation between a club and each individual player.
>
> To correct a misapprehension in the public mind as to the alleged "enormous profits" divided among stockholders of League clubs, it may be interesting to know that during the past five—and only prosperous—years, there have been paid in cash dividends to stockholders in the eight League clubs less than $150,000, and during the same time, League players have received in salaries over $1,500,000. The balance of the profits of the few successful clubs, together with the original capital and subsequent assessments of stockholders, is represented entirely in grounds and improvement for the permanent good of the game, costing about $600,000.
>
> They knew there was no urgency for the consideration of their claims and knowing that the League could not, without sacrifice of time, money and other conflicting interests, convene its clubs in midsummer and anticipating and desiring a refusal, to cover the conspiracy, which, it now appears, was then hatching they started the organization of a rival association, while receiving the most liberal of salaries from their employers. Under false promises to their brother players, that they would only secede in the event of the League refusing them justice, they secured the signatures of the latter to a secret pledge or oath to desert their clubs at the bidding of their disaffected leaders. Upon the publication of their plot on Sept. 7, 1889, they and their abettors denied, day after day, that there was any foundation for the story,

and repeatedly plighted their words, that the League should have a chance to redress their alleged grievances, before they would order a "strike."

How false their promises, how evasive, contradictory and mendacious have been their every act and deed, from first to last, we leave to the readers of the daily and weekly press for verification.

An edifice built on falsehood has no moral foundation and must perish of its own weight. . . .

On December 16, 1889, Colonel Edwin A. McAlpin, a New York real estate speculator, tobacconist and head of the New York club, was elected president of the Players' League. John Addison, a Windy City contractor and president of that city's franchise, was chosen vice president. Sportswriter Frank H. Brunell was named secretary-treasurer.

The eight clubs were represented thus:

New York—Edwin A. McAlpin, William "Buck" Ewing
Brooklyn—Edward F. Linton, John M. Ward, G. E. Andrews
Boston—Julian B. Hart, Daniel Brouthers
Philadelphia—J. M. Vanderslice, George Wood
Pittsburgh—John M. Beemer, Edward "Ned" Hanlon
Buffalo—Moses Shire, John E. Rowe
Cleveland—Albert L. Johnson, John "Cub" Stricker
Chicago—John Addison, N. Fred Pfeffer

Prizes for the upcoming pennant race were established, with $7,000 for to the champions, $5,000 to the second-place team, $500 for teams in third through seventh places and nothing for the team in the cellar.

On March 11, 1890, the P.L. met again at the Weddell House in Cleveland, with the following delegates in attendance: from Boston, Hart and Brouthers; from Chicago, Addison and Pfeffer; from Cleveland, Johnson and Stricker; from Buffalo, C. R. Fitzgerald, Shire and Deacon White; from Brooklyn, Linton; from New York, Colonel McAlpin, Edward B. Talcott and Ewing; from Philadelphia, J. Earl Wagner and F. S. Elliot; and from Pittsburgh, M. B. Lennon, John K. Tener and Hanlon.

The prize fund was now to be distributed thus: for first place, $6,250; followed by $4,800, $3,500, $2,500, $1,750, $800 and $400 awards.

The pitcher's box was moved from 45 to 51 feet from home plate, and a two-umpire system was instituted, the first time this had been mandated on a regular basis. Arbiters (one of whom would be Ross Barnes) were to be dressed entirely in white. Later in the season, when two teams of umpires showed up by mistake on the same day, four umpires were used for the first time.

A major portion of creating the new Players' National League was establishing ballparks at each franchise. In New York, McAlpin and Talcott found a site across from Day's ballpark. Originally a seventeenth-century grant

OUTFITTERS TO THE PLAYERS' NATIONAL LEAGUE

KEEFE OFFICIAL PLAYERS' LEAGUE BALL

ADOPTED BY THE PLAYERS' NATIONAL LEAGUE
BEWARE OF COUNTERFEITS
THE ONLY GENUINE KEEFE OFFICIAL PLAYERS' LEAGUE BALL IS PUT UP IN A BOX AS SHOWN IN THE ABOVE CUT MADE IN THE BEST POSSIBLE MANNER EVERY BALL GUARANTEED TO GIVE SATISFACTION
PRICE $1.50 EACH $15.00 PER DOZ.

1890.
PLAYERS' NATIONAL LEAGUE
BASE·BALL· GUIDE
·ALL·THE·OFFICIAL·FIGURES·
PUBLISHED BY
F.H.BRUNELL, Sec'y & Treas
927 Chicago Opera House, CHICAGO.
PRICE, 10 CTS.

of farmland from the English crown to John Lon Gardner, it was the property of James J. Coogan, an upholsterer who became Manhattan borough president. Just a few hundred feet from the Giants' Polo Grounds, this new "Brotherhood Park" was larger than its rival field and featured a bar, the "Seeley and Rappleyea Cafe," under its grandstand. Featuring "fine wines, liquors and cigars, whiskey and James Everhard's Celebrated Lager Beer," it was managed by Dasher Troy, whose contract had been so bitterly contested in 1884.

Chicago's "Brotherhood Park" was on West 35th Street, across from the future site of Comiskey Park. Rent was $1,500 per year. Boston played at "Congress Street Park." Buffalo expanded "Olympic Park" at Michigan Avenue and Ferry Streets from 3,500 seats to 5,000. Brooklyn operated at Eastern Park in the East New York section of the city, where stockholder George Chauncey, a noted financier, had large real estate holdings. Pittsburgh utilized the old American Association field, "Exposition Park."

As the Players' League was organizing, the existing circuits underwent major restructuring. On November 13, 1889, the American Association deadlocked in the choice of a new president to replace the ineffectual Wheeler C. Wikoff. Brooklyn, Kansas City, Baltimore and Cincinnati backed L. C. Krauthoff of Kansas City, while the others backed Zack Phelps of the horrendous (27-111) Louisville club.

On the way to the Association's session in New York, representatives of five A.A. clubs—Philadelphia, St. Louis, Baltimore, Columbus and Louisville—had gathered in Philadelphia for a secret conference. When the remaining clubs— Cincinnati, Brooklyn and Kansas City—found out about the back-room dealings, they were indignant. Charles Byrne of the champion Brooklyn Bridegrooms and Aaron Stern of the Cincinnati Reds marched across town to where the National League was holding its meetings. As the Association's bylaws allowed members to secede, they were within their rights to apply for National League membership. This was not the first time a club had jumped leagues, the Association's Pittsburgh and Cleveland clubs having gone over to the League in 1887 and 1889, respectively. Brooklyn and Cincinnati were accepted. The League was for the moment a ten-club circuit.

Further desertions rocked the Association. Kansas City enlisted in the Western Association (where Krauthoff became League president and where his club, not surprisingly, won the 1890 pennant). The Baltimore Orioles joined the Atlantic Association, playing alongside such cities as New Haven, Harrisburg and Lebanon, Pennsylvania.

There was some thought of consolidating the American Association with the P.L. John M. Ward attended a special Association meeting on December 4 which examined the possibility of a merger. Al Spink urged Von der Ahe to support the P.L., and when Chris attended the Players' December meeting, there were rumors the Browns would join that league. The Association seemed on the verge of extinction.

The National League faced a much different but still vexing problem: a glut of franchises. Its two weak links were the Washington Senators and the Indianapolis Hoosiers. The last-place Senators disbanded, but John T. Brush of Indianapolis demanded compensation for the Hoosiers to depart League ranks. He received $60,000 for a franchise he had purchased for just $18,000 a little more than a year before.

The American Association patched itself back together, adding teams in Brooklyn (the Gladiators), Rochester (the Hop Bitters), Syracuse (the Stars) and Toledo (the Maumees). Fortified by such second-rate franchises it took the field for 1890.

Organized Baseball's War Effort

When the Players' League finalized its playing schedule, it forwarded a copy to the League so that it might, "should it so choose, avoid conflicting with our clubs. . . ." Further, Brunell suggested to his rivals that they adopt a resolution allowing exhibitions with the Players' teams both during and after the regular season.

The result was a decision by the Nationals to fight to the bitter end. The N.L. adopted a schedule conflicting with the Players' at every turn. If the Players' would be in New York or Chicago or Pittsburgh on a given date, so would the League.

The National League continued to be incensed by its rival's progress. *Spalding's Guide*, edited by Henry Chadwick, was an official National League organ and provided a scathing analysis of the situation. Noting the Brotherhood had begun in New York, which "had petted its players for years," it castigated the "ingratitude" and "the ambitious efforts of a small minority," as well as the lust for "self-aggrandizement" characterizing the leadership of this "whole revolutionary scheme." Ward was mentioned only as the "mastermind" of the plot.

The *Guide* also heaped venom on the Brotherhood's supporters in the press, "the class of young base ball journalists . . . so free in censorious comments" regarding the League and its legislation.

To cap its case that charges of player "slavery" were a joke, the *Guide* printed a list showing the progression of salaries of several categories of National League players ("malcontents"), those of nine years' tenure, those of four to seven years', three, two and one. These figures, it was argued, illustrated "the justness and fairness of the much-abused, grossly misrepresented, but beneficial Reserve Rule." The *Guide's* list of nine-year players:

NAME	1881	1882	1883	1884	1885	1886	1887	1888	1889	TOTAL
King Kelly	1300	1400	1700	2000	2250	2500	4000	4000	4000	$23,150
Hardy Richardson	1250	1300	1500	2000	2100	4000	4000	4000	4000	$24,150
Ned Williamson	1400	1400	2000	2300	2500	2500	2500	3000	3000	$20,600
George Gore	1100	1200	1800	2100	2100	2100	2500	3000	3000	$18,900
Dan Brouthers	875	1200	1600	2000	2500	4000	4000	4000	4700	$24,875
Jim O'Rourke	2000	2000	2250	3000	4500	3000	3500	3500	3500	$27,250
Deacon White	1600	1600	1600	1600	2500	3500	3500	3500	3500	$22,900
Jack Rowe	1250	1400	1650	2000	2100	3500	3500	3500	3500	$22,400
Ned Hanlon	1200	1400	1500	1700	1700	2100	2100	2800	3100	$17,600
George Wood	875	1000	1400	1600	1600	1800	2000	2100	2500	$14,875
Pud Galvin	1200	1300	1700	2600	2600	2000	2100	3000	3000	$19,500
Fred Pfeffer	750	1000	1600	1800	1800	2100	2400	3000	3000	$17,450
Buck Ewing	1000	1200	3100	3100	3100	3500	3500	4500	5000	$28,000
Monte Ward	1700	2400	3000	3000	3000	3000	3000	4000	4250	$27,350
Tim Keefe	1500	1500	2809	2800	3000	3000	3000	4000	4500	$26,109
Roger Connor	900	1200	2000	2000	2200	3000	3000	3000	3500	$20,800
										$355,909

Adding to the National League strategies, Albert Spalding sought to counteract the opinions of Francis Richter's *Sporting Life* by installing O. P. Caylor and Harry C. Palmer at the *New York Sporting Times*. Caylor would not employ the rapier where a sledgehammer could be found, referring to the players as "drunken knaves" and "men without principle, who knew not how to keep their words and had no sense of shame." Palmer inquired why players should make carping criticism when they were lucky enough to be "in a business that is really a pastime and unquestionably a pleasure." The *Sporting News*, meanwhile, which supported the revolt, was bombarded with hate mail and threats to withdraw advertising. Its circulation plummeted.

Not all invective was on one side. The *Sporting News* caustically termed the *Sporting Times* "*The Spitting Times*" and labeled Palmer's relationship to Spalding "as a leech is to its appurtenant." Francis Richter called Spalding "the Windy City fake."

"In place of powder and shell, printers' ink and bluff formed the ammunition by both sides," A. G. Spalding summed up two decades later.

Over 100 players deserted the National League. Virtually every big-name League player joined the "conspiracy," among them Charlie Comiskey, Fred Pfeffer, Hugh Duffy, Connie Mack, Ned Williamson, Buck Ewing, Ned Hanlon, "Dummy" Hoy, Art Irwin, "Silver" King, Tim Keefe, John Montgomery Ward, King Kelly, Hoss Radbourn, Deacon White, John K. Tener, Roger Connor, Jimmy Ryan, "Patsy" Tebeau, George Van Haltren, George Wood, Hardy Richardson, Jack Rowe, Dan Brouthers, Ed Delahanty, "Lady" Baldwin, "Duke" Farrell and George "Piano Legs" Gore.

Coming over from the American Association were stars such as Pete

**Venerable Harry Wright, manager of the Phillies, inspired such loyalty among
his players that Philadelphia suffered the fewest Players' League defections of
any National League team.**

Browning, "Tip" O'Neill, Matt Kilroy, Harry Stovey, Arlie Latham, Henry
Larkin, "Yank" Robinson, Gus Weyhing, Michael Griffin, Louis Bierbauer and
Davey Orr. These desertions, noted the 1890 *Reach's Guide,* inflicted "a severe
blow upon the Association clubs with whom they had no quarrel. This was very
disastrous to the St. Louis, Athletic and Baltimore clubs, nearly ruining the latter."

Venerable Harry Wright remained Phillies manager despite advances
from the Players' camp. His still-considerable influence helped his team suffer
the fewest defections of any League team. An amazing example of the loyalty
he inspired was the case of young catcher George Stallings, future manager of

the 1914 "Miracle Braves." Stallings had been cut by Wright a few years before, and despite offers from three P.L. clubs begged for another chance with Wright. "Since leaving your team in '87," Stallings wrote, "it has been my ambition to make myself competent and play under your management again." In a year when the National League was hiring almost anyone off the street, Wright spurned his advances.

Cap Anson was the major star retained by the National League. Despite later admissions that the Players "were never so crooked or deceitful as the magnates were," Anson stuck with Spalding in Chicago. No doubt he was influenced not only by long-time loyalty to Spalding, but also by ownership of a share in the club. Most of Charlie Byrne's Brooklyn club, just transferred in from the American Association, also stayed; Brooklyn thus accomplished the unique feat of winning back-to-back pennants in two different major leagues. The Cincinnati Reds, also transferring from the Association, retained most of their players.

But these cases were not the norm. Charles Comiskey gave up management of the Browns to join the P.L. "I couldn't do anything else," he commented, "and still play fair with the boys," The legendary Anson could hold onto the loyalties of but two of his 1889 players, third baseman Thomas Burns and pitcher "Wild Bill" Hutchinson. Boston retained only pitcher John Clarkson and catcher Charlie Ganzel. Pittsburgh could hold but Billy Sunday and one minor player. Washington's roster transferred *en masse* to Buffalo.

King Kelly was one of the greatest of nineteenth-century stars. A real crowd-pleaser ("Slide, Kelly, Slide!"), Kelly would try anything once. One day he was managing, and a foul pop came his way. "Kelly, now catching!" he yelled to the umpire, as he bounded off the bench to make the grab. The rules did not prohibit what he had done, but they did the next day.

Kelly also knew the value of a dollar—that is, how much of a good time it could buy—but when Albert Spalding not only offered him a blank contract to sign with the National League, but also a $10,000 signing bonus besides, Kelly announced he was "going to take a walk" to think it over. It was a tempting offer, but when he came back a full 90 minutes later he stared at Spalding and announced, "I've decided not to accept."

"What! And pass up that $10,000?" stammered an incredulous Spalding.

"Oh, I want it badly enough, but I can't go back on the boys. . . . My mother and father would never look at me again if I proved a traitor to the boys," responded Kelly, who paused and added, "Neither would you."

Oddly enough, before Kelly left he asked for a loan of $500. Stranger still, Spalding gave it to him. "I think it was little enough to pay for the anguish of that hour and a half," wrote Spalding, "when Kelly was deciding to give up thousands of dollars on the altar of sentiment in behalf of the Brotherhood."

The National League attempted to recapture players through a series of lawsuits. All were unsuccessful. In January of 1890, the Giants sought an injunction against Ward, citing the case of opera impresario William Lumley, who had successfully restrained diva Johanna Wagner from performing elsewhere. It was denied by New York State Supreme Court Justice Morgan Joseph O'Brien on grounds that Ward's 1889 contract contained no valid restraint on his actions for any subsequent year. O'Brien did not find any mutuality in a contract which benefited one party, the club, indefinitely, while the other was guaranteed only ten days' pay. "We have the spectacle presented," O'Brien wrote with no little sense of scorn, "of a contract which binds one party for ten days, and of the party who is itself bound for ten days coming into a court of equity to enforce its claims against the party bound for years." A similar attempt at injunctive action against Buck Ewing also was struck down in March, this time by Judge William P. Wallace of the Southern New York District of federal court, who called the reserve clause's effect "wholly nugatory."

Outfielder "Orator Jim" O'Rourke, himself an attorney, could barely contain his joy. "He that hath committed inequity shall not have equity," he maintained. The unsuccessful suits regarding Ward and Ewing had cost the National League not only the two star players, but also $15,000 in lawyers' fees and court costs.

Also failing was an attempt by John I. Rogers' Philadelphia club to retain the services of infielder William Hallman. Judge M. Russell Thayer took offense at players' being "absolutely at the mercy of the owner" and released Hallman from any obligation to the National League club.

Rogers, an attorney who had a major hand in developing the standard player contract, was glum. "I have nothing further to say," he tensely informed the New York *Clipper,* "except that in Pennsylvania our 'reserve' clause may have to be rewritten, or it must disappear from future contracts."

Only in the case of outfielder John Thomas Pickett was a ballclub even marginally successful. Pickett had been sold by St. Paul of the Western Association to Kansas City of the American Association in May 1889 for $3,300, of which he received $800. In 1890 Kansas City had dropped down to the Western Association, but it still retained on its roster Pickett, who had been on the disabled list for a good part of 1889. Pickett had even signed with the team, receiving an advance of $200. Pickett had no wish to play in the Western Association, however, and signed another contract with Philadelphia of the Players' League.

Kansas City management sued in Philadelphia Common Pleas Court, seeking to enjoin Pickett from playing for the P.L. The court ruled in the team's favor, holding that the outfielder's "ingratitude being equal to bad faith, the equities are with the employer." However, Pickett did not return to Kansas City, settling with the club for $200 plus legal expenses. Pickett remained with the Quakers, hitting .280 in 100 games.

There were far less-legalistic methods of recapturing players, namely

Michael "King" Kelly, one of the most proficient and popular players of the 1880s, spurned a $10,000 offer to desert the Players' League. (Courtesy of National Baseball Library, Cooperstown, New York.)

offering them more money. During the 1890 season A. G. Mills, J. Walter Spalding (A. G.'s brother), and Cap Anson attempted to secure Buck Ewing's return. For whatever reason Ewing remained in the P.L., but henceforth was regarded with suspicion by fellow players.

Before the season opened, Ed Delahanty and third baseman Joseph Mulvey were lured away from the P.L. but returned before the start of play. Shortstop Jack "Judas" Glasscock did not, "double-jumping" back to Indianapolis. When that franchise folded, he won the 1890 N.L. batting crown with New York.

Coming over from the P.L. in midseason was Arlie Latham, who when suspended by Chicago for his usual riotous behavior, signed with Cincinnati of the Nationals.

The Players Take the Field

As the Players' season began, Boston, New York and Chicago were considered pennant contenders. Opening Day was April 19, 1890, with Brooklyn defeating Boston at Boston 3–2 before a crowd of 10,000. In New York, the Philadelphia Quakers outslugged the home team 12–11 before 12,013 chilled fans. Chicago humiliated Pittsburgh 10–2 before 10,000 customers in Pennsylvania.

This was the high-water mark for the Burghers, who would soon be playing to empty seats in Pittsburgh. "The Brotherhood treasurers don't need valises," jibed the local wags; "they carry the receipts in their vest pockets."

Their League counterparts, or what was left of them, lost 23 straight, including three in a single day to Brooklyn, and one crowd numbered but 25 very hard-core fans. Stung hard by defections, manager Guy Hecker's team, called the "Innocents" that year, won just 23 while losing 113.

Fred "Sure-Shot" Dunlap was released by the Innocents after hitting .172. He retaliated by accusing manager Hecker of drunkenness, card-sharping his players and being such a poor pitcher that his own sister could play better. Outfielder Billy Sunday backed Dunlap up, except that he could not vouch for the part about "Sure Shot's" sister, as he had never seen her play.

By late July attendance was so poor that all Pittsburgh's games were transferred to the road. At season's end the League would present Pittsburgh with a "Booby Pennant" festooned with 113 stars—one for each defeat.

By June the Players' League had to assess each club an extra $2,500 to remain solvent. On July 17, to bail out the weakening Buffalo club, two pitchers, one outfielder and an infielder were ordered sent in from competing teams.

Financed largely by attorney Moses Shire, former Sheriff Frank T. Gilbert and Charles R. Fitzgerald, the Bisons were dubbed the "Home for Respectable Old Men" by the Cincinnati *Enquirer*. The paper further predicted that "about one month after the season starts, the word 'respectable' will be changed to 'indigent.'" The club started out fast, besting Cleveland 23-2, 15-8, 19-7 and 18-15, but then petered out entirely. Pitching, hitting and fielding were equally ghastly. On June 27 the Bisons were humiliated 30-12 by Philadelphia, which scored 14 runs in one inning. Shortly thereafter a rookie pitcher named Lewis gave up 20 runs in just three innings as Brooklyn trounced Buffalo 28-16. He was never seen again. Left fielder Ed Beecher committed a record 55 errors for the season.

In July the Philadelphia franchise was rescued by two local butchers, the Wagner brothers. About the same time in the National League, Day's New York club threatened to collapse unless bailed out by his allies. Eighty thousand dollars was pumped in, mostly by Spalding. In exchange for $60,000 promised him for giving up Indianapolis, John T. Brush also received a share of the club. Things were little better for McAlpin and Talcott. During the season their Players' club took in a mere $59,000 while paying out $67,000.

In August the Boston *Globe* reported National League deficits were an estimated $201,713—a total reaching $300,000 by season's completion. At

The Chicago Pirates of the Players' League. At center is manager–first baseman Charles Comiskey. Second from right, top, is Arlie Latham, who became one of the first players to jump back from the P.L. to the National League.

year's end P.L. Secretary Brunell reported a loss of $125,000 for his circuit.

In the American Association, clubs were so wracked by desertions that the Louisville Colonels (now renamed the Cyclones), who had established a major league record with 111 losses in 1889, won the 1890 flag. The new Brooklyn team, the Gladiators, was so pathetic it folded in mid-campaign and was replaced by the Baltimore Orioles, who had completed their Atlantic Association schedule and now returned to the circuit for the last 34 games of the season.

The minor leagues were also hit hard, as the National League grabbed up almost all available talent to replace Players' League deserters. The minors suffered their worst season financially. The Texas League folded on June 10. The Indiana State League quit on June 24. The International League disbanded on July 10. The Pennsylvania State League died on July 23. By mid-August the Western New York, the Michigan State, Interstate, and Tri-State leagues also collapsed. Buffalo's minor league club, in direct competition with the Players' League and playing in a cheaply built new park, fled to Montreal on June 4. Losses for the minors as a whole may have exceeded $200,000.

**The woeful Buffalo Bisons lost 96 games and finished last in the Players'
League. (Courtesy of Joseph M. Overfield.)**

Interleague war disastrously affected attendance for both rival parties, but
particularly for the National League, which had been shorn of its star players.
Large numbers of passes were issued by both sides. "Major-league tickets,"
observed historian David Quentin Voigt, "were never so easy to acquire as in
1890." The Players' League sent many free passes out by mail. Ladies were
admitted free by both camps. A. G. Spalding initiated "Professional's Day," on
which members of the acting profession were let in without charge. This
widespread largesse particularly amused many former Boston players, who
could recall Arthur Soden's practice of charging their wives to get in.

Toward September, rumors of a merger were rife. One "well-known
player" was quoted as saying, "The Players' and American Association will
consolidate and then . . . will work in harmony with the National League as
the Association has in the past."

Attendance was impossible to estimate because both sides shamefully exaggerated. In mid–August one New York paper sent reporters to count the
houses at both parks. They reported exaggerations of 150 percent.

"If any party of this controversy," contended Albert Spalding, years later,
"ever furnished to the press one solitary truthful statement as to the progress

of the war from his standpoint; if anyone at any time during the contest made
true representation of conditions in his own ranks, a monument should be
erected to his memory. I have no candidates to recommend for the distinction."

One estimate of season attendance went as follows:

	NATIONAL	PLAYERS'
Boston	147,539	197,346
Brooklyn	121,412	79,272
Buffalo	–	61,244
Chicago	102,536	148,876
Cincinnati	131,980	–
Cleveland	47,478	58,430
New York	60,667	148,197
Philadelphia	186,002	170,123
Pittsburgh	16,064	117,123
	813,678	980,611

The Beginning of the End

As the season drew to a close, the baseball world was stunned by the sale
for $40,000 of the Cincinnati League club by clothier Aaron Stern to a consor-
tium of Players' League stockholders.

Initially, Stern denied he would ever sell to the Brotherhood. Then he
promised he would do so only for cash. When he did make the sale, it was only
for a portion in cash, with the balance in promissory notes. As baseball
historian Preston D. Orem observed, "Stern prided himself on being a practical
business man above all else, including such minor matters as selling out his
associates."

Buyers included McAlpin and Talcott of New York, George W. Chauncey
and Wendell Goodwin of Brooklyn, John C. Haynes and Julian B. Hart of
Boston, the Wagner brothers of Philadelphia, Al Johnson of Cleveland and Addison and P. L. Austin of Chicago. Plans called for ultimate transfer to local
ownership.

O. P. Caylor struggled to put the best face on events. "It is nothing short
of a confession of weakness," he snorted. "I have it from very good authority
that the Brotherhood is on the downward path, tobogganing so to speak."

But it was a stunning coup for the Players'. "It will not only bring into our
league one of the best ball teams in the country . . . but it will give us an ideal
circuit," crowed Ward, as he was about to launch a great blunder in strategy.

Flushed with success, Ward on October 3 invited his National League
counterparts to a peace conference, with recognition as a legitimate circuit his
goal.

Both sides were exhausted and wanted peace. "The pressure for a truce

. . . continues," wrote the *Sporting Life* on October 3. "The press, the players, and the public demand a cessation of the needless, costly and damaging conflict. . . ."

The National League met in New York on October 9. Allan W. "White Wings" Thurman, son of a United States Senator and a minor stockholder in the Columbus A.A. Club, was soon to emerge as a key figure in the peace process. He proposed consolidation of the three existing circuits into two leagues with different price structures. It was an odd peace plan because it left competing franchises in a number of cities. Fifty-cent admissions were planned for clubs in Boston, Brooklyn, Chicago, Cleveland, Columbus, Indianapolis, New York and Philadelphia, and a 25-cent admission would be set for other teams in Baltimore, Boston, Cincinnati, Louisville, Philadelphia, Pittsburgh, St. Louis and Washington.

While the National League debated Thurman's plan, three Players' League owners were at the St. James Hotel. Also converging on New York were representatives of the Association. Albert Spalding had just returned from a sojourn to Europe and was shaken to hear of Cincinnati's defection. Spalding started the conference by getting the Players' delegation to reveal the enormity of their financial losses. He realized their weakness and proceeded with a gigantic bluff, demanding "unconditional surrender." To his amazement they "greedily" accepted his proposal.

"We had been playing at two games all through—baseball and bluff," Spalding would recall. "At this stage I put up the strongest play at the latter game I ever presented."

The P.L. people said they would balk at abandoning the Players' League name, insisting the Senior Circuit allow its retention. Spalding sensed he had them on the run. Also discussed was the division of clubs on a basis similar to Thurman's plan. When Spalding carried this news back to the rest of the League, his fellow magnates were ecstatic. So cocksure was Brooklyn's Charlie Byrne that he attempted to re-institute the reserve clause. Spalding told him to wait just a while.

An informal secret peace conference convened, with three emissaries from each circuit. Spalding, John B. Day and Byrne represented the National; Von der Ahe, Vonderhorst and Thurman came from the Association; and Al Johnson, New York's Edward Talcott and Brooklyn's Wendell Goodwin represented the Players'. It may not have been coincidence that representatives of the rival Brooklyn and New York franchises were sitting down together. Soon a real deal—and the disintegration of the Players' League—was at hand.

Officially nothing had been settled except for a truce on player signings and the date of the conferees' next session, October 22. Almost immediately, however, McAlpin and Talcott attempted to get the best deal by consolidating with Day's Giants. By October 20 dispatches reported that a deal had been hammered out and that Buck Ewing was to manage the club. The two Pitts-burgh clubs were also reportedly near a merger.

Unease spread in the Players' camp. They suspected a sell-out, as did the Wagner brothers, owners of Philadelphia. On October 20 the Brotherhood met in New York, and unity between the Brotherhood and its financial backers was clearly unraveling. On October 21, on a motion from Chicago's John Addison, the P.L. moved to reassure the players, adding three Brotherhood repre-sentatives – Ward, Ned Hanlon and Boston shortstop Arthur Irwin, to its delegation for the upcoming October 22 session.

Although some immediate rumblings were heard from the N.L.-A.A. camp, P.L. Secretary Brunell maintained, "We shall meet with our six players or not at all. If they don't receive us that way, it ends all and the Players' League will stand where it is. There is nothing in the statement that the New York and Brooklyn clubs are anxious for this consolidation."

Whispers of P.L. owners' duplicity were fast turning into shouts, and most were probably correct. Still, the Brotherhood couldn't believe its dream was shattering, and sent to the P.L. Central Board of Directors a statement that despite "the many rumors current . . . their entire confidence" was in their magnates' "ability to safely conduct the [Players' League's] affairs."

Their naive faith was shattered at the joint session with the capitalists, when it became obvious that New York, Brooklyn, Chicago and Buffalo were less than solid. Buffalo, in fact, was on the verge of dissolution, and the P.L. was forced to assume responsibilities for its players' back salaries.

Under these circumstances, on October 22 the augmented P.L. delegation marched into New York's Fifth Avenue Hotel to resume negotiations. The League and Association denied the new P.L. delegation's validity because of its doubled membership. Albert Spalding bluntly stated, "Before the National League consented to any negotiations whatever, it was mutually decided that the question of a compromise should be settled between the moneyed men of both organizations on a purely business basis."

John B. Day added, "The Players' League cannot add to their committee at their own free will. Their present committee can represent player rights."

Ward rebutted, "Do these gentlemen wish to go on record as saying that the occupation of ballplayer bars him from business associations with respect-able men?" Knowing full well that Spalding and Barnie were former players, he addressed the former directly: "Mr. Spalding, are you willing to place such a stamp of infamy upon the profession of which for years you were a member?"

Much haggling went back and forth before Al Johnson allowed a vote of the original nine delegates to settle the issue. Not surprisingly, by a six-to-three tally, the Brotherhood was barred from the meeting, at which point the session broke up.

Formal negotiations were pretty much at an end; deals were being negotiated left and right as P.L. magnates endeavored to save what they could.

The Players' League Collapses

The next day, Johnson, Wendell Goodwin and Edward Talcott met secretly with Spalding and company at his Hoffman House suite. Word leaked out, but all three denied making concessions; their protestations did little to reassure anyone. John M. Ward now spoke openly of "dark corner" meetings and of "not treating the players in good faith."

By November 1, even Ward admitted consolidation was inevitable. He claimed to be supportive of it "if the principles of the Players' League are perpetuated," i.e., the end of the reserve rule and "an equal division of the gate receipts." J. Earl Wagner and Francis Richter were scurrying up from Philadelphia to meet with Colonel McAlpin to assuage their worries over his possible actions. Their fears were soothed.

"We are now of the opinion that the New York people do not intend to do anything that is unfair or dishonorable," reported Richter. ". . . I think that the players have been treated finely. They should not say too much. They cannot get the worst of it, no matter what is done." But as he spoke, Addison of Chicago was hurrying to New York, openly attempting his own deal with Spalding.

On November 5 the anti-consolidationists met in Philadelphia. Their faction was now down to three — Boston, Philadelphia and, despite Addison's negotiations, Chicago. They proposed suing Brooklyn and New York if they went through with their rumored secession. However, they were warned by counsel to the New York club, Judge Bacon, that such "a suit would be utter nonsense."

By November 10, McAlpin resigned as Players' League president, and when the circuit met at Pittsburgh's Monongahela Hotel on November 12, the New York and Brooklyn clubs formally announced consolidation with their N.L. counterparts. A committee of Ward, Johnson and Prince was to negotiate with the National League regarding consolidation, but it was too late. The once-intractable King Kelly signed with Soden's club. Ned Williamson and Jimmy Ryan telegraphed Albert Spalding, begging to return. Pittsburgh was consolidating on a 50-50 basis. Chicago was also on the block, although Spalding was nervous about the price. "All admit," reported the New York *Times*, "that the baseball war has been a failure."

Nonetheless, on November 13 the Players' League convened again, but was jolted to learn of Chicago's sale to Spalding for $10,000 in cash and a $15,000 interest in the White Stockings. Even before the session, the group was dispirited. Even Ward had gone hunting for the day, too "tired" from events to go on. Feelings were particularly bitter against Johnson, who was termed a "confidence man." One P.L. delegate mixed metaphors, telling the New York *Times* Johnson had "been trying to ride two horses, but now he is out in the cold."

The National Leaguers also met in New York that day and, basking in their triumph, were equally contemptuous of Johnson. "When they begin to call each other confidence men," chortled one magnate, ". . . we have them on the run, and we propose to keep them there. It is unfair, however, to speak disrespectfully of Mr. Talcott . . . a gentleman in all his dealings with our organization. Other men—one in particular, a very prominent member of the Cleveland Club, has been guilty of sharp practices in asking for secret conferences. . . ."

The League met again the next day to resolve the Cincinnati issue. Al Johnson appeared, unsuccessfully trying to cut a deal. Published reports stated that he offered both the Cleveland club and his share of Cincinnati to the N.L. for $40,000, but that offer was rejected as "ridiculous."

That same day, the Players' League met in rump session at New York's St. James Hotel, with Boston's Charles Prince taking charge. He expressed disappointment in Johnson ("I can't see why he deserts us all the time"), but with much bravado issued a not-very-realistic "Manifesto" contending that "notwithstanding the way many of the so-called capitalists have shown weakness," the P.L.'s ills had been "greatly exaggerated" and "the organization will remain whole." As Prince was issuing these brave words, Philadelphia's J. Earl Wagner was indicating a desire to join the American Association. He would eventually join forces with Prince himself to force their way into organized Baseball. Wagner got his wish to take over the forfeited A.A. Philadelphia franchise, while Prince was allowed to operate an Association nine in Boston, although Arthur Soden successfully insisted that it be under conditions designed to cripple it financially.

By November 22, Secretary Brunell was being evicted from his Chicago offices for non-payment of rent. It was all over.

Most Players' League parks were retained, as they were newer and more "modern" than the old League sites. The Giants moved across the street into "Brotherhood Park," renaming it the "New Polo Grounds." In Chicago, Albert Spalding similarly moved to Brotherhood territory, as not only was that park more modern, but rent was one-fifth what he had been paying. In Boston, Congress Street Park became the home of Prince's Association team in 1891 and of the League in 1894. Brooklyn's Eastern Park, after some haggling, became home of the Bridegrooms from 1891 to 1897. Exposition Park in Pittsburgh would be used by the National League until Forbes Field was opened in 1909. (It would later be rescued temporarily from oblivion by the city's 1914 Federal League franchise.)

Only P.L. parks in Cleveland and Philadelphia would never see big league ball again. Cleveland's nine would certainly not stray from Frank Robison's streetcar line.

Also left out in the cold were Al Johnson, Deacon White and his Buffalo partners, some minority Brooklyn stockholders—and the Brotherhood of Professional Base Ball Players.

Meanwhile, New York Players' League personnel had not been paid since

September 1. In late November they were told point-blank, "Well, sue the club if you think you can accomplish your object any sooner. You are a stockholder, are you not? Why don't you put your hand in your pocket like some of us and help settle up matters?"

Sadly opined the *Sporting News*, "Win in the lottery and you are a clever man, for he who triumphs is reveled. . . . Ward and those who fought with him might have been written down in history as great had that one word, Success, crowned their efforts. As it failed to follow them, however, there are no crowns for them and when they are gone they will be thought of as fellows of no great shakes after all."

Chapter 7
Failed Beginnings — Part I

Annihilation of the Players' League theoretically should have ushered in a new tranquility. It did not.

Collapse of the American Association

Relations between the National League and the American Association had never been warm. The Association resented the Nationals' dominance, and when two ex–P.L. men, second baseman Louis Bierbauer and outfielder Harry Stovey, were signed by Pittsburgh of the National League instead of their former Athletics team, all hell broke loose.

Technically, it was quite legal. Philadelphia had forgotten to reserve the two. But when the Association's own president, Allan "White Wings" Thurman, who was serving on the three-man Arbitration Board, "reluctantly" ruled against the Athletics, that was more than could be easily tolerated.

Also adding to the strain was confusion over the Cincinnati franchise. Both circuits desired the city, and Albert Johnson dealt with both in a slippery fashion. For 1891 each circuit would field a team in the Queen City, one backed by Chris Von der Ahe, the other by John T. Brush.

It was war to the death, and the Association cracked apart almost immediately. Milwaukee, Columbus and Louisville were total financial disasters. As early as June, Columbus was mumbling about peace. In August, Boston desperately cut admissions to 25 cents, a violation of the agreement made when Soden and company had allowed Tom Prince into Boston. To forestall desertions of any individual franchises (known in the slang of the time as a "dinky-dink"), the majority of stock in each club was transferred to the Association itself.

Brush and Von der Ahe conferred in Cincinnati in early August. Resulting were committees being named to discuss a settlement: Brush, Charles H. Byrne, and James Hart, representing the League, and Von der Ahe, Zack Phelps and Louis Kramer, representing the Association.

Throwing a monkey wrench into negotiations was the defection of the fading King Kelly from the American Association to the Boston N.L. team. This was regarded by the Association as a betrayal, and it appeared the war might continue another season.

But by mid–November talks were on again, and on December 15, at a session in Indianapolis, the four stronger A.A. franchises were brought into the League: Baltimore, St. Louis, Washington and Louisville joined with the eight N.L. clubs to form the "National League and American Association of Professional Baseball Clubs." To guarantee that none of the signatories would be readily betrayed, a ten-year pact banning any club disfranchisements was signed.

Louisville, Baltimore and St. Louis ownership simply transferred operations lock, stock and barrel into the new 12-club circuit. J. Earl Wagner, formerly the owner of the defunct Philadelphia A.A. franchise, was allowed to purchase the Washington club and became the first and only man in major league history to own franchises in three different leagues in as many years.

The remaining A.A. franchises were bought out for $130,000, an obligation assumed by the 12 survivors. A new era of "monopoly" baseball had begun, and it was a highly profitable one. By the conclusion of 1893, the full $130,000 debt was paid off, and a $25,000 surplus accumulated. Next season was even better. One or perhaps two of the 12 National League clubs only broke even, but the remainder turned profits ranging from $5,000 to $40,000, with Baltimore and New York particularly prosperous—even though the nation itself was in the throes of the Cleveland-era depression.

Talk of Reviving the American Association

Once again, prosperity bred threats of renewed competition. By September 1894 a revived American Association was openly being discussed in baseball circles. Prime backers of the scheme were Francis Richter, editor of *Sporting Life;* Albert L. Buckenberger, manager of Columbus (A.A.) in 1889–90 and Pittsburgh (N.L.) in 1892–94; Louisville second baseman Fred Pfeffer; and William Harrison "Billie" Barnie, a former billposter, catcher and roller rink operator, who managed the Baltimore club from 1883 to 1891, Washington in 1892, and Louisville since 1893.

In New York on October 17, 1894, Buckenberger, Al DeRoy and Al Pratt arrived from Pittsburgh to attend a closed-door session of Association organizers. Buckenberger gave the press a cheerful assessment of the situation: "At tomorrow's meeting [in Philadelphia] representatives from New York, Brooklyn, Philadelphia, Boston, Chicago, Providence, Buffalo and Detroit will be present. It will be a secret session, and we hope to complete our organization. A uniform admission fee of 25 cents will be charged in each city. Al Johnson is interested in the local club. The others we prefer not to mention

**National League magnates of the 1890s. (Courtesy of National Baseball
Library, Cooperstown, New York.)**

now. We have secured grounds all right in this city, Brooklyn [reputed to be
Ambrose Park] and elsewhere. We shall play as long a season as the National
League does. After our organization is effected we shall not hesitate to talk for
publication. Till then we have nothing to say."

On October 18 in Philadelphia the Association formally organized; franchises were awarded to New York, Brooklyn, Philadelphia, Pittsburgh,
Chicago, Milwaukee and Washington.

Existing contracts would be respected, but the reserve clause was not.
Player sales were banned. Sabbath ball was allowed, as were 25-cent admissions. A double-umpire system was to be employed.

It was rumored that former major league cities Providence and Buffalo
(now with the Eastern League) would transfer over, but that was soon
squelched. "Three or four people in the Eastern League came together [at the
Broadway Theatre in New York]," revealed Eastern League President Patrick
T. Powers, "and the cities of Buffalo and Providence pledged themselves to the
Eastern League."

Despite reports that Harry Wright, now serving as chief of National League
umpires, would head up the new circuit, W. S. Kanes of Philadelphia, a former

Athletics stockholder, was elected president and secretary. A *Sporting News* correspondent from Cincinnati named Mulford was not impressed by the choice or by prospects of the new Association. Kanes, he sniffed, "was never prominent in [the Athletics'] councils."

The Board of Directors would initially represent the following cities: Pittsburgh, Chicago and Philadelphia. No backers' names were immediately made public. "Until the gentlemen who control the purse-strings of the new organization come out of the high grass to be counted, the American Association will be looked upon as a curiosity," one observer concluded.

Yet names were soon leaking out. Billie Barnie would take the Brooklyn club; Fred Pfeffer, Chicago; and Al Buckenberger, Pittsburgh. Mike Scanlon (a veteran of the Union Association experiment), Fred Postal (later a president of the American League Senators) and Walter Hewitt were involved in Washington.

As Buckenberger revealed, one of the men the Association was attempting to involve was (of all people) Albert L. Johnson. Buckenberger, Pfeffer, Scanlon and "Pebbly Jack" Glasscock were all trying to lure the trolly magnate back to the game. Johnson, however, was uninterested.

George W. Williams, reputed backer of the Chicago franchise, seemed less than enthusiastic about the new grouping and did not favor war with the League. He was, however, certainly interested in operating a club in the Windy City.

"What I am in favor of is a Western League club in Chicago," he revealed. "I don't want [James A.] Hart [of the Chicago National League club] to have the franchise as that would be essentially unfair. Both teams would be controlled by one club, and people would lose confidence in the game. If the Western League would give me the Chicago franchise, I will guarantee to put a first-class team in the field. I can raise the necessary backing tomorrow."

"There is room for two organizations," contended W. H. "Buck" Becannon, a Madison Square Garden promoter and a backer of the proposed New York franchise. "We are convinced . . . that twenty-five-cent ball will find plenty of patrons in all the chief cities. It is not our design to fight anybody. We only want our share of the patronage, and we think we can get it."

Organized Ball Reacts

"They say they do not intend to antagonize the League," mocked O. P. Caylor in the *Sporting News*. "Why, of course not. They remind us of burglars who do not intend to antagonize society."

One newspaper in Pittsburgh was just as negative: "[S]uch a scheme would be folly of the maddest kind. There is not a good reason theoretical or practical, sentimental or otherwise, in support of it. The success of base ball, to a very great extent, depends on public sentiment, and we have seen what a base ball war did to that sentiment four years ago. There is one solid basis for all base ball organizations, and that is the reserve rule. The proposed organization ignores this fundamental and necessary principle, and consequently can only be compared to that foolish man who built a house on sand."

John T. Brush was equally intolerant: "If these Association people think they can get protection from us and at the same time invade our territory they are mistaken. No one denies them the right to organize, but the moment they infringe on our rights (and they will) there will be war. If any one tries to put another club in Cincinnati I will fight it dollar for dollar."

Spalding's Guide incredulously faced the thought of new competition so soon, terming it a "revolutionary effort" to revive not only the American Association but the Players' League as well. Predictably, it defended what even it termed "repressive measures" to defeat this "treachery."

As the new Association was organizing in October, reports from Boston further alarmed the establishment. One John J. Moore was in town representing the new Association's New York franchise, and was there to sign star Boston players Hugh Duffy, Tom McCarthy and Herman Long.

"It would surprise the base ball public," the well-respected Moore, the brother of a former Congressman, boasted, "to know the enormous salary that has been offered for these three great players."

Tommy McCarthy did little to dampen the rumors. Telling the press he would not comment on whether he or Hugh Duffy was signing with New York, McCarthy commented he "was in base ball and so is Duffy for the salary . . . ."

And Buckenberger had been telling the press that pitcher Amos Rusie was about to sign ("Pfeffer says he has him all right") and that other Giants were on the verge as well ("Well, three of them are disenchanted, we understand").

In St. Louis, former Browns manager Ned Cuthbert told the *Chronicle* he could obtain an A.A. franchise "for the asking" and would play at then-vacant Sportsman's Park. He claimed the backing of a local banker, John Mullaly, and stated further that "three of Von der Ahe's players are ready to sign with a new Association club . . . ."

In Washington on October 26, Nick Young added a new twist to events: "The members of the League do not want any more baseball wars, but they do stand ready to defend their hard-earned interests against what appears to be nothing more than a band of base ball speculators. The insinuation has been thoroughly made and we know every man, his social and financial standing, directly or indirectly interested in the new association. The impression prevails after looking over the field that they are proceeding upon the idea that the League, rather than to become involved in another struggle similar to that with the Brotherhood, will go down into its pocket and buy the rival organization. They will be sadly disappointed if they are entertaining any such idea. The

League has a well-balanced, compact organization and the market is stocked with desirable players.

"There is one thing that can be stated with all frankness, and that is that the present League does not intend to enter into a competitive test of dollars for the services of popular players in the League. If they are disposed to place their loyalty to the parent organization on the auction block, they are at liberty to do so. If they deliberately violate the terms of the National Agreement and desert the League, they must understand that they deliberately place themselves upon the blacklist, so far as the League is concerned, for all time to come."

Pressure Is Exerted

The National League thus instituted a policy of "massive retaliation," but was careful to avoid being labeled as the big bully beating up on the new kid on the baseball block. Instead it adopted the pose of protector of the minor leagues.

On November 15, 1894, Patrick T. Powers, president of the Eastern League, and Byron Bancroft "Ban" Johnson, secretary of the Western League, petitioned the National League on the issue:

TO THE NATIONAL LEAGUE AND AMERICAN ASSOCIATION OF PROFESSIONAL BASEBALL CLUBS;

Gentlemen; "We the representatives of the undersigned leagues, operating under the National Agreement, . . . respectfully submit the following: Your body is the recognized major base ball organization of the country, and have sole right to elect the National Board and control all bodies identified with the agreement.

It has been made known to us, and we have good and substantial reasons for believing that such knowledge is correct, that a new organization of base ball clubs is contemplated, which of necessity, must operate without the pale of the National Agreement. It appears also that it is the purpose of the new association, if it materializes, to attempt to take from our respective organizations and clubs players now held by us under the right of reservation accorded us by the National Agreement. We therefore request that you, as a body, take some action to protect us, so far as possible, against all outside organizations. We trust you will give this immediate attention, and we await your action.

On the following day a lengthy "Manifesto" was issued in response to the Western League's call for help by a special committee consisting of League President Young, Brush, Charles Byrne, Harry R. Vonderhorst and James A. Hart.

At the tail end of this document was appended the heart of the matter, the call for the suspension of Buckenberger, Barnie and Pfeffer "until such time as they or either of them can satisfy the National Board that they have in no way been engaged directly or indirectly in the organization of any club, league or association formed or to be formed in conflict with . . . the National Agreement." As would be expected, the League unanimously adopted the recommendations.

The National Board itself followed that up with a resolution "governed absolutely by a desire to comply with the letter and spirit of the requests made to this Board," declaring the accused trio "ineligible to be employed either as manager, player or in any other capacity by any club or organization identified with the National Agreement, and said provisions are hereby declared suspended."

Were they not to provide such proof by December 31, 1894, they would be "expelled and forever debarred" from Organized Baseball.

To *Sporting Life* this was a "tremendous bluff" by a League "arrogantly determined to maintain its monopoly and crush out opposition by any means. . . ."

Barnie and Buckenberger didn't see it that way, capitulating almost immediately and denying they had negotiated with the A.A. while under contract to any National League club. Buckenberger submitted an affidavit to that effect, and contended that what he really desired was an Eastern League franchise.

On December 20, 1894, Barnie attended a session with Arthur H. Soden, Charles Byrne and Nick Young where, with much "wild talk and gesticulation," he declined to sign a loyalty oath to the League. Nonetheless, the League somewhat incredibly stated it had discovered no "positive evidence" of disloyalty. Barnie was reinstated, serving as manager of Scranton of the Eastern League in 1895. By 1897 he was pilot of Brooklyn.

Pfeffer refused to attend the above session, and stated point-blank that as a released player he had every right to do as he pleased, although he denied attempting to entice any players to jump with him.

The League found his statement "extremely indefinite and unsatisfactory" and suspended him. "Pfeffer was up to his neck," argued the 1895 *Spalding Guide.* "He tampered with players and did all he could to hurt the League. That was too much, and the League had to take action." Pfeffer took the post of Princeton's baseball coach, although he publicly stated he wished to return as a League player. At this point, public opinion went to work. Ten thousand fans petitioned for his reinstatement, and Louisville, in violation of N.L. rules, tendered him a contract for 1895.

A compromise was reached. Pfeffer was reinstated on February 25, 1895, but fined $500 (a sum paid by his friends) and forced to sign a loyalty oath.

As the screws were turned on this trio, the revived American Association collapsed. It had signed no players, adopted no schedule, played not a single game, but the idea had not expired. In just a few years, it would spring to life again.

Syndicate Baseball

The basic impetus to this new scheme was a cut-back following the 1899 season by the National League from twelve teams to eight. The four clubs dropped were less-profitable ones in Louisville, Cleveland, Baltimore and Washington.

One reason the original American Association had succeeded where others failed is that there were any number of large American cities in 1882 without major league ball. Now that situation was coming to pass again.

Beyond that, a new evil gripped and weakened the National League: "Syndicate Baseball."

This was a practice in which an owner held portions of more than one competing club. By the turn of the century the practice was widespread in the National League, and was undermining public confidence in the game.

The most crushing abuse involved the Cleveland and St. Louis clubs, both owned by Frank de Haas Robison. In 1899 Robison moved the best players on the Spiders roster (including "Cy" Young, Bobby Wallace, "Nig" Cuppy, "Cupid" Childs and Jesse "Crab" Burkett) to St. Louis. Cleveland was left so weakened it finished the season with a 20-134 mark, a won-lost percentage of .130.

When Spiders manager Lave Cross informed Robison that he needed some help to win games, Robison was indignant.

"I'm not interested in winning games here," Robison growled. "Play out your schedule. That's your job."

A similar scenario played out in Baltimore. Owners Harry Vonderhorst and Ferdinand Abel, tired of declining attendance in Baltimore, transferred the cream of the great Orioles team to their other club in Brooklyn. Joe Kelley, "Wee Willie" Keeler, James McJames, "Smiling Al" Maul, Jim Hughes, Hughie Jennings and Dan McGann were all sent packing from Baltimore.

Harold Seymour has tracked down what he believes was the extent of "Syndicate Ball" in March 1900:

> John T. Brush: Owner of Cincinnati; stockholder in New York.
>
> Arthur Soden: Held one-third of Boston; principal minority stockholder of New York.
>
> Ferdinand A. Abel: Owner of 40 percent of both Brooklyn and Baltimore; stockholder in New York.
>
> Frank de Haas Robison: Owner of Cleveland and St. Louis.
>
> Harry Vonderhorst: Owner of 40 percent of both Brooklyn and Baltimore.

Ned Hanlon: Owner of 10 percent of both Brooklyn and Baltimore.
Charles Ebbets: Owner of 10 percent of both Brooklyn and Baltimore.
Albert G. Spalding: Owned a large portion of Chicago; stockholder in New
York.

The American Association of 1900

Al Spink, founder of the *Sporting News* and then sports editor of the St.
Louis *Post-Dispatch*, claimed credit for the idea of a new challenge to the National League. "The Fall seasons in baseball at this time," he wrote a decade
and a half later, "were absolutely devoid of interest and the conditions were
in marked contrast to those which existed when the champion clubs of the National League and the American Association battled each other each fall for a
world's championship."

He pointed out that such a new combination might rekindle interest in the
game, and wrote to his colleagues in the press to drum up support. The results
were not encouraging. "Most of the Eastern sporting editors made fun of the
proposed league," he recalled.

Supporting his idea, though, was baseball promoter and publicist Ted
Sullivan, Henry Lucas' right-hand man in organizing the Union Association.
Sullivan was "extremely impressed" with the concept. Spink introduced him to
St. Louis Alderman George D. Schaefer, who engaged him "to scout the coun-
try in search of cities for the new body."

On September 17–18, 1899, in Chicago an "American Association of
Baseball Clubs" was announced.

Franchises were hoped for in New York, St. Louis, Milwaukee, Detroit,
Chicago, Baltimore, Philadelphia and Washington. All enjoyed Organized Ball
in 1899, Detroit and Milwaukee in Ban Johnson's Western League, the remainder in the National.

Attending were Thomas Harlan, Chris Von der Ahe, George P. Heckel,
Schaefer and Spink representing St. Louis; Harry D. Quinn, formerly of
Milwaukee's A.A. franchise, and Alderman C. S. Havenor of Milwaukee
(Havenor would later be connected with Milwaukee's minor league American
Association franchise; in 1905 he was convicted of receiving a $200 bribe
while alderman and was sentenced to two years in the Milwaukee House of
Detention); Frank Navin of Detroit; Adrian C. "Cap" Anson and his son-in-law
W. H. Clough of Chicago; Assemblyman Frank Beckley of New York; Frank
Hough, sports editor of the Philadelphia *Enquirer;* and Michael D. Scanlon of
Washington. Letters were read by Spink from fiery third baseman John
McGraw of Baltimore and Billie Barnie, now of Brooklyn, indicating support.

Anson declined the presidency and Quinn was chosen as interim head of
the new group. Other temporary officers were Scanlon as vice president,

Schaefer as treasurer, Hough as secretary and Von der Ahe, Scanlon, Beckley and Havenor as directors.

A variety of motives propelled these men. Quinn formerly owned the Milwaukee club in the National League and was trying to get back into baseball. The same circumstance fit Von der Ahe, whose St. Louis club had been dropped from the circuit in 1898. Spink was no longer with the *Sporting News,* whose control had passed to his brother Charles, and he was looking for action.

Lurking in the vicinity were representatives of the powerful Western League—Ban Johnson, Charles Comiskey and Thomas J. Loftus—who were testing the waters, but noncommittal in joining.

"You're a Chicago boy," Spink chided Comiskey. "You belong down there and not in St. Paul.

"Yes," begged off Comiskey, now owner of the Western League's St. Paul club, "and I'm willing to go right down there with you now . . . in the furthering of this enterprise, but I have partners in the Western Association, not situated as I am, and I do not think it would be fair for me to quit them at this time."

"Honest competition, no syndicate baseball, no reserve rule, to respect all contracts, and popular prices" were the announced goals of the circuit.

"By abolishing the reserve rule," noted the New York *Times,* "the new league thinks it will get a hold on the best baseball talent, . . . and by catering to the public with lower prices [i.e., twenty-five cents] is certain to get to the masses. [League organizers] also argue that the evils engendered by forcing syndicate ball upon the public are too patent to be overlooked."

The *Times* further noted that the conferees "disclaimed any intention of going to war with the minor leagues, but they strongly intimated that it was war to the finish with the National organization."

In December, at another Chicago session, Francis Richter joined the cabal. Richter, an inveterate backer of rival leagues, charged that National League ownership was marked by "gross individual and collective mismanagement, their fierce factional fights, their cynical disregard of decency and honor, their open spoliation of each other, their deliberate alienation of press and public, their flagrant disloyalty to their friends and their tyrannical treatment of the players."

John McGraw was there in person, although somewhat pessimistic in that the league had little hope of the securing a team in New York because of the scarcity of playing grounds. Cap Anson was also sounding doubtful about the viability of his Chicago backing.

Only in his mid-twenties, McGraw had already become a force in the national game. The finest leadoff hitter in baseball, McGraw had distinguished himself as the on-field leader of Ned Hanlon's legendary Baltimore Orioles of the 1890s. That meant not only baseball "smarts" but also a style of play that verged on the homicidal. "McGraw," complained Arlie Latham, "eats gunpowder every morning and washes it down with warm blood." Spikings, cheating, fisticuffs and vituperation marked the "Oriole"—and the McGraw—way. It was with some risk that this new association was aligning itself with such an incendiary character.

The Search for Playing Fields

Parks were secured for the various franchises. Anson obtained the former Brotherhood Park; Boston's John Drewson signed a lease to the Charles River Park. Frank Navin attempted securing Van Derbeck's Grounds in Detroit.

In Baltimore in late January a physical battle took place for Union Park, former home of the Orioles. For $3,500 the Association group secured a lease on the site, but Ned Hanlon refused to relinquish possession. President Phil Peterson (owner of the Glosman Ginger Ale Company), his attorney Conway W. Sams and "half a dozen henchmen" advanced on the park. Peterson and the groundskeeper tangled. Deputy Marshall Farnan separated them, but "while all this was proceeding the balance of the Peterson crowd . . . leaped into the grounds. They ran for third base—McGraw's corner—and there pitched their camp. The Hanlon forces took possession of first base." Each side beseeched the law to evict the other, but without success. The Association followed this up with an injunction.

The National League Responds

Besides such farcical battles, the National League took other steps to deal with this upstart. The Senior Circuit's full name since 1891 was "The National League and American Association of Professional Base Ball Clubs," and it was not about to allow this new group to use any portion of its full title. The League was also giving serious consideration to setting up an "American Association" of its own to play in League parks when N.L. teams were on the road, thus giving continuous competition to their new opposition.

"The National League," commented President James Hart of its Chicago club, "paid something like $15,000 for the second half of its title, and intends to use it. The National League will protect itself. We have ballplayers enough . . . to have a second league if we want one, and find it advisable to start one. We have the grounds; there is nothing to do but start an American Association. The name is ours. We can put it into active operation if we want to."

Most Association men thought the idea of a League-backed Association to be mere bluff and somewhat absurd. Art Irwin termed it "foolish"; George P. Heckel observed, "The League plan seems to be figured on the basis that if there is not room for two teams in a city the situation will be improved by putting in three teams."

Sporting Life **editor Francis Richter, a backer of the American Association revival, among other rival leagues.**

Two prize catches for the new Association were third baseman John J. McGraw and catcher Wilbert Robinson of the Orioles, who were determined to continue in Baltimore. With the League dropping the city, they had to come up with another option. Both were highly popular locally, and beyond that had opened a profitable saloon, "The Blue Diamond," there. The National League responded with threats of a subtle "blacklisting" of both McGraw and Robinson. There would be no formal ban, but they would be "parceled out" to some N.L. club and "offered so low a salary that [they] could not in

Opposite: John McGraw, fiery on-field leader of the great Orioles teams of the 1890s and a backer of the American Association revival.

self-respect accept it" and thus be consigned to some "outer darkness" of baseball.

From January 30, 1899, to February 2, 1900, the new circuit met again, this time at Philadelphia's Continental Hotel. Among the first orders of business was a name change to the "New American Base Ball Association." Troubles persisted in getting a Philadelphia franchise in operation, as two groups of backers dropped out. And difficulties persisted in New York and Providence. In Manhattan political pressure made securing a field virtually impossible. In Providence, local ownership was supposedly sympathetic to joining forces with the Association, but was hedging its bet until it was a "go."

Any number of players of varying talents were at this conference including Napoleon "Larry" Lajoie, Ed Delahanty, Lave Cross, Mike Grady, Dick Harley, John Clements, Bill Shindle, Bill Hallman, Jimmy Fields, Gus Moran, Roy Thomas, George Wrigley, Harry Davis, Big Bill Massey and Joe Gunson.

George Heckel of the projected St. Louis club crowed: "The Continental Hotel was full of players, . . . and McGraw was continually receiving letters and telegrams from League players, telling him they were in sympathy with the Association. Players like Lajoie and Delahanty openly declared that they would sign, . . . and that they would do so at a reasonable figure. In fact, they gave us to understand that there would be no hold-up, but that they would sign with us for the very same figures offered by the National League."

John McGraw dominated events. "McGraw and Robinson were undoubtedly the whole thing," noted *Sporting Life*. "McGraw made a profound impression by the remarkable capacity for business he exhibited."

In late January the league was shaping up as follows:

CLUB	PRINCIPAL BACKER	MANAGER
Baltimore	Phil Peterson	John J. McGraw
Boston	Tommy McCarthy	Tommy McCarthy
Chicago	A. C. "Cap" Anson	A. C. "Cap" Anson
Detroit	Thomas J. Navin	Pat Donovan
Milwaukee	Harry D. Quinn	Hugh Jennings
Philadelphia	–	Joe Kelley
Providence	–	Billy Murray
St. Louis	George D. Schaefer	Bill "Scrappy" Joyce

The Fateful Session at Chicago

On Monday, February 12, 1900, delegates convened at Chicago's Great Northern Hotel under the leadership of temporary President Quinn to formally initiate the circuit.

Ill portents clouded the horizon. Boston's and Detroit's contingents were nowhere to be found. Their absence depressed everyone, "but particularly . . .

the Baltimore delegates, McGraw and [Phil] Peterson." No business was conducted on that Monday, as delegates pondered their fate. Those in attendance were:

CLUB	DELEGATES
Baltimore	Phil Peterson, John J. McGraw
Chicago	Adrian C. "Cap" Anson
Louisville	Colonel I. F. "Ike" Whitesides, Moore
Milwaukee	Harry D. Quinn, Charles S. Havenor
Philadelphia	George H. Regar, Francis C. Richter
St. Louis	George P. Heckel, Thomas Harlan, Al Spink

Neither Boston nor Detroit showed by Tuesday, but it was determined to advance nonetheless. Quinn declined the permanent presidency, and St. Louis nominated Anson to serve. The choice was unanimous despite misgivings by the Philadelphia delegation, which preferred former American Association President Zack Phelps of Louisville, and which felt the chief executive should not be connected with any club. Richter and Milwaukee's O'Brien declined to serve as secretary-treasurer, so Peterson was elected to that post. A four-man Board of Directors was established, consisting of Havenor, Schaefer, William J. Gilmore ("the well-known and wealthy theatrical man") of Philadelphia and a "director-to-be-named-later" from Boston. By this time a telegram had been received from Boston's Tommy McCarthy, indicating he was *en route.*

On the selection of the eighth club, each franchise was to deposit a $5,000 bond with the Association. If a suitable eighth member could not be chosen or if any club did not deposit its $5,000, the president was empowered to declare the Association suspended.

The season was to begin on April 16. Thomas Harlan and Francis Richter were to draw up a uniform player contract. No action was taken on adopting an official league ball, although several companies vied for the honor.

Franchises were awarded to St. Louis, Chicago, Louisville and Milwaukee in the West and Boston, Baltimore and Philadelphia in the East.

Originally, the Western end of the circuit was to consist of St. Louis, Chicago, Milwaukee and Detroit, but as Detroit had been absent from both the Philadelphia and Chicago meetings, Louisville, under Colonel Ike Whitesides, was admitted in its place.

Just one hour after Louisville's admittance the group received this telegram:

H. D. Quinn, Chicago
   Returned home this evening. Found your telegrams. Detroit stands ready to fulfill all obligations. Make your demands. We will comply.

THOMAS J. NAVIN

But it was too late, and Louisville's admission stood. McGraw and Peterson were appointed to select the eighth franchise (to be located in the East) within the next six days. Providence was considered a distinct possibility, but applications for membership had also been submitted by Washington, Worcester and Syracuse.

On Wednesday, after everyone but the Philadelphians had departed, McCarthy finally arrived. He brought exciting news. He had not left Boston until Monday night because he had been successfully organizing a stock company, capitalized at $75,000. McCarthy, thinking the Association would be in session for some time, stopped in Buffalo to sign some players, including third baseman Jimmy Collins.

This news buoyed Anson, Richter and George Regar ("a well-known local publisher and advertising agent"), and it was decided that in order to fill the gap, the Association as a whole would purchase the Providence club, "as any old place would do for a year."

McGraw and Anson Waver

Meanwhile McGraw and Peterson (who had left on Tuesday night), instead of trying to find an eighth club, were meeting with William J. Gilmore in Philadelphia to ascertain his intentions.

They were not impressed by his answers, particularly in regard to Philadelphia's ability to find a playing field for the 1900 season. Gilmore also refused to sign any papers committing funds to the Association before hearing from Regar and Richter. Why the duo pressed Gilmore for funds when the Chicago agreement called for the eighth club to be selected prior to all clubs depositing their $5,000 bond is not known.

The upshot was a cable from McGraw and Peterson to Anson: "Philadelphia looks bad. W. J. Gilmore will not sign agreement. No answer on grounds for three weeks. Not advisable to wait. Better call deal off."

McGraw then aggravated the confusion by talking to the press. "We had seven cities partially pledged," McGraw stated. "At the Chicago meeting . . . I was delegated to go to Philadelphia to get Mr. Gilmore's signature. . . . Mr. Gilmore refused to sign the agreement, saying that the grounds belonged to the city and that it would take at least two weeks to find out whether he could get them or not, and that he did not intend to pledge himself until he found out how he stood.

"We cannot wait that long so at Anson's request I telegraphed him . . . [that] the jig is up. The people back of this thing did not know how to handle it. If the right parties were behind it, it would have been a go. As to what I am going to do I cannot say. They will have to come to me. . . . I am sorry that the new Association fell through. Through the whole matter I have acted in an honest, straightforward manner, and have nothing to feel sorry for. At the Chicago meeting I demanded solid backing from the other cities, and when they could not show that, I knew then that the thing would not go through."

McGraw blustered about putting an Eastern (International) League team in Baltimore or even of organizing a barnstorming semipro team, but he was not yet ready to leave the National League.

Anson unilaterally issued a statement of total capitulation: "Off it is. The new American Association ceases to exist from now on, so far as I am concerned. I am its president and I declare it dead. . . . Had [Philadelphia] shown the proper financial backing and grounds there would have been no trouble. I am sorry it happened. . . . I really did not think there was much hope, . . . but I made up my mind that I would not desert the enterprise and was hoping at times that something might turn up that would make it look more favorable."

Francis Richter lividly declared that "President" Anson had "made an ass of himself." Of McGraw he wrote—with little gift of prophecy—"A pitiful ending, indeed, to a brilliant, if meteoric career as a leader of men."

William J. Gilmore fired off a telegram to McGraw:

Philadelphia, February 16

Dear Sir:—Since wiring you late yesterday afternoon I saw another gentleman last night, and I am satisfied that the ground question can be settled in a few days.

Messrs. Regar and Richter have just come in, and they say the meeting in Chicago was all satisfactory but that you seemed to show a disposition to hedge. That is too bad, as Philadelphia was in good shape to make its end good.

I see by the papers to-day that you have called the thing off. Is this so? . . .

Regar and Richter also wired McGraw:

Philadelphia, February 16

By what authority did you come to Philadelphia to see our people before our return from Chicago? And why did you advise Anson to act before prescribed time limit of ten days and before you made an effort to secure the eighth city?

McGraw answered that the issue was "not worth while to dwell upon," dealing, as the *Sporting Times* gently phrased it, mostly with "personalities."

More cables flowed as Richter and Regar attempted to shore up their rapidly collapsing circuit.

From Richter and Regar to all clubs in the circuit:

Philadelphia, February 16

McGraw lost his head and acted hastily. Philadelphia ready and anxious with $40,000 on authority of Mr. Gilmore.

George Schaefer of St. Louis sent off wires to Peterson, McGraw and Anson, urging them to not "show the white feather" and to continue the effort. When no positive response was received he threatened legal proceedings.

Meanwhile, McGraw was receiving large numbers of wires from players and other interested individuals urging his support, but he refused to rejoin the Association camp. McGraw is said to have "practically" admitted his mistake in a private letter to Francis Richter, but no such public *mea culpa* was ever produced, and the New American Association was reduced to ashes.

That, however, was not the end of the National League's troubles, for a far more dangerous threat was looming in the form of one Byron Bancroft "Ban" Johnson.

Chapter 8

The American League

As the New American Association crashed to earth, Ban Johnson's new "American League" was ready to take up the cudgels against the National League monopoly.

Hard-driving, hard-drinking Johnson was born on January 8, 1864, in Norwalk, Ohio, the son of a college professor. An 1887 graduate of Marietta College, young Ban took a job as a sportswriter for Murat Halstead's Cincinnati *Commercial-Gazette*. There he made the acquaintance of two individuals who would help shape his life: Reds manager Charles Comiskey and owner John Tomlinson Brush. Comiskey became a long-time friend (until an inevitable falling-out, that is), while Brush chafed under Johnson's journalistic criticisms.

Born in 1845, Brush made his fortune with a profitable Indianapolis department store, then one of the few such enterprises in the Midwest. He was a noteworthy figure even for those days. His devious ways were well-noted. "Chicanery is the ozone that keeps his old frame from snapping," noted one harsh observor, "and dark-lantern methods the food which vitalizes his bodily tissues." After the turn of the century he moved a crippled frame with two canes, as he was plagued by a locomotor ataxia, a nervous condition quite often associated with syphilis.

It is said that to rid himself of the youthful gadfly, Brush used his influence in the newly resuscitated Western League (Comiskey had actually come up with the idea for the circuit and Brush owned its Indianapolis franchise) to have Johnson elected its president—and thus kept far away from Brush's more-important Cincinnati holdings.

In any case, on November 20, 1893, in Detroit, Johnson was named head of the historically unprofitable Western League. At the time it represented Indianapolis, Sioux City, Detroit, Toledo, Kansas City, Milwaukee, Minneapolis and Grand Rapids.

In 1895 Johnson was joined by Comiskey. Brush had fired his manager at Cincinnati, and the "Old Roman" became manager of the Western League's Sioux City Huskers. The following year Comiskey purchased the club, moving it to St. Paul. Comiskey's debut as an owner was not auspicious. Brush had warned him that "St. Paul is a graveyard," and with the Saints losing 17 consecutive games in 1895, that prophecy seemed correct. Beyond that, a local ordinance barred profitable Sunday games in the city.

In 1897 another key figure, Connie Mack, joined the league as pilot of Milwaukee. Previously he had served as manager of Pittsburgh in the National League. On taking the Pittsburgh job, Mack exacted a pledge from owner Colonel William W. Kerr that there would be no second-guessing of his managerial moves; but Mack was skeptical the Colonel would abide by it. Sure enough, Kerr wired Mack one day questioning a decision. The normally mild-mannered Mack responded with a telegram reading, "Told you so."

That was the end of Mack's career in Smoke City. "I've followed your National League career pretty well, Connie," Johnson told the now-unemployed Mack, "and I long have admired your way of doing things. I've a managerial vacancy in Milwaukee that I would like to have you fill. If you are interested, we would give you an interest in the club. We're not a big league, but I've a strong, well-balanced circuit, and I think you will find real competition. What's more, I have plans for the future of the Western League. . . . You'll be your own boss up there; you'll run everything."

"The Western League was a pretty good league in the late nineties," Mack later recalled, "about the strength of the . . . American Association before the [Second World] War. I had some good men in Milwaukee, men who later played for me on the Athletics or with other American and National League teams—Dave Fultz, Rube Waddell, Wid Conroy, Frank Sparks, and Ginger Beaumont. Comiskey had Frank Isbell and Roy Patterson in St. Paul. Other Western League players who later made big-league reputations were Topsy Hartsel, Socks Seybold, and Ollie Pickering, all of whom played in my Athletic outfield; Jimmy Slagle, Harry Steinfeldt, Deacon Phillippe, George Davis, Sandow Mertes, Bill Coughlin, and some other good men."

Meanwhile, Johnson and Brush contained to wrangle, particularly over the magnate's habit of drafting Western League players ostensibly for Cincinnati, but actually for Indianapolis. When Brush alleged irregularities in the awarding of four Western League franchises (all with pro–Johnson owners) and brought his charges before the National Board of Arbitration, on which he sat as a member, he went too far. With the assistance of Brush's fellow National League owners, Johnson not only rebutted Brush's accusations but forced him out of the Western League. Brush would not forget the episode.

Johnson, through his imperious manner and strength of will, transformed the Western League into a decided success. He backed up his umpires, insisted on a dignified atmosphere and turned his circuit into the "strongest minor ever." The Cleveland *Leader* was typical when it noted it was "conceded on all sides that [Western] League games are better conducted than those in the [other] major organizations."

Johnson was far from a teetotaler, but he was death on public drunkenness by his charges. "A ball player, or manager, is a public figure," he informed

Byron Bancroft "Ban" Johnson, founder of the American League.

Connie Mack shortly after Mack joined the W.L. "Everybody knows him, especially if he is a success. And a player, or manager, who isn't known intimately by his public isn't worth his salt. Once a ball player gets drunk in public, it isn't long before the entire town knows about it. An average person gets drunk, and his friends quietly put him to bed. But once a player gets drunk and boisterous, he immediately is put down as a drunkard. He will make an error on the field, and everyone will say: 'Oh, yes, he was drunk again last night.' The ball player doesn't have to be as decent in his private life as the average man; he must be more so."

Changes continued as Ban Johnson attempted to build up his circuit. As early as 1896 Johnson was making no secret that he wished to challenge the National League's monopoly. However, the times were not propitious yet. One by one the franchises were altered. In 1899 Buffalo, owned by English-born Alderman Jim Franklin, a local butcher, dropped out of the troubled Eastern League and replaced Toledo in Johnson's circuit. Franklin, a mercurial but highly popular Republican, would fill in as Buffalo's manager in both 1899 and 1900. When the National League planned to drop Washington, Louisville, Baltimore and Cleveland following the 1899 season, and with the emerging threat of the planned American Association, Johnson was about to institute a series of moves which would gain his circuit major league status.

When this new American Association had first met in Chicago in September 1899, they offered the Western League an opportunity to merge with it. Johnson declined, but in October, on the motion of Indianapolis' President W. F. C. Golt, the Western League changed its name to the "American League," a first step in gaining for it a more national and less sectional character.

Then came a much bolder step. Johnson announced plans to encroach on National League territory in both Cleveland and Chicago. Although the N.L. had abandoned Cleveland, it still retained territorial rights, and it had an active and very prosperous franchise in Chicago. Normally, this would have translated into outright war with the Senior Circuit.

While Johnson coveted Cleveland, he did not immediately know how to secure the city. In the winter of 1900 Johnson paid a call upon the offices of Davis Hawley, president of Cayuhoga Savings and Loan and former secretary of the old Spiders. Johnson offered Hawley the presidency of a new Cleveland franchise, but Hawley declined, claiming he was too old to serve. Instead, he connected Johnson with suitable backing.

He introduced Johnson to two men who would play a vital role in the American League: Charles W. Somers and John F. Kilfoyle. Somers was a millionaire coal dealer, who would ultimately bankroll not only Cleveland, but Boston, Chicago and Philadelphia. Kilfoyle operated a men's clothing store on Public Square, and was such a rabid baseball fan that in 1908 he had to retire from the game when the strain of rooting for his Naps injured his health.

The National League reacted negatively — at first — to Johnson's plans, particularly his eyeing of Chicago. Arthur Soden clearly foresaw that if Johnson could place a team in Chicago, there was nothing preventing him from entering Philadelphia, St. Louis or, most importantly, Boston. Colonel John I. Rogers of Philadelphia drafted a resolution maintaining that an American League franchise in Chicago would be viewed by the Nationals as a declaration of war. And, with the threat of a rival American Association fast receding, the N.L. was in less of a mood to cooperate with Johnson.

Johnson responded: "All right; let them go ahead. I think it is a bluff to scare us out. Whether or not it is, we are going to come to Chicago. I believe the public will support us in an honest effort to furnish clean base ball. We seek no war . . . and only want an opportunity to exert our rights. If the National

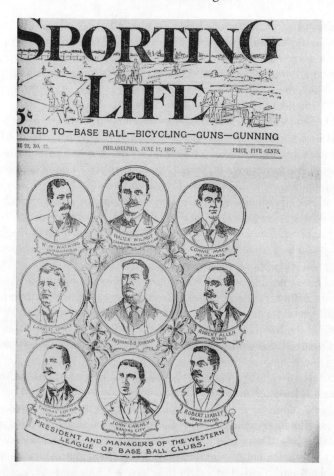

President and managers of the Western League, 1897. At top right is Connie Mack, at center left Charles Comiskey and at center Ban Johnson.

League starts a reserve organization it will only represent so much loss entailed in an effort to keep another league from getting established. I don't believe the public will sympathize with that sort of a thing. On the contrary I believe we will get the sympathy of the public if a fight is forced upon us. It seems to me, moreover, that the Chicago club might better be spending its money towards strengthening the ball club it has than in fighting other leagues which do not seek to injure it."

But these were not normal times. Anxious over the threat of the American Association, the Nationals had earlier indicated acceptance of Johnson's move to the Windy City.

There were precedents for placing minor league clubs in major league cities in time of war. The Eastern League's Monumentals had been allowed into Baltimore in 1884 in order to help thwart the Union Association challenge. And later in that very year of 1900, the National League would be seriously proposing to place an entire "American Association II" in its parks to help combat its new opponent.

But at this time the American Association threat was fading fast, and the National League was not quite so eager to see competition in any of its markets. Perhaps Cleveland or Louisville could be offered up, but by no means Chicago.

Johnson's league was not yet solidly behind him as he undertook this momentous step. Comiskey of Chicago and Somers of Cleveland supported the moves, of course, as well as Kansas City, Detroit and Milwaukee. But owners Billy Watkins (Indianapolis), Salspaugh (Minneapolis), and Jim Franklin (Buffalo) were less-confident. "Watty" Watkins would not even discuss the matter with the press. Franklin wanted no tangling with the National League and publicly stated he wished he were back in the Eastern League. Salspaugh admitted he was not looking for any trouble.

Even getting to this position was not easy. Johnson had faced opposition from owner Arthur Van Derbeck of Detroit on the Cleveland controversy, and in view of that and Van Derbeck's nasty divorce proceedings (which involved ownership of the ballclub), Johnson deposed him as franchise head, installing Wayne County sheriff and hotel keeper James D. Burns and field manager George Tweedy Stallings in his place.

To resolve the thorny issues of Cleveland and Chicago, Johnson met face to face with James A. Hart of the Chicago Nationals and hammered out an advantageous settlement. On March 3, 1900, they agreed the new American League could plant franchises in both Cleveland and Chicago for the upcoming season. All Johnson gave in return was a pledge to honor the National Agreement; a cash settlement to reimburse the League for improvements made to the Cleveland park; and Hart's right to select two American League players. Additional promises were made that the new Chicago team would not play north of 35th Street (thus committing the A.L. team to the stockyard area; "If Commy can play in that smell, he's good," said Hart), and that the name "Chicago" would not be employed by the franchise.

Comiskey's St. Paul club moved to the Windy City. Grand Rapids was transported to Cleveland. With teams now in Chicago, Cleveland, Indianapolis, Detroit, Buffalo, Kansas City, Milwaukee and Minneapolis, every city in the A.L. save for Minneapolis had at one time or another belonged to the National League.

Detroit was vacating its old Western League park at Lafayette Boulevard and Helen Avenue and moving to Woodbridge Grove at Michigan and Trumball. The area had been paved with cobblestones and only a few inches of soil had been lain over the base for the field. It was renamed "Bennett Field," after catcher Charlie Bennett, and seated 8,500.

Buffalo owner James Franklin was wary of war with the National League. (Courtesy of Joseph M. Overfield.)

During the season Johnson would strongly hint that he meant finally to advance to major league status, by, among other means, advancing into big league cities. In late August, he told *Sporting Life,* "We've expanded each year, and why shouldn't we continue to do so? We could do three times as much business in St. Louis as the National League. I like Cincinnati, and we may go further east than Buffalo even." But a week later Johnson retreated, denying any intention of challenging the National League.

In September 1900 Johnson decided to advance to the East. His immediate objectives were Washington, Baltimore and Philadelphia.

Jimmy Manning, owner and manager of Kansas City for the past seven years, planned to bring that club to Washington, and the locals there were jubilant. "The Eastward Ho! campaign of the new league forced that Missouri town into an undesirable corner geographically," crowed the Washington *Post*, "and Manning was offered the Pearl of the American League's new Eastern possessions—Washington."

Two points were wrong with that statement. Washington, of course, was *not* the "Pearl" of the Eastern baseball world, and Manning was not majority stockholder. Johnson brought in Fred Postal, owner of Detroit's Griswald House, to head up the new franchise, although Manning did obtain some stock.

The National League still retained the lease to its old ball yard, "The Boundary," at Florida Avenue and Seventh Street (the future location of Griffith Stadium), so the trio of Johnson, Manning and John McGraw scoured the city for a suitable site. They found one at Bladensburg and Fourteenth, and construction began in a fortnight.

In Baltimore, the "Baltimore Base Ball and Athletic Company" was formed with 400 shares capitalized in the amount of $40,000. Sidney Frank was president and held the largest percentage of stock. Insurance man and Police Court Judge Harry Goldman was secretary. John McGraw and Wilbert "Uncle Robbie" Robinson, Appellate Court Judge Conway Sams, James P. Shannon, owner of the Eutaw House, and Father John Boland (who had officiated at McGraw's first wedding) were also stockholders, McGraw was named player-manager at $5,000 per year, and Robinson received a $3,000 contract.

Securing a playing field took some effort. Ned Hanlon still held the lease on old Union Park, and sites at Electric Park and near Druid Hill Park were dismissed. A five-year lease on property at York and Pinckney Streets owned by Johns Hopkins University was obtained, and on Lincoln's Birthday 1901 ground was broken by contractor Harry S. Rippel. Within seven weeks an 8,500-seat park had been constructed.

Washington and Baltimore were relatively easy prizes, as they were *de facto* vacant territory. Philadelphia was not. Nonetheless, Johnson soon placed a team there. It ostensibly was backed by sporting goods magnate Ben Shibe, who took 50 percent of the stock. Connie Mack got 25 percent. Frank Hough, sports editor of the *Enquirer*, and Sam Jones of the Associated Press each held 12.5 percent. Interestingly, Shibe—now in the American League—was business partners with Alfred Reach, a stockholder in the crosstown National League Phillies. The above public accounting, however, ignored one major fact: in actuality Charles Somers was the team's most significant backer.

"We now had our franchise," recalled Mack in his autobiography, "but we had no team and no park. What I know about Philadelphia I learned from walking the streets of the city, inspecting every vacant lot. We were in such a hurry . . . we thought we might have to take a city playground. Finally we decided upon a site at Twenty-ninth and Oxford Streets, and got it on a ten-year lease.

"Columbia Park was the name we gave it. We had just five weeks left . . .

Benjamin Shibe, holder of 50 percent of the stock in the Philadelphia American League franchise.

to put up stands in order to keep the franchise. It didn't take us very long to construct a single-decked wooden grandstand. . . ."

Johnson's real goal was Boston, but even he drew back from that action. His proposed circuit for 1901 would now be:

WEST	EAST
Chicago	Baltimore
Cleveland	Buffalo
Detroit	Philadelphia
Milwaukee	Washington

By October 1900 Johnson was noticeably negligent in his signing of the National Agreement for another season. On October 31, 1900, he wrote to Nick Young, citing the spectre of the American Association as a reason for his impending actions:

> . . . The plan of the American League to occupy Eastern territory has been well defined, and I think the men in the National League thoroughly understand our position in the matter.

For two years we have been menaced by the possible formation of a league hostile to our interest [the American Association] and detrimental in many ways to Organized Baseball. This annual agitation is hurtful and we propose to shape our organization as to check it in the future.

In extending our circuit to the far East, it is unreasonable to assume we could continue along the old lines prescribed by the National Agreement. New conditions must alter, in part, our relations with the National League. This is a matter I have discussed informally with some of our members.

Yet Another Attempt by Francis Richter

Incredibly, still another try to resurrect the American Association was indeed being bandied about. On September 16–17, 1900, at Baltimore's Rennert Hotel, many familiar names gathered with that purpose in mind. The cities involved and the parties representing them were:

Baltimore—Phil Peterson, Harry Goldman
Philadelphia—August A. Koch, Francis Richter
Boston—John Quinn, representing Messrs. McCarthy and Splaine of the
    Charles River Amusement Company
Chicago—Charles Havenor
Milwaukee—Harry D. Quinn
St. Louis—Joseph D. O'Brien

Denying any involvement, and noticeable in their absence, were John McGraw and Wilbert Robinson. Each city's delegation promised to raise a club capitalized at $50,000. Five thousand dollars was deposited by each club with the league and turned over to the Mercantile Trust Company of Maryland for safekeeping.

Naturally, such maneuvering met with some skepticism. The Cincinnati *Commercial Inquirer* stated bluntly:

> The new league is a fake. It is not likely that the promotion of the new league, which was "organized" in Baltimore a few weeks ago, will get as much free newspaper notoriety out of their pet scheme as they did last. Few indeed are the cities who take any stock in that organization. The very fact that the men who met in Baltimore are almost to a man the same crowd that made such a dismal failure last winter has caused men who were willing to "boost" such a scheme along to come to weaken.

Charles Comiskey branded such talk of reviving the Association as "bosh," saying it "wasn't worrying anybody." He doubted the cities that National League had dropped—Louisville, Baltimore, Washington and Cleveland—

were "good towns" and declared that Louisville wasn't "even a good minor league city."

"The Association," he concluded, "would be compelled to take on a circuit of losers, and losers do not breed baseball enthusiasm."

Francis Richter defended the viability of the new circuit (now called the "National Association") in *Sporting Life:* "It makes little or no jot of difference . . . whether the entire press take much, little or no stock in the new rival league."

Further he disparaged the chances of Ban Johnson's American League, terming its 1900 campaign "a season of comparative failure." Johnson, Richter alleged, faced a "threatened invasion of three of its best cities by the new National Association" and was trying to find a way out of its "desperate situation."

To back up Richter's charges, *Sporting Life* released data it alleged reflected the American League's attendance and profit and losses for 1900:

CLUB	ATTENDANCE	PROFIT/LOSS
Chicago	124,000	+$10,900
Detroit	104,000	− 1,000
Milwaukee	88,000	+ 6,771
Kansas City	84,000	+ 2,331
Indianapolis	76,000	− 300
Cleveland	60,000	− 5,661
Buffalo	56,000	− 3,496
Minneapolis	40,000	− 4,995
TOTAL	632,000	+$ 4,550

The Senior Circuit Reacts

At the National League's winter meeting in New York, no action was taken on permitting Johnson to enter Washington, Baltimore and Philadelphia. The N.L. did not even bother to summon Johnson and Charles Somers to their conference, and beyond that they themselves were now reviving talk of an "American Association II," this time with a goal of checkmating Johnson.

Additionally, they were now confronting the American League on its Western front, assigning its Kansas City and Minneapolis territories to a new Western League that Thomas Jefferson Hickey had organized for the 1900 season.

Now that the die was cast, Johnson discarded his supposed shyness about invading Boston (actually the decision had been made on January 29). Somers provided most of the capital, with Johnson also owning some stock. Connie Mack, fresh from his task in Philly, was dispatched to find suitable grounds. Originally he looked at land leased by former shortstop and pennant-winning manager Art Irwin. The Charles River site was used by Irwin as a bicycle track. However, Irwin was soon approached by the new American/National Association group. Johnson quickly learned of his rivals' actions and instructed Mack to keep on looking. In January, Mack obtained a five-year lease from the Boston Elevated Railway Company on a former carnival and "Shoot the Chutes" site on Huntington Avenue.

To seal the deal Mack presented the railway with a check signed by Charles Somers. The company's agent, not aware of the Clevelander's reputation, wired Somers' bank for a credit check. They wired back, "Draw on us to the extent of $100,000."

The American Leaguers constructed a 7,000-seat grandstand not far from Soden's South End Grounds. Ground was broken on March 6, 1901. The first order of business was filling the large pool which was the grand finale of the "Shoot the Chutes."

A casualty of the Boston decision was Jim Franklin's Buffalo team, which now beat a hasty retreat to the Eastern League. As a parting courtesy to Franklin, the American League agreed to refrain from raiding Buffalo in the coming war.

Meanwhile, the National League was pushing the American/National Association scheme as a counterweight to Johnson's moves, and in Boston Soden gave Art Irwin permission to operate an Association club in Beantown. It was to be called the Reds and would play at Irwin's Charles River site.

In February 1901 Ban Johnson again indicated there was no turning back: "The National League has taken for granted that no one had a right to expand without first getting its permission. We did not think that this was necessary, and have expanded without even asking. . . . If we had waited for the National League to do something for us, we would have remained a minor league forever. The American League will be the principal organization of the country within a very short time. Mark my prediction."

John McGraw was letting out reports that the National League was suing for peace. It wasn't exactly true, but Johnson was not at all displeased by the tactic, as witnessed by this correspondence:

> American League
> Professional Base Ball Clubs
> 1203 Fisher Building
> Chicago
>
> February 12, 1901
>
> Mr. John J. McGraw
> Baltimore, Md.
> DEAR SIR:
>   I can only guess your motive in giving out the story of a peace conference

between the American and National Leagues. Possibly you wanted to crowd the League players in the matter of getting them under contract. At all events it was a good scheme, and put the National League fellows way up in the air. They knew, of course, no peace negotiations were on, and they were at a loss to explain the purpose of that Baltimore story. It put a kink in the American Association contingent, and from this out they will be looking for a "throw down."

The American League teams, with possibly the exception of Boston and Philadelphia, are about completed. The Milwaukee team is made up, and Comiskey has all his players in line with one exception of Padden. Griffith and Wallace are signed. Comiskey hopes to get Fielder Joes [Jones], of the Brooklyn club. Flick is willing to sign for $2,800, but the clubs are afraid to touch him on account of his Philadelphia contract. I will leave for the East tonight. Will be in Cleveland tomorrow and hope to be in Washington by Thursday.

With kind regards I am—

Yours truly,

B. B. Johnson

Among other locations the National League had endeavored to place a rival American Association club in Detroit. On the 16th of the month its backers announced, "We are going to buy Jimmy Burns out, and not allow another American League game in Detroit."

The locals were not swallowing this scheme, however. On February 23 the *Sporting News'* Detroit correspondent reported: "There is no one here who inclines to an American Association club except Van Derbeck, who has an ax to grind, and the board of directors of the [Detroit Athletic club]. The owners of the property around the [proposed A.A.] park have united in a petition to the mayor to withhold a license, and have retained counsel to bring injunction proceedings unless the project is dropped. Any one who backed an American Association club in Detroit would have no more chance than a prizefighter in Cincinnati."

Johnson's lineup for 1901 was as follows:

CLUB	PRESIDENT	MANAGER
Baltimore	Sidney S. Frank	John J. McGraw
Boston	Charles W. Somers	James J. Collins
Chicago	Charles Comiskey	Clark Griffith
Cleveland	John F. Kilfoyle	James R. McAleer
Detroit	James D. Burns	George T. Stallings
Milwaukee	Matthew Killilea	Hugh Duffy
Philadelphia	Benjamin Shibe	Connie Mack
Washington	James Manning	James Manning

A key figure joining the American League, despite his ignominious role in the stillbirth of the New American Association, was John McGraw. McGraw, his sidekick, Wilbert Robinson, and second baseman Billy "Wagon Tongue" Keister had been sold to St. Louis prior to the start of the 1900 season for the staggering figure of $15,000. At first both McGraw and Robinson refused to report, but McGraw soon worked out a deal with St. Louis. Both would report for duty, but in an unprecedented move both would have the reserve clause stricken from their contract for 1901.

During the season the duo often played indifferently, and McGraw was in constant negotiations with Ban Johnson regarding an American League club in Baltimore. With the season complete, McGraw and Robinson were so overjoyed to bid farewell to St. Louis they tossed their uniforms in the river as their train crossed the Mississippi.

Johnson gave the two more than just an opportunity to play in Baltimore. Both would be stockholders, although the largest investor was Sidney S. Frank, a 29-year-old stockbroker with $40,000 in the team. McGraw would manage again, and he would cajole such players as pitchers Jack Dunn and "Iron Man" Joe McGinnity, infielder Bill Keister and catcher Roger Bresnahan to join him.

The alliance of McGraw and Johnson was not destined to endure. When Johnson formally converted the American League to a major league, he issued the following statement of principles:

> CLEAN BALL is the MAIN PLANK in the American League platform, and the clubs must stand by it religiously. There must be no profanity on the ball field. The umpires are agents of the League and must be treated with respect. I will suspend any manager or player who uses profane or vulgar language to an Umpire, and that suspension will remain in force until such time as the offender can learn to bridle his tongue.

The rabidly umpire-baiting McGraw soon ran afoul of the imperious Johnson. Throughout 1901 and into the beginning of the 1902 season, Johnson had repeatedly fined McGraw for such encounters. Finally in July of 1902, McGraw was suspended indefinitely. At this point, John T. Brush proposed to McGraw that Brush purchase the fifth-place Baltimore club.

Originally, McGraw had been slated by Johnson to lead an A.L. invasion of Manhattan. Along with his suspensions, however, McGraw received the impression (or so he would later say) that Johnson was about to pull a doublecross. He was, however, still determined to go to New York—and now had an alternate plan.

"I knew what Ban Johnson was up to," McGraw later contended. "As far back as midseason of 1902, he made secret plans to drop Baltimore and move . . . to New York. That was all right with me, as I expected to go along as manager, with a share in the club. But, when I learned . . . he was ready to ditch me at the end of the 1902 season, I acted fast. He planned to run out on me, so I ran out on him, and beat him to New York by nearly a year."

On June 18, McGraw left the Orioles under the command of Wilbert Robinson and headed for New York to meet with Giants owner Andrew Freedman. The two met several more times, and also involved in the scheme was Cincinnati owner Brush. McGraw clandestinely conferred with Brush at his lavish Indianapolis estate "Lombardy." The trio hatched a Byzantine plot not only to shift McGraw to the Giants but to deal a body blow to Ban Johnson's upstart circuit.

McGraw had been out of the Baltimore lineup with an infection resulting from a spiking. When he returned to the field on June 28, he and outfielder Joe Kelley seemed to go out of their way to antagonize umpires Tom Connolly and Jimmy Johnstone. The result was a forfeit and the indefinite suspension of both Orioles by Johnson.

"No man likes to be ordered off the earth like a dog in the presence of friends," fumed McGraw. "Ballplayers are not a lot of cattle to have the whip cracked after them. . . . There is an end to self-sacrifice. A man must look out for himself."

McGraw was now about to leave Baltimore. Freedman dispatched Giants club Secretary Fred M. Knowles to Baltimore, and McGraw cleverly set upon gaining his release. "Muggsy" (a nickname McGraw loathed) had advanced the foundering Baltimore club $7,000 to meet expenses, largely player salaries. Now he demanded it back. When the club could not come up with the cash, McGraw told the club he wanted his freedom.

He got it on July 7. That evening he left for New York and by the next morning had signed with Freedman for $11,000 a year for four years. "I appreciate the kindliness which has prompted the Baltimore club to give me the release I asked for," McGraw told the New York press corps, "and I wish to assure them publicly that in consideration . . . I shall not tamper with [their] players."

Instead McGraw endeavored to deliver the whole club, bound and gagged, over to the National League.

It was a complicated scenario. Ultimately 201 of the 400 Oriole shares were gathered up. McGraw traded his half of the "Blue Diamond Cafe" to Wilbert Robinson in exchange for Uncle Robbie's Orioles holdings. These McGraw transferred to fellow stockholder John J. Mahon, a politician and father-in-law of outfielder Joe Kelley. Mahon, who had replaced Frank as president in 1902, then purchased the interest of Father Boland. Mahon now had control and turned it over to Freedman's Baltimore agent, attorney Joseph C. France, who then transferred power to Brush.

Brush released pitchers Joe McGinnity and Jack Cronin, first baseman Dennis "Dan" McGann, catcher Roger Bresnahan and outfielders Cy Seymour

John J. McGraw, ally-turned-enemy of American League founder Ban Johnson.

and Kelley. Bresnahan, McGinnity and Cronin signed with the Giants. Kelley and Seymour inked with the Reds.

The Oriole roster was denuded of players; against St. Louis on July 17 it could not even field a team. Johnson declared the franchise forfeit, appointed Wilbert Robinson its new manager, and transferred in reinforcements from other clubs. The Orioles skidded from fifth to last.

Despite this fiasco one could not but surmise that Johnson was relieved to be rid of "Muggsy" McGraw. "McGraw was one of the hardest men in the league to control," Johnson informed the press, "and now that he has left I cannot see how the American League has lost anything."

Johnson Cleans House

McGraw was not the only manager Johnson dueled with. Detroit's George Stallings was if anything even more fiery than the "Little Napoleon."

As time wore on, Detroit owner Jimmy Burns also felt less than friendly towards Stallings. As early as September 1900 Johnson charged with typical bluster: "Stallings is no good and Burns is a cheap sport. He ain't got a drop of sporting blood in his veins. We want good managers in this league, and not men who are always talking to newspapers about their wrongs. There are two or three cheap skates in this league, and I'll put them out of business."

Recriminations continued to fly during 1901, and by November 13 of that year Johnson publicly vowed again that Stallings must be expelled from the league, this time charging outright treachery on his part during that season. Burns shared Johnson's sentiments. Johnson charged: "Stallings put a proposition before Burns for the transfer of the club to the National League, and Burns was very mad about it. That was the origin of the trouble between Burns and Stallings. Burns then decided to take everything possible into his own hands, and as he was the treasurer, clamped upon the funds. He has got the money put away where it is safe, and it will be produced at the proper time. Stallings will get back every dollar that he put into the club; and that wasn't very much."

Others contended Stallings held the majority of Tigers stock and was the club's largest creditor to boot. *Sporting Life* reported that the manager wanted $22,500 to sell out. Johnson threatened to move the club out of Detroit. Both Stallings and Burns eventually sold out to Samuel F. Angus, a Detroit railway contractor and insurance man.

Also getting the boot at 1901's close was Washington's Jimmy Manning. Originally, it was announced that Manning had retired to pursue other business interests, but it was soon revealed Johnson had forced him out as well.

"Mr. Johnson's nature," said Manning, "is such that he brooks no opposition whatsoever. I wasn't even invited to confer when Mr. Johnson called in representatives of other league clubs. I asked for funds from the league's reserve fund, to which I had contributed, in order to buy new players and he refused me."

Manning sold out to Postal for $15,000. Replacing him as manager was Tom Loftus, former manager of the Western League's Columbus club and in 1900–01 manager of Chicago in the National League. Some said that it was Johnson who actually made the choice of Loftus.

Another Effort at Organized Labor

Rampant labor discontent played a part in the American League's success. Major grievances included a $2,400 salary cap, unreasonable fines, and the practice of "farming" or optioning players to the minors. Being "farmed" was particularly onerous in those days, in that it voided the player's contract in regard to salary yet still bound him to his former club.

On June 10, 1900, at New York's Sturtevant's House delegates from each N.L. team instituted a "Protective Association of Professional Baseball Players." Pittsburgh catcher Charles "Chief" Zimmer was elected president, Chicago hurler Clark Griffith vice president, Boston catcher Bill Clarke treasurer and Brooklyn first baseman Hughie "Ee-Yah" Jennings secretary.

"The wonder is that the union for self-protection against intolerable oppression has been so long delayed," commented *Sporting Life*. Samuel Gompers of the American Federation of Labor tendered his support and dispatched organizer Dan Harris, but the players, fearing the taint of union involvement, declined affiliation.

Management was not enthusiastic over these developments. "I do not believe in labor organizations or unions, . . . " bluntly remarked Arthur Soden. "When a player ceases to be useful to me I will release him."

Within a month the PAPBP had the support of over 100 National, American and Eastern leaguers. At this point Buffalo attorney Harry Leonard Taylor, a former major league first baseman, stepped into the picture.

Taylor soon formulated a platform:

1. The ten-day clause would be applied to both owner and player.
2. The club would bear physicians' fees for players injured on the field.
3. A three-man arbitration board would be created to resolve disputes.
4. No player would be traded, sold or "farmed" without his consent.

In December 1900 — on the eve of the American League's break-away — a National League committee of Soden, Brush and Rogers met with Taylor, Zimmer, Jennings and Griffith at New York's Fifth Avenue Hotel.

As the players entered the room, Griffith noticed that Nick Young was attempting to gain their attention. "Son," he whispered, "they ain't gonna give you anything in this meeting. I just wanted to tell you."

Soden immediately revealed that serious negotiations would not occur, stating his committee had no authority to make any concessions. Griffith found his attitude "condescending."

Later Soden, attempting to avoid the lobby, ran into the players in hotel bar. Griffith invited him to join in a beer, and Soden claimed he had left the Players' Association demands with his fellow owners. Griffith, however, noticed his petition was visible from the owner's coat pocket. The pitcher then openly called him a liar. The magnate stammered he would give the petition full consideration and beat a hasty retreat from the establishment.

"They treated us," complained Taylor, "as if we had been unruly kids who had to be lollipopped and put to bed."

Despite such treatment the PAPBP still was not willing to jump wholeheartedly into the American League camp. Said Zimmer: "We don't want a baseball war, and to show that we have no secret agreement with the American League, we have ordered all . . . players to keep from negotiations with Ban Johnson for the present at least."

Johnson, however, took the wind out of Zimmer's sails by agreeing to the Association's demands, and by February 1901 the National League was back at the bargaining table, albeit with its traditional regressive attitude. "Don't bring your lawyer," Zimmer was told—and in the spirit of the times he did not.

The owners granted some relief—most notably that "farming" without the player's consent was prohibited. Other provisions included a meaningless one-year "option-to-renew" on player contracts (renewable in perpetuity at the club's discretion) and requirements for the transfer of minor league teams.

In return the PAPBP agreed to expel any member who signed with the American League, "pending final action by the Protective Association as a body."

Many thought Zimmer had been "bunkoed" by the magnates into agreeing to "blacklist" the Association's own members. Taylor, however, pointed out that the "pending final action" clause gave the Association an important out. In any case, restraining players from jumping to the American League was now akin to attempting to hold back the tide. This inability to keep players from jumping was indicative of the group's impotence. Soon Johnson was publicly terming Zimmer "one of the worst characters in baseball," and the N.L. was also showing little use for the PAPBP.

By the beginning of 1901, Zimmer was out as Association president, replaced by former Brooklyn second baseman Tommy Daly, who not only had jumped to Charles Comiskey's White Stockings, but had violated the terms of his existing N.L. contract, which ran to 1902. By year's end the PAPBP was defunct.

National Leaguers Jump in Droves

From the very beginning the American League succeeded in enticing National Leaguers. Third basemen Jimmy Collins and Lave Cross; pitchers Cy Young, Clark Griffith, Joe McGinnity, Harry Howell, George "Nig" Cuppy and Jimmy "Nixey" Callahan; catchers Lou Criger and Roger Bresnahan; second basemen Jimmy Williams and Billy Keister; outfielders Sam Mertes, "Chick" Stahl, Buck Freeman, "Turkey Mike" Donlin and Fielder Jones all made the jump. Only the Pittsburgh club was largely exempt from this exodus, as Ban Johnson was hoping to entice Barney Dreyfuss to deliver his whole club to the new circuit.

Spalding's Guide for 1902 admitted that 74 N.L. players had jumped. Hall of Fame historian Lee Allen, on the other hand, noted that of 182 players appearing in A.L. games for 1901, 111 were former Senior Circuit chattels.

The greatest player coming over to the new league was Phillies star second baseman Napoleon "Larry" Lajoie. Lajoie was receiving a $2,600 salary from owner John I. Rogers but wanted to be compensated to match roommate Ed Delahanty's $3,000 stipend. Connie Mack quickly lured him across town.

Various sources have placed Lajoie's Athletics salary at either $4,000 or $5,000. "We paid Larry $4,000," recalled Connie Mack, "but he was cagey, and made sure we would pay him that much money. He had us deposit the entire sum in a Philadelphia bank in the name of Frank Hough, sports editor of the Philadelphia *Enquirer*, and a man named Johnson, with whom Larry boarded. On payday, they would draw checks against the amount and pay Larry."

In five National League seasons, the slick-fielding Lajoie had hit .326, .361, .324, .378 and .337 for Rogers, who promptly went to court to retrieve his three contract jumpers—pitchers "Strawberry Bill" Bernhard and Charles "Chick" Fraser had joined Lajoie.

At first the Common Pleas Court of Philadelphia refused to grant Rogers an injunction, citing the standard contract's well-known lack of mutuality. Rogers, however, appealed to State Supreme Court, where on April 2, 1902, just two days before the start of the American League season, he won.

Lajoie pleaded, among other things, that his services were not "unique." Judge William P. Potter responded that while the Frenchman "might not be the sun in the baseball firmament, . . . he is certainly a bright, particular star," and thus his absence constituted a definable loss to Rogers. With Lajoie having batted .426 with 14 homers and 125 RBIs to win the A.L. triple crown, there was some logic to that.

Beyond that, it was found that Lajoie's Phillies contract was not as nebulous as the standard pact. For one thing, he had signed for three years, starting in 1900, and was specifically enjoined from playing with any other team.

The National League was elated. Nick Young termed it "a great legal victory," and Chicago's James A. Hart contended that the second baseman would land behind bars if he remained in the new circuit.

Chick Fraser immediately returned to his old club, while Bernhard and Lajoie sat tight (despite a $3,000 offer from the outlaw California League). Finally, two months into the season, it was noted that Potter's jurisdiction extended only to the state of Pennsylvania.

Connie Mack remembered Charles Somers' generosity in setting up not only the Athletics but also half the new league. Seeing the woeful state of his Cleveland club, Connie sold both Lajoie and Bernhard to the Bronchos. Lajoie signed a new pact with Somers that gave him $25,000 for three years (or $30,000 for four seasons, depending on which account you believe). The contract was guaranteed, no matter what any court ruled. The Phils did appeal to

HARRY S BRESSLER

Napoleon "Larry" Lajoie, triple crown winner for the Philadelphia Athletics in 1901, the American League's first season as a major league.

Cleveland's Common Pleas Court, but their motion for an injunction was denied for lack of jurisdiction.

Now the duo could play anywhere in the American League—except Philadelphia. When Cleveland arrived in the City of Brotherly Love, sheriff's deputies boarded the train to search for Lajoie, but he would never be found. "I guess he took French leave," manager Bill Armour joked, while Lajoie and Bernhard relaxed at nearby Atlantic City.

In other court decisions the N.L. did not fare as well. In May 1902 St. Louis City Court Judge John A. Talty cited the Fourteenth Amendment and the Sherman Antitrust Act in allowing pitcher Jack Harper, shortstop Bobby Wallace and outfielder Emmett "Snags" Heidrick to remain with the St. Louis American League club.

Almost Breaking the Color Bar

Another potential source of talent was the nation's increasing number of black ballplayers. Although a few blacks had played in the American Association in 1884 and in a variety of minor leagues, the early 1890s, since a campaign of exclusion had slowly tightened on blacks aspiring to a professional career. By 1901 there were no blacks in Organized Ball.

John McGraw was never one to let *anything*—let alone the racial mores of his time—stand in his way. In spring training 1901 he spied a bellboy at Little Rock's Eastland Hotel, Charles Grant. Grant was a fine second baseman who the previous year had performed with the Columbia Giants, a black team from Chicago.

McGraw thought him to be of major league caliber and soon launched a scheme to get him on the Orioles. "Charlie," he explained to his find, a light-skinned black, "I've been trying to think of some way to sign you for the Baltimore club and I think I've got it. On this map there's a creek called Tokohama. That's going to be your name from now on, Charlie Tokohama, and you're a full-blooded Cherokee."

Grant went along with the story, alleging his father was white and his mother a Cherokee, but White Sox owner Charles Comiskey would have none of the charade. "I'm not going to stand for McGraw bringing in an Indian on the Baltimore team," he promised. "If Muggsy really keeps this Indian, I will get a Chinaman of my acquaintance and put him on third. Someone told me that the Cherokee of McGraw is really Grant, the crack Negro second baseman from Cincinnati, fixed up with war paint and a bunch of feathers."

McGraw forgot about the idea, and by April the talented Grant was back with the Columbia Giants.

The Effect on the Minors

By August 1901 the National League was so short of talent that it unilaterally abrogated the National Agreement with its minor league partners so it could raid their rosters for players. This was a shocking, desperate and unprincipled move for the Nationals, who were the reputed guardians of baseball law and order.

In response, the Western League's Thomas Jefferson Hickey, on September 5, 1901, at Chicago's Leland Hotel, united the 11 existing minor leagues (the Western Association and the Eastern, Western, Pacific Northwest, Three-I, New England, New York State, Connecticut, North Carolina, Southern and California leagues) in a new "National Association of Professional Baseball Leagues" to protect their interests. Eastern League President Pat Powers was named president.

Convening again on October 24–25, the new group adopted the familiar A, B, C and D classification system for the minors, strict reserve clauses, and roster and salary restrictions.

The American League opened for business on Wednesday, April 24, 1901, with the Cleveland Bluebirds at the Chicago White Stockings' South Side Park. All other games (Washington at Philadelphia, Milwaukee at Detroit and Boston at Baltimore) were rained out.

Ironically, Ban Johnson was not in attendance (he was in Philadelphia), but rival owner James Hart was. Also missing was Mayor Carter Harrison, who was called away by William Jennings Bryan's unexpected visit to the city. But aside from these absences, it was seen as "the most auspicious beginning imaginable." Good feeling abounded so much that the bleacherites "indulged in a merry cushion fight all through the concluding inning by way of celebration."

The box score at Chicago:

CLEVELAND						CHICAGO					
	R	H	PO	A	E		R	H	PO	A	E
Pickering, rf	0	1	0	0	0	Hoy, cf	0	1	3	0	0
McCarthy, lf	0	2	4	0	0	Jones, rf	2	1	4	0	0
Genins, cf	0	0	1	0	0	Mertes, lf	2	1	4	0	0
LaChance, 1b	1	1	12	0	0	Shugart, ss	2	0	4	4	0
Bradley, 3b	0	0	2	5	0	Isbell, 1b	1	2	8	0	1
Beck, 2b	0	2	1	2	0	Hartman, 3b	0	1	0	7	0
Hallman, ss	1	0	1	2	1	Brain, 2b	0	0	1	4	0
Wood, c	0	1	2	1	0	W. Sullivan, c	1	2	2	0	0
Hoffer, p	0	0	1	1	0	Patterson, p	0	0	1	1	0
	2	7	24	11	1		8	8	27	16	1

									R	H	E
Cleveland	0	0	0	1	0	0	1	0	0–2	7	1
Chicago	2	5	0	0	0	0	1	0	x–8	8	1

Two base hit—Beck. Total bases—Chicago 8; Cleveland 8. Sacrifice hit—Shugart. Struck out—Patterson. Bases on Balls—Off Hoffer, 6; off Patterson, 2. Double plays—Hoffer, Hallman and LaChance; Brain, Shugart and Isbell. Left on bases—Chicago, 5; Cleveland, 5. Passed Ball—Wood. Time—1:30. Umpire—Tom Connolly. Attendance—9,000.

Opening Days at the various A.L. cities staggered on until early May. On April 26, the American League followed up at Baltimore's American League Park (Baltimore 10, Boston 6), and at Philadelphia's Columbia Park (Washington 5, Philadelphia 1); on April 28, at Detroit's Burns Park (Detroit 14, Milwaukee 13, with the Tigers scoring 10 runs in the bottom of the ninth), at Washington's American League Park (Washington 5, Baltimore 2, before 9,772 fans) and at Cleveland's League Park (Cleveland 4, Milwaukee 3); on

May 4 at Milwaukee's Lloyd Street Ball Park (Chicago 11, Milwaukee 3); and finally on May 8 at Boston's Huntington Avenue Grounds (Boston 12, Philadelphia 4).

Charles Comiskey's Chicago White Stockings, managed by Clark Griffith (who went 24-7 on the mound), won the first A.L. pennant by four games, as Jimmy Collins' Boston club (variously called the Puritans, the Americans and the Somersets—after Charles Somers) ran into pitching troubles the last two weeks of the season and tailed off badly. More importantly, both Boston and Chicago outdrew their National rivals. The Puritans drew 289,448 and bested Arthur Soden's Beaneaters by over 100,000 customers.

National and American League attendance for 1901:

	NATIONAL	AMERICAN
Baltimore	xxx	141,952
Boston	146,502	289,448
Brooklyn	189,200	xxx
Chicago	205,071	354,350
Cincinnati	205,728	xxx
Cleveland	xxx	131,380
Detroit	xxx	259,430
Milwaukee	xxx	139,034
New York	297,650	xxx
Philadelphia	234,937	206,329
Pittsburgh	251,955	xxx
St. Louis	379,988	xxx
Washington	xxx	161,661
	1,911,031	1,683,584

The Syndicate Plan

During the summer of 1901 Andrew J. Freedman invited John T. Brush, Arthur Soden and Frank de Haas Robison to a fateful meeting at his Red Bank, New Jersey, estate. There the three plotted to implement Brush's scheme for "syndicate baseball."

Until the advent of Charles O. Finley and George Steinbrenner, Freedman was widely considered the most unpopular owner in the history of the sport. A German-Jewish bachelor who grew rich in dry goods and real estate, Freedman became the trusted crony of Tammany Hall's Richard Croker, even serving as his best man. Together the two engineered the election of Robert A. Van Wyck as the first mayor of the consolidated City of New York. With financier August Belmont, Freedman helped finance and control the new Interborough Rapid Transit subway.

By all accounts Freedman was highly unpleasant. Frank Graham termed

Charles Comiskey (in suit) poses with his 1900 American League champion Chicago White Stockings. The Sox repeated as champions in 1901, the A.L.'s first season as a major league, and drew more fans to their South Side Park than saw the National League rival Cubs play on the West Side.

him "Course, vain, arrogant and abusive." Albert Spalding found him "obnoxious." Pittsburgh *Sporting Life* correspondent A. R. Cratty recalled that it was his duty to interview Freedman on each trip the Giants made to that city. "No job was ever harder," he wrote on Freedman's death, "unless it be the same act with the late John Tomlinson Brush as the target. Freedman never let you get away from the idea that he was a New Yorker. His whole attitude demanded a sort of homage because he was from the big burg on the island. That high bearing cost him many friends on the circuit, or rather in the provinces. Some old and young feared him."

Freedman once physically assaulted Brush in the barroom of New York's Fifth Avenue Hotel. In return he was given a pasting by Brush's friend, Bert Dasher. He once ran into J. Walter Spalding (A. G.'s brother), and so vociferously insulted him that Walter resigned from the Giants' Board of Directors.

Freedman's teams were chronic tail-enders, as he fired managers with abandon (he had three in 1895 alone, including Harvey Watkins, an actor whose only qualification was his status as a long-time Giants fan). In July 1898, after an anti–Semitic remark by Orioles outfielder "Ducky" Holmes, Freedman even precipitated a near-riot at the Polo Grounds by pulling the Giants off the field and forfeiting to Baltimore.

Brush had developed a scheme to turn the National League into one giant corporation, the ultimate baseball cartel. The plan remained secret until the National League's annual meeting began in New York in December 1901. On December 11 the New York *Sun* broke the story of "the organization of the National League Base Ball Trust, to be divided into preferred and common stock to draw a dividend of 7 per cent; all of which is to belong to the National League, as a body. . . ."

Common stock according to the plan would be parceled out among the various clubs as follows:

New York	30%
Cincinnati	12%
St. Louis	12%
Boston	12%
Philadelphia	10%
Chicago	10%
Pittsburgh	8%
Brooklyn	6%

A five-man "Board of Regents," to be elected by the stockholders, would govern the corporation. It would choose a president (to be paid $25,000 annually) and a treasurer (to be paid not more than $12,500). All managers (at $5,000 each) were to be hired through the Board. All players were to be "licensed" by them.

Brush's scheme for such centralized, overreaching control emerged from an earlier plan of his to crush the American League. In midseason, he had plotted to lure the weak Detroit and Baltimore clubs away from the A.L. He would then force Ban Johnson to agree to a new 12-club circuit, "dominant and in full control of baseball in this country."

It would be, wrote Brush to Spalding, "conditioned upon business principles, with charter perpetual, subject to such modifications as good business judgement would suggest, . . . and with a code which will absolutely control player, manager, umpire, and club official."

Earlier, Spalding circulated a plan for a similar trust so he could negotiate peace with Johnson. Nothing, however, came of the idea. In any case, Spalding was strangely pacific toward the American Leaguers. "The more I think it over," he wrote to Brush, "the more I am impressed with the unwisdom of such a move [i.e., luring away Baltimore and Detroit]. . . . The public will hold the National League responsible . . . and it will prove a boomerang . . . and

forever belittle the two clubs . . . guilty of such a Judas-Benedict Arnold act,
and then again what does the National League gain by it? . . . I think you very
much mis-estimate the . . . strength of the American League if you think such
a move would kill it off. . . ."

Spalding even had his business partner Alfred Reach arrange a meeting
with Johnson at Atlantic City. "Spalding," recalled Johnson, "asked me if the
American owners would meet peace overtures in a fair spirit. I said they
would."

Brush's plan drew the resentment of the four owners left out in the cold.
It also raised the hackles of an American public decreasingly tolerant of
"trusts" and monopolies.

As soon as the League meeting began, Pittsburgh's Barney Dreyfuss
nominated Spalding for president. As early as February rumors had Spalding
replacing the ineffectual Nick Young, to strengthen the circuit's hand in the
coming war. It was thought Spalding would certainly have the support of the
four non–"Red Bank" owners, as well as Soden, a long-time friend. Many
viewed Spalding's election as a foregone conclusion. "It would not be surprising
to see his election made unanimous," noted one Brooklyn paper.

It was a false prophecy. The "Red Bank" faction (as they were now called)
raised all sorts of technical objections to the nomination and ended up standing
firmly against Spalding, voting to retain Young.

On the second day of the session, Spalding himself appeared to address
the gathering:

> I am told that this is the last day of the National League. Rumor declares
> that it will not outlive this day. Gentlemen, I was present at the birth of this
> organization. I saw it when its eyes were first opened to the light of day,
> twenty-six years ago next February, in this city. If it is to be buried today . . .
> I ask, gentlemen, the privilege of closing its eyes in death. I claim that not
> only as a privilege but as a right. . . .
>
> This National League has two fathers: William A. Hulbert – God bless his
> memory – and the other – myself. Twenty-six years ago this month I spent
> thirty days in Mr. Hulbert's house with him, writing the first constitution; and
> I claim, because . . . I have been unanimously elected an honorary member
> of this body, that I have the right to speak in its councils.
>
> We have a very sick patient here. . . . I think it is time that somebody asked
> some questions to find out what has brought it to this condition. Emaciated
> in form, pulse weak, heart fluttering; and yet we see a few motions of the
> muscles that indicate that life is not extinct. Gentlemen, as an honorary
> member of this League, if it is to die, I propose to stay by that corpse until
> it is buried. I sincerely hope I am misinformed.
>
> I object to any more daggers being thrust into that body in my presence.
> At least I have the right to demand that. Let us stand by . . . for a few minutes
> and see if we cannot fan it to life. . . .

Cincinnati Reds owner John T. Brush, mastermind of the monopolistic "National League Base Ball Trust."

I have no personal feelings against any man in this room. In fact, I can say some of the best friends I have in the world are here. But when it comes to the question of personal friendship for one of you, or two of you, or all of you combined, I think more of the National League than I do of any one of you or of all of you.

. . . The eyes of the nation are upon you, and somehow or other the people have an idea that you are a band of conspirators, talking about nothing but gate receipts. You have got into a fight with the American League; you have lost players, I understand; I certainly judge from the papers that you have lost their support, and I am told that some have violated the confidence that was reposed in them by this League.

I accuse you of violating a trust in having abrogated the National Agreement. The most damnable thing that was ever done in baseball was the way that was done. . . .

Spalding's oratory failed to sway his opponents, however, so he took his case to the members of the working press.

"I will assure you gentlemen," a perspiring and wildly gesturing Spalding thundered to a huge assemblage of reporters, "that in the event of my election to the office of president of the National League, before I will accept the same, I will impose some conditions . . . that will be of lasting benefit to the game. One of them I will make bold to state . . . I will demand that Andrew Freedman . . . be eliminated from the councils of the body. This will be the first and most important condition. . . .

"The issue is now between Andrew Freedman and A. G. Spalding, and when I go back actively into baseball Andrew Freedman gets out. He gets out right away or I'll get out. . . ."

But despite Spalding's stirring oratory, the deadlock continued for 25 ballots, Spalding holding the votes of Chicago, Philadelphia, Brooklyn and Pittsburgh, while Nick Young just as consistently held the other four.

After the 25th ballot, Freedman, Robison, Soden and Brush left the room, leaving Nick Young with their proxies. Young then ruled a quorum no longer existed, while Colonel John Rogers insisted that "once a quorum, always a quorum."

Young then left, but the others remained and elected Rogers chairman pro tem. He called for another vote, and Albert Goodwill Spalding, who was sound asleep in his hotel room, was "elected" president of the National League—four votes to none.

At 4 a.m. Spalding ordered Young to immediately surrender League records and papers to him. Young at first demurred, allowing that he would turn the trunkful of documents over to his son Robert. As negotiations proceeded, a porter hired by Spalding spirited the trunk away.

Spalding then called a League meeting and proceeded to move in for the kill. Only his four supporters answered his call, but Spalding noted that Giants Secretary Fred Knowles was lurking in the doorway while all this was going on. A. G. ruled that by Knowles' "presence" New York was represented. Thus, a "quorum" was created.

Spalding next called for a vote on the Brush-Freedman "Syndicate" plan, which, not surprisingly, was quickly rejected. While Young was probably relieved to be out of all this turmoil, Andrew Freedman had no intention of surrendering so easily. Freedman went to court, and although his first motion was denied, on March 29, 1902, a Judge Truex of New York ruled Spalding's election invalid.

Deadlocked balloting proceeded once more. Soden, John Montgomery Ward and Colonel William C. Temple of Philadelphia were all nominated, but to no avail. Finally on April 3, 1902, a compromise of sorts was reached. A triumvirate of Brush, Soden and Hart was named to guide executive functions as the second year of war commanded. Brush chaired the unwieldy group. Nick Young, the eternal Nick Young, was back as secretary-treasurer. Some allege that as part of this deal, Andrew Freedman sent word to A. G. Spalding he would retire from baseball as soon as he gracefully could.

Ban Johnson, of course, was elated by such dissension in the opposition ranks. In every previous struggle, the National League had been firmly united, while its various interloping competitors had lacked cohesion. Now, the shoe was on the other foot.

"If they fight like a bunch of Kilkenny cats among themselves," Johnson chortled, "I know we have them licked."

Following the 1901 season, the American League looked still more viable, as Johnson shifted his weak Milwaukee franchise to St. Louis (which, next to Chicago, was the largest city allowing Sunday ball). The new franchise would utilize old Sportsman's Park.

Owners Henry and Matthew Killilea hired Jimmy McAleer, who had ably assisted Johnson in recruiting National League players, as manager, replacing Hugh Duffy. The Killileas soon sold out to Ralph L. Orthwein, who in turn transferred the club to Robert Hedges. Augmenting the Browns, as they were now called, was a raft of deserters from the crosstown Cardinals: pitchers Jack Powell, Charles "Jack" Harper and "Wee Willie" Sudhoff; the keystone combination of Bobby Wallace and Dick "Brains" Padden; and outfielders "Snags" Heidrick and Jesse "Crab" Burkett.

And even more players deserted the National League. The Phils took heavy losses: outfielders Ed Delahanty and Elmer Flick, shortstop Monte Cross and pitcher Bill Duggleby. The Cards lost first baseman Dan McGann, Topsy Hartsel left the Cubs, and Boston bade goodbye to right-hander Bill Dinneen.

Ban Johnson even attempted the biggest catch of all, Honus Wagner. In the process he visited Pittsburgh, and had to beat a hasty retreat from Wagner's hotel room as Pirates owner Barney Dreyfuss was irately advancing onto the scene.

Despite losing Lajoie and Bernhard, Connie Mack made a remarkable comeback in 1902, helped initially—but only temporarily—by the acquisition of Flick, Hartsel, Cross and Duggleby. Flick was soon shifted to Cleveland along with Lajoie and Bernhard, and Duggleby returned to the Phils.

Having lost so many players, Mack sought reinforcements. In midseason he picked up second baseman Danny Murphy, a Philadelphia native who had played briefly for the Giants. Murphy responded by hitting .313 in 76 games. Next he signed George Edward "Rube" Waddell, a more-than-slightly eccentric Cubs property who had been farmed to Los Angeles of the Pacific Coast League. Waddell did not join the Athletics until June 26 but went 24-7 the rest of the way and remarkably led the circuit in strikeouts with 210.

The A's took the pennant by five full games.

The year saw the American League pull away from its rival in attendance:

	NATIONAL	AMERICAN
Baltimore	xxx	174,606
Boston	116,960	348,567
Brooklyn	199,868	xxx
Chicago	263,700	337,898
Cincinnati	217,300	xxx
Cleveland	xxx	275,395
Detroit	xxx	189,469
New York	302,875	xxx
Philadelphia	112,066	189,469
Pittsburgh	243,826	xxx
St. Louis	226,417	272,283
Washington	xxx	188,158
TOTALS	1,683,012	2,206,457

Late in the 1902 season, Andrew Freedman, much to the relief of his fellow magnates, bowed out of the game. He sold the Giants to John T. Brush, who in turn disposed of his Cincinnati holdings to the political boss of Hamilton County, Ohio, George B. Cox, ex–Mayor Julius Fleischmann (whose fortune came from Fleischmann's Yeast) and August "Garry" Herrmann, who was named president. Herrmann was a virtual tool of Cox. Journalist Lincoln Steffens told of seeing Cox interrupting Herrmann and another flunky, Rudolph Hynecke, with the taunt: "When I whistle you dogs come out of your holes, don't you?"

There was an awkward silence.

"Don't you, Garry?" Cox repeated his query.

"That's right," responded the docile Herrmann.

Ban Takes Manhattan

After the 1902 season, jumping to the American League continued. Brooklyn outfielder "Wee Willie" Keeler, Brooklyn pitcher "Wild Bill" Donovan, Cincinnati outfielder Sam Crawford, Boston pitcher Vic Willis, Pittsburgh pitchers Jack Chesbro and Jesse Tannehill, Pirates catcher Jack O'Connor and Pittsburgh infielders "Wid" Conroy and Tommy Leach all signed with Johnson's league. Even Christy Mathewson and catcher Frank Bowerman were hopping from the Giants to the Browns. The N.L. would later win contract disputes and retain Willis, Leach, Mathewson and Bowerman.

The American League's invasion of Manhattan was now—minus John McGraw—about to occur. Obtaining a field in Manhattan was always the major issue delaying the incursion, as Andrew Freedman enjoyed considerable favor from the local politicians, so much so that any site considered would soon have a street cut through it by the city fathers.

In December 1902 Johnson located a promising site bordered by 142nd and 145th streets, Lenox Avenue and the Harlem River. It was, moreover, near a new station of the Interborough Rapid Transit subway. Johnson's agents convinced John B. McDonald, an IRT contractor, to purchase the land and lease it to the A.L. McDonald persuaded financier August Belmont II to come aboard. However, an IRT director—one Andrew Freedman—soon killed the plan.

"You know that I am out of baseball, having sold my controlling interest in the New York club to Mr. Brush," gloated Freedman to the press in early January 1902, "but you may quote me as saying that someone has been stringing these Western fellows all along."

That situation was changing, however, and fast. On February 18, 1902, the estate of one Josephine Peyton had auctioned off 12 parcels of land for $377,800 to John J. Byrne, a nephew of "Big Bill" Devery. Devery, one of the Big Apple's foremost gamblers, was a very active Democrat in Manhattan's Ninth District, and a former city police chief.

Devery soon was in business with Frank Farrell, another major operator. Ex-saloonkeeper Farrell owned 250 pool halls in the city and was closely connected to "Boss" Sullivan, an even greater star in New York's underworld firmament.

Coal dealer Joseph Gordon, acting as front man for Farrell and Devery, approached Johnson, telling him his group could easily arrange for a park to be built if given a franchise. Devery and Farrell paid $18,000 for the Baltimore franchise and installed Gordon as president. Devery's name was missing from those listed as stockholders, although it was well-known he had contributed approximately $100,000 to the enterprise.

"Me a backer!" Devery modestly, if somewhat dishonestly, exclaimed. "I only wished I did own some stock in a baseball club. I'm a poor man and don't own stock in anything. Besides, how could I pitch a ball with this stomach?"

That's one version of the story. Frank Graham in *The New York Yankees* tells another. According to sportswriter Graham, Johnson and his new ownership group were brought together by the New York *Sun*'s Joe Vila. Vila had known Johnson since the A.L. president's own sportswriting days and introduced him to Frank Farrell.

Farrell was more than eager to purchase the Baltimore franchise, although Johnson was unsure about his prospective new club owner. His reticence evaporated when Farrell produced a $25,000 check and handed it over to Johnson, proclaiming, "Take this as a guarantee of good faith. If I don't put this ballclub across, keep it."

"That's a pretty big forfeit," replied an amazed Johnson.

August "Garry" Herrmann became president of the Cincinnati club after John T. Brush sold the Reds and bought the New York Giants in 1902.

"He bets that much on a horse race, Ban," Vila informed him.

In any case the deal was made between the American League and its somewhat shady triumvirate. For $75,000 in actual construction costs (plus $200,000 in excavating the rocky, hilly terrain) rickety, wooden, 16,000-seat Hilltop Park was constructed. A local Democratic politico, Thomas McAvoy, received contracts for both phases. A full 500 workmen went to work, excavating 12,000 cubic yards of bedrock, replacing it with 30,000 cubic yards of fill. On May 30, 1903, the Highlanders opened before 16,243 fans and defeated Washington 6–2 behind "Happy Jack" Chesbro.

To help shore up the weak New York roster—which after all had finished dead last in Baltimore—Ban Johnson dispatched reinforcements. Clark Griffith, his pitching career winding down, would manage. Outfielder "Wee Willie" Keeler was lured from Brooklyn for a sizable sum. "I signed Keeler myself," boasted Johnson, "and I found him an easy man to deal with." The strengthened club would finish a respectable fourth in 1903.

The National League Sues for Peace

If more player defections and a successful A.L. invasion of New York weren't bad enough, news on the attendance front was even more depressing for the Nationals. While the Senior Circuit had easily outdrawn its rival in 1901, in 1902 the Americans had surged ahead. The figures:

	1901	1902
National League	1,920,031	1,683,012
American League	1,683,584	2,206,457

Such losses could no longer be tolerated, and in December of 1902 at the National League's annual meeting at New York's Victoria Hotel, a series of steps were taken which would lead to peace.

Not everyone expected a speedy resolution. The New York *Times* believed the N.L. was prepared to carry on the fight "relentlessly" and "as bitterly as ever," but that was not to be the case.

The Cardinals' Frank de Haas Robison was the first to crack. He quickly found support from Dreyfuss of Pittsburgh (who rightfully feared an invasion of his city; Johnson was preparing to shift the weak Detroit team there), Rogers of Philadelphia, Herrmann of Cincinnati and Hart of Chicago. Even Boston and Brooklyn gave grudging approval, leaving John T. Brush as the solitary "bitterender."

The resolution, adopted on December 10, read:

> Whereas, It has been stated in the public prints that the President of the American League has declared that his organization has been in favor of, and that the National League has been opposed to, a peaceful settlement of the so-called baseball war, therefore,
>
> Resolved, that a committee of three be appointed for the purpose of conferring with representatives of the American League now in this city if they so desire, to ascertain upon what basis such a result can be accomplished.

Herrmann (a friend of Johnson's dating back to Ban's Cincinnati newspaper days), Hart and Robison were appointed to meet with the American League. Eventually Harry Pulliam would join this group.

In addition, the deadlock regarding N.L. leadership was broken. Henry Clay "Harry" Pulliam, 32-year-old secretary of the Pittsburgh club and a former Louisville newspaperman, was elected league president.

Perhaps by prearrangement, Johnson, Somers and J. F. Kilfoyle were in New York, ostensibly to close the deal on Manhattan playing grounds. Herrmann dispatched a letter to Johnson at Broadway's Criterion Hotel, urging a meeting and transmitting the League's resolution to him.

The two sides agreed to meet on January 9, 1903, at Cincinnati's Grand

Hotel. The A.L. delegation was composed of Johnson, Comiskey, Somers and Henry Killilea of Boston (Somers had just sold out to the former Milwaukee and St. Louis magnate). But the session almost ended before it began. Johnson on January 3 charged that the National League delegation "had no authority to act conclusively on anything" and that "for the present there will not be a meeting. . . ."

Harry Pulliam responded this was an "erroneous impression."

"It has been intimated that the Committee has not . . . authority to act," he noted in a prepared statement the following day. "The contrary is the fact. . . . The Committee, however, prefers not fully and finally to exercise that judgement without reserving the right on their part to confer with their colleagues. . . .

"The National League wants peace. In obtaining it there will be no objection on our part to have a fair, a frank, and open discussion of all the points about which there may be a difference of opinion."

The two sides did meet, and the idea of consolidation was quickly advanced—and rejected.

"This war is very costly to both sides, and the National League is willing to make concessions," advanced James A. Hart. "We would be willing to return to the old twelve-club National League, taking in four of your clubs, absorbing the others." This was the tried-and-true National League method of survival, working perfectly in the cases of the Players' League and the American Association.

"Any such thought is repugnant to the American," responded Johnson. "We're standing on our own two feet, and have no thought, not the slightest intention, of being absorbed. We are a major league, just as fully as is the National, and we are in the field to stay."

The negotiations went quickly. "No one imagined it was such a sweeping victory for the American League," noted an incredulous New York *Times*, "as it proved to be when the details arrived later on."

The full text of the agreement:

> First—Each and every contract hereafter entered into by the clubs of either League with players, managers or umpires shall be considered valid and binding.
>
> Second—A reserve rule shall be recognized by which each and every club may reserve players under contract, and that a uniform contract for the use of each League shall be adopted.
>
> Third—After full consideration of all contract claims by each and every club, it is agreed that the list hereto attached, marked exhibits "A" and "B," is the correct list of the players legally awarded to each club. Exhibit "A" being the list of American League players and Exhibit "B" being the list of National League players.
>
> Fourth—It is agreed that any and all sum of money received by any player

Henry Clay "Harry" Pulliam became National League president in 1903, at age 32.

from other than the club to which he awarded by the exhibits hereto attached shall be returned forthwith to the club so advancing said sums, and until all said sums of money so advanced are returned said player shall not be permitted to play with any club in either league.

Fifth—The circuits of each League shall consist of the following cities:

American League. Boston, New York, Philadelphia, Washington, Cleveland, Detroit, Chicago and St. Louis.

National League—Boston, New York, Brooklyn, Philadelphia, Pittsburgh, Chicago, St. Louis and Cincinnati.

Neither circuit shall be changed without the consent of the majority of clubs of each league.

It is further provided that there shall be no consolidation in any city where two clubs exist, nor shall any club transfer or release its players for the purpose of injuring or weakening the league of which it is a member.

Sixth—On or before the first day of February of each year the President of each League shall appoint a schedule committee of three, who shall be authorized to prepare a schedule of the games to be played during the championship season by each club in each league. This schedule shall be submitted by the committee within three weeks after its appointment to the League for adoption and ratification. Each committee shall be authorized if it deems advisable to provide for a series of games between all of the clubs in both leagues.

Seventh—On or before the first day of February of each year the President of each League shall appoint a Committee on Rules of three each who shall be authorized to prepare uniform playing rules. These rules shall be submitted by the committees within three weeks after their appointment by each league for their ratification and adoption.

Eighth—It is further agreed that the said two leagues heretofore mentioned shall enter into a National Agreement embodying the agreements and conditions heretofore set forth and it is further agreed that Presidents Ban B. Johnson [sic] and Harry C. Pulliam be and they are hereby appointed each a committee of one from each league for the purpose of making, preparing and formulating such National Agreement and it is further agreed that they invite President P. T. Powers of the National Association of Professional Baseball Leagues to confer with them in the formulating of said National Agreement.

Ninth—It is hereby agreed that each member hereby binds himself and his respective league by signing this agreement this tenth day of January 1903.

> HARRY PULLIAM
> AUG. HERRMANN
> JAMES A. HART
> FRANK DEHAAS ROBISON
> B. B. JOHNSON
> CHARLES A. COMISKEY
> CHARLES W. SOMERS
> H. J. KILLILEA

John T. Brush was incredulous. "The report seems incomplete," he sarcastically told the press in Indianapolis when shown a report of the agreement. "There surely must be more to it than I have read. There should be some account of the National League committee loosing their pocketbooks to the committee from the American League, and I don't care to discuss the report until I have it all before me."

In regard to the A.L. fielding a club in New York, there remained some disagreement—centering on whether the team could be placed anywhere except Manhattan. Fred Knowles of the Giants was insistent this was the case, although the agreement held no specific limitation to that effect. Since Andrew Freedman had just squashed Johnson's Lenox Avenue plans, the *Times* reported that "the American League [was] virtually powerless to hold games on Manhattan island next year." With Johnson having solid plans to evade the Giants' political pull (by aligning himself with Farrell and Devery), the issue was clearly less important, however, than the daily press believed.

If it were true, however, that the Americans could not go to New York, others were prepared to fill the breach. Buffalo was making a bid to leave the

Eastern League once more and join up with Johnson. Also affecting the Eastern League was Ned Hanlon's attempt to locate a franchise in the A.L.'s vacated Baltimore territory. Hanlon would be successful in snapping up the old American League park for just $3,000 and in relocating the Montreal franchise to that city.

An Arbitration Committee had been appointed to decide the fate of disputed players (i.e., those who had signed conflicting contracts). Larry Lajoie, Ed Delahanty, Sam Crawford, Harry Davis, Kid Elberfeld, Willie Keeler, Wid Conroy, Wild Bill Donovan and Dave Fultz were all awarded to the American League. Returning to National League clubs were Vic Willis, Tommy Leach, Harry Smith, Rudy Hulswitt, Sam Mertes, Frank Bowerman and — last, but not least — Christy Mathewson.

"A glance at the list of players awarded to each club," summed up the New York *Times*, "shows at once that the American League conceded very little and had all the better of the distribution."

At one point, even a discussion of interleague play "informally" occurred and was alluded to in Article Six — "so that fifteen instead of seven visiting clubs would be seen at each place." But, of course, nothing came of the idea and nothing has come of it to this day.

Peace with the American League was thus largely concluded. Brush attempted to block the settlement in court and even refused to have his Giants play the American League in the 1904 World Series, but basically it was all over.

Ban Johnson had succeeded where Henry Lucas and John Montgomery Ward had failed. He had welded together a strong coalition and held it together against the National League's fiercest attacks.

When the next challenges to Organized Baseball appeared on the horizon, Johnson would find himself on the other side of the barricades.

Chapter 9

Failed Beginnings—Part II

Baseball entered into yet another profitable era following the peace Johnson and Pulliam hammered out. Major league profits grew, and interest exploded in the minors as well. From 1903 to 1914 the minors expanded from 13 to over 40 leagues. Even the intractable John T. Brush caught the spirit of cooperation. "Here's to the American and National leagues!" he toasted after the 1905 World Series. "May they both live long and prosper."

Thrive they did, with a fairly steady upward progression in attendance:

	NATIONAL LEAGUE	AMERICAN LEAGUE
1903	2,390,362	2,344,888
1904	2,664,271	3,024,028
1905	2,734,310	3,120,752
1906	2,781,213	2,938,076
1907	2,640,220	3,398,078
1908	3,512,108	3,611,366
1909	3,496,420	3,739,570
1910	3,494,544	3,270,689
1911	3,231,768	3,339,514

To disguise the majors' profitability, the *Spalding* and *Reach* guides in the teens stopped reporting attendance, but the new stadium-building boom that began in 1909 with Shibe Park could not easily be hidden.

In August 1910, for example, the *Sporting News* ran an article extolling the profitability of big league ball. Utilizing "very conservative" estimates, the publication developed a profit and loss projection for a hypothetical team:

RECEIPTS

13 Saturdays (at home)	$8,000	$104,000
54 week days (home)	2,000	108,000
7 Sundays (abroad)	4,000	28,000
12 Saturdays (abroad)	4,000	48,000
56 week days (abroad)	1,500	84,000
Privileges on home grounds		10,000
		$382,000

EXPENSES

Players' salaries	$75,000
President's salary	25,000
Secretary and assistant salary	8,000
Rent of ball park	20,000
Employees	5,000
Southern training trip	8,000
Traveling expenses	12,000
Incidentals	5,000
Losses by postponements	24,000
Total Expenses	$182,000
Net profit	200,000

Competitors to Organized Baseball arose—so-called "outlaw" leagues—such as the Pacific Coast, Tri-State, California State, Tidewater and Atlantic leagues.

The Burlesquers' League

None of these involved circuits pretending to be of major caliber, but by 1910 real challenges to baseball's monopoly were on the boards.

In August 1910 Ed Butler, a St. Louis theatrical producer, announced formation of a new 12-team major league, featuring New York, Pittsburgh, Philadelphia, St. Louis, Boston, Cleveland, Cincinnati, Louisville, Chicago, Kansas City, St. Paul and Milwaukee. Other backers besides the wealthy Butler included millionaires H. C. Minor of New York and J. E. Fenley of Cincinnati.

"We have been working on this proposition for more than a year," Butler stated, "and . . . we will be ready to get into harness at the opening of the 1911 baseball season. Some of the leading theatrical men of the country are associated with me in this enterprise, and we have the backing of fifty million dollars. . . . It is our plan to draw players from the best circuits in the country on a co-operative basis."

Butler claimed the partnership of George H. Rife of Philadelphia, Colonel J. H. Whalen of Louisville, Herman H. Fehr of St. Paul, H. Wittig of Milwaukee, Harry H. Martell of Brooklyn, James E. Fennessey of Cincinnati, Drew Campbell of Detroit and Cleveland and the Edwards Amusement Company of Boston.

Harry Martell, owner of Brooklyn's Casino and Empire burlesque houses, seemed less confident of the scheme. At first wary of questions, Martell eventually admitted, "If the plan materializes I am in on it. But I had no idea things were in such fine shape." He claimed—and most observers believed him—that he had no plan as to where he would construct a park.

Meanwhile in Pittsburgh, Pirates owner Barney Dreyfuss mocked the idea of Butler's league: "Of course, there is nothing in the story of a new league breaking in here or anywhere next year. It's all a bluff. . . . A bunch of theatrical men are after some advertising, and they have seized upon this baseball stall as a good way of getting it.

"Let them come in if they want to play here. I'll not try and stop them. In fact, I'll even help them. I'll even save them the trouble of finding grounds. . . . I still hold the lease on Exposition Park . . . and I am willing to turn this park over to the new league for exactly the same rental I pay for it. I don't want a cent of profit. The prospective invaders can have it for what it cost me. I don't believe for a second that they will accept the proposition, however. It's the same old wild tale we hear every year, and I am surprised any person yields any credence in the yarn."

Soon the circuit was being tagged the "Burlesquers' League" and ridiculed by such as Horace Fogel of the Phils and Ben Shibe of the Athletics. A's Secretary Frank Hough snorted: "So a lot of theatrical men with a measly $50,000,000 in capital are going to organize a new twelve-club league, eh! Doubtless these gentlemen are successful showmen, but manifestly they have no idea of baseball, or they could have never thought of founding a twelve-club circuit. . . . The National League tried that when it had an absolute monopoly of all the big cities, and it was a most dismal failure."

Hough was exactly right; nothing further was heard from Butler. But in that very same month, events transpired that would lead to yet another threat, as it was announced that fight promoter "Tex" Rickard—the brains behind the Jim Jeffries-Jack Johnson fight—had packaged an ambitious tour of barnstorming big leaguers.

Daniel Fletcher's League

Twelve games, featuring an impressive roster of talent, were to be played following the 1910 World Series between the A's and the Cubs. Players, to be paid $500 to $1,200 each to participate, included outfielders Ty Cobb, Tris Speaker, Clyde Milan, Solly Hofman, Sam Crawford and Sherwood Magee; pitchers Walter Johnson, "Chief" Bender, Orval Overall, George "Wabash" Mullin and Mordecai "Three Finger" Brown; second basemen Johnny Evers and Eddie Collins; shortstops Joe Tinker and Donie Bush; catchers Johnny Kling, Bill "Rough" Carrigan, Oscar Stanage and George "Moon" Gibson; and third basemen Harry Lord and Art Devlin.

John McGraw and Detroit's Hugh Jennings would manage their respective league squads. Trainers from the Cubs and Tigers were engaged to accompany the teams, and it was hoped a "well-known New York surgeon" would also come along.

Cubs second baseman Johnny Evers, a target of Daniel Fletcher's raid on major league talent. (Courtesy of Edward Kennedy.)

Rickard's involvement was controversial. *Sporting Life* was against him and "the intrusion of any prejudicial foreign element into the domain of organized ball." Organized Baseball responded by announcing its own opposition to the tour.

On August 27 the real figures behind the scheme became known. Two Cincinnatians, E. H. Wilbern, "a hotel man, a capitalist, a globe trotter and a seasoned fan," and Jefferson Livingston, head of a preserving company, were prepared to put up between $50,000 and $75,000 to back the tour. A Toledo promoter named Daniel A. Fletcher was business manager for the venture. *Sporting Life* now was impressed by the prospects. It found Wilbern and Livingston "entirely responsible and therefore able to go through with the scheme . . . regardless of the financial outcome."

Nonetheless, it was a time when the magnates frowned on outside sources of income for players; for example, ghostwriting for prominent players was banned. At a special National Commission session on September 1 the door was slammed on the tour. "The National Commission opposes the playing of the series," read a terse statement. "The National League and the American League oppose it. We will not allow it to be played." Baseball simply locked the promoters out of every O.B. park and ordered the return of any advance checks received.

On September 26 Fletcher announced from Cincinnati that the tour was proceeding and that he had letters from Evers, Hofman, Collins, Mullin, Crawford, Stanage, Bush, Johnson and McGraw saying they would honor their contracts. Only one of 34 checks, he claimed, had been returned.

That same day Garry Herrmann charged Fletcher with attempting to form a new major league and claimed he was in possession of copies of contracts Fletcher was circulating for that purpose. "Five or six players," said Herrmann, "have signed contracts offered by the new league. I do not think the new league can exist if it proposes to offer contracts like the one I have seen. The players . . . have been offered bonuses of $10,000 and will become free agents after a few years. . . . [S]uch a league offering such inducements cannot exist very long." The Pittsburgh *Leader* reported that Honus Wagner had signed with Fletcher and that Johnny Evers was about to. The Detroit *Times* reported a conversation between Fletcher and pitcher George Mullin in which Fletcher offered to match Mullin's $5,000 Tigers salary.

Fletcher emanated confidence. "The time for the formation of a new league is ripe," he averred. "I find that many players are greatly dissatisfied. Those who have all-star checks, which the National Commission had advised them to return, are especially sore . . . and are aiding me in my efforts to secure players for the new league."

Fletcher boasted he had letters of support from two of the game's most prominent stars, and despite whispers he would not be able to obtain qualified managers, the promoter insisted he would indeed have no appreciable problem in that regard.

"I have signed no managers whatever," Fletcher admitted. "I will sign none until I get all the star players in line. The heads of the two major leagues claim the third venture will not be a success [because] it has no 'baseball brains' back of it. Well, all I have to say is that they are dead wrong. When I produce contracts signed by all the star players of the two leagues I will have no trouble in the world to get the managers I want."

Walter Johnson, visiting at Comiskey Park, freely admitted he'd signed with Fletcher and that shortstop George McBride, outfielder Clyde Milan and catcher "Gabby" Street had also gone over.

"I do not know exactly how many players have been signed up [but we] will each get a $10,000 bonus if everything goes through all right," commented the pitcher, "and we have assurances from Mr. Fletcher that the possibility of a hitch is past. We will also get an increase in salary, varying from half as much again as we are being paid in the American League. I can't say for sure, but I would bet money on it that every man who has signed a contract for the all-star tour also has a contract to play in the new league next year. As each of us four will pull $10,000 spot cash, I suppose all the others will do the same."

**Walter Johnson (right, shaking hands with Boston's Smoky Joe Wood) admit-
ted signing with Daniel Fletcher, but the great right-hander stayed with the
Senators. (Courtesy of National Baseball Library, Cooperstown, New York.)**

Johnson further explained that the projected league would begin with only
six clubs, as Fletcher desired high quality ball. "Fletcher hasn't any money to
speak of himself," said Johnson, "but I understand he has several millions of
backing. Fletcher isn't a capitalist, as many have been led to believe, but a
promoter—and he's a good one."

When the above was printed, however, Johnson, Milan and Street all wired
Washington's newspapers, denying they'd cast their lot with Fletcher.

On October 3, at a special National League meeting in Cincinnati, N.L.
President Thomas Lynch warned players to return Fletcher's checks or face
severe penalties. "If any attempt is made," he promised, "to cash any of the

certified checks sent out by the promoters of the all-star tour, the Commission will see to it that the original backers of that plan don't suffer any loss. I understand that most of the players have already returned their checks. If this man Fletcher tries to hold up Messrs. Wilbern and Livingston, he will find himself very much up against it. But I don't believe that any big league ballplayer would be guilty of such a dishonorable act. . . . If a man would do a thing like that, I would be in favor of blacklisting him."

The Highlanders' Frank Farrell dismissed the whole plan: "Why it's true that certain players have been approached by Fletcher, . . . but if he doesn't give them cash on February 10 the thing will go up in hot air. It takes big money to organize a . . . league in the leading cities already represented, and I don't believe any capitalists are anxious for a fight with the organized leagues. I am not worrying at all." Reds Business Manager Frank Bancroft echoed Farrell's sentiments: "When the showdown comes, Fletcher will back up."

That same day, October 3, Fletcher was personally feeling the power of Organized Ball. In Cincinnati he resided at the Havlin Hotel, which housed National League teams visiting that town. He was ordered to vacate the premises. In late September Fletcher had been seen buttonholing visiting Cubs at the hostelry.

"It would be a bad business policy," explained the hotel's manager, a Mr. O'Dowd, "to keep Fletcher here when ballclubs are staying with us. The magnates would grow tired of having him approach their men right in front of their eyes. The baseball patronage is a big item with us. For that reason, I asked Fletcher to leave, and he did."

The next day an undaunted Fletcher bragged he would easily have $5,000,000 in capital behind him and that $10,000 advances were no problem at all. Garry Herrmann named pitcher "Three Finger" Brown, catcher Johnny Kling, outfielder Solly Hofman, pitcher Orval Overall and second baseman Johnny Evers of the Cubs, and shortstop Honus Wagner and outfielder Tommy Leach of Pittsburgh as having signed with Fletcher. Some members of the Highlanders and Giants were also said to have received offers.

On Saturday, October 15, Fletcher grandly announced from Cincinnati: "If I were to name all the men who have already signed my contracts I would have the old leagues running up and down in complete despair. . . . I can positively show that I have [Ty] Cobb, [Russell] Ford, [Gabby] Street and [Walter] Johnson. Just these four is a sample, and pretty fair specimens at that."

That same day in Washington, Manager Jimmy McAleer keenly observed, "People have the wrong idea of what this man Fletcher is trying to do in baseball. He is not signing players to contracts. He is merely signing them to options on contracts. If he gets enough options he will probably go to some capitalist or group of capitalists, if he can find them, and say: 'For so much money I can guarantee you certain players with whom to form a new baseball league. If you are willing to produce the cash we can do business. No cash, nothing doing.' In other words, there is no new league in sight, but a promoter who is willing to be liberally recompensed for putting together a new league, providing that he can get anybody to help him out."

October 29 was a big news day. In Chicago Fletcher claimed he had 92 players under contract. In Pittsburgh the United States Realty Company announced that Recreation Park, on the city's north side 20 minutes from downtown, along with several adjacent houses, had been purchased by an agent of the new league for $60,000. Word from Pittsburgh had the circuit including that city, Columbus, Toledo, Louisville, New York, Philadelphia, Cincinnati and St. Louis. It was also alleged that the American Association, long restive, would be supporting Fletcher's league, and that Pittsburgh businessmen were being solicited to purchase stock in the local franchise.

The *Sporting News* was not impressed by news of the Recreation Park transaction. "How puerile!" the paper editorialized. "A couple of hundred dollars for a deed and a little mortgage is really all is required to be able to say, 'I own a park worth hundreds of thousands.'"

By October 31 it was revealed that most of the players signed for Fletcher's barnstorming tour—now reduced to only 10 games at a Kansas City amusement park—had lost confidence in the scheme and were returning their checks. These included Ty Cobb, George Mullin, Solly Hofman and "Three Finger" Brown.

Nonetheless, that same day Fletcher was in Chicago, again displaying his 92 "contracts" and confidently stating, "I will be in a position in the near future to give the players assurance of significant capital to carry the proposition to a successful state." Fletcher maintained he would take control of land in Chicago and construct a park over the winter. Franchises in the league were now promised for Chicago, New York, Boston, Cincinnati, Cleveland, Washington and either St. Louis or Kansas City.

A November 1910 report held that Fletcher had signed 12 members of the Chicago Cubs. Cubs President Charles W. "Chubby Charlie" Murphy fired off an angry statement, saying that Cubs fans "will not lose any sleep over the fear of losing any of their favorites . . . if what our attorney says is true. We have options on their services for next season. . . . These options would probably be held to be prior to the ones signed with Fletcher and which attorneys say are not worth the paper they are written on." Murphy threatened anyone backing Fletcher with suits in every state having a National League team.

"Promoters who are dashing around," concluded Murphy, "making wild statements and changing their linen in newspaper offices, being minus hotel bills, naturally fell in with such players and take advantage of the restive condition which is marked by avarice and greed."

This was the season of the "third league." A November report had the American Association on the verge of becoming a rival. Association President Thomas M. Calvington and Kansas City President George Tebeau strongly backed the scheme. It was even thought Organized Baseball would give the A.A. its blessing so as to forestall Fletcher's threat. Association magnates contended, reported the *Sporting News*, "that it is not necessary to declare war on the major leagues, believing that in another year they will be able to show . . . that a third major league is bound to come into the field, either outlaw or protected, and that they will agree to allow it to enter the field or trouble will occur."

By late November the established clubs had signed most of their personnel to contracts, and in January 1911 Fletcher conceded his prospects for the new season were dim, but insisted that he would be on the field for 1912.

"Magnates of the major leagues would like to convince people, and to make themselves believe, that I am through fighting," opined the still wildly optimistic promoter in an interview with the Pittsburgh *Leader*. "I have only just begun. One year hence the real war will be fought out. My project is a legitimate business undertaking that the baseball trust can neither checkmate nor gobble up. I am not promoting a third big league, but forming one real major league of star caliber. The magnates like to refer to me as a joke. Let them smile now — my laugh comes later. The star players, the fans, and the press made baseball. Greedy club owners are reaping all the profits. We will emancipate the players from their bondage and furnish patrons of the game the high-class article of sport to which they are entitled. When our league is formed, of star players only, all of whom have expressed their eagerness to become affiliated, . . . the National and American leagues' clubs will be unable to muster forces sufficiently strong to hold their own with the Eastern [International] League and American Association clubs. It is a fact easily proven that [their] reserve clauses will not hold in court. In fact, I believe the stipulations contained in these documents are contrary to the Constitution of the United States. For want of sufficient time and capital I was unable to get my league under way for this year, but we will start in 1912 with a strictly all-star organization. I have the players, and have secured splendid sites for grounds in every desirable city."

Shortly afterward his erstwhile backers, Wilbern and Livingston, were reported heading for Australia to plan a "major league" as well as bring a big league team, possibly Clark Griffith's Cincinnati Reds, to tour there under official auspices.

At the same time it was announced that $5,000 in checks for their unsuccessful barnstorming tour were still unreturned. Christy Mathewson and Ty Cobb both held certified checks in the amount of $1,000, while Gabby Street, Harry Lord, Chief Bender, Johnny Evers, Tris Speaker and Art Devlin still possessed drafts for $500 each.

Fletcher was done, eventually "flying the coop" to avoid paying $200 in printing bills. But soon two seemingly real threats were on the horizon: the Columbian League and the United States League.

SPORTING LIFE

DEVOTED TO BASE BALL AND TRAP SHOOTING

Vol. 58—No. 24   Philadelphia, February 17, 1912   Price 5 Cents

IS BUILDING ON SAND!

The President of the Proposed Outlaw United States League Announces a Policy as Regards Contracts With, and Reservations of, Players Which Foredooms the Organization to Utter Failure.

JACOB DAUBERT.

SPORTING LIFE

DEVOTED TO BASE BALL AND TRAP SHOOTING

Vol. 58—No. 21   Philadelphia, January 27, 1912   Price 5 Cents

WARNING TO PLAYERS!

Ball Players Under Contract or Reservation to Clubs in Organized Ball Should Not Permit Themselves to Be Blinded or Cajoled By the Specious Promises of Promoters of Shadowy Outlaw Leagues.

FRANK L. BODIE,
Outfielder of the Chicago American League Club.

The Columbian League

Both enterprises sent initial shock waves through Organized Baseball. *Sporting Life* headlined in January 1912, "WARNING TO PLAYERS! Ball Players Under Contract or Reservation to Clubs in Organized Ball Should Not Permit Themselves to Be Blinded or Cajoled by the Specious Promises of Promoters of Shadowy Outlaw Leagues." The *Sporting News* printed a cartoon in reference to the Columbian League questioning the ability of fans to support a third league.

The Columbian League was the brainchild of John T. Powers, organizer of the Class D Wisconsin State League in the fall of 1904. That work was not easy. Said Powers at the time: "I hadn't anticipated what a thorny path I had before me, and I attribute my staying powers to the several years' experience I had in . . . a score or more of local amateur leagues in Chicago."

In February 1912 Powers announced the Columbian League's formation, with clubs in Cleveland, Chicago and St. Louis. In St. Louis, the *Sporting News* correspondent used the visit of Powers in February to tweak Browns and Cardinals owners for their closed-door policy toward the press.

"If the Columbian League should establish itself in St. Louis," he noted, "operated by men who evidently know the value of publicity and are keen for it, the Cardinal and Brown owners would awaken to the realization of what it means to be on the soft side of the boys who boom or blast base ball by the typewriter route."

Meanwhile Powers continued onward. "We are not fighting capital with capital," said Powers, "and do not seek a fight with any person or combination. But we have the right to exist and compete with the 'baseball trust.'"

In March, however, his scheme collapsed when one of his prime backers, St. Louis brewer Otto Steifel, backed out. Powers put his idea—temporarily—into mothballs.

The United States League Organizes

Meanwhile a United States League (not to be confused with an identically named league back in 1910; that circuit threatened to break baseball's color bar) was propounded by William Abbott Witman of Reading, Pennsylvania.

Born on October 19, 1860, Witman began as a machinist but soon became a highly successful contractor and dealer in coal and sand. As a builder he left his mark on Reading, erecting a seven-story Japanese-style pagoda atop Mount Penn and an incline railway to that peak. An active Democrat, Witman was first

Opposite: *Sporting Life* **made its position on "outlaw" leagues clear in these two Page 1 headlines early in 1912.**

William Abbott Witman, mastermind of the United States League.

elected to the City Council from the Eighth Ward in 1886 and would unsuccessfully run five times for mayor.

Witman had backed a Reading club in the Pennsylvania State League of
the 1890s. He owned a ballpark at Eleventh and Exeter Streets, grandly called
the "Circus Maximus" and "considered at the time of its completion in 1909
one of the best athletic fields in the East." It later became the stadium for
Albright College.

Witman would face no competition in placing a United States League team
in his home town. Reading's Tri-State League club had come to an end on
July 4, 1911, when the stands at Lauer's Field had collapsed.

Witman was elected president and secretary-treasurer of the USL. Captain
Marshall Henderson of Pittsburgh was elected vice president. The lively
Goldsmith ball was adopted as official, as was a 128-game schedule. Except
for territorial rights, the rules of the National Agreement were in force.

Cap Anson endeavored to purchase either the Washington or New York
franchise and wanted badly to manage in the circuit. Anson later attempted to
buy the Reading franchise for relocation to Buffalo, but Witman refused to sell.
At first glance, Anson's backing would seem desirable, but Cap had fallen on

hard times. Elected Chicago City Clerk in 1905, Anson came under official investigation in 1906, and was turned out of office in 1907. Soon afterward he would declare bankruptcy.

In January 1912 as the United States League unveiled plans to invade Brooklyn, Charles Ebbets announced the purchase of land for a new park for his National League team. "Oh yes," chortled the *Sporting News,* "anybody can start a major league, all he needs is to get the ear of a base ball scribbler who has space to fill. But what is the counter of the 'third major league' to Mr. Ebbets? It seems to be its next move and the place has been set."

At the same time the paper noted the Class C Wisconsin-Illinois League was facing a rumored "outlaw" competitor. "Is it possible," it jibed, "that the United States League has again changed its base? Will it bob up its threatening head in [this] territory next? Well, it will cost less to build a grandstand in Clarinda than in Gotham."

In February Witman issued a statement designed to upset the baseball world: he would honor existing contracts but would ignore the reserve clause.

Witman, mocked sportswriter Jimmy Isaminger, "has announced . . . an emancipation of all base ball slaves. As the United States League hasn't signed a single player up to date and has no control over any organized players, it is hard to see who this new Abraham Lincoln emancipated."

Sporting Life ran a banner headline: "IS BUILDING ON SAND! The President of the Proposed Outlaw United States League Announces a Policy as Regards Contracts With, and Reservations of, Players Which Foredooms the Organization to Utter Failure."

Witman, the *Sporting News* charged, either "does not expect his organization to be a permanent one, or he is woefully ignorant of the chief bulwark of permanency. . . .

"Any one with brains enough to provide for the morrow—and the Lord takes care of only the lilies of the field—realizes the reserve rule, rigidly enforced and honestly obeyed, is vitally essential to the life of the game. . . ."

"We have no right to object to them, no right to annoy them," placidly observed Garry Herrmann, but few other O.B. figures had anything even remotely kind to say about the United States League.

"Why, these fellows talk as if they could start a new league on a postage stamp," commented National League President Thomas J. Lynch on December 30, 1911. "Can they not realize that before they put a team in the field they would have to spend $5,000,000? Sounds big, doesn't it? However, they would have to spend every penny of it. . . . If they want . . . to fight the big leagues they must play big league ball in big league plants. . . .

"Where do these leagues expect to get their players? Do they think men who are now drawing big league salaries . . . will fall for their offers? They might offer special inducements, but well does the big leaguer know what a hopeless chance the new concern would have. Would he take a chance of being

Thomas J. Lynch, National League president, 1910–14.

placed on the blacklist for a few hundred dollars more than he is getting? Besides what demand is there for a third big league? There is none. . . .

"Who would stand a war of this sort better—we, with our modern plants, fast teams and patronage, or those promoters, who have neither plants nor teams and are not even sure that the public will take kindly to them?"

"The [Columbian and United States] leagues have no financial backing as far as I know," commented Ban Johnson. "You cannot build ballparks in a night, and neither league is in condition to start the season. It is preposterous to think that either will prove a success when . . . it takes millions of dollars nowadays to finance a major league or even a good-sized minor. Then where are they going to get their players? Practically every man in the major leagues has been signed, and fans are not likely to patronize prairie leaguers."

"We have not taken Mr. Johnson into our confidence," replied Powers, "in securing our financial backing, and for that reason he knows nothing of our finances. Very little is known about the money back of the prominent major league clubs. There is no reason to suppose that we would be any more indiscreet. . . . As for the class of players on our lists, Mr. Johnson is equally ignorant. We have not announced the . . . players . . . whose signatures we hold. All that will be done on time. Until then Mr. Johnson's judgement of them is of little value to himself or to prospective patrons of the games we will play."

In mid–February at a United States League meeting in Cleveland, bad news started to seep out. It was announced that Charles White, backer of the New York franchise, was having difficulty in obtaining a playing field. Even more ominous was White's absence from the session, pleading the press of "politics."

The *Sporting News* conceded there was "unusual enthusiasm" for the league in Richmond and Reading, but that these localities were "very inferior" minor league towns. "In Washington, Pittsburgh, Cleveland and Cincinnati, where the big leagues are now doing business, there is not a great deal of interest."

Witman had to admit the quality of his players was not exactly big league— in fact, it was between that found in A and B classification leagues.

Brooklyn owner Amos Hussey, backer of a successful semipro team in the borough, was incensed:

> It's major league ball or nothing. That was the understanding when I cast in my lot. I can make a good living at my park under conditions that have existed—more money than could be expected from any dinky league. If the United States League backs down now it can go crash. And I'll do all in my power to help it on its fall. I have five former major leaguers under contract and I'm willing to put a club of major league class into Brooklyn. If the rest of these fellows have been fourflushing, the sooner I find out the better. I'm willing to take chances on a new venture, but I'm not going to toss off a sure thing on a joke.

"This is no dream league," Witman advanced from Reading on March 23. "We have a compact circuit and financial backing that assures at least one full season. In Cleveland, Washington, Pittsburgh and Cincinnati there will be few, if any, conflicting dates with major league clubs already in those cities. . . . The report that some of our cities are shaky is absolutely untrue."

Witman's strategy was to field teams with "name" managers (such as "Deacon" Phillippe at Pittsburgh and "Rowdy Jack" O'Connor at Cleveland; O'Connor had been let go as Browns manager after the 1910 batting race controversy in which St. Louis went out of its way to give the crown to Larry Lajoie). Rosters would be filled out with either promising newcomers (often just local semipros) or with washed-up former marginal major leaguers. Reports did exist, though, of contracts being offered to such as the Braves' Harry Steinfeldt (a rather paltry $300 a month to manage and play for the U.S.L.'s Cincinnati team).

The players lured to the United States League (which unlike the previous attempts actually got off the ground) were a motley crew. Perhaps the biggest name was 1909 Giants 18-game winner Arthur "Bugs" Raymond, who pitched for its Cincinnati club. Raymond was a pitcher of some talent, but his dipsomania had caused John McGraw no end of worries. A favorite trick of his when called on to warm up the Giants bullpen was to take the ball he had been given across the street to a saloon and trade it for a few shots of booze.

Shortly after the 1912 United States League campaign ended, Bugs came to an unfortunate but appropriately pathetic end. Reduced to pitching semipro games in Chicago, he was at a field on the Windy City's northwest side, where he became embroiled in an argument with several neighborhood hooligans. Knocked to the ground, the former big league star was kicked repeatedly in the head. He suffered a fractured skull and expired two days later in a seedy hotel room he shared with his long-suffering wife and children. His United States League teammates would be his pallbearers.

Former Giants and Superbas catcher Joe "Gummy" Wall signed with New York. "Wall was a fabulous character," wrote Al Schacht. "He was about thirty then and built solid, and always wore a dirty old New York Giants uniform. When he was managing semipro teams, he used to send the box scores to the New York *Press*, which . . . carried all the box scores of Sunday's semipro games. According to the *Press*, Wall batted about .950. Every time he reported a game, he listed himself as hitting 4-for-5 or 5-for-5. The funny part was, we found out later, Joe couldn't read or write, but dictated his reports to his brother."

Schacht (the papers referred to him as "Shack") later went on to pitch for the Washington Senators. For the U.S.L. he played for the Cleveland Forest Citys. His previous experience had been as batting practice pitcher at the Polo Grounds and earlier that year at Erie in the Class C Ohio-Pennsylvania League.

Schacht relieved in the home opener at Chicago's Gunter Field, striking out 11 and getting the win as Cleveland rallied to win 15–8.

"Tom Murphy," recalled Schacht, "owner of the Cleveland club, was so elated that at a victory party at the Sherman Hotel that evening he presented me with his very own beautiful gold watch and chain as a token of his appreciation. Believe it or not, the next morning after breakfast, while proudly wearing the watch on my vest, I was leaning out the window of my room on the seventh floor of the hotel, idly watching traffic below, when the chain slipped loose and the watch fell out. It was smashed to a million pieces on the sidewalk. And I felt that my heart went with it."

Former American League home run king Ralph "Socks" Seybold and ex–A's reserve catcher Bert Blue signed with Richmond. Seybold was 41 and had last appeared in the big leagues in 1908, when he had mustered only a .215 average for the A's. In spring training of 1909 he had broken a leg and was released. Blue had appeared in only 17 major league games. In 1911 he'd led the Class D Ohio State League with a .347 average in 126 games.

Cleveland's roster included ex–Senators first baseman Jerry Freeman, catcher Howard Wakefield (father of outfielder Dick Wakefield) and pitcher "Doc" Moyer. They also featured ex–Cardinals outfielder Joe Delahanty.

Washington inked former White Sox second baseman Gus Dundon, ex–White Sox backstop Frank Owens (who would surface again in the Federal

Former Pirates pitching star Charles "Deacon" Phillippe was tabbed to manage the Pittsburgh club in the United States League.

League), and ex–Cubs and Braves pitcher Big Jeff Pfeffer (he lost 22 games in 1906).

Reading's personnel included Charles Malay, who had played second for Brooklyn in 1905; 38-year-old Jack Cronin, who had hurled in the majors as long ago as 1895; third baseman Artie Brouthers (who would also play for Pittsburgh of the U.S.L.), who had hit .208 in 36 games for the 1906 A's; and Sam Fletcher (0-1 for Brooklyn in 1909), who would surface with two games for the 1912 Reds.

The Chicago Green Sox signed 37-year-old outfielder Louis Gertenrich. Lou had last appeared in the big leagues in 1903 with Pittsburgh for one game; his previous record had been two games with Milwaukee of the 1901 American

League. Chicago's most-talented player was shortstop Ernie Johnson, who went on to play 810 games in 10 seasons in the Federal and American leagues.

The U.S.L.'s Brooklyn roster was constituted largely of the local Ridgewood semipro team. All players signed were free agents.

The U.S.L. talent pool was not impressive. While any high minor league can boast of having a sprinkling of ex- and future major leaguers, it is still worthwhile to note which players of those categories appeared in U.S.L. uniforms. U.S.L. expert Frank Phelps provides the following list:

PLAYER	USL TEAM	POS.	MAJOR LEAGUE CAREER
Bill Bartley	Cincinnati	p	1903 N.Y. (N.L.), '06–07 Phil. (A.L.)
Bert Blue	Richmond	c	1908 Phil.-St. L. (A.L.)
Artie Brouthers	Reading	1b	1906 Phil. (A.L.)
George Browne	Washington	of	12 yrs. 1901–12
Frank Bruggy	New York	c	5 yrs. 1921–25
Kid Carsey	Washington	Mgr.	10 yrs. 1891–1901 (as pitcher)
Jack Cronin	Reading	p	7 yrs. 1895–1904
Lee Dashner	Cincinnati	p	1913 Cleve. (A.L.)
Joe Delahanty	Cleveland	of	1907–09 St. L. (N.L.)
Gus Dundon	Washington	if	1904–06 Chi. (A.L.)
Hack Eibel	Reading	1b	1912 Cleve. (A.L.), '20 Bos. (A.L.)
Charlie Fallon	Washington	of	1905 N.Y. (A.L.)
Sam Fletcher	Reading	p	1909 Bkln. (N.L.), '12 Cinc. (N.L.)
Lou Gertenrich	Chicago	of	1901 Milw. (A.L.), '03 Pitt. (N.L.)
George Hogan	Cincinnati	p	1914 K.C. (F.L.)
Sam Hope	New York	p	1907 Phil. (A.L.)
Ernie Johnson	Chicago	ss	10 years, 1912–25
Burt Keeley	Chicago	Mgr.	1908–09 Wash. (A.L.) (as pitcher)
Harry Kirsch	Cleveland	p	1910 Cleve. (A.L.)
Charlie Malay	Cleveland	if	1905 Bkln. (N.L.)
Ed McDonough	Chicago	c	1909–10 Phil. (N.L.)
Hexmas McFarland	Richmond	of	5 yrs., 1896–1903
Tom McGuire	Chicago	p	1914 Chi. (F.L.), '19 Chi. (A.L.)
Bob Meinke	Chicago	ss	1910 Cinc. (N.L.)
Fred Mollenkamp	Cincinnati	1b	1914 Phil. (N.L.)
Jack O'Connor	Cleveland	Mgr.	21 yrs. 1887–1910 (as catcher)
Frank Owen	Washington	p	8 yrs., 1901–09
Big Jeff Pfeffer	Washington	p	6 yrs., 1905–11
Deacon Phillippe	Pittsburgh	p	13 yrs., 1897–1911
Bugs Raymond	Chicago-Cincinnati	p	6 yrs., 1904–11
Claude Ritchey	Pittsburgh	2b	13 yrs., 1897–1909
Al Schacht	Cleveland	p	1919–21 Wash. (A.L.)
Ralph Seybold	Richmond	of	9 yrs., 1899–1908
Ben Taylor	Cincinnati	p	1912 Cinc. (N.L.)
Howard Wakefield	Cleveland	c	1905, '07, Clev. (A.L.), '06 Wash. (A.L.)
Joe Wall	New York	1b	1901–02 N.Y. (N.L.), '02 Bkln. (N.L.)

On March 25 *Sporting Life* reported that Charles White of the projected New York franchise had admitted failure in finding grounds on Manhattan and was throwing in the towel.

"You can say that the Brooklyn club is undecided whether or not to stay in the circuit or not," an increasingly nervous Amos Hussey of Brooklyn declared on March 26. "Buffalo was the logical selection because it broke the long jump from here to Cleveland, Cincinnati and Pittsburgh. There was good backing for a club in Buffalo, and we regret that Witman did not accept it. . . . The United States League has been botched so far, and doesn't look any too good for Brooklyn."

Clubs for the upcoming season were shaping up as follows:

CLUB	PRESIDENT
Chicago	William C. Niesen
Cincinnati	John J. Ryan
Cleveland	W. L. Murphy
New York	William Jordan
Pittsburgh	William T. McCullough
Reading	William A. Witman
Richmond	E. C. Landgraf
Washington	Kohley Miller

Rumors circulated that Brooklyn demanded each club post a $5,000 bond with the league, something the others were loath to do. Brooklyn was also dissatisfied with the condition of the Washington franchise, and its resignation was reputedly coming in a few days. Despite reservations, Brooklyn momentarily remained, only to drop out before Opening Day.

Umpires named by Witman were George Goodhart of Reading, Bill Massey of Philadelphia, Joe Bailey of St. Louis, John Quinn of Chicago, Arlie Latham of New York and Henry Tone of New York. The first five had been ballplayers, and Latham was quite well-known. Tone was described by the New York *Times* as having "considerable experience as an umpire in semi-professional games."

U.S.L. Ballparks

Pittsburgh played at Exhibition Park, the old American Association, Players' League and National League park; New York finally settled in at the rough Bronx Oval at 163rd Street and Southern Boulevard; at Richmond, Rebels owner E. C. Landgraf built 7,000-seat Lee Park in just 27 days at Altamont Street near Moore Street, since Broad Street Park was in use by the Class C Virginia League; Reading played at Witman's "Circus Maximus," Brooklyn at Ridgewood Park, Cincinnati at Gilbert's Park, Chicago at Gunther Park at North Clark Street and Leland Avenue and Washington at Union League Park.

Cleveland Forest Citys owner W. L. Murphy set up offices at the city's Gillsy Hotel on April 10 and soon signed a lease with Luna Park, a popular and fairly new local amusement park four miles to the East of downtown at Woodhill Road and Woodland Avenue. In mid–April construction began, and by month's end a 4,600-seat facility was completed for $15,000. Anyone purchasing either a 25 or 50-cent ticket to the Forest Citys would be admitted free to the rest of the park. Monday and Thursday afternoons were designated as Ladies' Days.

The United States League Season of 1912

To the amazement of observers the League was actually launched on Wednesday, May 1, in Washington, where Richmond triumphed 2–0. At Cincinnati, Chicago won 5–4, and at Cleveland Pittsburgh took an 11–7 contest.

At the Bronx Oval, Reading and New York opened up with a band from the Catholic Protectory playing; a local dignitary, James A. Delehey, Clerk of the Bronx Supreme Court, throwing out the first ball; and President Witman wearing "a contented smile throughout the afternoon." Between 2,000 and 2,500 fans were in attendance. The teams played to a 10–10 ten-inning tie, called at 6:25 p.m. on account of darkness.

The local press displayed different degrees of tolerance for the new league, but indications were the quality of play was distinctly poor. The New York *American* noted with great forbearance that the league "did not look like the joke organized baseball has been prone to regard it. The opening day exercises assumed big league character. The teams were rigged out in the classiest style. . . . The game wasn't the greatest but fairly interesting nevertheless. . . . Good ball would be impossible at the grounds just yet. The field is in very bad shape because a mountain had to be removed from the north wall. . . . The outfielders took their lives in their hands every time they went after a fly. . . ."

The New York *Sun* was less tolerant: "It wasn't major league or minor league ball. . . . It was outlaw ball masquerading under a high sounding name . . . and barring two men, Joe Wall, a local semi-professional, and Jack Cronin, who once pitched for the Giants and Brooklyn, not a player in uniform was familiar to the fans."

Besides poor baseball, this game was plagued by further low comedy: "A lone taxicab containing women rolled through the left field gate. The chauffeur, in spite of noisy warnings, drove to a point behind second base, where suddenly the wheels sunk to the hubs in the loose earth. Much chug chugging. Then . . . 20 laborers to the rescue. The cab was slowly dragged back upon solid ground and the crowd stood up and cheered."

The New York *Times* emphasized the fashions of the day. "The New York Players," its reporter noted, "were nattily attired in cream colored uniforms, trimmed with narrow black braid, black stockings with white stripes and black caps. The name 'New York' adorns the front of the blouse. They also have gray sweater coats with the monogram 'N Y' on them. The Reading players wore uniforms of blueish gray with black trimmings. On the left arm of the shirt was a red and blue shield on which was printed a white R."

The box score:

READING	AB	R	H	PO	A	NEW YORK	AB	R	H	PO	A
Sheckard, cf	5	1	2	0	0	Noyes, 3b	4	1	0	4	4
Malay, lf	4	0	1	3	1	Freyer, ss	6	2	3	3	6
Brouthers, 2b	4	3	2	3	4	Wall, 1b	6	1	1	7	1
Dieters, 3b	5	2	1	0	1	Bruggy, c	5	1	3	8	3
Beal, rf	6	1	3	1	0	Young, rf	2	1	0	0	0
Pettit, 1b	6	0	3	7	1	Hynes, 2b	2	1	1	7	1
Broderick, ss	2	1	0	3	2	Tierney, cf	2	2	0	1	0
*Cronin	1	0	0	0	0	Hope, p	0	0	0	0	0
Manning, ss	0	0	0	0	0	Peterson, p	4	1	1	0	1
Porte, c	3	1	2	2	2						
Fletcher, p	2	1	2	0	1						
Milliman, p	3	0	0	1	3						
	41	10	16	30	15		39	10	10	30	18

Reading	2 2 1	0 1 1	0 0 0	3 – 10
New York	0 0 0	4 0 1	2 0 0	3 – 10

Errors – Noyes, Brouthers, Beal, Manning, Porte, Fletcher
* – Batted for Broderick in 9th inning

Two-base hits – Freyer, Bruggy (2), Beal, Pettit. Sacrifice hits – Young (2), Malay, Porte. Stolen bases – Bruggy, Malay, Brouthers, Dieters (2), Broderick, Porte. First base on errors – New York 3; Reading 1. Left on bases – New York 11; Reading 11. Double plays – Malay, Broderick, Pettit and Brouthers; Bruggy and Hynes. Struck out – By Peterson, 6; by Fletcher, 6; by Milliman, 4. Bases on balls – Off Hope, 1; off Peterson, 6; off Fletcher, 3; off Milliman, 5. Hit by pitches – By Peterson (Broderick); by Fletcher (Bruggy, Hynes). Wild pitches – Milliman 2. Passed ball – Porte. Hits – Off Hope 2 in one inning (at bat 5); off Peterson 14 in nine innings (at bat 36); off Fletcher 2 in three and one-third innings (at bat 11); off Milliman 8 in five and two-thirds innings (at bat 28). Umpire – Mr. Tone. Time of game – 2 hours and 50 minutes.

Not much improvement in play occurred in the next few games. Reading's Doc Cronin beat New York's Sammy Smith 5–2 and struck out 12 before 300 paying fans while 200 others peered on for free from beyond the fence. The *Times* observed, "The veteran [Cronin] wore a much larger belt than in the days when he last showed his slants to a New York crowd...."

In the ninth inning a delivery wagon parked beyond right field pulled away, and some fans "of the deadhead variety" were sent flying.

N.L. President Lynch (left) and his A.L. counterpart Johnson seemed confident the United States League would go up in smoke.

Reading won again (6–2) on Friday, May 3, as the *Times* headlined, "SMALL CROWD IN BRONX/ New York Not Enthusiastic Over Invasion of New United States League." The big news of the game was Heine Dieters, the Reading third baseman, slugging umpire Harry Tone after a called third strike in the first inning. In the sixth, New York first baseman "Gummy" Wall became so upset over being charged with an error that he dispatched the bat boy to the official scorer to protest the decision, alibing that the sun was in his eyes. "Wall," noted the *Times* with some sarcasm and a little confusion in tenses, "would make a great first sacker in the old Cloudy Day League."

The 1912 season featured perhaps the most bone-chilling weather in baseball history. Take for example, the experience of Cleveland. After a decent

Opening Day crowd of 3,697, the following days' crowds numbered just 562 and 423, respectively. The weather was atrocious. In the season's first three weeks the Forest Citys played ten dates at home and four away but lost six more to the climate—including, most unfortunately, three Sundays.

While the established leagues had the capital to survive, the U.S.L. did not. "We have enough money to pay salaries for the entire season," said Witman in one of his less-lucid moments, "even if not a single fan comes into our grounds." Soon attendance was averaging between 300 and 400 fans—then even less. Within two weeks crowds were so sparse in Cincinnati that the team was forced to play all games on the road. On May 23 Cleveland collapsed. The following day Manager George Browne of Washington, as well as most of his players, quit in disgust over back pay. Witman labeled Brown a "troublemaker."

In mid–May, an incident involving the American League's Detroit Tigers gave rise to rumors of major player defections to the United States League. The cause was a unique incident in major league annals. On May 12, 1912, at New York's Highland Park, Ty Cobb became engaged in a brawl with a fan who had been razzing him mercilessly. When Cobb was suspended indefinitely by Ban Johnson, his teammates rose to his defense, contending a "grave injustice" had been committed, and on May 18 the team staged an unprecedented strike. Rumors arose that the strikers would jump to the U.S.L., and it is believed five (Cobb, Jim Delahanty, Sam Crawford, George Mullin and Donie Bush) actually were tendered contracts. However, the revolt soon fizzled, and all players were soon docilely back with Detroit.

Witman attempted placing the Washington franchise back together; meanwhile, Marshall Henderson, president of the Pittsburgh franchise, tried to lure wealthy St. Louis brewer Otto Steifel into purchasing the defunct Cleveland club and giving it a home in St. Louis.

Only Pittsburgh and Richmond were making money. Pittsburgh enjoyed the best press coverage in the league. With good crowds at Richmond, more U.S.L. games were rescheduled there, but the glut of contests caused attendance to taper off.

On May 27 New York forfeited a game on its own field to Chicago when just 50 fans showed up. Owner Tom Cronin, a Bronx politician, gave up the next day, and Witman declared the franchise forfeit. He called an emergency meeting in Pittsburgh for May 29 to explore the following options:

1. Continue on with only six clubs.
2. Replace the New York and Cleveland clubs.
3. Retreat from the East by moving Reading and Washington to the West.
4. Go out of business.

On Memorial Day, Reading played its last home game and was preparing to pull up stakes for a new location. Attendance was so poor that on May 30

Cincinnati, despite having another game to play at Reading the next day, simply headed home.

Reading started the season with a 12-3 record, then collapsed into a nine-game losing streak. Players such as Charlie Malay (who Witman said was released) deserted the franchise when they weren't paid.

O.B. scouts began to descend on Reading, hoping to pick up the pieces. The better Reading players contracted with various clubs. Sam Fletcher was signed by Cincinnati, Hack Eibel by Cleveland, Frank Sheckard by Providence, George Pettit by the St.Louis Browns, Doc Milliman and Ed Porte by York of the Tri-State League, Bollinger by London of the Class C Canadian League, Berkel by a Class C Western Association club and Dieters by a Virginia League team. Even Reading Manager Leo Groom was signing a contract to scout for the Browns.

"The fact that many of the United States League's leading players were signed even before the league disbanded is proof the quality of the ball wasn't the worst," contends scholar Frank Phelps.

On June 1 Witman filed for voluntary bankruptcy in United States District Court in Philadelphia. His assets were listed at $52,030, including the Reading ballpark, valued at $50,000, while liabilities amounted to $53,806, including $750 in unpaid player salaries.

"This step," averred Witman on June 6, "was taken for the protection of those of my creditors who have honest claims that might have been jeopardized when they became due." He alleged a "combination of Organized Baseball and political forces" had been organized to "trim" him.

That same day, Richmond dropped out. At Pittsburgh on June 3–4, the remaining cities met to try to finish out the season. Indianapolis and St. Louis were designated to replace Washington and New York. Pittsburgh's Marshall Henderson was named league president, but it was too late. On June 3 New Yorker John J. Ryan, the owner of the Cincinnati club, threw in the towel. It was thought at the time that his was the only club not behind in salaries, but on June 4 14 Cincinnati players—Harry Armbruster, James Barton, Fred Bierman, Leo Witterstatter, William J. Bartley, Thomas Crowe, Lee Dashner, Dennis Hicks, Ben Taylor, George Hogan, Fred Mollenkamp, Ollie Chapman, Fred Badel and Harry Cornell—filed suits for a total of $1,200 in back pay.

Meanwhile at Exhibition Park, the Pittsburgh and Reading teams played five games just to keep busy—it was a sorry postscript to a sorry league.

Yet there was still one more fading gasp to this circuit. On June 17 at New York's Olympic Field, a Negro club, the Lincoln Giants, behind the great Dick "Cannonball" Redding, defeated a team titled the "All Leaguers," composed of the remnants of the United States League, mostly from its Washington and New York teams. Al Schacht pitched for the "All Leaguers." Redding struck out 24 and allowed only three hits in just one hour and twenty minutes.

"This organization," summed up the 1913 *Reach Guide*, ". . . went the way of all 'houses builded on sand,' after just one month of wretched existence. The organization had neither officials, circuit, or magnates to commend themselves to the public; or players to attract or hold patronage. Furthermore, there was no baseball brain to plan and direct, no courage to combat and circumvent adverse conditions, and no capital to help the organization over the inevitable losing initial season."

The United States League of 1913

Witman was not a man to be easily defeated, however, and he spent months reorganizing for another effort. On January 5, 1913, a new eight-club circuit was announced. A meeting was held on May 4, 1913, in Philadelphia to draw up a schedule. Witman was again elected president; Hugh McKinnon of Lynchburg, vice president; and Harvey C. Boyer of Reading, secretary. A 126-game schedule, beginning Saturday, May 10, and ending September 27 was drawn up. No games were to be played on the Sabbath. Rosters were made up "almost 100 percent of unknowns, sandlotters," according to Frank Phelps.

Presidents of the 1913 version of the United States League:

CLUB	PRESIDENT
New York	David Driscoll
Brooklyn	Leo Groom
Newark	James A. Timony
Reading	William A. Witman
Philadelphia	George Brubaker
Baltimore	A. N. Elrod
Washington	Wilfred Carsey
Lynchburg	Harvey C. Boyer

The League started as planned on May 10, 1913, but that was the last thing that went right for this star-crossed circuit. On Sunday, May 11, New York refused to take the field in Newark because that club had not paid the $75 guarantee owed New York for the season's opener.

A similar incident occurred with Brooklyn, which opened against Washington in the nation's capital on May 10. Brooklyn refused to play on Monday, May 12, due to Washington's failure to deliver its guarantee.

On Sunday night, May 11, in Washington both that city and New York were expelled; the U.S.L. would continue with six clubs. However, attendance on Monday was so sparse the league collapsed immediately, with even Witman disgusted. "This," summed up *Sporting Life*, "proved the quickest and most ridiculous failure in the long history of base ball, a history teeming with ill-advised club and league ventures and with failures of small and great degree."

Only one performance of note occurred in this abbreviated season. On Opening Day, a Reading pitcher named Yerkes tallied three of the team's 11 hits and picked six runners off first. He had plenty of opportunities to work on his move, having put 18 runners on base with six hits, 11 walks and one error.

And thus ended the United States League, one of the most pathetic ventures in baseball annals. But as the U.S.L. was expiring, the Columbian League was reconstituting itself under a new name—the Federal League.

It would not pass on as quietly as Witman's circuit.

Chapter 10

The Federal League

As the United States League collapsed, John T. Powers moved steadfastly ahead with plans to revive his Columbian League.

The 1913 Federal League

On February 17, 1913, in Grand Rapids, Michigan, Powers announced a resuscitated circuit consisting of Grand Rapids, Detroit, Chicago, Indianapolis, Kansas City, Cincinnati, Cleveland and one unnamed other city; the league was to begin play that season. While in Grand Rapids, Powers leased Ramona Athletic Field and spoke with Mayor George Ellis, a former owner, about backing a franchise.

"The field," said Powers, "is large enough for two teams in all the cities in which we propose to place teams. They call the Columbian an outlaw league because we invade territory under Organized Baseball's protection, yet in a number of cities permission is granted by American Association clubs for smaller league teams to play non-conflicting dates. The Columbian League proposes to respect contracts, but will not recognize reservation. . . . It does not believe a man should be held as chattel year after year. . . . There will be sufficient number of players of real major league caliber on each team of our league to make us able to compete successfully for patronge. . . . Grand Rapids will be given faster ball than it has seen in years if the company is formed here. I cannot see how it can help but appeal to Grand Rapids lovers of baseball. Several major league players will be on the team here if our plans materialize. . . ."

Less than a month later Powers' plans had radically changed. On March 8 in Indianapolis a new "Federal League of Baseball Clubs" was established, with Powers as president, M. F. Bramley of Cleveland as vice president, John A. George of Indianapolis as treasurer and James Ross of Indianapolis as secretary.

The board of directors was composed of William T. McCullough of Pittsburgh; Michael Kinney of St. Louis; Charles X. Zimmerman of Cleveland; John

209

A. Spinney of Cincinnati; James A. Ross, John A. George and John S. Powell of Indianapolis; and Charles I. Sherlock of Chicago.

Events in Covington, Kentucky, indicated the jerry-built nature of the circuit. In January 1913 local interests were after a franchise in the Class D Blue Grass League along with other Kentucky cities; but the nearby Cincinnati Reds, exercising their territorial rights, vetoed the plan. In fact, not only was Covington denied a place in Organized Baseball, but the Blue Grass League was expelled from the National Association for having even considered the idea.

In March Covington's hopes had shifted toward the Feds. A "Covington Amusement Co.," capitalized at just $12,000, was formed, with bank vice president Charles Eugene Clark as head. Former A's pitcher Bill Bartley (0-1 in 19 big league games) was the "prize" catch on the "Blues" roster.

The lineup for the 1913 Feds:

CLUB	OWNER	PARK
Chicago	John T. Powers	DePaul University
Cleveland	M. F. Bramley	Luna Park
Covington	Charles E. Clark	Riverbreeze Park
Indianapolis	J. Edward Krause	Riverside Beach Park
Pittsburgh	M. Henderson	Exposition Park
St. Louis	Otto Steifel	St. Louis University

Parks were found for the infant circuit. Pittsburgh's Exposition Park was again pressed into service. So was Cleveland's Luna Park. In Chicago "a little cigar box of a place" at DePaul University was utilized. Right field was only 255 feet away. Indianapolis' Riverside Beach Park held parking for 200 cars.

Covington's Riverbreeze Park at Second and Scott streets was actually closer to downtown Cincinnati than was the Reds' Redland Field. Riverbreeze Park was originally built for 4,200 fans but was soon expanded to 6,000. It featured a very small playing field, however. Games were high-scoring affairs and "home run posts" were installed beyond the fences. Anything not reaching them was deemed a two-base hit.

Enthusiasm ran high in Pittsburgh, where "the opening . . . was successful beyond all expectations" and where conveniently located Exposition Park was still considered by the locals to be "one of the finest baseball fields in the country." For Covington's May 9 opener, the throng was "so great that the stands would not accommodate all who attended."

Covington's joy was short lived, and attendance soon dwindled. By June the *Kentucky Post* implored fans to "Show them you are loyal to Covington and their baseball team."

Opposite: The 1913 Covington Blue Sox would not survive the season; in July the franchise was transferred to Kansas City.

In July the franchise (with a 21-31 record) bit the dust. After some discussion of a move to Toledo or Baltimore, the club was hastily transferred to Kansas City. Attorney C. C. Madison, a former teammate of Joe Tinker's, took over the club presidency. Kansas City's Gordon & Koppel Field, situated near Brush Creek, seated an estimated 12,000.

The quality of play in the Federal League was not overwhelming. Most players came from deep down in the talent barrel. The Cleveland Green Sox (or "Youngsters") were so hastily organized they fielded a largely local semipro cast on Opening Day. Most of the team was soon replaced. St. Louis was similarly composed of locals, in this case members of the Mound City's "Trolly League." One of these "Trolly Leaguers" was pitcher "Chief" Raymer, who against Pittsburgh on May 16 recorded one of the stranger no-hitters in pro annals. He surrendered Pittsburgh's only safety in the fourth inning to a third baseman named Warren. Warren, however, had batted out of turn, and his hit was nullified.

When the league began its concerted efforts to improve in 1914, most 1913 Feds fell back to their natural level. For example, St. Louis catcher Waring returned to Peoria of the Class B Three-I League. Indianapolis pitcher Eli Cates was reduced to trying out with South Bend of the Class D South Michigan League.

The Advance to Major League Status

On August 2 in Indianapolis the Feds ambitiously agreed on advancing to major league status for 1914. Expansion was also discussed, with several schemes being considered; the most traditional involved expansion to eight clubs. Investors representing New York, Baltimore, Philadelphia, Brooklyn, Detroit, Milwaukee and Cincinnati were all supposedly interested.

Former Phillies owner Horace S. Fogel (who had been expelled from N.L. ranks in 1912 for charging that that season's pennant race had been fixed in favor of John McGraw's Giants), claiming to represent interests in Baltimore, Philadelphia and New York, proposed a more ambitious agenda. He suggested a grand scheme of an Eastern and a Western Federal League. The east would include New York, Buffalo, Brooklyn, Philadelphia, Washington, Baltimore, Rochester and Boston. The West would comprise Detroit, Milwaukee, Chicago, Cleveland, Indianapolis, Kansas City, Cincinnati and St. Louis. It was not clear which wing Pittsburgh would enter.

Colonel Charles Zimmerman, Ed Steininger and James Gilmore were appointed to accompany Fogel east to scout promising franchises.

Exit Powers

On Sunday, August 3, 1913, John T. Powers was deposed as president. One reason given was that he wanted to transfer a Pittsburgh-Chicago game to his home city of Sheffield, even securing a large guarantee, but Chicago refused. Others felt Powers was removed for too "timid" an attitude toward the move to major league status.

Officially, Powers was said to be overworked, and a "vacation" was offered in appreciation of his "generous" contributions to the league. James A. Gilmore of Chicago was to serve as acting president until September 20, to be assisted by league Secretary Lloyd Rickart.

Powers threatened to initiate a new circuit to rival the Feds, this time supposedly under "Organized Ball auspices"—and viewed it as a third major league. He saw possible franchises in St. Louis, Chicago, Indianapolis, Cleveland, Pittsburgh, New York, Baltimore, Toronto, Buffalo and Montreal. It was the last anyone heard of him.

Gilmore had arranged this revolutionary conference, calling for Powers' dismissal and for putting the Feds on a sound footing. He demanded that each club make a sizable deposit in a sinking fund. To those who demurred he shouted, "All right, get out!"

"I went in . . . [with] the assurance that I was to take charge," recalled Gilmore. "John T. Powers, the president, was not progressive enough to suit my notions. He seemed to avoid rather than to seek publicity. But it took me fourteen hours to convince . . . the various clubs of the wisdom of making a change."

In response to the Feds, the majors, particularly Brooklyn's Charles Ebbets, circulated talk of yet another "continuous ball" scheme, i.e., planting minor league teams in big league parks to help stave off a challenge. "Capital for outlaw undertakings would be rather difficult to find if such a plan was put in force," noted one New York paper. "Its adoption would, of course, involve the dropping of several cities now in the American Association and the International circuits, substituting the major league cities now occupied by but a single club."

Such a plan met with vigorous objection from International League President Edward G. Barrow. Barrow even issued a threat of his own, stating unequivocally that he planned on major league status himself.

"I don't take any stock in the proposition, . . ." he stated. "I have something . . . which I think will make [the I.L.] a third big league without any outside influence. There is altogether too much major league influence in the International League anyway, and we don't want it to become any larger." Barrow indicated he had a plan for buying the existing big league interests (Detroit's, Brooklyn's and the Highlanders') in I.L. clubs. Rumors also floated that the practice of "farming" was about to be banned by the National Commission. The Newark *Evening News* contended a third big league could emerge from a combination of stronger I.L. and A.A. franchises.

On August 18 Organized Baseball faced yet another challenge. An "outlaw" Dixie Base Ball League was formed by Memphis Police Court Judge

James Gilmore became Federal League president near the beginning of the circuit's push for major league status.

W. J. Bacon and Harry N. Pharr, also of that city, with franchises in Memphis, Chattanooga, Atlanta, Birmingham, New Orleans, Little Rock and Shreveport. In six of the eight cities the new circuit would be challenging established minor league clubs.

On August 19 the Federal League met again in Indianapolis, adopting a resolution mandating each club to deposit a $25,000 bond by September 20. This was to guarantee player salaries and incidental expenses in the coming war. New parks were to be constructed in Cleveland, Indianapolis, Chicago and St. Louis. Baltimore and Buffalo were being considered as potential members.

The Players Fraternity

On September 10 David Fultz of the Players Fraternity, a union of the time, issued a statement of neutrality regarding the Federal League controversy. "They must fight it out themselves. As an organization we refuse to be drawn into the controversy. . . . There seems to be an abundance of money ready for investment in the base ball business, but this can have no effect upon our . . . maintaining a position of neutrality as long as there is a possibility of obtaining a square deal from the magnates."

Organized ball viewed this as a veiled threat. *Sporting Life* said some saw it as "little short of treason." The paper claimed: "No matter how viewed President Fultz's declaration has made a bad impression on magnates and public and should be repudiated by the players."

"Fighting Jim" Gilmore

Horace Fogel, Lloyd Rickart, and Ned Hanlon were believed by outside observers to be front-runners to replace Powers at the September 20 session, but it was, of course, James Gilmore who emerged as president. Gilmore, a Chicago coal dealer, was an energetic figure. He had become the controlling force in the Chicago franchise by assuming the moribund club's outstanding debts.

"It came about in August 1913," he recollected. "I was on my way to the Chicago Golf Club for a tilt with Eugene R. Pike, now comptroller there. In his company was E. C. Racey, then treasurer of the Chicago club of the Federal League. . . .

"Now at this time my baseball experience was limited in the extreme. I was a fan of White Sox convictions. Like most fans I considered myself wise in the game. That day for the first time I learned of the Federal League.

"Racey was full of it; simply bubbling over. . . . The Pittsburgh team was in Chicago. W. C. [W. T.] McCullough of the visitors with E. R. Pike collared me three days later at the Chicago A. C. and simply talked me blind. The upshot was that . . . I would take a flyer. Without his knowledge or consent I declared Charlie Williams in with me. We assumed liabilities with Pike and A. Moran. There were twenty-two games remaining on our schedule. They cost Williams and myself just $14,000."

Born in Portsmouth, Ohio, on March 2, 1870, Gilmore was the son of a dry goods merchant. The family moved to St. Louis when Jim was just two and to Chicago when he was six. Gilmore was "change pitcher" for Marquette School on the West Side.

His first job was a $3-a-week messenger with Armour & Company. He asked for a $4-per-week raise; when that was refused, he quit and landed a

Cy Young managed the 1913 Cleveland Federal League club.

$7-a-week post with his brother at a local coal company. Gilmore volunteered for service with the First Regiment of the Illinois National Guard in the Spanish-American War and got as far as Santiago and Manila. He contracted malaria while in Santiago and lost 70 pounds in 46 days. On his discharge he had reached the rank of commissary sergeant.

He returned to Chicago, finding employment as a coal salesman. In 1910 he became president of his own firm, the Kerchnen Company, manufacturers of ventilators and ventilating engines.

One of Gilmore's strengths was an ability to bring in well-healed club backers. He pointed out to them the "Half Million Dollar World Series" of 1912, in which the Giants and Athletics netted $490,000 for eight games, as proof of the lucrativeness of big league ball.

Newly elected Chicago Mayor William Hale "Big Bill" Thompson gave Gilmore his first big tip when he advised him to go after Charles Weeghman as a backer.

Charles Weeghman and the Chicago Federals

The 40-year-old Weeghman had first come to Chicago as an 18-year-old "penniless adventurer," jumping at the first job offered him—$8 a week at the Kings Restaurant. Eight years later, he was part-owner of his own establishment and on his way to becoming owner of a successful chain of "armed chaired lunch counters, where waiters are eliminated and each patron shifts for himself." He became a millionaire.

When the Federal League established itself in Chicago, Weeghman later told *Baseball Magazine*, it was "an unrecognizable miniature of its present size. No one of its promoters even dreamed of national expansion at that time. The club, like all new enterprises, lost money. Mr. Gilmore . . . undertook to finance the club, but after he dropped seven or eight thousand dollars with no visible returns, he began to look around for reinforcements. Spotting me as a likely victim, he came to me with a proposition. . . ."

Gilmore convinced Weeghman to invest $26,000, assuring him, "There won't be any other expenses. That will be all the money we will require." Soon Weeghman realized the venture was a "bottomless well." Much in the fashion that Gilmore had cajoled him into investing, Weeghman turned to another wealthy Chicagoan, William Walker, owner of the Midwest's largest wholesale fish market.

"He didn't have to interest me in baseball any, as I had always been interested in that," the heavyset Walker admitted, "but he did rope me into this magnate thing, and I haven't got used to the feel of it yet. They say it's a show business, and an owner is in the public eye, . . . but I had rather be back with my fish—I know more about them—for that is my business."

"Since we were launched out as a national league, we knew it was no time to spare expenses and we didn't," Weeghman recalled. "Before we opened the gates of our new park we had invested four hundred and twelve thousand dollars."

At Indianapolis on November 2, Buffalo and Baltimore were admitted to the circuit.

J. Edward Krause and company erected a new $100,000 "Federal Park" in Indianapolis seating 19,964, although an estimated 25,000 could be let in "without anyone getting on the field." Hoosiers business manager would be former Indianapolis Western League and American Association manager Billy Watkins.

Backers of the Buffalo team included local real estate developer Walter Mullen, Oliver Cabana, and William E. Robertson. On March 22 ground was broken on Northland Avenue for 20,000-seat Federal Park, costing an estimated $130,000.

Carrol Rasin served as Baltimore's president, and Ned Hanlon, the most famous of its directors, owned the property on which new "Terrapin Park" was

By August 1913 the sporting press was proclaiming the Federal League's intent to become a "major."

constructed. Secretary of the city's short-lived American League franchise, Harry Goldman, served the Feds in the same capacity. A self-proclaimed "33rd degree rooter," Goldman had fought to keep the old club from moving to New York and even attempted buying the Senators and shifting them to Baltimore.

Construction for Terrapin Park began on February 1, 1914. A wooden park in the new age of concrete and steel, it cost $82,000 and seated 15,000.

Gilmore attempted to interest Otto Steifel, the wealthy St. Louis brewer, in bankrolling the franchise there. Steifel, however, refused to commit himself until an eight-club circuit was in order. Almost instantly, the dynamic Gilmore contacted some Toronto interests and announced a franchise there. Steifel was now aboard.

On November 15 in Chicago, Gilmore was elected permanent president.

More Major Backers: Robert B. Ward and Philip De Catesby Ball

"I was in Toronto about to close for a site on King Street on which I held an option," recalled Gilmore. "This was in the first week of February 1914. The Toronto people had pledged $125,000. At the King Edward hotel in Toronto I met a Chicago friend, Harry Herrindon."

"Nix on Toronto," Herrindon told Gilmore. "I'll put you up against a live one." He introduced Gilmore to Robert B. Ward. By Lincoln's birthday, Ward had thrown in his lot with the new league. Born in New York in 1852, Pittsburgh's Robert B. Ward was the millionaire owner of the Tip Top Bakeries and of the Brooklyn franchise. Although from a family of bakers, he amassed his own fortune. "I never inherited a five-cent piece," he bragged. "All that I have, I have made myself, and I believe honorably and fairly." In 1913 his 13 bakeries produced 249,992,325 loaves—40,000 linear miles of bread: "Bread from Baker to Consumer, untouched by Human Hand." To further promote his product he endeavored to name his new team the "Tip Tops," but outraged sportswriters threatened to boycott the tag, and the team became the more prosaic "Brookfeds."

Even Charles Somers had to admit Ward's addition to Federal League ranks was a coup. "He is the kind of man any league would go a long way to get," the Cleveland owner allowed. "When I think of the ability that man has shown and the things he has pulled off, . . . I am lost in wonder that Gilmore pulled him in. You have to hand it to him. He is one clever promoter."

"I was not impressed by the financial picture in Pittsburgh and intimated as much to Mr. Ward," recalled Gilmore of the barely solvent William W. Kerr. "I'll fix that quick," responded the baker, who introduced Gilmore to a former classmate of Ward's brother and partner George, railroad contractor Edward W. Gwinner. Within an hour Gwinner had committed to support of the franchise.

"He's got $10,000,000," Gilmore crowed. "Guess that's pretty bad backing, eh?" Gwinner probably was worth only $500,000, but he was joined by prominent New York architect C. B. Comstock, who did a lot of designing for the Ward brothers, including their new Brooklyn park.

Philip De Catesby Ball, manufacturer of artificial ice plants, took over from Otto Steifel when St. Louis' losses became too much for the brewer to bear. Despite his high-toned, French-sounding middle name, Ball was a pretty tough

Charles Weeghman, president of the Federal League's Chicago Whales.

character. Born in Keokuk, Iowa, in 1864, Ball was almost named after Al Catesby, a famous Welchman. That was his father's wish. His mother balked, and "De Catesby" was chosen as a compromise. He had always been interested in baseball and was a catcher for Shreveport until a barroom knife fight cost him use of his left hand. After that he punched cows and worked on the railroad. He saved $1,000 by the most frugal of living and bought his first ice plant. From there he was off and running.

"Why, that first year," noted Gilmore, "I travelled 55,000 miles. I had to break into several fortunes with a conversational jimmy."

"I believe that man Gilmore," said National League President John K. Tener, "not only can convince a millionaire that the moon is made of green cheese, but he can induce him to invest money in a cheese factory on the moon."

Talent Begins to Jump

The first player jumping to the 1914 Feds was the 35-year-old manager-first baseman of the Browns, George Stovall. "No white man ought to be

The 1914 Buffalo Federal League club. (Courtesy of Joseph M. Overfield.)

bartered like a broken down plow horse," argued the Missouri-born Stovall when Browns owner Robert Hedges refused to give him his outright release. He became player-manager of the Kansas City squad.

In December 1913 the baseball world was shocked by the defection of legendary shortstop Joe Tinker. He had been sold from the Reds to Brooklyn for $15,000, but demanded a share in the purchase price. When that was refused he signed to manage Weeghman's Federal League team.

On January 17, 1914, a report out of Chicago had Gilmore offering Ty Cobb a five-year $75,000 contract. His 1914 salary was to be paid in advance, with the remainder in an escrow account. Cobb telegraphed back saying he had already signed with Detroit and was unable to accept the Fed offer.

Rumors floated that the Feds would invade Washington and that Walter Johnson would play there. The league quickly moved to scotch them. "Washington cannot support one team, let alone two," sniffed Robert B. Ward.

Also current were whispers that Ben Muckenfuss, a former associate of Chris Von der Ahe's, would locate a Fed team in the Corona, Queens, section of New York for the 1915 season.

Yet another "name" was added to the Fed lineup when John Montgomery Ward, former star player and leader of the 1890 Players' League revolt, and

more recently president of the Boston National League team, signed on as Brookfed business manager.

Nonetheless, Organized Ball remained confident regarding Fed competition. Garry Herrmann dismissed the upstart's 1913 campaign as lacking in either "prosperity or prestige." He promised a "passive" policy toward the interlopers if National Agreement "contractual and reservation rights" were respected.

"Rivalry will not be resented," he noted in his official report for 1913, "as long as league and club rights are not ignored, but illegal and unsportsmanlike interference with and utter disregard of established privileges of National Agreement clubs will justify the adoption of vigorous defensive methods."

In January, Charles Weeghman began to develop cold feet. "Unless six of the eight clubs in the Federal League can show me the goods, I will withdraw from the organization," he threatened. ". . . I am in this thing hook, line and sinker, providing the lineups are satisfactory, and I cannot make this assertion too emphatic. However, I am greatly surprised after reading the list of players rounded up by the other cities."

Nonetheless, the Feds pulled themselves together, and Weeghman announced he was staying. Gilmore revealed that 29 major leaguers had signed, and Weeghman went forward with plans to build a fireproof 20,000-seat park at Seminary and Addison on Chicago's populous North Side.

The main parcel Weeghman purchased had originally been put together by the De Cantillon brothers back in 1909, when they had purchased the site in order to place an American Association franchise in the city. Nearby residents petitioned Mayor Carter Harrison II, claiming the enterprise would "disturb the peace and quiet of the neighborhood and destroy the district as residential property," but they failed in their endeavor.

However, Weeghman ran into other, more expensive roadblocks. "Some time ago," he revealed, ". . . I had bought the vacant site at Addison and Clark, but I did not possess one little strip 16 feet wide near one end of the property . . . owned by one of my friends, and I had been assured of getting it, but had neglected to close the deal. About a week ago this friend of mine was approached by some unknown man and offered $25,000 in cash. . . . Of course, that is a fabulous sum for it and he came to me. I know it was Organized Baseball behind that offer. I didn't want to see my friend lose a chance to make so much money, if the offer was on the square, and I thought it was a bluff all the time. I told my friend to go ahead and sell it. The party then asked for time to close the deal, and agreed to pay the $25,000 on Saturday afternoon at 4:30 or lose his chance to buy. Well, the result was no one showed up . . . with the $25,000."

Opposite left: Robert B. Ward, millionaire baker and owner of the Brooklyn Federal League club; right, Ward's brother and club vice president George S. Ward.

The signing of Joe Tinker was a coup for the Federal League. Here, Tinker and his sons model Chicago Whales uniforms.

Rumors floated that Weeghman had been given an opportunity to purchase the Browns from Robert Hedges. He admitted he'd been offered the chance to buy a non–Chicago big league club, but refused to say which one. Ban Johnson denied the Browns were for sale, and the Cubs' Charles Murphy charged that Weeghman was already secretly out of the outlaw circuit.

Word also came from Pittsburgh that "Deacon" Phillippe, former Fed League pilot, was suing his old club for back pay. He charged the circuit had just merely survived the 1913 season and was a threadbare operation.

Each club was mandated to deposit a $25,000 guarantee with the league, and to sign at least five major leaguers to contracts.

To obtain players, a variety of tactics was employed. Fed agents were ready at the dock in New York in March 1914 when players from Charles Comiskey's World Tour returned. Only Steve Evans and Mike Doolan were signed, but Fed overtures forced O.B. to grant hefty raises to retain the others.

Joe Tinker was wiring to players: "You are invited to come to the Federal

Opposite: Washington Park, Brooklyn, home of the Brookfeds. The park was designed by C. B. Comstock, a member of the Pittsburgh club's board.

League headquarters in Chicago and discuss terms. Even if you do not sign a contract, all your expenses will be paid by the Federal League."

A bonus to signing with the Feds was that they employed a modified reserve clause, much more favorable to the individual player. To exercise his "reserve," a Fed owner had to disclose his intentions September 15. A player thus "reserved" would receive at least a 5 percent raise. In addition, any player having served in any part of ten Federal League seasons could receive his unconditional release for the asking.

Players jumping for the 1914 season included:

PLAYER	FROM	TO FEDERALS
Mickey Doolan	Phils	Baltimore
Otto Knabe	Phils	Baltimore
Tom Seaton	Phils	Brooklyn
Ad Brennan	Phils	Chicago
Howie Camnitz	Phils	Pittsburgh
Doc Crandall	Giants	St. Louis
Grover Hartley	Giants	St. Louis
Claude Cooper	Giants	Brooklyn
Rebel Oakes	Cardinals	Pittsburgh
Steve Evans	Cardinals	Brooklyn
Claude Hendrix	Pirates	Chicago
Mike Simon	Pirates	St. Louis
Skipper Roberts	Cardinals	Pittsburgh
Tex McDonald	Braves	Pittsburgh
Jack Quinn	Braves	Baltimore
Bill Rariden	Braves	Indianapolis
Dutch Zwilling	Braves	Chicago
Walter Dickson	Braves	Pittsburgh
Hap Myers	Braves	Brooklyn
Al Bridwell	Cubs	St. Louis
Ward Miller	Cubs	St. Louis
Earl Moore	Cubs	Buffalo
Mysterious Walker	Dodgers	Pittsburgh
Baron Knetzer	Dodgers	Pittsburgh
Ben Meyer	Dodgers	Baltimore
Joe Tinker	Reds	Chicago
Mordecai Brown	Reds	St. Louis
Chief Johnson	Reds	Kansas City
Gene Packard	Reds	Kansas City
Armando Marsans	Reds	St. Louis
Frank Harter	Reds	Indianapolis
George Suggs	Reds	Baltimore
Al Wickland	Reds	Chicago
Willie Adams	Browns	Pittsburgh
George Stovall	Browns	Kansas City

PLAYER	FROM	TO FEDERALS
Byron Houck	Athletics	Brooklyn
Danny Murphy	Athletics	Brooklyn
Russell Ford	Yankees	Buffalo
Rollie Zeider	Yankees	Chicago
Bill McKechnie	Yankees	Indianapolis
Cy Falkenberg	Indians	Indianapolis
Norman Cullop	Indians	Kansas City
Vic Moseley	Red Sox	Indianapolis
Bob Groom	Senators	St. Louis
Frank LaPorte	Senators	Indianapolis
Ted Easterly	White Sox	Kansas City

In the course of the Federal war, estimated historian Harold Seymour, 264 players donned a Fed uniform—81 major leaguers and 140 from the minors. Of these, 18 broke major league contracts; 25 disregarded minor league pacts; 63 ignored big league reserve clauses and 115 abandoned minor league reserve lists. Of the remainder, 25 had previous pro experience but were free agents, and 18 had no professional background at all.

The Federal League Goes to Court

The case of Phils catcher Bill Killefer was vexing to the Feds. Paid $3,200 in 1913, Killefer gave his word to the Phils he would return for 1914. Instead, in January he signed with Charles Weeghman's Chicago Whales for a three-year $17,500 contract with a $525 advance. Then Killefer jumped back to the Phils for a $19,500 pact. One sportswriter penned the following doggerel to commemorate the controversy:

> Weeghman Weeghman Federal Man
> Make me a contract as fast as you can,
> Pad it and sign it and mark it O.K.
> And I'll go to the majors and ask for more pay.

The Federal League sued in Federal District Court at Grand Rapids, Michigan, but was not upheld. Judge Clarence W. Sessions categorized Killefer "as a person upon whose pledged word little or no reliance can be place, and who, for gain to himself, neither scruples nor hesitates to disregard and violate his express engagements and agreements." He returned the catcher to the National League.

Nonetheless, Sessions did not uphold the uniform player contract, finding it "lacking in the necessary qualities of definiteness, certainty, and mutuality." The Feds appealed, but the Sixth Circuit Court of Appeals concurred with Sessions.

CAMNITZ, PITTSBURG

GROOM WASHINGTON AMER.

LA PORTE, N. Y. AMER.

In February, Gilmore and Ban Johnson secretly conferred in order to avoid war. Johnson denied there was any room for a third major league, and nothing came of the session. The established leagues settled in for a protracted conflict, deciding that the National Commission would be the focal point of their resistance.

In May, Ban Johnson warned: "No player of the Federal League can ever play in the American League. A man may be reinstated by the National Commission, but can never hope to get into the American League. The National and other leagues may accept him, but as for the American League, never."

To prevent the Feds from invading Cleveland, Charles Somers moved the Toledo club of the American Association to League Park for a two-season experiment in "continuous ball." Players such as Billy Southworth, Elmer Smith, Jay Kirke, "Sad Sam" Jones and Josh Billings all shuttled between the A.L. and the American Association. Hurting the Indians more than the Feds was their woeful caliber of play—eighth in 1914 and seventh in 1915—and attendance plummeted.

Play Begins

Opening Day for the Feds as a major league came on April 13, 1914. The Buffeds took on Baltimore at Baltimore's Terrapin Park, with 27,692 fans, including both cities' mayors, in attendance. Visible from the site was Oriole Park, where only 1,500 saw John McGraw's Giants take on Jack Dunn's Orioles.

The box score for Baltimore's 3–2 victory:

BUFFALO	AB	R	H	PO	A	E	BALTIMORE	AB	R	H	PO	A	E
Hanford, cf	4	0	2	2	0	0	Meyer, rf	4	0	1	2	0	0
Downey, 2b	3	0	0	2	2	0	Knabe, 2b	4	0	1	0	4	1
Louden, ss	4	0	0	1	1	1	Zinn, cf	2	1	1	1	0	0
Bonin, rf	4	0	0	2	0	0	Simmons, lf	4	0	0	0	0	1
Delahanty, lf	3	0	1	1	0	0	Swacina, 1b	4	1	2	11	0	1
Smith, 3b	3	0	0	1	0	0	Walsh, 3b	3	0	0	1	3	0
Agler, 1b	3	0	1	5	0	1	Doolan, ss	2	1	1	4	1	0
Blair, c	3	1	1	10	2	1	Jacklitsch, c	4	0	1	8	3	1
Moore, p	2	0	0	0	0	0	Quinn, p	4	0	0	0	2	1
*Young	0	1	0	0	0	0							
Krapp, p	1	0	0	0	2	0							
TOTALS	30	2	5	24	7	3	TOTALS	31	3	6	27	13	5

*Batted for Moore in fifth inning.

Opposite: Four who jumped to the Federal League in 1914; clockwise from upper left, Ennis "Rebel" Oakes, Howie Camnitz, Frank LaPorte and Bob Groom. (Courtesy Edward Kennedy.)

The schedule for the Feds' first season as a "major" league.

											R	H	E
Buffalo	0	0	0	0	2	0	0	0	0	–	2	5	3
Baltimore	0	0	0	3	0	0	0	0	x	–	3	6	5

Two-base hits—Knabe, Jacklitsch, Swacina, Hanford, Zinn, Meyer. Sacrifice hits—Smith, Walsh. Stolen bases—Bonin, Doolan. Double play—Krapp, Blair and Agler. First off balls—Off Quinn 1, Moore 1, Krapp 1. Hit by pitcher—By Krapp 2. Struck out—By Quinn 8, Moore 3, Krapp 5. Wild pitch—Moore. Left on base—Baltimore 4, Buffalo 4. First on errors—Baltimore 2, Buffalo 3. Time 3:30. Umpires—Bush and Mannassau.

The next day Pittsburgh opened before 12,000, while on April 16 the St. Louis Terriers and the Kansas City Packers both had their openers. At

Handlan's Park, 20,000 saw the Terriers and the visiting Hoosiers. Nine thousand patrons overflowed tiny Gordon & Koppel Field to view Chicago at Kansas City, twice the size crowd the American Association Blues were drawing the same day. "The stockyards declared a half holiday," reported the Kansas City *Star*—half and whole holidays are popular at the yards—and several hundred dealers in pigs and steers were in the stands."

On April 23 Indianapolis and Chicago opened. St. Louis lost to the Hoofeds 3–0 as 15,000 watched, and Indiana Governor Ralston threw out the first pitch. In Chicago 20,000 jammed Weeghman Park to see Chicago trim Kansas City 9–1.

Kansas City might have fared better had not the Cincinnati Reds served an injunction on its starting pitcher, George "Chief" Johnson, in the second inning. He was forced to leave the game. Judge Foell of Chicago's Superior Court ruled Johnson had to return to the Reds, but was overruled on appeal.

Buffalo did not open at home until May 11 (construction had not begun until March 22), and 14,286 saw the first game.

Litigation Continues

In June Judge Walter Sanborn ruled against Cuban-born St. Louis outfielder Armando Marsans. Marsans had signed to play with the Reds for 1914, then jumped to the Feds. The court did not rule on the reserve clause but returned Marsans because he violated a signed contract. His Federal League career lasted just nine games.

On June 15, 1914, the White Sox's Hal Chase jumped to the Buffeds after giving Charles Comiskey ten days' notice that he intended joining the Feds. At first, the authorities of O. B. could not reconcile themselves to the defection. "I don't believe it," said Ban Johnson. ". . . The Federal League can't get sensible players to climb aboard a sinking ship. Hal Chase above all others. The Federals are running to cover. They're through."

Comiskey got an injunction against Chase. To prevent "Prince Hal" from being served, the Buffeds secreted the first baseman away at an undisclosed local site and even seriously considered having aviator Glenn Wright fly him to a field near Federal Park so he could approach the field undetected. Wright was unable to obtain a plane in time, and Chase arrived at the park on June 25 by less-dramatic methods and was served in the second inning.

The injunction was overturned on July 21 by New York State Supreme Court Judge Herbert Bissell, who termed the reserve system "peonage" and "the dominion of a benevolent despotism through the operation of the monopoly established by the National Agreement."

"The Chase contract with the Chicago club," said Federal League counsel Edward E. Gates, "is not enforceable in a court of equity for lack of mutuality in that the player is not only bound for a period of years, but that he is also bound by the terms of the National Agreement, which he [Bissell] holds to be a monopoly . . . and in violation of common law, in restraint of his free right to contract with any of the parties to the National Agreement, which is all of Organized Baseball, except that club which holds him upon their so-called reserve list. . . .

"This is indeed a victory and one which means a good deal to the ballplayers who have for years been . . . restrained in their basic right of free contract. This decision is by far the most far-reaching one that has been decided against Organized Baseball as yet. The fact that Judge Bissell held that the baseball business was not trade within the meaning of the Sherman Act relieves the parties to the National Agreement of any charge of violating the federal statute, and hence they would not be amenable . . . to those penal statutes, but the manner of . . . the National Agreement is held to be a monopoly and in violation of the common law. We feel this opens up the field for the Federal League. . . ."

Salary Escalation

The cost of players signed by the Feds was not cheap. One paper printed this comparison of O.B. and Fed salaries of selected players:

PLAYER	O.B.	FEDS
Joe Tinker	$5,500	$12,000
Arthur "Vin" Campbell	3,200	8,500
Claude Cooper	2,500	7,500
Cy "Jinx" Falkenberg	4,000	8,500
Benny Kauff	2,000	7,500
Tom Seaton	2,600	8,200
Hal Chase	6,000	9,000

Even players remaining in O.B. profited greatly. A comparison of 1913 and 1915 salaries is instructive:

PLAYER	1913	1915
Ty Cobb	$12,000	$20,000
Rabbit Maranville	1,800	6,000
Jake Daubert	5,000	9,000
Ivey Wingo	2,600	6,500
Ray Caldwell	2,400	8,000

In June reports appeared of Organized Baseball's forming its own "Third League" to defuse the Federal threat. Meeting in New York, the magnates discussed taking four cities each from the International League and the American Association to form a new circuit. Others held that this plan was a sham, that the actual proposal would involve placing "second" teams in Brooklyn, Pittsburgh, Cincinnati, Detroit and Washington. A round-robin World Series was even discussed, but nothing came of either scheme.

One of the aspects of war between the two sides was possible favoritism in umpiring. SABRmetrician Craig Wright, in *The Diamond Appraised*, notes that over the years the homefield advantage has been relatively stable, but that in times of crisis it has been known to increase sharply. This had occurred during the founding of the American League. In 1902 A.L. home teams had won an all-time high 63 percent of their contests. When peace was declared the advantage soon shrank to more normal proportions.

From 1911 to 1913, the average major league home-team winning percentage was .520. In 1914 it catapulted to .553 in the A.L. and N.L. and was only slightly below that in the Federal League (.542). "There may have been," observed Wright, "subtle encouragement in one form or another, perhaps in an occasional philosophical hint about the need to entertain the troubled masses."

In late September rumors circulated that the Northwestern and Pacific Coast leagues were about to defect to the Federal cause. Fielder Jones contended he would not be surprised to see them "jump at the chance" to align with the new league.

Also that month, Weeghman and Garry Herrmann secretly conferred. Nothing resulted from the meeting, as Herrmann informed his National League colleagues, because the Feds demanded too much from a settlement.

Meanwhile, the Feds were fighting a strong battle at the turnstiles. Still in the pennant race on the last Sunday of the season, the Chicago Whales took in 34,461 paid admissions, and over 38,000 fans were actually at the park. It was a particularly proud moment, for at the same time both their O.B. rivals were at home, drawing nowhere near that amount. The crowd at Comiskey Park was less than 3,500, while the Cubs drew fewer than 2,000 fans.

Connie Mack's American League champion Athletics soon felt the sting of the Federal raiders, losing ace pitchers Chief Bender and Eddie Plank after the close of the 1914 campaign.

"Even though we won," Mack admitted, "it was my unhappiest season. . . . Federal League agents, and one of them was my old player, Danny Murphy, dogged our players all season. In some cases we had to tear up two and three contracts to hold our stars, and I was disgusted and discouraged with the lot of them. Time heals many wounds; the players were trying to get all they could, just as they did in the American League's early days, but I was too close to a bad situation to have much patience with it."

Mack sold off his great team. Eddie Collins, Jack Coombs, Jack Barry, Jimmy Walsh, Herb Pennock, Eddie Murphy, Jack Lapp, Bob Shawkey,

Carroll Brown and Frank "Home Run" Baker all were sent packing from the once-proud A's by the end of 1915.

The Johnson Incident

An even greater shock came when the Feds announced the signing of Washington's Walter Johnson with the Whales.

In July, Johnson had been approached in New York City by an agent of Robert Ward's. That evening Johnson met with Ward, promising he would not sign with the Senators until at least granting the Feds full consideration.

Johnson informed Senators Manager Clark Griffith of the meeting, and the two haggled over the summer but came to no agreement. At season's end, Griffith offered Johnson a contract of $16,000 for either one or two years. Walter requested $20,000; Griffith said no. But on the way to his Coffeyville, Kansas, home, Johnson was approached by Fielder Jones, who said the St. Louis Federals would pay him that amount for three years. Johnson deferred, responding that he was not much interested and further that he believed Griffith would eventually tender him an acceptable offer.

Johnson wrote twice to Griffith without reply. He then received a tactless letter from Senators President Harry Minor, informing him that he was Washington property, the offer was now $12,500, and that if Johnson did not accept the offer, his pact would be extended automatically. "I did not like it, . . ." was Johnson's response. "When I received that letter from Minor it put a different appearance on the case."

Shortly thereafter, Charles Weeghman wrote Johnson. Then Joe Tinker journeyed to Coffeyville: "It didn't take us long to come to terms—about twenty minutes, I guess." The "Big Train" was to receive $17,500 a year for three years, with a $6,000 advance.

Later that same day, Johnson received a letter from Griffith, telling him to ignore Minor. Griffith then met with Johnson in Kansas City.

Reports said Griffith arrived with high-powered lawyers to bludgeon Johnson into returning, an assertion Johnson denied. Griffith informed the pitcher his absence would wreck the Senators staff and would drop the team from a contender into the second division. "He said that he didn't deserve any such treatment from me, as he had always done well by me," Johnson told the Washington *Post*. "I cannot tell here the arguments he used, but . . . he convinced me that I ought to have remained with Washington and ought to return even then."

Johnson uneasily returned to the American League. "I did not treat the Federal League right," Johnson admitted to *Baseball Magazine*. "I broke my contract with them. But . . . only because I was convinced that by not doing so I would be doing a greater injury to Washington. Perhaps I was wrong, but

I at least acted for what I considered best. . . . I bungled it, no doubt, but it is done. . . ."

At about the same time, Giants hurler "Rube" Marquard (24-7 in 1911; 26-11 in 1912; 23-10 in 1913) signed with the Brookfeds after being denied a $1,500 advance on his two-year New York pact. He convinced Robert Ward he was free to sign—even swearing out an affidavit—and received a two-year Fed contract for $10,000 per year.

"Marquard will rue this day," vowed the secretary of the Giants, a Mr. Foster. "Why, only the other day he came in the office asking to see his contract, and he has the audacity to say he is a free agent."

"That is the worst of Organized Baseball's methods," responded Ward. "We give our players copies of contracts, which the other side does not, and their players never know where they stand. I am confident of one thing, . . . Marquard acted with me in good faith."

But the Giants were right, and Marquard returned to them, lucky not to be prosecuted for fraud.

The Feds Go to Judge Landis

On January 5, 1915, the Federal League brought suit in United States District Court for Northern Illinois against Organized Baseball for violation of the Sherman Antitrust Act. In part the suit was retaliation for rebuffs in the Walter Johnson, Armando Marsans and Rube Marquard matters.

Seeking relief on 11 points, the Feds accused Organized Baseball of being a conspiracy and a monopoly. The defendants submitted a 47-page affidavit in their defense.

The Feds were coming before Judge Kenesaw Mountain Landis, a jurist most widely known for his record-setting $29,000,000 judgment against Standard Oil, but also an avid baseball (particularly Cubs) fan. The plantiffs clearly believed "trustbuster" Landis would serve their cause.

The Federals were represented by Edward E. Gates, the American League by George W. Miller and the National by George Wharton Pepper.

"I have gone just about far enough in this case," Landis snapped at Gates. "The time has come when I should ask you gentlemen just what you want me to do. . . . Do you want me to stop the teams from going on spring training trips? Do you want me to break up the clubs or what do you want me to do?"

"Both sides," warned Landis, "must understand that any blows at the thing called baseball would be regarded by this court as a blow to a national institution."

"As far as I can see," said Gilmore, "there is nothing which might drag matters over any extended period. We are ready now, and there is no reason why the other side should want any delay. The sooner this fight is over the better it will be for the game."

Gilmore's assessment was incorrect. Landis, a true ball fan, knew that if he rendered a decision based on the law it would go against Organized Baseball. This he was not prepared to do, and so he sat on the case for months.

The Colonial League

Also in January 1915 the Feds lashed out on another front, endeavoring to form their own farm system. In early 1914 John Montgomery Ward had proposed "eastern" and "western" circuits, but nothing came of his pronouncement. In June of that year rumors circulated that the Feds were out to lasso the Class D Atlantic League, centered largely in New Jersey. Again nothing happened, and the Atlantic League folded at season's end.

The league they did choose was the existing New England–based Colonial League. Each club in this economically operated Class C "trolley league" had travelled by interurban transit to its games and returned home by nightfall to cut down on travel expenses. Its franchises were Brockton, Fall River, New Bedford, Pawtucket, Taunton and Woonsocket—all one-time members of the New England League.

Reports persisted throughout 1914 that the Colonial League was playing footsie with the Feds. In August 1914 the Boston Red Sox cancelled an exhibition with Woonsocket due to the Fed rumors.

In January 1915 Gilmore and Ward met with representatives of the circuit in New Haven to formalize matters. Woonsocket was dropped and three clubs—New Haven, Hartford and Springfield—from the defunct Class B Eastern Association were added. The Feds would supply six players to each club; in return each Colonial League team would recompense the Feds $200 per month per player. If the player's salary exceeded that amount, the Feds would pay the difference.

Most of the Feds' deficit for 1914 ($25,000), it was revealed, had been picked up by Brooklyn's Ward brothers. In 1915 the arrangement was formalized with a member of the family, William S. Ward, being named league treasurer.

The Colonial League still avoided overnight trips, but was, nonetheless, in poor financial shape. Minor league ball—whether organized or outlaw—was in the doldrums in 1915. By July 10, both Fall River and Taunton had disbanded.

Standings on July 10:

The Federal League failed to find sympathy in U.S. District Court's Judge Kenesaw Mountain Landis.

CLUB	W	L	PCT.
Hartford	23	18	.561
New Bedford	23	18	.561
New Haven	24	19	.558
Springfield	21	19	.525
Brockton	21	21	.500
Pawtucket	19	20	.487
Fall River	22	24	.478
Taunton	14	28	.333

Play resumed as a six-club league on July 11, but without much improvement at the gate. Pawtucket drew so poorly it had to play all of its last month's games on the road and was renamed the "Orphans."

Playing talent was fair at best. Former major league second baseman Jim Delahanty (he'd started the 1915 season with the Brookfeds) managed the strong Hartford club and paced the circuit in batting with a .379 mark. United States League alumnus "Big Jeff" Pfeffer had managed Pawtucket in 1914. Former A's outfielder Danny Murphy appeared for both New Haven and Pawtucket in 1915.

The most-noteworthy player to graduate from Colonial ranks was hard-hitting Brockton outfielder Merwin "Jake" Jacobson, who became a star for the great Orioles teams of the 1920s and eventually made it briefly to the big leagues. Also graduating to higher ranks was outfielder Mike Menosky, farmed to New Haven by Pittsburgh, who played nine seasons of major league ball.

Second half standings:

CLUB	W	L	PCT.
Hartford	55	42	.567
Brockton	57	44	.564
New Bedford	56	45	.554
New Haven	52	50	.510
Springfield	47	50	.485
Pawtucket	37	57	.394

Peace, Peace, But There Is No Peace!

Peace talks were held again in April 1915. *Sporting News* editor J. G. Taylor Spink arranged for Ban Johnson and Phil Ball to meet at McTeague's Restaurant in St. Louis. Two weeks later the duo got together again at Comiskey Park. Ball was heard to mutter something about the pity of the battles being fought in the courtroom and not on the diamond, but nothing came of the conferences.

Player raids continued in 1915. From the A's the Feds got pitchers Chief Bender and Eddie Plank; from the Braves outfielder Leslie Mann and third baseman Chuck Deal; from the Cardinals versatile Lee Magee; from the Pirates, first baseman "Big Ed" Konetchy and third baseman Harry "Mike" Mowrey; from the Phils infielder Milton Reed; from the Giants, pitcher "Hooks" Wiltse; from the Red Sox, pitcher Hugh Bedient and second baseman Steve Yerkes; from the Reds, infielder Marty Berghammer; from the Tigers, pitcher Alex Main; from Brooklyn, catcher Bill Fischer and outfielder Jack Dalton; from the White Sox, infielder Harry Lord; from the Senators rapidly aging second baseman "Germany" Schaefer.

The Feds Gain Another Major Backer

The major difference in the Fed lineup for 1915 was the addition of Tulsa oil millionaire Harry F. Sinclair. "I was considering the purchase of a club in Organized Baseball when opportunity came for me to study all the phases of the present baseball war," said Sinclair. "From early childhood I have been a fan, and as such many of the intricacies of the political side of the sport were

Federal League
Notables—

Edward Plank

Pitcher of the St. Louis Federal Club
This Famous Pitcher USES

Ⅴ ICTOR
TRADE
SPORTING GOODS CO.
MARK

EDWARD PLANK
Pitcher of the St. Louis Federals

Adopted on merit
Manufacturers of the Official
Federal League Ball

Victor supplies are sold by all leading dealers—Insist on the brand made by

Victor Sporting Goods Co. Springfield Mass

The 284 pitching victories Eddie Plank had accumulated for the Philadelphia Athletics made him attractive to the Federal League, and to advertisers.

covered up because of my intense interest in the game itself. The turning point came after a close study of men and methods.

"The Wards of Brooklyn and Messrs. Ball of St. Louis and Weeghman and [Vice President William M.] Walker of Chicago were known to me, and in ten minutes James A. Gilmore was able to show me why the Federal League would succeed. His proposition looked too good to be turned down. Founded on business decency with men of substantial standing and wholesome love of baseball, the Federal League appealed to me as the league of the future."

"I was in Cincinnati on the Bill Killefer case in the spring of 1915 with John M. Ward," Gilmore recalled. "John told me he had heard that Pat Powers had a friend who had made a fortune in the Western oil fields who had been trying to break into baseball. That was Harry F. Sinclair."

Gilmore found Sinclair to be "an enthusiast from the start." The millionaire mentioned that he knew Phil Ball, so "Fighting Jim" immediately telegraphed Ball for more information on Sinclair's finances.

"All right," Ball replied, "Rockefeller has half the money in the world, Sinclair the other half."

Meanwhile Sinclair was also checking the Feds out. He wired Ball: "How does baseball look to you?"

Another 1915 jumper: Washington Senators veteran Germany Schaefer signed with the Newark Peps. (Courtesy Edward Kennedy.)

"Come in and get your feet wet," Ball wired back.

Sinclair endeavored to move the sorry Kansas City Packers to Newark, but was blocked by a stockholders' court action. "Kansas City is going to keep its franchise," vowed club Director D. J. Haff on the eve of the decision, "and we will not accept any money settlement if Judge Baldwin's decision is for us." Instead the pennant-winning—but poorly drawing—Indianapolis franchise was transferred to Newark.

Patrick T. Powers would be involved in the actual operation of Sinclair's Newark "Peppers." The New Jersey native had been managing as long ago as 1884 and in 1892 piloted the New York Giants. From 1893 to 1905 and again from 1907 to 1911 he served as Eastern (International) League president. In 1901 he was first president of the National Association.

To manage Newark, Sinclair offered John McGraw $100,000 (or, another story has it, a blank check). McGraw would have no part of the bargain. Later he would charge the Feds had tried to "wreck baseball."

Newark's park was actually in nearby Harrison. One hundred thousand dollars was invested in the 20,000-seat field.

Harrison Mayor John J. Daly requested that businesses in the town close at noon on Opening Day, April 16, 1915. A Federal League–record crowd of 26,032 saw the Peppers defeat Baltimore 7–5. Five thousand more were turned away.

Benny Kauff Attempts to Defect

At the same time, in an attempt to give Organized Ball some more competition in New York City, the Hoosiers' Benny Kauff, star of the 1914 Federal season, was transferred from Indianapolis to Brooklyn by Jim Gilmore.

Kauff dominated the 1914 season and had once boasted, "I'll make Cobb look like a bush leaguer if I can play for the Giants." Such confidence caused one scribe to write:

> Though I hate to pull the chatter,
> I admit that I'm some batter;
>   If I play I'll make a sucker out of Cobb:
> I'm a one-man batting rally,
> And I knock 'em down the alley,
>   I'm modest little Benny-on-the-job.

Kauff signed a three-year contract with the Brookfeds but then informed the Giants he had no contract with Brooklyn. His grievance was that Brookfed Business Manager Dick Carroll had deducted $500 in salary which Kauff had previously received as an advance from Indianapolis. Gilmore immediately suspended Kauff for ten days and fined him $100.

"I am through with the Federal League for good," vowed Kauff. "I consider myself a free agent, and I will report to McGraw . . . tomorrow. The Tip Tops have held up part of my salary. If I can't play with the Giants I'll quit the game for good and all."

The Braves' James E. Gaffney protested to the National Commission, charging Kauff was still ineligible. When Boston visited the Polo Grounds for Kauff's first scheduled game, Gaffney pulled his team off the field. Umpire Mal Eason telephoned National League President John Kinley Tener, who agreed with Gaffney that Kauff was still legally bound by his three-year Federal League contract (Organized Ball had long since learned certain lessons in the courts). However, while Eason and Tener conversed, umpire Ernie Quigley had declared a forfeit to New York. The next day, Tener reversed Quigley's decision, ruled that an "exhibition" the Braves and Giants had played after the "forfeit" was an official League game (the Braves won 13–6) and decreed Kauff benched.

Kauff applied to the National Commission for reinstatement but was refused. Weeghman's Chicago Whales expressed interest in the outfielder.

Tulsa oil millionaire Harry F. Sinclair bought the Indianapolis Hoosiers and moved the 1914 Federal League champions to Newark for 1915.

Brooklyn was not immediately disposed to take Kauff back, but when the outfielder threatened to sue (former Brookfed Business Manager John M. Ward was now his attorney), he was returned to the lineup.

Rumblings of New Territory

During the season, the Feds made noises of a move into Boston. In June, Gilmore, Sinclair, Robert Ward, Edward W. Gwinner and C. B. Comstock journeyed to the Hub to meet with prospective backers and to survey locations for a club. Reportedly available was a Forest Hills site which James E. Gaffney had eyed before building Braves Field, farther out in the Alston area. "These Boston men," said Gilmore, "have been after me for some time, and, after investigation, we found them to be reputable businessmen of high financial standing." Gilmore denied there would be any midseason invasion of New England or that a move to Boston in 1916 would mean the league would not go to New York.

Further underscoring its intentions to conquer New York, in July 1915 the

League announced its intention to shift its headquarters from Chicago to Gotham. Rumors also continued of invasions of Boston, Detroit and Cleveland. As for cities the Feds would abandon, Gilmore tersely said, "If a city hasn't the gumption to show it appreciates our baseball, it will have only itself to blame...."

One of the franchises Gilmore was referring to was Newark. Despite its record-setting Opening Day, attendance fell off quickly. By July the Peppers were drawing poorly, and Sinclair, despite Powers' objections, was threatening to move immediately if trolly service was not extended to his park.

The Effect on the Minors

The minor leagues were hard hit by the Federal War, particularly Buffalo, Indianapolis, Newark, Kansas City and Baltimore, all of which were in direct competition with the Feds. Ed Barrow's International League was known as the "Belgium of Base Ball." In Baltimore, Jack Dunn's team was rocked immediately. Despite being 5½ games up in early July, Dunn was $28,000 in the red. For example, only 200 fans saw Babe Ruth's debut. The league refused to allow Dunn to move, and in response he sold off ten of his best players (including Ruth) and skidded to sixth place. In 1915 Dunn fled to Richmond in midseason.

In Buffalo, the International League Bisons were a very strong team, second in 1914 and first in 1915. In 1914 exhibitions they beat both the Braves and Athletics — the two participants in that year's World Series. In 1915, Bisons manager Patsy Donovan challenged the Buffeds to one game — the winner to take the territory. The Feds refused. Yet the Bisons barely drew over 100,000 each season.

In early August 1914, Ban Johnson subsidized the Buffalo I.L. club payroll to keep it afloat, sending $3,218.65 via Ed Barrow to owner Jacob Stein. The following year was not much better. Both the American League and the National Association stood ready to purchase the club. More subsidies came through, and the club survived the year when Stein sold out to Red Sox owner Joseph J. Lannin.

In Newark the International League could not survive even a full season of Federal competition. The franchise shifted to Harrisburg, Pennsylvania, on July 2.

In mid-1915 a motion was made to drastically cut Fed ticket prices, but it was defeated 6–2, with only St. Louis and Newark in favor. But in August the decision was reversed after a four-game experiment at Newark. On Saturday, August 8, 18,000 fans jammed the park, and Newark, St. Louis, Pittsburgh, Brooklyn, Baltimore and Chicago all announced cuts, with bleacher admissions 10 cents, 25 cents for the pavilions and 50 cents for the grandstands. Box seats remained $1.

A scorecard for the 1915 Chicago Whales, who won the Federal League pennant by a mere two percentage points over St. Louis and one-half game over Pittsburgh.

By August, Gilmore abandoned plans for a Boston franchise, and he, Ward, Sinclair and Comstock visited brand new Braves Field as guests of James Gaffney. "Next year [we] will have a team in New York," said Gilmore. "The object of our visit . . . was to get some ideas on the building of an up-to-date plant. Comstock is ready to lay out the field when we get ready to invade New York." Gaffney even treated the quartet to lunch.

Following Chicago's capture of the 1915 pennant, Charles Weeghman challenged Organized Baseball to some post–World Series competition, with Chicago playing the winner of the Phils–Red Sox match-up. Harry Sinclair offered to bet $200,000 on the outcome. If Weeghman's challenge was not accepted, said Chicago Mayor Thompson, "public opinion will be with the Whales anyway, for the public will look with suspicion upon any sport who fails to accept a challenge."

On to New York!

Rumors continued to swirl of a Fed invasion of New York, with President Gilmore saying a location had been selected. "We not only have the grounds," bragged Gilmore, "we have drawn plans for a concrete stadium to seat 55,000 persons—even bigger than Braves Field. . . . We are getting up the cost sheets now, and may . . . make an announcement very soon." Most believed the site was at First Avenue and 41st Street, although Gilmore refused to confirm that.

After the season, Kansas City turned in its franchise to Gilmore, and it was announced the club would operate in New York for 1916. In December definite word was received that an $800,000 ballpark (the stands themselves would cost $475,000) would be erected at 145th Street, between Lenox and Fifth avenues. The plot of land on which the park would be built contained 183 building lots and 547,000 square feet of ground.

C. B. Comstock had designed a double-decked, postless grandstand. Originally a 55,000-seat stadium was announced, but that was soon scaled back to 35,000, with possible expansion to the former number. It would be 450 feet from home plate to straight-away center and 388 feet down each line.

Construction would start on January 15. *Sporting Life* reported Braves President James Gaffney would likely receive the construction contract "if he cares to make a bid."

Harry Sinclair backed the club and would divest himself of his Newark holdings. "I'll stand at the Battery," said Sinclair of his Giants and Highlanders rivals, "and I'll match any of them in pitching dollars into New York Harbor. We'll see who quits first." Fielder Jones, George Stovall and the Tigers' Hughie Jennings were rumored candidates for the manager's post.

That this new club would be competitive was all but assured. The Feds would transfer talent in to give it credibility, and Frank "Home Run" Baker of the Athletics was reportedly being offered a contract.

The Feds threatened further raiding for 1916. In August, Gilmore announced, "As there is no telling when Judge Landis will make known his decision, we are forced to go after players now, so as not to be left in the hole." As late as December 9 White Sox hurler Eddie Cicotte was negotiating with Pittsburgh manager Rebel Oakes.

And in Brooklyn, Business Manager Dick Carroll was promising a night baseball experiment for either October or November, using both major league and semipro players. If the trial succeeded, Gilmore promised, his 1916 schedule would see all afternoon games until June, when all Monday, Tuesday, Thursday and Friday contests would be under the lights.

Moves Toward a Settlement

Yet despite such outward displays of confidence, the Feds were quietly negotiating for peace. On October 9 a secret meeting was held at Philadelphia's Bellevue-Stratford Hotel with the National Commission.

Despite increased costs in terms of salaries, the established major leagues

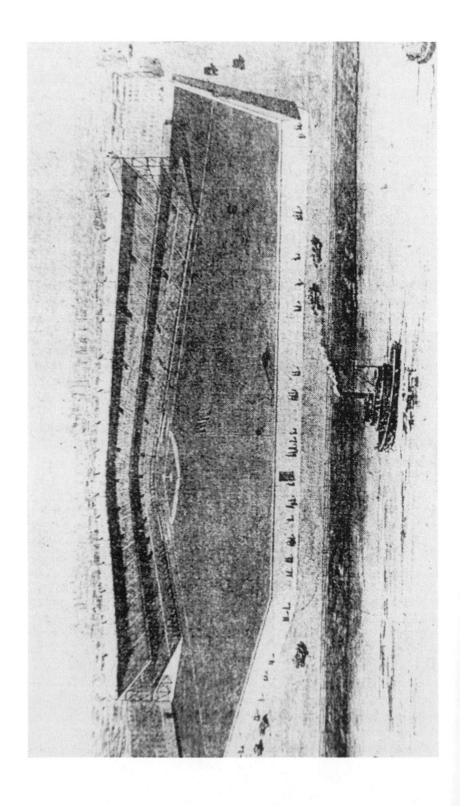

had not been significantly hurt at the gate by the Feds. While some clubs facing
direct Fed competition showed attendance drops—such as the Browns,
Dodgers and Pirates—other clubs which faced no such competition, such as
the Reds and Senators, also showed declines. It is difficult to find any pattern.
A much more telling factor, as is usually the case, was where a club finished.
The dramatic box-office decline of the A's from 1914 was not based on any Fed
competition—there was none—but rather on their disastrous on-field performance.

Attendance for the period:

CLUB	1913	1914	1915
Boston AL	437,194	481,359	539,461
Boston NL	208,000	382,913	376,283
Brooklyn NL	247,000	122,671	297,766
Cleveland AL	541,000	185,997	159,285
Chicago AL	644,501	469,290	539,461
Chicago NL	419,000	202,516	217,791
Cincinnati NL	258,000	100,791	218,791
Detroit NL	398,502	416,225	476,105
New York AL	357,351	359,477	256,035
New York NL	630,000	364,313	391,850
Philadelphia AL	571,896	346,641	146,223
Philadelphia NL	470,000	138,474	449,898
Pittsburgh NL	296,000	139,620	225,743
St. Louis AL	250,330	244,714	150,358
St. Louis NL	203,531	256,099	252,666
Washington AL	325,831	243,888	167,332

The Federal League was dealt a major blow on October 19 when Robert
Ward died of a heart attack at his New Rochelle mansion.

"If you think we can win," Ward had told Gilmore, "I will put up another
million." Gilmore responded, "The best . . . we could get out of it was whatever
mercy Organized Baseball could be bluffed into granting."

"Ward's death," thought Gilmore, "did not effect the final situation.
Doubtless with him we might have exacted more reasonable terms. But no one
could have avoided the inevitable. There was no room for three major leagues."

Figures from both sides converged on Philadelphia for the 1915 World
Series ("[We] . . . were not chasing any officials of Organized Ball," maintained Gilmore. "We wanted to see the games, and being broad enough to
recognize the fact that the national sport may be legally played by other than
Federal League teams, we were there as fans to see the games"), and talk of
peace ensued. On December 13, just prior to the National League annual

Opposite: A proposed New York City Federal League park.

meeting, Senior Circuit magnates met with Gilmore and Sinclair in John K. Tener's New York office. Dinner at the Republican Club followed, and a rough agreement was hammered out.

Still to be heard from were the American League and the minors. Pittsburgh's Barney Dreyfuss was dispatched to meet with Ban Johnson in Chicago. Shortly thereafter an American League committee arrived in New York. Yet publicly Johnson still appeared intractable. "Principles will prevail, . . ." he stated, "rather than mere money or personal consideration."

Two sessions were held at the Waldorf Astoria on December 17. Time drew short, as the Fed option on its New York site would expire on December 23. First the two majors met. Then in the evening a conference was held with John Farrell of the National Association, Ed Barrow of the International League and Thomas Chivington of the American Association.

On everyone's mind was the Federal League suit still before Judge Landis. Would Landis consent to dismissal? After all, the Feds had charged Organized Baseball with a monopolistic conspiracy; now they were endeavoring to join that monopoly. "It is the most absurd thing I have ever heard of," snorted National League counsel J. Conway Toole.

But Landis did dismiss the case, and in Cincinnati on December 22, 1915, a settlement was reached. A complicated plan saw the Federal League go out of business and its suit against Organized Baseball withdrawn, but the establishment paid a heavy price as well.

A Complicated Agreement

Roughly, the terms of the settlement were as follows:

1. Charles Weeghman was allowed to buy the Chicago Cubs from Charles B. Taft. Rosters from the clubs would be combined. Joe Tinker would manage, and Weeghman Park (eventually better known as Wrigley Field) would become the new home of the Cubs.

2. Phil Ball would be allowed to buy the St. Louis Browns from Robert Hedges and John E. Bruce. Again, rosters would be combined. Terriers pilot Fielder Jones would replace Branch Rickey as Browns manager.

3. Edward W. Gwinner of the Pittsburgh Rebels was bought out for $50,000 over five years. He attempted to purchase the Indians from Charles Somers (who was $1,750,000 in debt) but was unsuccessful.

4. The Wards of Brooklyn were bought out for $400,000 over twenty years. O. B. was given control of Washington Park.

5. Newark's Harry Sinclair was bought out for $100,000 over ten years. O. B. was given control of Harrison Park. Sinclair was allowed to sell the more-valuable Fed players, collecting $35,000 from the Giants for Kauff and $22,500 from the Yankees for Lee Magee. Others such as Hal Chase, Edd

F. JONES, CHICAGO AMER.

As part of the peace settlement between the Federal League and Organized Baseball, St. Louis Terriers Manager Fielder Jones took the reins of the Browns.

Roush, Bill McKechnie, Bill Rariden, Germany Schaefer and Fred Anderson fetched smaller prices.

6. Baltimore was awarded $50,000, but thought the payment too little. A seven-man committee was to resolve the matter at a meeting to be held in Cincinnati on January 3, 1916.

7. Buffalo (which had lost $170,000) and Kansas City, both of which had both operated at severe losses in 1915 and required subsidies from the league to finish the season, were given nothing. Buffed owner William E. Robertson wanted the Buffalo slot in the I.L. but was refused.

8. Fed players were reinstated. Originally, the American League balked at this, and the settlement nearly foundered over the issue, but eventually Johnson's league agreed to rescind its blacklisting of Federal personnel.

It was rumored that other Federal owners would soon be back in the picture. Harry Sinclair (in partnership with James Gaffney, who had just sold his interests in the Braves) was reputedly the next owner of the Giants. It was even believed Gilmore would be his club president. According to Gilmore, Sinclair did offer $1,000,000 for the club, but Harry Hempstead (the late John T.

Brush's son-in-law) would not sell for less than $1,300,000, and Sinclair "would not stand to be stung."

On January 13 details of the St. Louis and Chicago transfers were finalized. The Browns were sold for $525,000 to Ball, Steifel and company. Ninety percent of the Cubs went to Weeghman for $500,000 – $100,000 in cash and the rest in notes. Further, Weeghman was to take over the Cubs' $12,000-per-year lease on old West Side Park, although former Cubs owners Charles Taft (brother of ex–President William Howard Taft) promised the new management assistance in dumping the property.

Baltimore Challenges the System

Baltfed stockholders continued to be upset by the terms of the settlement. In New York on December 17, they tried buying into the major leagues for $250,000, but the magnates scoffed at the city's "pretension" to big league status. "Baltimore is a minor league city and not a hell of a good one at that," jeered Charles Comiskey. "You have too many colored population to start," added Charles Ebbets. "They are a cheap population when it gets down to paying their money at the gate."

The Terrapins next tried shifting their franchise to Ed Barrow's International League, but as Jack Dunn was moving his team back into Baltimore, the scheme failed. Then they offered their "franchise" to Dunn for $100,000. Again, the answer was no. Finally, they offered Dunn the post of managing their club if they were allowed into the I.L. Still, that was refused.

When the Federal League met in Chicago on February 19, 1916, to dissolve itself, Baltimore refused to have anything to do with the session. It also refused to withdraw from the suit before Landis. Selling its ballpark to Jack Dunn for $25,000, it raised $50,000 for a suit against Organized Baseball filed on March 29, 1916, seeking damages in the amount of $900,000, charging conspiracy to destroy the Federal League and to establish a monopoly.

The suit reached United States District Court in Philadelphia on June 11, 1917. Representing the American and National Leagues were George Wharton Pepper, Frank Pritchard and Samuel M. Clement, Jr. Stuart S. Janney and Chester Farr, Jr., were counsel for Baltimore.

Janney startled the court by announcing the suit was being withdrawn as the Baltfeds were now convinced that "representatives of Organized Ball had not entered into a conspiracy to destroy the business of the Baltimore Club."

The defendants claimed not to be surprised by this development. One O.B. source claimed that Baltimore had dropped its suit after having seen a copy of the stenographic record of the December 1915 peace conference in New York, which the defense had placed on the record.

Yet in Federal District Court in Washington on September 21, 1917,

Baltimore sued again, claiming violation of the Clayton Antitrust Act and seeking $900,000 in damages. Also charged in this case were Gilmore, Weeghman and Sinclair.

The Court finally ruled in April 1919, and it came down in favor of Baltimore, awarding $240,000 in damages and lawyers fees. An appeal was heard in October 1920, with Pepper claiming the game was "a spontaneous output of human activity . . . not in its nature commerce, [and] that, therefore Organized Baseball cannot be interstate commerce." Pepper argued that baseball was a local enterprise, denied the existence of farm systems, held that Congress had not meant for baseball to be governed by either the Sherman or Clayton and, surprisingly, admitted that the reserve clause was a mere "honorary obligation," not legally binding on players.

In April 1921 the Appellate Court overturned the lower court decision. Baltimore then took its case to the United States Supreme Court. On May 22, 1922, Justice Oliver Wendell Holmes, speaking for the majority, held that the game was not interstate commerce. "The business is the giving of exhibition games," wrote Holmes, "which are purely state matters."

Then baseball received a bonus it had never expected, upholding of the reserve clause. It was justified, ruled Holmes, because it was "intended to protect the rights of clubs . . . to retain the services of sufficient players."

Cost of the War

Estimates of Federal League losses varied wildly. Some put the total at $10,000,000. Historian Harold Seymour counted up the Fed deficit at $2,500,000, with Brooklyn taking an $800,000 bath. Phil Ball claimed he lost $182,000 but "had a lot of fun." In December 1916 Gilmore said total Fed losses were only about $500,000 and even contended that Harry Sinclair made money after player sales were complete. Pittsburgh, he estimated, lost $150,000 but received $50,000 in the settlement and recouped $35,000 from sale of "players, equipment, etc." Baltimore, he stated, made $9,000 in 1914, but lost roughly $75,000 overall.

And what did Gilmore himself think of his failed enterprise? "There is no room for three major leagues," he commented in 1916. "There is no public demand for more than two. Take it from me, there will never be more than two first-class circuits. And no pity need be wasted on the downtrodden player. The reserve clause, . . . to which I objected, is vitally important to clean promotion of the sport. It might not be if the moral sense of some players and (I regret to say it) some magnates were more highly developed. But in this age of commercial competition baseball could not live a year without [it] . . . .

"How I fell I cannot figure yet. But I wouldn't trade the experience for a fortune. That surely was the life."

How strong a league was the Federal? In terms of financial backing it was very strong, although ultimately not durable enough. Artistically, there are many interpretations. In an April 22, 1978, letter to the *Sporting News*, sports statistician Pete Palmer contended Fed players were largely not of big league caliber.

Defining a "regular" player as one who played 77 or more games as a position player or 17 games as a pitcher for two prior years, Palmer found that of 107 Fed 1914 regulars only nine qualified as "major league" regulars. In 1915 it was only 14 of 111. By comparison, of the 113 National League "regulars" in 1915, 46 qualified by the Palmer definition.

Further, of the 147 players Palmer termed as Federal League "regulars" in either 1914 or 1915, 79 never again played a single major league game. Only eight Fed "regulars" went on to appear in 500 or more big league games. Those in the majors in 1916 had a composite batting average 50 points lower than their 1915 Federal League mark.

While the Feds put up a game fight and held key advantages such as the Jim Gilmore's dynamic leadership and unusually strong financial backing, they basically failed in the face of cohesive opposition led by Ban Johnson, and because there was no real demand for additional big league teams.

Finally, despite signing scores of major leaguers, the Feds lassoed few true stars—the Cobbs, the Johnsons, the Speakers. Benny Kauff was the "Ty Cobb of the Federal League," but he was no real superstar.

So the Feds stumbled, but other incredibly diverse challenges would follow in the decades to come.

Chapter 11

The Continental League of 1921

Following the Federal League's absorption, baseball faced and survived—although just barely—the challenge of the First World War. In fact, the 1918 season was shortened, ending at Labor Day, and the World Series was barely played. Only the collapse of Imperial Germany saved baseball for the 1919 season.

The game then emerged into the lively ball era of Babe Ruth, with increased hitting and attendance, and as it did it was met with yet another of the short-lived, farcical rivals that had marked the early 1910s. This time the "challenge," the "Continental League," emanated from Boston.

Championing it was George Herman "Andy" Lawson, whom the *Sporting News* characterized as "famous as [a] baseball promoter in the past." Announcements Lawson distributed described him—albeit, in somewhat exaggerated terms—"as the father of the old United States League, which later developed into the Federal League." Others recalled him as the organizer of another recent flop called the "Greater Boston League."

Despite these claims, as we saw in the chapters covering the United States League and the Federal League, Lawson's name was not prominent. If he had a role to play, it must have been a supporting part.

Assisting him in this new endeavor were James Nelson Barry and George Maynard Riley, also of Beantown. Barry, whose residence was given as 433 Shawmut Avenue, was moderately well-known as a promoter of New England area semipro teams. He had also functioned as a sort of talent scout or "bird dog" for big league clubs. Riley, of 15 Park Square, was unknown in baseball circles.

The *Sporting News* termed Lawson an "Old Friend" and seemed to be taking the announcement at least semi-seriously, reporting the circuit would be a "big league" and "a real rival of the American and the National," although details of how it would obtain its players were not discussed.

On December 28, 1920, the Continental League was chartered under the laws of the State of Massachusetts, capitalized at $60,000. Lawson held 4,000 shares of its common stock; Barry held 3,000, and Riley owned 2,000. The following day an organizational meeting was held.

253

On December 31, Lawson announced that his league would represent not cities as had been the traditional manner, but states (shades of the Minnesota Twins, Texas Rangers and California Angels). The Massachusetts club would operate in Boston; New York State's in either Brooklyn or Buffalo; New Jersey's in Camden; Pennsylvania's in Pittsburgh; Maryland's in Baltimore; Michigan's in Detroit; Ohio's in Cleveland; and Indiana's in Indianapolis. In no case would there be more than one team per state.

Offices of the new circuit would be at 27 School Street, opposite the Boston City Hall.

Major league baseball was prosperous, and in any case was not about to be cowed by a circuit capitalized at a mere $60,000 (although there was talk of the Maryland franchise's being backed by $2,000,000).

"Let 'em come along into Brooklyn," challenged Robins Secretary Charles H. Ebbets, Jr. "If they have two or three million dollars to invest in grounds and a plant, they will have everything they need except ballplayers—and, of course, that is only a minor item in getting a team of major leaguers together.

"I don't think there is much to get excited over in this proposition. Evidently somebody up Boston way is having a Happy New Year."

Ebbets heaped further ridicule on the Continental League's choices of Camden ("When [it] is included as one of the cities in the new league, there is no hesitation in regarding the circuit as something as a joke") and Indianapolis, which he recalled as a city which won a Federal League pennant and then saw its team move to Newark.

"It is difficult," concluded Ebbets, "to consider a major league without teams in New York, Philadelphia, Chicago or St. Louis, but they do try some odd things in baseball now and then."

The *Times* took care to point out further difficulties Lawson and company would be facing. The courts had recently given grudging backing to the standard player contract. Parks were now more expensive. After the Feds' failure, men of wealth would be less inclined to back a third league. "It is not likely," the *Times* reasoned, "that major league club owners will view the proposed organization with any great alarm. . . ."

However, restiveness was in the air within Organized Baseball's ranks. The International League and the American Association were grumbling about breaking away from the National Association. Controversy centered over the draft prices paid by big league clubs for minor league players.

"The Indianapolis club," said Indians manager Jack Hendricks, "is solidly back of any move that President [Thomas Jefferson] Hickey may take to lead the American Association from the smaller loops into a larger one."

Nonetheless, Lawson seemed to make no moves to take advantage of this discontent.

On January 4, 1921, "Andy" Lawson was officially named president of the mysterious new circuit. Along with this news, came another of what would soon be a whole series of conflicting news releases concerning prospective franchises. Now missing was any mention of a Pennsylvania franchise. In its place was the possibility of one for "the Province of Toronto, with a team at Toronto."

Lawson was off and rolling in any case. There would be no salary limits on Continental League clubs, and Lawson extended a fantastic offer to financially hard-pressed Red Sox owner Harry H. Frazee to purchase Fenway Park. He added nonchalantly: "In the event of the Red Sox not accepting the offer to sell, a park will be built in Boston."

Other names now emerged. Fred Lundy was awarded the Boston franchise, although it was said he was a mere agent for others. The Indiana slot was given over to Indianapolis' Donald Jones; the New Jersey franchise to Philadelphia's Charles H. Mack.

On January 9 the New York *Times* reported that Lawson was surveying the New York metropolitan area for possible playing sites. Old Federal League locations at Newark (Harrison Park) and Brooklyn (Washington Park) were examined, although Lawson indicated that either city might be replaced as its state's prospective representative—Newark by Camden; Brooklyn by far-off Buffalo. In fact, the possibility of any Garden State club now seemed iffy.

In terms of player personnel Lawson indicated that the Continental League (which the *Times* alternately termed the "Continental Baseball Association") had already signed several "prominent" players, as well as some umpires, although he would not reveal their identities. Players would be engaged for one season only—i.e., there would be no reserve clause. Despite rumors to the contrary, players involved in the recent Black Sox scandal were not being considered.

The *Times* was intrigued and amused by another of Lawson's ideas, that he would be engaging "Negro or Cuban" talent, primarily for his Massachusetts, Pennsylvania and New Jersey squads. The paper noted that such a move would "ensure him the 135th Street and Lenox Avenue [Harlem] vote quite solidly." Lawson himself commented that both Philadelphia and Boston contained large black populations, hinting that these could be a significant percentage of his gate. "He asserted," reported the *Times*, "that there were at least 100 [black] ball players in this country who were the equal in playing skill of the average sound player in the two major leagues. . . ." It was not a popular opinion for the time, but it was, of course, true.

Regarding franchises, Lawson claimed that three of the eight possible clubs had already been assigned, the aforementioned Indianapolis and Boston teams, plus Toronto. Lawson piously hoped to have as many players from the state or province that each club represented as possible. He also hoped to buy existing clubs and or stadiums if they were available.

Capital for the new circuit, Lawson maintained, was now at the $75,000 level.

Lawson's next stop was Philadelphia. From the City of Brotherly Love, he announced that the Continental League's season would commence on May 1 and end just after Labor Day. Franchises would now be awarded to Massachusetts (Boston), Indiana (Indianapolis), New York (Brooklyn), New Jersey (Newark), Pennsylvania (either Philadelphia or Pittsburgh), Maryland (Baltimore), Ohio (Cleveland) and either Ontario (Toronto) or Michigan (Detroit).

Aside from the daily shifting of franchises, other statements by Lawson were guaranteed to raise eyebrows. Each C.L. club would be affiliated with the American Federation of Labor, and, of course, there would be no reserve clause, "as the Continental does not recognize such contracts."

Lawson continued his campaign to obtain the former Federal League stadia, firing off a telegram to Cincinnati Reds President Garry Herrmann (the former National Commission Chairman), ordering him to "cut the strings" on the Newark and Brooklyn fields. "Otherwise," the promoter threatened, "I shall immediately sign four American League players who wish to jump to the Continental League."

Still in Philadelphia a few days later, Lawson contradicted himself once more. Now he stated that he would indeed sign the disgraced (but still not tried in a court of law) Black Sox players.

Other announcements were to come, but were not calculated to inspire the baseball public. Minor league catcher Harry O'Donnell (an Athletics property) was dickering with the Continentals—amazingly, it was said he could virtually name his price. Former Red Sox and Buffeds infielder Clyde "Hack" Engle was negotiating to become pilot of the C.L. Boston team. Darby, Pennsylvania, resident Eddie Bohon was attempting to secure the Camden franchise.

More interesting was Lawson's continuing flirtation with black talent. The Chicago American Giants were mentioned as a prospective franchise, although that club was already a member of Rube Foster's new National Association of Colored Professional Base Ball Clubs. Two other black teams, the obscure Boston Tigers and the Knoxville Giants, were also mentioned as possible C.L. members.

By early February two more franchises were formally awarded: to shoe manufacturer Warren L. Patterson in Buffalo (this meant Brooklyn was out of the running) and to Captain Raymond C. Warner in Philadelphia (this spelled *finis* for Pittsburgh).

Therefore, shortly Lawson was on the move again, heading for Pittsburgh, Cleveland and either Cincinnati or Chicago to line up backers. Again he was hinting of black participation, boasting that four Negro clubs were knocking on his door.

As Opening Day approached less and less was heard of Andy Lawson and his Continental League. By late April, he popped up announcing that play would not begin on May 1, but would instead start on May 20.

It never did.

Chapter 12

The Mexican League

Following the Second World War, major league baseball enjoyed yet another era of great opportunities. Millions of fans returned from military service, more than eager to take in a game. Attendance soared. Also returning were hundreds of professional players. Not since the Federal League's absorption had such a talent surplus existed. The game's magnates seemed securely in the driver's seat.

True, there were the traditional harmless labor rumblings, but little seemed destined to rock the boat—at least until invaders appeared from Mexico.

Baseball originally came to that nation in the 1880s when American railroad men taught the game to the locals. The first Mexican-born big leaguer was Baldomero "Mel" Almada, a 20-year-old center fielder for the 1933 Red Sox.

Since 1925 a *Liga Mexicana de Béisbol* had functioned south of the border, quietly operating apart from the restrictions of American Organized Baseball.

The Pasquel Family

In the late 1930s, however, the league was given fresh drive by the five wealthy Pasquel brothers, who had a personal fortune of an estimated $60,000,000.

The Pasquels were among the most powerful people in Mexico. Their father operated a prosperous cigar factory, but they really hit their stride when one son, Jorge, married the daughter of Mexican President Plutarco Calles. Jorge was appointed customs broker, and his fortune grew. Soon he discarded his wife but grew still more powerful.

The Pasquels were also close friends of Calles' successors, General Manuel Avila Camacho and Miguel Aleman. In fact, it was widely rumored that Mexican government funds partially backed their new league.

While Jorge was the family's driving force and dominant personality, the others had their roles to play as well. The eldest brother, Bernardo, handled

257

From left: Ray Dandridge, Jorge Pasquel, Mexican President Plutarco Calles and unidentified player. (Courtesy John Holway.)

negotiations with American ballplayers. Twins Gerardo and Alfonso largely stayed out of baseball, restricting themselves to the family's more traditional enterprises. Mario, the youngest brother, according to pitcher Tom Gorman, "met the stars from the United States and put them on the train for Mexico City."

Jorge and Bernardo were no strangers to the U.S. State Department. Back in December 1941, according to muckraking columnist Drew Pearson, both were placed on the U.S. "blacklist" for trading with Hitler's Germany. They got off by signing affidavits they would refrain from that practice in the future.

In 1945 Jorge Pasquel spent six months in the United States observing American *béisbol.* He was not all that impressed: "That caused me to wonder why these leagues set themselves up as governing bodies for the sport. Don't they know we play fine baseball in Mexico?"

In 1946 the addition of San Luis Potosi and Torreon made the Mexican League an eight-team circuit. Populations of the various franchised cities varied wildly. To wit:

CITY	POPULATION
Mexico City	1,448,422
Monterrey	185,833
Puebla	138,491
Tampico	81,312
Torreon	75,796
San Luis Potosi	57,353
Vera Cruz	54,225
Nuevo Laredo	28,872

Most of the circuit's fields, with the exception of Mexico City's Parque Delta (capacity 23,000), were crude. Puebla's was described as "one of the poorest diamonds" in the league—"a barren strip of prairie with a wire fence around it." In Tampico a railroad cut across the outfield. "Game called end of 8th. Slow freight," daydreamed one American scribe. Torreon's and Nuevo Laredo's parks were set up for night ball, but their systems were less than adequate.

"Mexico City had the only decent accommodations," observed Gorman. "There was little or no provision for dressing or showering. They were all skin infields."

The league operated on a syndicate basis. To create a "balanced" circuit, a central committee assigned players to clubs most in need of them. Further, 55 percent of all gate receipts were funneled into the league for distribution at season's end. Additionally, the Pasquels owned the Mexico City Reds and the Vera Cruz Blues. Both teams played in Mexico City's Parque Delta, although Vera Cruz was 200 miles away. The league being a family affair, Jorge was president, while Bernardo served as vice president.

The Prior Black Presence

Before the Pasquels lured white major league players to Mexico, American blacks had begun a steady exodus south. Beginning in 1939, Pasquel took the cream of talent from the American Negro leagues.

Besides money, the dropping of the color bar was a mighty lure for these men. "We are heroes here, . . ." said former Newark Eagle shortstop Willie Wells, who first went down in 1940. "In the United States everything I did was regulated by color. Well, here in Mexico I am a man."

The Negro leagues' hand-to-mouth operators could not compete with the Pasquels' pesos. "The first player they got after on my team was [third baseman Ray] Dandridge," recalled Eagles owner Effa Manley. "He came to me with this thousand dollars in his hand, and said Mr. Pasquel had just given him this to play with his team, and if I'd just give it to him he wouldn't go." Manley realized she couldn't win "a bidding war," so she advised Dandridge to head south.

While most historians accept the above account, researcher James Overmyer has unearthed documents which prove Manley and other black magnates were far less-gracious—and sometimes just downright cheap—about letting their talent slip away to Mexico.

In the spring of 1943 young Monte Irvin was barnstorming his way north with the Eagles. At Washington, for a doubleheader against the Homestead Grays, he received a telegram from Jorge Pasquel offering him $500 a month plus $200 per month for housing expenses. The first month's stipend would be paid in advance.

Irvin's $150-per-month Eagles salary couldn't compare with that offer, but he didn't savor the thought of going to Mexico. So he left for his Orange, New Jersey, home, informing Effa Manley of the facts of the case.

Effa showed up in his living room to convince either Monte or his mother that he should remain in the Negro leagues. Irwin was almost sold; he asked for just a token $25-a-month raise in order to stay.

Effa refused, replying she had to save her money to pay the team's "stars." Irwin finished packing and headed for Mexico.

Aside from persuasion, however, tougher measures could be employed. Correspondence recently discovered by Overmyer reveals that these owners were not above attempting to manipulate the draft status of players to keep them from playing ball for the Pasquels.

A February 20, 1943, letter from Effa Manley to the Chicago American Giants' Dr. J. B. Martin includes this point:

> Now the main reason for this letter, I want you to get me the names, addresses, and draft board number if possible of all the ballplayers who are planning to go to Mexico. I am working on something that might do us some good. There is no question they are planning to go if they can. One of my men has already left his defense job, and is taking a rest before leaving. Isn't that something? I expect to go to Washington and see someone important. Could you arrange to meet me there if it is done?

A March 7, 1943, a letter from the Homestead Grays' Cum Posey to Abe Manley (Effa's husband) asked, "Kindly send me the address of the local draft boards at which Wells and Dandridge are registered."

After the war, when the Pasquels' raids became more serious, Effa Manley was still attempting to secure government intervention, as the following October 8, 1945, letter from her attorney, James A. Curtis of Newark, reveals:

Dear Mrs. Manley:

> I had the conference with Senator [H. Alexander] Smith and his secretary, Ab Herman [a former infielder with the Boston Braves], . . . October 5th in Washington, concerning the hi-jacking of Negro Major League ball players by the agents of the Mexican Leagues. . . .
>
> When Senator Smith arrived I explained the predicament of the Negro League owners and their desire for the protection of their investment. He was obviously surprised and amazed at the size of this business conducted by Negroes. He was sympathetic and interested. However, clever politicians as he and Herman are, he immediately saw the weak point in urging the State Department to intervene by refusing visitors permits to Negro ball players. He pointed out that such action would be discriminatory.
>
> Another point I was questioned on was the action taken by the ball clubs and the league against the offending players. I did not admit the true state

of affairs there because I knew that, if known by them, they would advise a house cleaning within the league itself.

It was agreed at the end of the discussion that this was a problem in which Senator [Albert "Happy"] Chandler [newly elected baseball commissioner] might be of service. Therefore Senator Smith will take up this matter with him when he returns from the World Series and arrange a conference for me with him within the next few weeks.

It was an impressive group of players who abandoned the Negro Leagues. Talent Jorge Pasquel recruited included Wells, Dandridge, catchers Josh Gibson, Quincy Trouppe and Roy Campanella; pitchers Roy Partlow, Chet Brewer, Theolic "Fireball" Smith, Nate Moreland and Leon Day; shortstops Sam Bankhead and Silvio Garcia; second baseman Sammy T. Hughes; outfielders "Cool Papa" Bell, Lloyd Davenport, Bill Wright, Alex "Home Run" Crespo, Santos Amaro and Monte Irvin; first baseman Buck Leonard; and third baseman Pat Patterson.

The great Josh Gibson abandoned Cum Posey's Homestead Grays, first for Venezuelan ball in 1940 (where he hit .419), then for the Mexican League in 1941, pacing Vera Cruz to a pennant with a .345 average. Gibson had been on the verge of rejoining the Grays, but at $800 per month (Posey offered $500) Mexico was too good a deal to turn down. Joining him were Homestead pitchers Roy Partlow and Terry McDuffie.

In Gibson, Pasquel had one of the finest players—black or white—in the game, but even that could not give him an appreciation of baseball's finer points. One day he walked into the Vera Cruz locker room after Gibson had gone 4-for-4—two singles, a double and a triple. "What's amatter Jipson?" he asked with discomfort. Josh held up four fingers and beamed: "Four-for-four. Four-for-four." That wasn't good enough: "No home run? I got Wells and Dandridge for doubles and triples. I got you for home runs."

But when you came through for Pasquel, he came through for you. He bought Ray Dandridge a house in Newark after his career was over. At other times he brought instant gratification. Once with two outs and the sacks loaded, he shouted to Mexico City batter Monte Irvin: "If you win this game I'll give you $200." Irvin peered down to catcher Roy Campanella and whispered: "Give me a fastball and I'll give you half." There followed a duel of wits. Campy agreed but signalled for a curve—as Irvin fully expected—and Monte walloped it over the fence. Jorge was there with cash in hand.

Campanella came to Mexico in 1942. He started the season with the Baltimore Elite Giants, but when he was fined $250 by Negro National League president and Baltimore owner Tom Wilson, he received a telegram:

I HAVE HEARD ABOUT YOUR DIFFICULTIES ... WOULD YOU CONSIDER FINISHING OUT THE SEASON IN THE MEXICAN LEAGUE STOP YOUR PAY WILL BE ONE HUNDRED (100) DOLLARS A WEEK

The Vera Cruz team (ca. 1939–41) included Josh Gibson (4th from left), Ray
Dandridge (5th from left), LeRoy Matlock (6th from left), and Johnny Taylor
(8th from left). (Courtesy of John Holway.)

PLUS EXPENSES STOP PLEASE ANSWER PRONTO STOP JORGE
PASQUEL.

Campanella played for Monterrey under Manager Lazaro Salazar for the
rest of 1942 and all of the 1943 season. He intended to return to Mexico in
1944, but when Wilson forgave his fine and offered him a raise to $3,000 for
the year plus a $300 signing bonus, Campy returned to Baltimore.

Pasquel's influence was pervasive. Quincy Trouppe and Theolic Smith ran
into draft troubles in 1943. Trouppe returned to Los Angeles to take a job in
a defense plant but soon received a visit from the Mexican consulate. "The
respresentative from Mexico told me," said Trouppe, "they had loaned the
United States 80,000 workers to fill the manpower shortage caused by the war
and all they wanted in return was two ballplayers by the name of Quincy
Trouppe and Theolic Smith."

Longtime Negro league catcher/pitcher Ted "Double Duty" Radcliffe
played for Vera Cruz in 1946. He received a $3,000 bonus from Jorge Pas-
quel. "I didn't do much catching," he recalled. "I was relieving and saved quite
a few games. Then every time I hit a home run they gave me a watch and a
suit of clothes. I hit seventeen home runs, batted .344 and made the All-Star
team at the age of forty-six!"

Another source of talent was Cuba. In 1946 40 Cubans could be found
on major league rosters, but it had been a vein long mined by the Mexican
League.

The great Martin Dihigo joined the Mexican League back in 1937. The

Cuban still holds the league mark for lifetime won-lost percentage, .717 (119-47). A great strikeout pitcher for the Aguila club of Vera Cruz, on July 29, 1939, he struck out 16 Monterrey batters. Versus Tampico in his next start on August 5 he K'd 18. In June 1938 against Comintra he fanned 22 in 13 frames. As a batter he was no slouch either, connecting for six hits in one game in 1937. All are still league records. In 1938 he led the circuit in batting, and in 1942 he managed the Union Laguna club of Torreon to a pennant.

The Major League Influx

Jorge was not satisfied with this rich harvest of black talent and coveted the rich talent of the U.S. major leagues. He began by talking of pouring $30,000,000 of his huge personal fortune into baseball. He planned to lure Joe Medwick to play and Babe Ruth to manage. Soon he would be pushing offers at scores of American players.

But it was not until February 1946 that Pasquel began raiding American rosters. Dodgers outfielder Luis Olmo, a Puerto Rican who hit .313 in 1945 with a league-leading 13 triples, signed for $40,000 for three years. Soon he was followed by Danny Gardella, Napoleon Reyes, Rene Monteagudo, Bobby Estalella, Adrian Zabala (who had led the Mexican League in winning percentage in 1944), Roland Gladu and Jean-Pierre Roy. With the exception of Gardella, none was an American citizen.

Gardella's signing set off a rush of Giants players to Mexico. Reyes, Zabala, Sal Maglie, George Hausmann and Roy Zimmerman would all eventually follow. Rumors of these defections soon reached Giants manager Mel Ott, who called a clubhouse meeting and grilled Maglie on whether he was heading south. Maglie, then a minor leaguer battling to make the Giants, admitted he was. Ott fumed, and tempers mounted. Meanwhile, back in the showers, pitcher "Big Bill" Voiselle, blissfully unaware of events and chronically hard-of-hearing, started whistling the then-hit song, "South of the Border, Down Mexico Way." The hitherto grim assemblage burst out in startled laughter, but the incident was serious to Giants management. Owner Horace Stoneham summoned Zimmerman and Hausmann to his office. Both said they would depart "if the price was right."

"Then," the magnate responded, "you're through with the Giants."

In March 1946 raiding went the other way. Alex Pompez, owner of the Negro National League's New York Cubans, announced that three top Mexican League stars—shortstop Silvio Garcia and outfielders Santos Amaro and Alex Crespo—were all returning to the Cubans. Garcia had hit .350 for Vera Cruz in 1945, Amaro .330 for Tampico and Crespo .311 for Nuevo Laredo.

Despite promises of big pay, the trio reported they were getting as little as

$300 per month in Mexico. Further agitating them were reports of the salaries that players such as Olmo, Gardella and Reyes pulled down.

"They all jumped my club to go to Mexico," Pompez told the press. "Now they have jumped the Mexican League to return to the Cubans."

Another Mexican League setback was a boycott by American sporting goods manufacturers. Top-quality bats, balls and gloves were in short supply. "Many bat companies in the United States have come to our support, offering us their best product," Jorge complained, "but we want only genuine Louisville Slugger bats. We are a big league; we want big league bats and . . . balls, no substitutes, and we have been unable to obtain them."

The Mexican National League, a Class B circuit affiliated with Organized Baseball, was feeling uneasy about the Pasquels' competition and hoped for assistance from *El Norte*. "We'd like to form part of a chain of some big league club," said Alejo Peralta, part-owner and manager of the league's Mexico City club. Later in the year the league would request an upgrade to Class A or A-1 status so that it might obtain better players and compete more evenly with the Pasquels.

It was not until April, when Brooklyn catcher Arnold "Mickey" Owen jumped to Mexico, that an established American player defected. When Branch Rickey did not respond to his pleas for a salary increase, Owen became increasingly intrigued by Olmo's talk of Mexico. And when Pasquel offered a $12,500 signing bonus and $15,000 per year for five years, Owen was on his way. At the border he was met not only by Alfonso Pasquel but by a message to call Rickey back in Brooklyn.

Rickey's persuasive powers were such that Owen made a 180-degree turn, rushing back to Brooklyn. He kept on driving until he picked up a paper that reported on Rickey's vow to trade Owen. Once again, the catcher reversed direction, and this time he did not stop until he got to Mexico City.

In Havana, Jorge approached Ted Williams, offering him $300,000 for three years. Williams, then making $40,000 with the Red Sox, was not impressed, despite Jorge's many diamonds. "Every one of them three- or four-carat, . . ." recalled Teddy Ballgame in his autobiography. "He absolutely glittered. The thing is it all seemed phony to me."

The Red Sox were in Havana for two games against Washington. Bernardo Pasquel took quarters in the Sevilla Biltmore, just a block away from the Senators' hotel, and approached several of their players. Catcher Mike Guerra, a Cuban, nearly jumped, but Clark Griffith came through with a salary increase. Pitcher Roger Wolff and outfielder Stan Spence were also approached. Wolff admitted he was "seriously considering" a Pasquel offer of $100,000 for three seasons, plus a generous $15,000 signing bonus. None, however, defected.

Pasquel also offered Bob Feller $300,000 for three years. "Sorry I cannot accept your generous offer due to present obligations," the pitcher wired back.

Pasquel was impressed by Rapid Robert's courtesy, promising to contact him once again when his "obligations were fulfilled."

The Mexicans were stung by criticism implying that theirs was an outlaw circuit. "We treat our players right here," said Gerardo Pasquel. "We don't treat them like slaves." an important daily sporting paper, *Esto*, charged O.B. with having "established their own rules, decided on their own salaries, [creating] the system of being proprietors of the men, like of any object."

"I will not hear any proposals or attend any meeting pertaining to baseball which is not discussed here in Mexico City," said Jorge Pasquel at a joint press conference with Mexico's President Manuel Avila Camacho on March 25. "Branch Rickey, Clark Griffith and some of the others in the United States have insulted us and made a lot of misstatements. . . .

"These offenses can only be washed out if they come to my home in Mexico and give us satisfaction. Unless these people send me a cable, giving me a satisfactory explanation and retract . . . calling our league an 'outlaw league,' I shall never speak to any of them — and that goes for their commissioner, Senor Chandler, as well."

When asked whether he was interested in having a big league team come to Mexico to establish "good will," he became livid. "Absolutely not," he shouted. "I don't have any interest in having them come to Mexico to play, as the Yankees did in Panama. We have our own Mexican League to promote and can't be bothered with American teams visiting Mexico."

Meanwhile, back at Daytona Beach, Florida, Pasquel's agents made the rounds of the Brooklyn camp, offering contracts to the likes of "Dixie" Walker and Jackie Robinson. Robinson was offered $6,000 plus transportation and expenses by a "Senor Jaime."

"Not interested at all," responded Robinson, who was only on the Montreal roster. "I've got too much at stake. I wouldn't care if you offered me as much as you offered Ted Williams. I still wouldn't go."

Senor Jaime was later accosted by Branch Rickey in the stands of City Island Park. "I'm an old man," howled Rickey, who was not about to see his great experiment interfered with, "but you get out of here or I'll beat you up to within one inch of your life."

Mexican overtures to the Dodgers continued, and in early May "Pistol Pete" Reiser was offered $100,000. Fifteen thousand dollars a year for five years, plus a $15,000 signing bonus, was the first offer. When that was refused it became $100,000 for three years "and $50,000 on the line." Infielder Stan Rojek, pitchers Hal "Skeets" Gregg and Jean-Pierre Roy (a 25-game winner with Montreal in 1945) and first baseman Augie Galan were also actively courted. Rojek had been offered $8,000 per year for three years plus a $10,000 signing bonus. Both Leo Durocher and Branch Rickey hurried to the rookie's home to talk him back to the Dodgers, and it was believed he was rewarded with a new contract.

Rickey was so upset that he brought suit on May 6 in United States District Court of Eastern Missouri (home territory of Owen and Reiser) against Jorge and Bernardo Pasquel, their agents, Robert Janis and Mario Lousac, and St. Louis *Times-Star* sportswriter Ray J. Gillispie.

Charges against the first four were dismissed by Judge Ruben M. Hulen on May 31 on grounds that they were not served within the Court's jurisdiction. Charges against Gillispie were dropped as Hulen found no evidence to prove he was part of any conspiracy. Instead he ruled that Gillispie was motivated solely by his zeal for a story.

Gillispie was named for one reason: it was he who in the *Times-Star* offices had signed Owen on behalf of the Pasquels. Further, he had contacted other players and umpires and even secured equipment and hotel reservations for the Mexicans.

"As a witness," Hulen ruled, "Gillispie impressed the court as fair, frank, informative and honest. On his uncontraverted testimony that he did not know Owen was under contract, we will not presume the converse. Having been assured by Owen he was not under contract, there was no obligation on Gillispie to seek confirmation of Owen's statement."

Rickey was not the only executive charging the press with assisting the Pasquels. The Yankees' Larry MacPhail alleged that New York *Herald-Tribune* sportswriter Rud Rennie had brought the Mexican League's offer to Phil Rizzuto in the Yankees' home clubhouse. Rennie termed the charge, "the silliest thing. I am no Mexican agent, never have been and cannot understand what all the shooting is for."

On May 9 MacPhail sought an injunction again Jorge and Bernardo, Mario Lousac, Carlos Baz (Bernardo's interpreter), sports columnist and attorney Ralph Ober and Rennie in New York State Supreme Court as well as in Pennsylvania, Massachusetts, the District of Columbia, Illinois, Michigan, Ohio and Missouri. All were charged with being part of the effort to hijack American players.

American players (with their 1945 major league records) corralled by the Pasquels included:

PLAYER	POSITION	AMERICAN TEAM	GAMES	RECORD
Ace Adams	pitcher	Giants	65	11-9
Alex Carrasquel	pitcher	Senators	35	7-5
Tommy de la Cruz	pitcher	Reds	0	— —
Roberto Estalella	outfielder	A's	126	.299
Harry Feldman	pitcher	Giants	35	12-13
Murray Franklin	shortstop	Tigers	0	— —
Al Gardella	first baseman	Giants	16	.077
Danny Gardella	outfielder	Giants	121	.272
Roland Gladu	outfielder	Dodgers	0	— —
Chile Gomez	second baseman	Senators	0	— —

PLAYER	POSITION	AMERICAN TEAM	GAMES	RECORD
Tom Gorman	pitcher	Braves	0	– –
George Hausmann	second baseman	Giants	154	.279
Red Hayworth	catcher	Browns	56	.194
Chico Hernandez	catcher	Cubs	0	– –
Lou Klein	infielder	Cardinals	19	.228
Max Lanier	pitcher	Cardinals	4	2-2
Sal Maglie	pitcher	Giants	13	5-4
Fred Martin	pitcher	Cardinals	0	– –
Rene Monteagudo	outfielder	Phillies	114	.301
Luis Olmo	outfielder	Dodgers	141	.313
Mickey Owen	catcher	Dodgers	24	.286
Nap Reyes	third baseman	Giants	122	.288
Jean-Pierre Roy	pitcher	Dodgers	0	– –
Jim Steiner	catcher	Red Sox	38	.190
Vern Stephens	shortstop	Browns	149	.289
Adrian Zabala	pitcher	Giants	11	2-4
Roy Zimmerman	first baseman	Giants	27	.276

The Vern Stephens Affair

In March, the Pasquels made a major catch—1945 American League home run king, Browns shortstop Vern "Junior" Stephens.

The slugger was flown to Mexico City and along with Danny Gardella was an overnight guest at Jorge Pasquel's luxurious five-story mansion—one floor of which was a gym, another of which housed his huge wardrobe.

"I slept under velvet sheets," marveled Stephens. "The rugs were so thick you couldn't see your toes when you walked around barefoot. It was like out of *Arabian Nights*."

Stephens signed a five-year $250,000 Vera Cruz contract. A certified check for $25,000 was mailed to Stephens' wife to seal the bargain.

At Mexico City's Delta Park, Stephens debuted in heroic fashion. Before 35,000 screaming fans he singled in two runs in the bottom of the ninth to deliver a 5–4 win.

Stephens was treated royally, flown to each location, wined and dined. But he immediately grew uneasy. First, he was constantly tailed, and his mail was opened before he received it. Then there were charming local customs such as the *excusado*, where fans relieved themselves on the outfield wall. Stephens also had grave doubts of the circuit's continued financial viability. "I knew after three days I wanted to go home," the shortstop once recalled. "But the question was *how?*"

His fears were not unfounded. When Ray Dandridge wished to leave, his train was stopped near Monterrey by Mexican troops. So in true cloak-and-dagger fashion, Vern's father and a Browns scout named Jack Fournier arranged for his escape. In a Monterrey hotel lobby an American approached Stephens and told him he could return to the Browns, who would not only meet his salary demands but arrange for a trade to a contender. The duo promised to whisk him across the border if he could evade his ever-present bodyguard.

He soon got his chance. His "protector" was badly hung over and at breakfast asked for permission to visit a restroom. Stephens readily agreed. When the detective went in the restroom, "Junior" skipped out the front door, and within minutes the trio was speeding away on a nervous 3½-hour drive to the border. They were all too aware that if the Pasquel brothers knew what was occurring, they would do everything they could to prevent Stephens' escape. It was a fingernail-biting drive to the border, but the trio made it, and Stephens rejoined St. Louis. The Browns kept their promise; Vern was soon traded to the contending Boston Red Sox.

In April, Bernardo Pasquel surfaced in New York, unsuccessfully propositioning Yankees shortstop Phil Rizzuto ($100,000 for three years), pitcher Spud Chandler and second baseman George Stirnweiss. Bernardo still fumed over Vern Stephens' loss ("I intend getting back the $5,000 he owes us even if it takes five times the amount to get it. We don't need the money but we like fair dealings") and threatened to sign at least one big Yankee star.

"And what would you say if I told you we will have Ted Williams . . . next year?" bragged the league vice president. "He said OK in Havana this year and then the arrangements fell through—but we'll have him next year."

And Pasquel was corralling the biggest name of all. Babe Ruth would be returning home with him—"solely for a visit—we have no set position in mind. . . ."

In mid–May the Babe flew to Mexico for two weeks, amid rumors he would emerge as commissioner.

"I've just been invited by the Pasquel brothers to have a good time down there," revealed the man they called "El Rey Jonronero." "I've heard that Jorge is a pretty good golfer and I'll probably take him on. The chances are I'll be back."

The Babe denied that any pressure had been put on him not to go. "No," said Ruth, "nobody asked me not to come. But that doesn't make any difference. I go where I please anyway."

Responding to the now-familiar question as to whether the Babe would become league commissioner, Bernardo Pasquel impolitely responded, "Are you crazy?"

At tour's end on May 30, Babe consented to a home run hitting exhibition before a Mexico City–Vera Cruz game. Sadly past his prime, Ruth waved at nearly 30 pitches. Finally he lined a ball against the right field wall 375 feet from home and then launched a 390-foot blast into the right-center field stands.

That was not the real story of the evening. Vera Cruz's pitcher-manager,

Phil Rizzuto, shown in a 1989 photograph, spurned offers to join the Mexican League.

Cuban-born black Ramon Bragana, had pitched to Ruth. Mexico City manager Ernest Carmona felt Bragana had borne down too hard on the Bambino. He went to the mound, but Bragana shoved him off. Later Carmona charged into the clubhouse after Bragana. He didn't get in, but moments later there was a fearful noise at the door.

"Somebody wanted in pretty bad," recalled Mickey Owen. "The hasp went flying off and in ran this character with an old-fashioned six-shooter. He turned out to be the manager's brother. He forced Bragana to get down on his knees and told him to apologize. I guess he got the apology. I didn't wait to see."

Bragana was suspended for 30 days. "Bragana," the league executive committee ruled, "tried to make it a pitching exhibition and by refusing to cooperate is subject to discipline."

On June 2 another bizarre incident occurred. At Mexico City, Mickey Owen, now Vera Cruz's acting manager, was embroiled in a vicious argument with home plate umpire Amado Maestri.

Maestri had a reputation for roughness. As Owen approached the volatile ump, Vera Cruz outfielder Bobby Estalella cautioned: "Don't get too close, Mickey! He'll crack you over the head with his mask."

Maestri thumbed Owen and then found himself jawing not only with Owen, but also with Jorge Pasquel. True to form Maestri threatened Jorge with his mask, and Pasquel's bodyguard—who had also come down from the stands— pulled his knife on the ump.

"I'm through with the league forever, . . . " vowed Maestri, who along with his umpiring partner Raul Atan departed for Cuba after the game. "I'll walk out of anybody's league when the president can come in and take sides."

It was Pasquel who in the ninth inning of that game ordered Max Lanier in for his first appearance. Pasquel trod across the diamond and entered the Vera Cruz dugout. "He . . . says to Mickey Owen, . . . " recalled Lanier to Don Honig, "'I want Max to go in.' Mickey didn't say anything; he just looked over at me and shrugged, as if to say, 'It's his money.'"

The Breadon "Peace" Mission

Also in June, Cardinals owner Sam Breadon—much like some baseball Rudolf Hess—took off on an unauthorized peace mission to Mexico City.

"I had hoped," he later stated, "that my visit . . . would be unobserved. When I left by plane from St. Louis, I did not think anyone would recognize me."

His plan soon went awry. He was spotted by Cleveland *Plain-Dealer* sportswriter Gordon Cobbledick (who was tipped off by Owen). The news was soon relayed to the American and Mexican press. But "even if Cobbledick hadn't seen me," Breadon reflected, "I doubt if I could have gotten away with it. While I made no effort to contact any of our former Cardinals when I entered the Mexican park, one of the other players spoke to me, and said: 'How do you do, Mr. Breadon? Glad to see you in Mexico!' He spoke English very well. I didn't recognize him, but I asked who he was, and I was told he was Danny Gardella. . . ."

Breadon was very impressed by the Pasquels, finding them worthy opponents for Organized Baseball. He further believed that the Mexican League's greatest threat was the leverage it afforded American players in contract negotiations. As a courtesy to a guest, Pasquel promised Breadon he would take no more players from the Cards.

Jorge even put in a pitch to the magnate for a Mexican–U.S. World Series: "It can't be a World Series unless your champion plays our Mexican pennant winner. You know, we also are in the world."

Commissioner Chandler was livid about Breadon's visit and ordered him to Cincinnati. Breadon refused: "I can't. I've given my word to the Pasquel brothers that I did not represent Organized Ball. If I came now, it would give the appearance that I was such a representative." Chandler fined him $5,000 and barred the Cardinals for 30 days from any official transactions through the Commissioner's office. Only National League President Ford Frick persuaded Chandler to remit both punishments.

Nonetheless, Breadon hinted strongly he would be willing to travel south again. "If after I have had my say, you still want to send Breadon to Mexico it will be OK with me," Chandler told Frick. "Breadon's visit down there made us lose face. The people in Mexico got the impression that we were begging for mercy, that we were scared, in a panic. Another visit by Breadon would intensify that feeling."

Whereupon the Cubs' Phil Wrigley introduced a motion barring any further unilateral "peace" missions. It was adopted unanimously.

The Continuing Black Presence

In June, pitcher Tomas Quinones, a Puerto Rican black, returned home from the Vera Cruz Blues charging Mickey Owen with "racial prejudice." "Things got bitter down there when Owen arrived," the hurler alleged. "Owen resented colored ballplayers and said he didn't like to catch them. When he did, he acted in such a way as to upset the pitcher and make him lose confidence." He further contended that other American whites there showed little enthusiasm for playing with blacks.

Despite the influx of white major leaguers, blacks continued to be a major force on Mexican League rosters. The Tampico squad was entirely black. The Baltimore *Afro-American*'s Sam Lacy journeyed down to Mexico and reported on the large number of black stars and the frustration Pasquel felt in that his expensive white talent was, as he put it, being "thoroughly outclassed by tan performers. . . ."

Former Negro leagues personnel in the 1946 Mexican League included:

Torreon: Martin Dihigo (manager), Avelino Canizares (shortstop), Hector Rodriguez (third base).

San Luis Potosi: Jesse Williams (shortstop), Booker McDaniels (pitcher), Cecil Kaiser (pitcher), Leonard Geraro, Conrad Perez.

Mexico City: Ray Dandridge (shortstop), Bill Wright (outfield), Theolic Smith (pitcher), Jesse Douglas (outfield), Carlos Colas (second base).

Nuevo Laredo: Lloyd Davenport (center field), Carlos Blanco (third base).

Monterrey: Lazaro Salazar (manager), Art Pennington (first base), Ramon Heredia (third base), John Taylor (pitcher), Claro Duany (right field), Ed Stone (left field).

Jorge Pasquel and pitcher Johnny "Schoolboy" Taylor circa 1939–41. (Courtesy of John Holway.)

> Vera Cruz: Ramon Bragana (pitcher).
> Puebla: Pete Pages (first base).
> Tampico: Barney Serrell (second base), Ray Brown (pitcher).

Not only quantity but quality distinguished black representation. Ray Dandridge, formerly of the Negro National League's Newark Eagles, was given a midseason bonus for being the circuit's "No. 1 shortstop." Center fielder Lloyd "Ducky" Davenport, formerly of the Negro American League's Cleveland Buckeyes, was awarded a trophy as the league's "outstanding center fielder."

In the Mexican League All-Star Game played in July, ten ex–Negro leaguers participated. The Southern division (which won 11–8) featured Dandridge, Bill Wright, Theolic Smith, and Booker McDaniels. Toiling for the

North were Avelino Canizares, Hector Rodriguez, Lloyd Davenport, Martin Dihigo, Claro Duany and Art Pennington.

The Musial Scare

On June 6 Alfonso Pasquel was pursuing Stan Musial. Pasquel visited St. Louis with Mickey Owen to tempt "Stan the Man" with an offer of $130,000 for five years, with $65,000 to be paid in cash up front. Owen peddled the joyous life of a ballplayer south of the border: "We are so sold on Mexico that my wife and I have decided to live there permanently."

Musial followed his meeting by packing up his family's belongings out of the Fairgrounds Hotel, where they resided during the season. Reporters wildly speculated that Stan was heading for Mexico, but in actuality he was merely moving across town to a home formerly used by recently traded Cards first baseman Johnny Hopp.

Stan said no, but did so coyly: "I told him I would not go with him at this time. . . ."

A Violent Circuit

The Mexican League was marred by violence on the field. Mexico City pitcher Theolic Smith once knocked umpire Irv Wimer out cold. Mickey Owen and Monterrey Industriales outfielder Claro Duany went at it hammer and tongs following a bone-jarring plate collision. On August 11 Tampico pitcher Lazaro Medina, a Cuban, fuming over abuse from Mexico City fans, hurled his bat into the stands. A young girl, Elisa Velasquez, was injured. Medina was arrested and fined $40 dollars (200 pesos). And when Tampico pitcher "Loco" Torres refused to leave the mound, manager Armando Marsans returned with a fungo bat, whacked him a few times, and had him arrested by the local constabulary.

There was off-field violence as well. In his memoirs, Tom Gorman recalled one incident at a cocktail party in Bernardo's back yard. "I saw Bernardo kill a guy," wrote Gorman. "He just pulled out a gun and shot him and that was that. . . . This guy was climbing over the fence. I don't know what the hell he wanted. But Bernardo shot a hole in him as big as a cucumber and everybody walked away and left him lying there as if it were a perfectly natural thing."

Other Frustrations

Other conditions preyed on the Americans' nerves. Detectives were dispatched to make sure Jorge Pasquel's American investments weren't out carousing. "Every night they checked us in," revealed Mickey Owen. "That is, at midnight, one of his agents would pound on your door and make you sign a note signifying that you were home and in bed."

Travel was another issue. "The buses were driven by madmen," contended Sal Maglie to interviewer Don Honig. "They used to push those old wrecks as hard as they could on those narrow, winding roads in the mountains."

The heat was devastating. "I'd be so tired after pitching a game [in Tampico] that I couldn't talk above a whisper," Max Lanier told Honig. "There was no air conditioning, for one thing. Didn't even have screens in the windows."

Mickey Owen Defects

In August 1946 Mickey Owen returned from Mexico in dramatic fashion. First he wrote to Commissioner Chandler asking if he could return. He received no reply, but on August 5 he booked airline reservations from Mexico City to Brownsville, Texas. The most-direct route was through Nuevo Laredo, but with Alfredo Pasquel at that city, Owen's chances of making it through there were almost nil. Besides that, customs officials would never let the well-known Owen through.

Owen traced his dissatisfaction to Jorge's interference, particularly his relieving the catcher of the Vera Cruz managerial duties. "Mickey, you have dissension on your team. I am going to help you," Pasquel informed Owen. "I'll put on my uniform and give you a lift."

The following day Jorge Pasquel took the field in his full Vera Cruz Blues uniform. Right after Owen gave the home plate umpire that day's lineup, Jorge presented another one. Jorge put Owen on first base, a position he would play that day for the first time. He shifted other players around just as haphazardly and when Owen went out to his customary position as third base coach, Jorge replaced him there as well. It was just too much for Owen — and so was the local cuisine.

"Look who is disgusted," shot back *Esto*, following Owen's defection. "Dishes which are as rich and varied as any in the world are insulted by Mickey Owen, an unhappy eater of hot dogs."

The Pasquels hit Owen with a lawsuit in Federal District Court, claiming $127,500 damages. They also vowed a new round of raids, but in recognition of Jorge's pledge to Breadon, promised to spare the Cardinals. Supposedly, Stan Musial had expressed renewed interest in joining the Mexican League. In New York, Bernardo waved a letter allegedly from Stan, promising to send it to Breadon. It was a laughable hoax, postmarked Wingdale, New York, on a date when the Cards were at Sportsman's Park. Further, it was signed "Stanly Musiel."

Not just gringos were itching to get out. Back on July 9, Luis Olmo had his lawyer write Ford Frick asking for reinstatement, pleading that unlike Mickey Owen, Olmo had not been under contract for 1946.

Estimates of 1946 league losses ran to $250,000. Only Mexico City was profitable. "Make money?" wailed Puebla owner Castor Montoto. "Not a chance! Gate receipts are averaging approximately $10,000 a month, which gives me approximately $80,000 for the season. There's just no way out." San Luis Potosi did not even finish out the season. In 1947 both Torreon and Nuevo Laredo were dropped as the league reverted to six clubs.

After the 1946 season, grumbling increased by the lower paid Mexican Leaguers, incensed over the huge salaries paid to such American stars as Gardella, Zimmerman and Lanier. Four groups of malcontents emerged— white North Americans led by Jean-Pierre Roy and Roland Gladu; black players led by outfielder Lloyd Davenport; Cubans led by pitcher Tommy de la Cruz; and native Mexicans captained by infielder Bobby Avila.

They wanted pay increases to bring them closer to the stars, but the Pasquels had another idea of how to achieve parity. In 1947 the stars' salaries were slashed. Max Lanier, for example, was cut from $20,000 a year to $10,000. Jumping from the Mexican League began *en masse*. Finding alternate employment became a necessity. In the winter of 1946–47 the Max Lanier All-Stars (including Lanier and Danny Gardella) played 81 games and won them all, but opponents became harder and harder to find as Organized Baseball promised to blacklist anyone playing them.

An offer from a team sponsored by Cleveland's Rosenbloom Jewelers was looking pretty good to Lanier. Gardella hooked on with a New York City semipro team, the Gulf Oilers. Scheduled to play the black Cleveland Buckeyes on Staten Island, the Oilers suddenly found themselves without an opponent. With Jackie Robinson getting his chance with Brooklyn, the Buckeyes were unwilling to jeopardize their big league chances.

The outlaw Provincial League in Quebec Province was a safe haven for many baseball men-without-a-country. Roberto (Bobby) Estalella, Alex Carrasquel and Jean-Pierre Roy played for its St. Jean team; Al Gardella for Farnham; Danny Gardella, Sal Maglie, Max Lanier, Quincy Trouppe and Roy Zimmerman for Drummondville; Adrian Zabala and Harry Feldman for Sherbrooke; and Roland Gladu and Fred Martin for St. Hyacinthe and Sherbrooke.

Meanwhile far to the south, Luis Olmo was with Pastora of the Venezuelan League and Roberto Ortiz was with Maracaibo. Mickey Owen found work managing semipros in Winner, South Dakota.

Some players remained in Mexico for 1947. Monterrey's George Hausmann set the all-time record for sacrifices with 27. Mexico City's Ray Dandridge paced the circuit in hits (169). San Luis Potosi's Roberto Estalella led in doubles (29). Alejandro Crespo returned from the New York Cubans and led in RBIs (96) for Puebla.

Danny Gardella, who had been reduced to the position of a $36-a-week

Decades after baseball's "Mexican Revolution," the Mexican League survives as an independent circuit accorded Class AAA minor league classification by Organized Baseball.

hospital orderly to supplement his Provincial League income, had won the support of Frederick A. Johnson, an attorney whose family had long been involved in baseball. In October 1947 Gardella and Johnson brought suit against O.B., seeking to overturn Danny's five-year suspension. Johnson charged Baseball was "a conspiracy in restraint of trade and commerce" and sought triple damages of $300,000 for his client.

In July 1948 the suit was dismissed, but Johnson appealed; on February 10, 1949, the Second Circuit Appellate Court in New York ruled 2–1 that Gardella's case justified a trial. Further, Judge Jerome N. Frank took a potshot at the 1922 Holmes decision which gave Organized Baseball exemption from antitrust action, terming it "an impotent zombi." He also called baseball's labor system virtual "peonage." Judge Learned Hand was equally skeptical of the existing system, finding "all restraints of trade unlawful at common law and one of the oldest and best-established of these is a contract which unreasonably forbids anyone to practice his calling."

Organized Baseball trembled to think of the possible results from Gardella's action. Even many of his fellow jumpers expressed public outrage.

"Baseball didn't force us to go to Mexico," said Mickey Owen. "We went because of our weaknesses." Lanier and Fred Martin went to visit Gardella at his Bronx home to urge him to drop the matter, feeling that Commissioner Chandler was about to declare an amnesty. Instead Gardella won both over.

Gardella, Martin and Lanier sued in the Southern District of New York for Organized Baseball to show cause why they should not be reinstated. Their action was a direct frontal assault on the legality of the reserve clause. In April Federal Judge Edward A. Conger ruled against them. The Appellate Division affirmed Judge Conger's decision, adding that to reinstate them "would restore them to positions they had resigned voluntarily."

Nonetheless, Gardella's original suit remained and was slated to come to trial in November. Ford Frick and several National League owners pressed Chandler for a settlement.

On June 5, 1949, Chandler lifted the ban against the Mexican League jumpers, ruling that any player could return merely by asking to: "Application for reinstatement is tantamont to reinstatement itself."

Chandler informed Mickey Owen, "Get your bags packed, boy, and get to your club right away."

Owen responded he would return to the Dodgers within 48 hours, but he was not paying close enough attention to the commissioner's words. Chandler had not said "Brooklyn"; he had said "your club." Branch Rickey, who had vowed never to take Owen back, was a man of his word, trading him to the Cubs.

Gardella persisted in his suit, although now Johnson was counseling caution. On October 8, 1949, Gardella settled secretly for $60,000 and was allowed back into baseball for a single game with the Cardinals in 1950.

And so the "Mexican Revolution" ended, with baseball breathing a sigh of relief over yet another close call regarding the legality of the reserve clause.

Chapter 13

The Continental League

Between the 1903 shift of the Baltimore Orioles to New York and the 1953 move of the Braves to Milwaukee, the two major leagues enjoyed a remarkable surface stability.

Not one franchise shifted, but many individual clubs were sick. Worse, the Braves' announcement was indicative of an overall downturn in attendance in the 1950s. Major league gates for 1952 dipped an overall 8.2 percent and 9.2 percent in each league—the fourth straight year of decline. The Braves had sunk to a Depression-era-level attendance of 281,278 for their last year in Boston.

Milwaukee was followed by other moves—the Browns to Baltimore, the A's to Kansas City, the Dodgers to Los Angeles and the Giants to San Francisco. The last two sent shock waves through the baseball world. For the first time in nearly 80 years the National League would *not* be represented in the New York City area.

New Yorkers were outraged. In the 1950s both the Dodgers (National League champions in 1952, 1953, 1955 and 1956) and the Giants (pennant winners in 1951 and 1954) seemed like ideal franchises. Yet on-field success masked financial troubles. Both played in aging parks in decaying neighborhoods. "I see a long, long line of poor Puerto Rican people getting their welfare checks," commented Walter O'Malley as he observed the scene across from his Montague Street offices. Despite their winning ways, attendance was declining for both:

	DODGERS	GIANTS
1947	1,807,526	1,600,793
1948	1,398,967	1,459,269
1949	1,633,747	1,218,446
1950	1,185,896	1,080,876
1951	1,282,628	1,008,876
1952	1,088,704	1,059,539
1953	1,163,419	984,940
1954	1,020,531	1,155,067
1955	1,033,589	824,112

278

	DODGERS	GIANTS
1956	1,213,562	629,179
1957	1,028,258	653,923

So when Los Angeles and San Francisco beckoned, owners O'Malley and Horace Stoneham cast tradition to the winds and headed west. As National League President Warren Giles supposedly cracked, "Who needs New York?"

The desertion stunned New Yorkers. An upstate Congressman, Kenneth B. Keating, who was campaigning for a United States Senate seat, observed the psychological damage: "Baseball. All these people seem to be interested in is the fact that the Dodgers have gone to Los Angeles. They have no civic enthusiasm. This is our problem. There is only one team in New York City now. Well, I know New York. It is not a city used to having a single team. This is a city which must have divided interests. All this apathy we are seeing is because of the baseball situation."

New York wasn't the only area affected by changing demographics. Major league ball had remained unchanged since 1903, but the nation had not. Big league clubs were still concentrated in the Northeast, but significant growth had taken place in the West and South. Besides Los Angeles and San Francisco, cities such as Atlanta, San Diego, Denver, Houston, Dallas, Oakland, Toronto and Montreal clamored for major league status.

The situation was akin to those which facilitated formation of the American Association and the American League. Yet certain factors favored the establishment: the greater stranglehold the majors now possessed over playing talent (through the farm systems) and the fabulous increase in the cost of stadium construction. No longer could cheap parks hastily be thrown up. The cost of stadiums was beyond the resources of the even wealthiest sportsmen.

But operating positively toward a possible insurgency was a more liberal attitude on the part of the public and the government. The era of business monopoly in which Spalding, Mills and Ban Johnson operated was dead. Baseball's legal status was hanging by a thread — and that thread was about to be cut.

William A. Shea: Father of the Continental League

In New York, disgusted baseball fans and civic leaders first reacted to the loss of National League ball by trying to hijack another Senior Circuit team.

In December 1957, New York Mayor Robert F. Wagner, up for re-election, appointed a four-man committee consisting of former Postmaster General James Farley, department store king Bernard Gimbel, real estate executive Clint Blume and high-powered attorney William A. Shea to engage a new team.

Shea would become the key figure in this drama. Born in New York on June 21, 1907, Shea grew up on a steady diet of baseball, attending Bushwicks, Ivanhoes and Farmers semipro games. In high school, he was offered Yankees tickets as an incentive to excel in Spanish by a teacher who was an aunt of pitcher Herb Pennock. Shea became proficient *en Español* and a fixture at the Polo Grounds, where the Yankees still played. Since his mother forbade him to take part in high school football, Shea put his energies into baseball, where he caught and played second base, and into basketball, in which he was a superior player. His school, George Washington High, did not have a basketball team, so Shea and his friends created "Fort Washington Prep," which booked contests against real scholastic squads. Eventually, the scheme was exposed, which did not keep the popular Shea from being elected president of the school's General Organization by the largest margin ever.

The six-foot-tall Shea attended New York University, where he was good enough at football to win a four-year scholarship from Georgetown University; he also played basketball. More importantly, he gained his law degree.

After graduation, his interest in sports continued. He played lacrosse for the Crescent Athletic Club, rated the nation's best. His father-in-law, Thomas Shaw, had been one of biggest bookmakers in New York during the 1920s—a legal activity back then. In the early 1940s Shea operated the Long Island Indians, a farm club of the Washington Redskins football team; he also had a share in an N.F.L. franchise in Boston. His first job after graduation from Law School in 1931 was with the firm of Cullen & Dyckman, where he met George V. McLaughlin, President of the Brooklyn Trust Company, whose patience kept the foundering Dodgers afloat for years. After that Shea worked for the New York State Banking and Insurance Departments and in 1941 became a founding member of the real estate and corporate law firm of Manning, Hollinger & Shea.

By the time Wagner tapped Shea, he was one of the city's most prominent attorneys. Now he was fighting the city's battle in the baseball wars. As an inducement for teams to move, Shea and company could dangle a projected new stadium in Flushing Meadows, Queens—an option O'Malley had rejected.

The quartet approached National League clubs in Cincinnati, Pittsburgh and Philadelphia. The first two expressed some interest, but eventually said no. Philadelphia wasn't paying any attention to Shea.

"In talking to [Bob] Carpenter [of the Phils]," Shea recalled, "I began to realize one thing. This fellow is just like me. He doesn't want to move. Philadelphia is his town and he is going to stay there. He's not going to pick up and leave the place just for money. There are other things which are more important to him. Civic pride? Sure, you can call it that. And when I'm talking to him, I begin to see that I am placing myself in the position of asking him to do the very thing I would never do. Pull out of your own town. That cured me. From then on, I stopped bothering other teams. I was not going to be a party to moving any club, so long as that city had people willing to support it."

The committee, now under Shea's leadership, tried a new tack: expansion. "At this stage," noted Shea, "my problem is that I am silly enough to think that the National League owed New York something. Here we supported two teams for all those years. Well, the National League didn't feel that way at all. They didn't feel anything. They couldn't have cared less."

So Shea's next gambit was the Continental League.

The Major Leagues Endorse Expansion

The Continental League Shea envisioned would feature strong financial and political backing, and word soon leaked out to the major leagues that a formidable threat was emerging.

In May 1959 a select group of Organized Baseball executives—Commissioner Ford Frick, American League President Joe Cronin, National Association President George Trautman, the Indians' George Medlinger, the Yankees' Dan Topping, the Pirates' John Galbreath and the Phils' Bob Carpenter—gathered in Columbus, Ohio, ostensibly to confer regarding the effect of major league broadcasts on minor league attendance. Soon, however, they adjourned to Galbreath's Darby Dan Farm, some 15 miles to the west.

The topic: Expansion.

This new session involved a much wider cast of characters: Commissioner Frick, A.L. President Cronin, National League President Warren Giles and representatives of all 16 big league clubs.

"The major leagues," said Frick, "recognize the desire of certain groups to obtain major league franchises, and since there is no existing plan to expand the present major leagues, the two leagues hereby declare they will favorably consider an application for major league status within the present baseball structure by an acceptable group of eight clubs which would qualify under ten specifications."

The group developed a program for expansion, the key feature being that expansion would not come within the two existing major leagues, but would involve the creation of an entirely new eight-club circuit. Theoretically any new league (but in practicality only the Continental League would be affected by this program) would have to meet the following criteria:

> 1. Responsibility for all of its financial obligations, including those involving territoriality.
>
> 2. With the league's membership application, statements including "stock ownership, financial ability, and character" for those involved with both the individual clubs and the new league itself shall be presented to Organized Baseball.

3. No city would have a smaller population than that of the smallest existing major league city, Kansas City, which had a population of 456,662 and a metropolitan area of 814,357.

4. Possession of—or a commitment for—a park with minimum seating of 35,000.

5. Development of a "balanced" 154-game schedule.

6. Acceptance of existing major league minimum salary of $7,000—with no maximum limit.

7. Acceptance of the existing Major League Agreement and the Professional Baseball Agreement.

8. Adoption of the existing uniform player contract.

9. Adoption of the existing major league pension plan.

10. Filing for acceptance by Organized Baseball at least six months before the session in which it would be considered and at least ten months prior to the start of the first season in which they proposed to operate.

At initial glance, such a plan seemed quite reasonable, but hidden within it was a major stumbling block, the issues of territorial compensation.

Some observers were immediately suspicions of what was offered. International League President Frank "Shag" Shaughnessy was one: "I think the idea was brought out just to stop talk of expansion [within] the American and National leagues."

Shea, however, was upbeat. "At last," he crowed, "we know we were thinking right. I'm only sorry we didn't do it sooner. We will be able to present a plan for a league within five weeks."

Formation of the Continental League

There was no shortage of applicants for Shea's new venture. "Our problem from the first," he explained in July 1959, "was one of cutting the number of applicants down, not finding them. I must have talked to hundreds of individuals and dozens of groups, most of them people I had never heard of before. I got letters and calls from mayors and governors and multimillionaires. We investigated. We surveyed. We probed and questioned. Sometimes the telephone at my house would ring all night long. It still keeps ringing. My wife says that when this is over she never wants to hear the word 'baseball' again. I think the third league has already lost one fan."

Already operating behind the scenes was 77-year-old Branch Rickey, semi-retired from his chores as general manager of the Pittsburgh Pirates, but still chairman of its board of directors. Two years earlier he had suffered a mild heart attack.

Rickey was a living legend, the founder of the major league farm system and widely credited as the greatest judge of baseball talent that ever lived. A former catcher and field manager of the Browns and Cardinals, he earned a law degree from the University of Michigan Law School. Joining the St. Louis Browns front office in 1916, he emerged as the foremost executive in the game, eventually creating dynasties for both the Cardinals and Dodgers. It was he who ended the color bar in baseball by signing Kansas City Monarchs infielder Jackie Robinson.

Bounced from his job as Pirates general manager in 1955, Rickey had been mulling over the thought of expansion since the end of the 1957 season. Pirates General Manager Thomas Johnson was incredulous at the news. "Disloyal," he fumed, "that's what he [is], disloyal—to the league and us. Here he is working for me and out generating support for a competitor with Shea."

Rickey argued that placing a major league franchise in a hitherto minor league city resulted in an attendance bonanza, citing the following statistics:

	MINOR LEAGUES	MAJOR LEAGUES	INCREASE
Milwaukee	1952–195,839	1953–1,826,397	833%
Baltimore	1953–207,182	1954–1,060,910	412%
Kansas City	1954–141,905	1955–1,393,268	882%
Los Angeles	1957–220,547	1958–1,845,268	737%
San Francisco	1957–284,532	1958–1,272,625	347%

"The traditional concept of 'major league' and 'minor league' cities is now changing," Rickey announced. "Houston, Dallas, Minneapolis, Toronto, Buffalo, etc., are not going to accept the 'minor league' label any longer. They belong in the majors and want 'major league' merchandise—baseball as well as all other products. This is the basic reason for the sports revolution that is now under way."

Another key player on the Continental League's newly installed board of directors was Edwin Carl Johnson. Reared on a Nebraska cattle ranch, Johnson moved to Colorado at the age of 17 and eventually became involved in Democratic Party politics, becoming a member of the State Legislature, lieutenant governor, governor and by 1936 United States senator. He fought FDR on his court-packing scheme and on the entrance into World War II, but after V-J Day was more willing to use our new-found atomic power "to compel mankind to adopt a policy of lasting peace or be burnt to a crisp."

In 1946, while a member of the Senate, Johnson became President of the Class A Western League, serving without pay until it went under in 1958.

On July 27, 1959, at New York's Hotel Biltmore, Shea unveiled his new Continental League. Franchises were granted to New York, Houston, Minneapolis–St. Paul, Toronto and Denver. Each deposited a $50,000 guarantee and pledged $1,500,000 in working capital plus another $1,000,000 in reserves. The league was to be an eight-team circuit, with Opening Day scheduled for April 1961.

The New York franchise was the Continental League's pride and joy. Its well-heeled financial backers were Mrs. Joan Whitney Payson, Mrs. Dorothy Killiam, Dwight F. "Pete" Davis, Jr., G. Herbert Walker, Jr., William Simpson and M. Donald Grant.

Mrs. Payson was the prime source of funds. In 1957, *Fortune* estimated her net worth at $100–200 million, making her one of the wealthiest women in the world. A Barnard College graduate, she maintained homes on Fifth Avenue; in Manhasset on Long Island; in Falmouth Foreside, Maine; in the horse country of Kentucky; and at Hobe Sound, Florida. Her grandfather, John Hay, a one-time aide to Lincoln, had been Secretary of State under McKinley and Theodore Roosevelt. It wasn't only her inherited fortune that gave Mrs. Payson her millions. Everything she touched seemed to turn to gold. Her investments in stage and film productions yielded such hits as *Rebecca, A Streetcar Named Desire* and *Gone with the Wind.*

She was a great sports fan. Co-owner of Green Tree Stables with her brother John Hay "Jock" Whitney, she distinguished herself in racing circles, but baseball was her true love. She often bestowed baseball monikers on her racehorses—"One Hitter," "Hall of Fame," "Gashouse Gang," "Third League" or "Shutout." She frequently attended Giants games, and by the time they headed west she owned 10 percent of the stock. Her vote—through M. Donald Grant—was the only one against the move.

Her wealth was so great that when her ownership of the Mets necessitated disposal of her Giants stock, she donated it to New York Hospital.

Mrs. Killiam, a resident of Montreal, had formerly enjoyed getting up a private railroad car to take her to World Series games at Ebbets Field. G. Herbert Walker's namesake was future politician George Herbert Walker Bush. Davis was the son of the donor of tennis' Davis Cup. Exactly what he did for a living was not clear. "He clips coupons," explained another member of the syndicate. The Montreal-born Grant, a former hockey player, was a senior partner in the brokerage house of Fahnestock & Co.

It was an upscale group.

So were the backers of the other franchises. Jack Kent Cooke of Toronto was a 45-year-old manufacturer who owned not only the Toronto Maple Leafs of the International League but also the similarly named franchise of the National Hockey League. Cooke claimed he was willing to spend $2,500,000 on the new team. "That is twice the amount I offered to buy the Detroit Tigers," he noted at Shea's press conference. "It is my money. It is not the city's."

Craig Cullinan, Jr., of Houston was a grandson of the founder of Texaco. His group, the Houston Sports Association, had negotiated with four existing franchises (including the Philadelphia A's and St. Louis Cardinals) for a move to Texas. Their last offer had been $6,000,000 for the Cleveland Indians.

The possibility of major league baseball in Minneapolis–St. Paul had long been considered. The Athletics had looked at Minnesota before settling on

Kansas City. The Cleveland Indians had mulled over moving there, as had Calvin Griffith's Washington Senators. Only the American League's failure to approve Griffith's idea had kept the Senators in the nation's capital. And in 1957 Horace Stoneham had been primed to move there before Walter O'Malley had cajoled the Giants owner into joining him on the West Coast.

In 1956 the Minneapolis Millers abandoned old Nicollet Park and moved to $4.5 million Metropolitan Stadium in suburban Bloomington. The park was designed to be expanded into a major league facility, and Stoneham was about ready to sign a lease. "OK, go ahead and order the steel," he told the city fathers just before he settled in San Francisco.

Meanwhile, the old rivalry between Minneapolis and St. Paul was slow to die. Baseball backers in St. Paul had not agreed on the Bloomington site and in 1957 erected 10,000-seat Midway Stadium for the Saints at a cost of $2 million. The impasse was not even close to being settled when Wheelock Whitney, Jr., of Minneapolis, a 33-year-old investment banker and a director of the Susquehanna Corporation, put together the group that was awarded a Continental League franchise. Even then, St. Paul City Commissioner Severin Mortinson was announcing, "We still hope to move a major league club to our own Midway Stadium. We don't plan to give up until the third league is definitely under way."

In Denver, Bob Howsam, Edwin Johnson's son-in-law and former administrative assistant and general manager of the American Association's Denver Bears, headed the group for that city.

In terms of where the teams would play Shea outlined the following scenario:

> Denver—Existing Bears Stadium would be expanded from 19,000 to 40,000 or 45,000 seats.
>
> Houston—Buff Stadium would not be used. A new stadium would be constructed, seating 37,000 to 40,000 patrons.
>
> Minneapolis–St. Paul—Metropolitan Stadium would be expanded to 40,000 or 45,000 seats.
>
> New York—Construction of a 52,000-seat stadium at Flushing Meadows would be undertaken by the city. Shea indicated if the new park were not ready on time, the team would play at either the Polo Grounds or Ebbets Field. He ruled out any chance of playing at Yankee Stadium.
>
> Toronto—Maple Leaf Stadium would not be used. A new stadium would be built to accommodate 37,000 to 40,000 fans.

Shea dismissed any idea that there would not be enough qualified players to stock a new league.

"If the major leagues co-operate with us," he commented, "we won't have a bit of trouble getting players. There are enough good players around right now to staff a new league.

A survivor of the Continental League campaign: the New York Mets' William A. Shea Stadium.

"Actually, the supply of young players can be unlimited. They haven't been coming up now because they haven't been given the opportunities. The risk of a big league career with only sixteen teams has been too great. The big leagues keep too many old players around now simply to profit from their names and reputations. The young players have to wait too long for their chance. With twenty-four big league teams—or maybe more—they'll get their chance.

"After a year or two, people will realize what can be done. This is the sort of thing which America does best. No one ever heard of an atomic scientist fifteen years ago. Now they're coming out of the woodwork. You can't tell me that a nation of a hundred and sixty million people can't produce two hundred more big league ball players."

It had been Edwin Johnson who had named the new league. Other names that had been considered included "The Third League," "The United States League" and "The International League."

Organized Baseball's reaction was decidedly unenthusiastic. Newly elected American League President Joe Cronin alleged that talk of taking over minor league cities "hurts" the minors. "Just branding a league 'major' doesn't make it one," added Cronin. "They have to come up with major league talent."

Warren Giles agreed that the C.L. would spell trouble for the minors and failed to see how a group "with five clubs" could be called a league. Horace Stoneham (an opponent of expanding the existing circuits), on the other hand, was enthusiastic, saying the C.L. had the "makings of a fine league."

Tigers manager Jimmy Dykes was skeptical over the league's prospects. "There just aren't enough major league ballplayers for three leagues," he candidly told reporters. "I don't see how the Continental League can make it.

"Oh sure, everybody will say they're willing to help the third league to keep Congress off their backs, but you won't find anybody willing to give up anything they could possibly use."

"Clubs coming into Houston with Toronto or Denver on their shirts," contended Houston Buffs manager Marty Marion, "would mean little to Houston fans. They won't come out to the park. But let the Yankees or White Sox or Braves come into Houston with players Texas fans know about and you'll see the stadium fill up."

Congressional Involvement

On July 28–31 Senator Estes Kefauver of Tennessee held hearings on the question of baseball's antitrust status. He was not impressed by statements Cronin, Giles and the Yankees' George M. Weiss had made following Shea's announcement of the Continental League. "I hope these gentlemen will have a change of heart," he stated. He more than hinted that how Organized Baseball treated the fledgling league would help determine his view as to whether it should be exempt from antitrust laws.

Edwin C. Johnson testified that if there was an unrestricted draft of minor league players, there would be no talent shortage at all and that the Continental League could move forward. He alleged "Phony deals . . . phony contracts . . . phony purchases" by the majors in their dealings with the minors.

This was something Branch Rickey, founder of the farm system—and alleged practitioner of a thousand phony deals—could not countenance.

"You can be a fish in a puddle," he told Kefauver's committee, "and think the world is made out of water, but you can't take the Western League and think baseball should be castigated as 'phony.' This is basically an honest game, supported and owned by honest men.

"Gentlemen, there has been maligning of some very great sportsmen in this country and that is unfair and leads the general public to believe amiss about them."

Had Rickey more time to research the topic, he might have quoted Johnson's 1951 testimony before Emmanuel Cellar's House Subcommittee: "Baseball has adopted itself a code of ethics worthy of emulation by any God-fearing group."

On August 2, a bid was submitted by the Jersey City–Newark area. Bennett Davies, an investment broker, announced that he was applying for membership. He hoped to play at vacant 23,000-seat Roosevelt Stadium in Jersey City and add on seats to meet the 35,000-seat minimum requirement.

Enter President Rickey

On August 18, 1959, Branch Rickey was named president of the fledgling circuit. Rickey was still under contract to the Pirates as an advisor, so the Continental League assumed the remaining 16 months of his pact. Also to be resolved was the issue of the 958 shares of the Pirates Rickey owned; John Galbreath purchased them for a reported $200,000.

There was, of course, concern about the aged Rickey's health. The veteran baseball man shrugged that off. "My doctor says he thinks I'll live just as long active as inactive," Rickey snorted. "Judas priest! I'd rather die ten minutes sooner than be doing nothing all the time."

His assumption of the presidency, startled many, including his own son, Branch, Jr., who was still farm director of the Pirates. "Are you sure?" asked a startled son, when told the news. "It surprises me. I didn't think he'd take it."

"We felt he was the only man who could conclude the operation we have undertaken," said Bill Shea. " He didn't want the job. We had to plead with him. The position required a man of great dignity, great ability and a man with a pioneer background.

"Mr. Rickey realizes the great toll the job might exact from him. We pray the good Lord spares him so he can see the Continental League champion in the World Series."

"Our new league," Rickey pledged, "won't pretend to be major the first year, but by the end of the third year that won't be unthinkable. The Pittsburgh team was castigated for its failures, but the same team finished second a year later [1958]. Were they minor league one year and major league the next?

"I am alarmed at the subtle invasion of professional football, which is gaining pre-eminence over baseball. It's unthinkable.·

"My friends think it's foolish of me to undertake such a venture as this at my age. But I'm actuated by a sense of duty, a debt I owe baseball. I could have sat back and collected my salary at Pittsburgh for doing nothing. I don't have to work. But now I'll be collecting the same salary for working hard. All I want is a couple of years to get this third league on its feet and then I'll let some young fellow take over."

Reporters pressed Rickey and wanted to know where the league offices would be established. Rickey exhaled a puff from his trademark cigar before responding: "In my coat pocket. Where else?"

Immediately following Rickey's interview, he, Edwin Johnson and Bill

Shea headed for the Warwick Hotel to confer with a committee representing Organized Baseball—Ford Frick, Joe Cronin, Warren Giles, Tom Yawkey, Arnold Johnson, Lou Perini and Bob Carpenter.

The meeting was merely an exploratory one. At its close Frick named Rickey, Cronin and Giles to investigate the vital—but unresolved—issue of how to stock the new clubs with players.

"The major leagues," stated Frick, "are going to help the third league get players as far as they can. But they are not going to give the Continental anybody for nothing. The player committee is not to set any prices on players."

After Rickey's ascent to leadership, offers from a variety of cities were reported—Honolulu, Buffalo, San Juan, Atlanta, Miami, New Orleans, Indianapolis, Portland, Seattle, Dallas–Fort Worth and Montreal.

The existing American Association and International League showed little enthusiasm for losing prime territory to the Continental League.

American Association President Ed Doherty demanded an indemnity of $1,000,000 for each territory lost. With Dallas, Fort Worth, St. Paul, Minneapolis, Denver and Houston all having American Association franchises, this would mean the possible loss of six of the league's eight franchises. "If they take those six cities from us, the American Association is dead," Doherty claimed.

Frank Shaughnessy, head of the International Association, demanded the same price for the loss of either Buffalo, Toronto or Montreal. "The founders of the Continental League claim to have millions," he blustered. "Well, they better get ready to spend some of it."

New developments occurred regarding possible playing fields. Prospective Montreal investors—Hy Richman, Kermit Kitman, Charles Mayer and Frank Hanley—outlined plans for a 45,000-seat stadium with parking for 10,000 cars. The New Orleans Pelicans proposed to continue using existing Park Stadium. At 26,000 seats (substantially under the 35,000 minimum Shea had originally established), Park Stadium was the largest facility in the Class AA Southern Association.

On October 22, the New York City Board of Estimate approved a $170,000 appropriation for preliminary engineering plans for a new $15 million, 55,000-seat stadium in Flushing. Included in the work were estimates for a movable dome and expansion to 80,000 seats. The unanimous vote was seen as major step forward for the C.L.

A Different Form of Expansion

On October 21 the Continental League suffered a major blow. The American League, meeting at New York's Plaza Hotel, announced it was study-

ing the request by Gerald Moore of the St. Paul–Minneapolis group for an A.L.
expansion team for that area. Just days before, Calvin Griffith had abandoned
plans to shift the Senators to Minnesota.

Also at the session, an expansion committee consisting of George Weiss of
New York, Bill DeWitt of Detroit and Hank Greenberg of Chicago was instituted.

It was later learned that the American League was considering expansion
to just nine teams, with the National League also going to nine clubs (adding
one in New York). An interleague schedule would be developed.

Such talk played havoc with Continental League plans, as prospective
members now were lured by possible berths in the established leagues. Bill
Shea thought the Continental League could have filled its membership to eight
clubs by now, but for this activity. "We sat down in good faith with these
gentlemen," said Bill Shea, "and thought they had entered into a co-operative
plan with us." There was even a mild hint from him that the Continental League
might go "outlaw."

Branch Rickey was far more explicit. He indicated that the C.L. would go
its own way in the case of further "interference"—"It would be a case of survival
or surrender, and we propose to survive."

He further contended that travelling the independent route would be "a
quicker and a more economical procedure." This was interpreted to mean
in terms of territoriality, but—even more ominously—it could have meant a
desire to rip up the reserve clause.

On December 7 the National League scotched the American League's
plans, however, when it indicated there was "not sufficient sentiment" for expansion. The American League, momentarily wedded to the idea of a nine-
team circuit, could not go forward with interleague play without a nine-team
National League.

With that, events began to move quickly again for the C.L. Atlanta was
granted membership on December 8 when a group consisting of Joe Fine,
Eaton Chalkley and Hughes Spalding, Jr., was admitted. Another group consisting of Chicago attorneys Robert Chatz and Jack Schaeffer and investor Lee
Stern had pursued the Atlanta franchise, even reportedly obtaining an option
on Les Mann's Class AA Atlanta Crackers (the asking price was an estimated $1,200,000). Rickey had never been too enthusiastic about this latter
group.

Later that month came Dallas–Fort Worth, under the leadership of contractor J. W. Bateson, president of the Dallas Eagles of the American Association, and Amon Carter, Jr., a Fort Worth publisher. In November it had looked
like Bateson and Dallas were both out of the picture, as Bateson had withdrawn
his bid.

Buffalo Bisons President John Stiglmeier was skeptical about aligning the club with the Continental League. (Courtesy of Joseph M. Overfield.)

Power Struggle in Buffalo

The final franchise was awarded in January 1960 to the existing Buffalo Bisons of the International League. The events leading to that move were filled with controversy.

Since 1955, when the Detroit Tigers had bailed out of operating the Bisons, the club had been community-owned, with over 3,000 shareholders possessing its 183,511 shares. Despite this spread-out ownership, there were several significant individuals involved in operating the franchise — and not all were enthusiastic over the Continental League's prospects.

First, there was rough-hewn club President John C. Stiglmeier. Stiglmeier, an insurance man and long-time area Democratic politician (22 years as mayor of the small town of Sloan, just east of Buffalo, and 17 years on the Erie County Board of Supervisors), held but 100 shares of stock, but his forceful political skills and hard-driving interest in the game (he had been general manager from 1940 to 1944) put him into a leadership position.

Second, there was Stiglmeier's total opposite, Yale-educated millionaire Reginald B. Taylor. Taylor, an accomplished horseman whose family fortune sprung from real estate holdings on New York's Broadway, had been a major financial angel for the transition to community ownership. He had been forced out as club president in 1957 in a power struggle with Stiglmeier, but still retained 10,100 shares of Bison stock. It was he who would put up the $50,000 deposit the Continental League had demanded.

Just as significant were the Jacobs brothers—Marvin, Charles and Louis, owners of Sportservice, Inc. The Jacobses were major power brokers in Organized Baseball, at one time operating concessions in over 100 facilities, including 12 big league parks. Sportservice owned 63,462 shares (nearly 35 percent) of all Bisons stock, along with Offermann Stadium, where the Bisons played. Offermann had been leased to the ballclub for 25 years at $1 per season—plus concession rights.

Stiglmeier was highly skeptical of the whole Continental League idea. He preferred that Buffalo—a leader in minor league attendance figures—achieve major league status through co-operation with Organized Baseball. Besides, he had experienced previous run-ins with Reginald Taylor, most notably over the firing of General Manager Danny Carnevale. The Continental League viewed Stiglmeier's attitude with alarm. Jack Kent Cooke termed it "a terrible state of affairs" and warned Buffalo that "without Reg Taylor, you will have nothing and will wind up with nothing, a ghost town."

To achieve major league status Buffalo would have to abandon 13,000-seat Offermann Stadium and embark on a $700,000 renovation of cavernous War Memorial Stadium to seat 42,000 (the renovation was indeed carried out; the results can be seen in the Robert Redford film *The Natural*, which was shot there), but making that transition was not easy.

The War Memorial lease contained a clause that any concession at the park would be operated directly by the franchise. If that were not the case—say, they were operated by Sportservice—city approval would be necessary. It is not hard to see that the Jacobses would not view this as a progressive measure.

Secondly, the club could end up with leases to the two stadiums— Offermann and War Memorial. The club was eventually assured by the city that this was not possible. The city, which was to construct a new junior high school on the site of Offermann Stadium, gave written assurances that it would let the club out of the War Memorial Stadium lease if necessary. A lease for the new park was signed in January 1960. "I don't think there is any question of doubt about Buffalo now," exulted Branch Rickey.

Still, John Stiglmeier dragged his feet on calling a meeting to turn over power to Taylor and to vote on making a Continental League bid. "Apparently someone has talked to Stiglmeier in the meantime and also to the Jacobs brothers," Bill Shea speculated. "Stiglmeier is a close friend of Frank Shaughnessy, and Shaughnessy hasn't done anything at all to help us, nor has he been available to us at any time." Shea further believed that pressure had been put on the Jacobs brothers by the American League. Louis Jacobs was "not available" for comment when the Buffalo *Evening News* called to query him on that point.

The Continental League used the possibility of a Montreal franchise as a threat to Buffalo, citing a "tremendous group" of backers there. The threat was most likely a hollow one. Montreal lacked a ballpark. Although the group was promised land and tax-free status for the project, it would have to build the structure itself. Beyond that, there appeared little likelihood construction could be accomplished by the start of the 1961 season.

Finally, a meeting concerning Buffalo's status was called for January 26, 1960; by this time Sportservice had thrown in its lot with the Continental League. By a 7–1 margin, shareholders authorized changes in the club's articles of incorporation to reflect a shift to the new league, turning over power from Stiglmeier to Reginald Taylor, and borrowed the $50,000 franchise fee from Taylor. Further, Taylor was responsible for raising another $1,500,000 to get the club ready for the majors.

The Continental League now had a full complement of eight clubs— Atlanta, Buffalo, Denver, Houston, Minneapolis, Dallas–Fort Worth, New York and Toronto.

Despite having a set lineup, in the spring of 1960 the Continental League negotiated with the Los Angeles Dodgers for the rights to their AAA Montreal territory. There seemed to be no problem over the $150,000 purchase price, but discussions broke down over a proposed $75,000 annual rental fee for Royals Stadium. "If they can't afford to operate where a minor league has been operating, then I don't know," chortled Walter O'Malley.

In July of 1960, owners of the Kansas City Athletics were offering their club to both the Dallas–Fort Worth and Houston C.L. syndicates. In some sense the proposal was a ploy to split Continental ranks, since it was rumored the A.L. would not oppose a move to Texas. The asking price, however, was $5,000,000, and that was considered an "exorbitant" price, since it did not include any real estate.

Failure of the Kefauver Bill

By late 1959 it was becoming clear that the Continental League was far behind schedule if it wished to open for business for the 1961 season.

The American League's expansion plan was one roadblock. Commissioner Frick's refusal to allow the Continental League to tie into a working agreement with the Class D Western Carolinas League was another. Bill Shea responded by threatening that Organized Ball should either "help us or face the consequences—affirmative steps on our own."

Branch Rickey explained just what that meant, when asked to comment on the possibility of the C.L.'s raiding Organized Baseball's talent supply. "I would be in favor of that," said the Mahatma, "if forced to do that. We've got to be forced to do that. I don't want to operate outside the canopy of baseball."

Organized Ball was not amused by the Continental League's threats. Both Ford Frick and Warren Giles issued heated statements in response. Giles' was the more incensed of the two (Note that he never referred to the Continental League as a league):

> If Shea thinks his implied threats will scare the National League into any action they would not otherwise take, he just does not know the National League. I'm fed up with his public statements unjustly criticizing the very organization he seeks to become part of.
>
> So far as I know, the Continental group has not offered any substantial evidence that they have met any of the fundamental requirements declared by the major leagues last May and which were accepted by them. It seems these requirements should be met before there could be any discussion of player acquisition, and before we should be asked to ignore our present rules to permit the organization of a Class D league under conditions not now permitted our own clubs.
>
> Most every obstacle they encounter is described by them as a roadblock purposely put there by the major leagues. This is unfair, misleading and untrue.
>
> If their prospective operators had been fully informed of the problems with which they were bound to be confronted in such a big undertaking, there would be less inclination to now blame someone else.
>
> There are enough experienced baseball men in their group to know that getting players with sufficient ability to be presented to the public as major league players would be an almost insurmountable task. If they do not know, all they have to do is to look at the very costly and sometimes frustrating efforts of some of the major league clubs. They, with astute baseball men, good organizations, large scouting staffs, farm systems and plenty of money, find it most difficult to accomplish what the Continental group apparently feels it can accomplish by criticism, threats and "Gilded Lily" statements about how plentiful players are and how formidable they will be in a short time.
>
> I have felt that a third major league or the expansion of either or both the present major leagues could contribute to the welfare of the entire baseball structure, but the atmosphere created by Mr. Shea's public statements is not helpful.
>
> The record will show that the National League has been more considerate of the Continental group and their problems than Mr. Shea has been of us.

Actually, neither Rickey nor Shea was so foolish as to want to go "outlaw." What they really counted on was baseball's talent pool being forced open by legislation prepared by Senator Kefauver. Basically, Kefauver's bill would do two things crucial to C.L. success: first, it would exempt the new league from idemnifying the minors for territory, and secondly, it would limit each major league club to control of just 100 players. All other personnel would be subject to an unrestricted draft at half the regular draft price. To clubs controlling many farm clubs (such as the Dodgers, Braves, Phils and Cardinals; the Dodgers in 1960 still owned three AAA clubs), this would be a heavy blow and would open up a vast talent pool to the upstart Continentals.

Further, Section 204 of the bill made any opposition to the Continental League — or virtually any other new league — a violation of federal antitrust measures:

> Any contract, agreement, rule, course of conduct or other activities by, between or among persons conducting, engaging in or participating in the organized professional team sport of baseball which prevents, hinders, obstructs or affects adversely the formation, organization or operation of additional major leagues not presently in operation or in existence, provided such addition major league or leagues shall consist of a group of not less than eight communities which group has a total metropolitan or territorial population of not less than 12,000,000 and expressing in their constitution, by-laws or rules the willingness to observe and comply with maximum major league standards respecting retirement programs, and playing schedules equal to existing major leagues, shall be in violation of the acts named in section 201 of this title.

Ford Frick and Organized Ball were unalterably opposed to this legislation. "This measure," Frick alleged, "is pernicious and vicious, the most dangerous bill yet introduced in Congress."

Referring to the draft of players under the Kefauver bill, Frick said, "The incentive for any club to build up talent, especially at the expense now involved, would be killed.

"Scouting staffs would be disbanded. Bonuses to young players would be eliminated. Farm systems would be done away with. We would be left hanging on the ropes. Does the Congress want this? I know it doesn't."

A rare meeting of all of the major league owners held at the exclusive Chicago Club in the Windy City on May 17 gave Frick their total support. Cubs owner Phil Wrigley denied earlier rumors that he supported the Kefauver Bill ("I was in favor of new legislation, not necessarily the Kefauver bill"). Yankees owner Dan Topping again repeated the O.B. line that the Continental League had not met the qualifications ("Those were our ten commandments") set down by the majors in May 1959.

Not only were Frick and the owners opposed. The press chimed in as well. Rochester sportswriter George Beahon said the bill would "complete the butchery of the minor leagues." The New York *Times*' Red Smith ripped apart the Kefauver measure, terming it a "bad bill," one that "requires respectable businessmen to welcome burglars into their lodge" since there were no financial or character requirements specified for new club owners in the legislation.

Smith also took issue with the Kefauver proposal's requirement that any new league have an aggregate population area of 12,000,000. He found this compared unfavorably to Organized Baseball's dictum that no new city would be smaller than the smallest existing big league city, Kansas City: "A league could put one team in New York and the other seven in towns named Oshkosh." He observed that neither Denver nor Atlanta was larger than Kansas City.

Smith also objected to the bill's lack of provisions for territorial rights or suitability of ballparks. "It is a stinker," Smith summed up.

Estes Kefauver introduced his bill on May 6, 1960. On May 24 the Continental forces received a setback when the Senate Antitrust and Monopoly Subcommittee accepted a motion by Michigan Democrat Philip A. Hart to strike out a key provision. Hart had several ties to organized sports. The brother-in-law of Detroit's former owner Walter O. "Spike" Briggs, he was a former vice president of the Tigers and counsel to the N.F.L.'s Detroit Lions. Hart amended the bill's Title II to allow an unlimited draft of players, but limiting control of players to the traditional 40-man roster. Ford Frick viewed it as "the lesser of two evils," and many saw it as a body blow to the C.L. Nonetheless, to the surprise of many, the Continental League endorsed the measure.

Even legislators from states benefitting from the new league's founding were wary of Kefauver's ideas. New York's Kenneth Keating, while conceding it gave "a shot in the arm" to returning National League ball back to his state, had to be pressured to support letting it out of committee. He warned the C.L. "not to count on Congressional intervention as a crutch or an excuse."

On June 28, the bill came to the floor of the Senate, and the forces supporting Organized Baseball moved into action. Wisconsin Senator Alexander Wiley, with Hart's backing, moved to amend Title I of the bill to grant baseball limited immunity from antitrust legislation, a feature he had been unsuccessful in backing within the Judiciary Committee. The original Kefauver measure mentioned football, basketball and hockey, but pointedly omitted the national pastime. Wiley's motion passed 45–41.

With this vote, Colorado's Senator John A. Carroll, a supporter of the Kefauver measure, saw the handwriting on the wall and moved to re-commit Kefauver's bill to committee. The Senate effectively killed the measure—and the Continental League's 1961 season—by voting 73–12 to do so.

"It was a severe blow, but we are not finished," declared Shea, who in mid–May reported that the C.L. would either have to throw in the towel or go "outlaw" if the bill failed.

Buffalo's Reginald B. Taylor was among those discouraged by the news. "We'll have to determine," he said, "if there is any hope for starting operation in 1962 or 1963 or just quit."

In regard to his "outlaw" plans, Shea had confidence that the courts would throw out baseball's reserve clause: "They [the majors] wouldn't have a leg to stand on."

"It was a bad piece of legislation," said Frick of the failed Kefauver measure, "which would have hurt the Continental as well as the American and National League." Although Organized Baseball had won a round, the close margin on granting antitrust exemption made it extremely edgy and caused many to look for a compromise.

Indemnification of the Minors

After the skirmishes on Capitol Hill, the two sides resumed negotiations. At a series of meetings in New York on July 20–21, 1960, it appeared that the Continental League might yet survive. Serious discussions finally began on the issue of minor league indemnification. Previously, the sides had been far, far apart.

Back in May, Bill Shea charged the minors with highway robbery: "Despite the fact that only two years ago the American Association acquired the franchises of Houston, Dallas and Fort Worth for less than $100,000, when the Continental League proposed to place teams in [5 A.A. cities] it was asked to pay $5,000,000 . . . for the franchise thus eliminated.

"The International League demanded $850,000 each for the Buffalo and Toronto franchises.

"When the St. Louis Browns moved their franchise to Baltimore several years ago [1954] the International League asked for and received $48,000 indemnity."

On June 4, Frank Horton, Rochester Red Wings president and counsel to the International League, fired back, branding the C.L. as "bush league" and "insincere." The International League, now demanding $750,000 each for its Toronto and Buffalo territories, was not pleased by the C.L.'s May 12 offer of $60,000 each.

"They said they would put this offer, asinine as it is," Horton, a future Congressman, said, "in writing . . . then submit it to our league directors at our June 27 meeting. We have not seen the letter."

Branch Rickey termed the I.L.'s demands "unreasonable," and commented that its intransigence might lead to the C.L.'s not opening as scheduled in 1961.

"These people have the nerve to blame us for inability to negotiate," charged Horton. "They are trying to use the International League as a whipping boy to cover up their own failures."

In July the Continental League offered to pay an indemnity equivalent to 40 cents on each adult paid admission in a club's last year of operation. As noted earlier the International League demanded $750,000 per franchise and the Southern Association $1,000,000. The American Association demanded $5,000,000 for its Denver, Houston, St. Paul, Minneapolis and Dallas–Fort Worth territories.

To see the vast difference between the two offers, an examination of *total* paid admission for these franchises for 1960 is in order:

CLUB	LEAGUE	PAID ATTENDANCE	C.L. PROPOSED INDEMNITY
Denver	A.A.	209,783	$83,913.20
Houston	A.A.	118,584	$47,433,60
St. Paul	A.A.	119,926	$47,970.40
Minneapolis	A.A.	115,702	$46,280,80
Dallas–Fort Worth	A.A.	113,849	$45,539.60
Buffalo	I.L.	278,352	$111,340.80
Toronto	I.L.	203,700	$81,480.00
Atlanta	S.A.	154,143	$61,657.20

When negotiations broke down once again (the lowest figure the American Association publicly considered was $800,000 per territory), it was not clear what would develop, although at Walter O'Malley's suggestion a meeting between all parties was scheduled for August 2.

Victory in Defeat

It was Lou Perini of the Milwaukee Braves who convinced the Continental League's backers of the difficulties in founding a third circuit. He further asked whether they would give up their league if four of its members were absorbed in the National and American leagues.

On July 10–11 the American League secretly reopened discussions regarding its own expansion. A.L. owners agreed to go ahead once they received assurances that the National League would also proceed.

Within a week, the Senior Circuit also came out for expansion. It notified Rickey of its action and warned him that unless the Continental League resolved the indemnification issue, A.L.-N.L. expansion would involve a number of areas having Continental League cities.

Not all N.L. members favored a ten-team league. Walter O'Malley preferred the earlier American League scheme of two nine-team majors playing an interlocking schedule—a decision no doubt influenced by a desire to avoid any expansion in the Los Angeles area. Phil Wrigley of the Cubs, on the other hand, cast his vote for a 12-team National League.

At the August 2, 1960, meeting, held at Chicago's Conrad Hilton Hotel, the Continental League agreed to Perini's suggestion. Handwritten notes taken by Walter O'Malley recorded the Milwaukee owner's motion:

> Will the American League and the National League committees agree to recommend to their respective leagues immediately, in 1961 if possible and

1962 if 1961 is not possible, to include two clubs each to be taken from the member clubs of the Continental League, with the understanding that, after this plan has been in effect for a reasonable number of years, a new look will be taken at the situation, this is to be done in conference and negotiation between American and National and Continental?

In a four-hour meeting, the Continental League became history, but major league expansion had been accomplished.

"My principal mission from the start," commented an elated Bill Shea, "has been to assure New York of having everyday baseball again. Today's action gives us that assurance and makes it more urgent than ever to proceed with the construction of the new stadium in Flushing Meadow."

Immediately, the various C.L. groups endeavored to gain entrance to major league ranks. Toronto and Dallas–Fort Worth applied for American League membership; Houston and New York moved to obtain National League franchises. To placate the remaining C.L. backers, the American League on October 26 announced an agreement to expand to 12 clubs "as soon as possible" – most likely within four seasons, but possibly as early as 1962.

On October 17, 1960, the National League admitted the New York and Houston Continental League groups. While it may have been a foregone conclusion that the Payson consortium would get the New York franchise, others coveted the rich prize. Frank Stevens, president of Harry M. Stevens concessionaires, called in Dodger General Manager Emil "Buzzie" Bavasi during the 1961 World Series with a lucrative proposition. Handing Bavasi a check for $1.8 million to purchase the New York franchise, Stevens' group indicated no interest in running the club, but wanted rights to the New York concessions. A stunned Bavasi turned them down.

On October 26, the American League double-crossed the C.L. by voting in two new franchises, Los Angeles (a move which the powerful and influential Yankees had insisted on) and Washington (to replace the club Calvin Griffin had finally been given permission to move to Minnesota). Originally bidding on the Los Angeles franchise was a consortium made up of Hall of Famer Hank Greenberg, White Sox owner Bill Veeck, Los Angeles banker and San Diego Padres owner C. Arnholt Smith and future Hall of Famer Ralph Kiner (Gene Autry was not part of the original consortium). This group, however, would not meet Walter O'Malley's demand of a $450,000 indemnification for the territory. (It is interesting to compare this $450,000 figure for Los Angeles with the million-dollar demands of the International League and the American Association.)

Meanwhile, Buffalo's Reginald Taylor would soon pay the price for his support of the Continental League, being deposed by Stiglmeier and the Jacobs brothers as Bisons chairman in December 1960.

Rickey was not pleased by this partial inclusion of the Continental League into O.B. "Their action," he wrote, "was not only unfair to the Continental League . . . but it was unfair to the American public in defeating any proper concept of major league expansion into a number of great cities throughout our country. . . . It is difficult to understand how reputable gentlemen will explain this breach of good faith."

In New York, a suggestion was made that the new ballpark be named in honor of Rickey. He modestly declined, proposing instead that the stadium be named after Bill Shea. He wrote to the City Council: "The first one to agree with me about a third league was Shea. By George, he leaped into action. He was like a turkey in a tobacco patch, not caring if he knocked down the stalks to get the worm. That's when I got to know the man. The better I knew him, the more I admired him and his effort. He's a marvelous unselfish person, asking and expecting no credit. By Judas priest, he worked. He neglected his law practice for two years. He showed intelligence and tenacity. He brought back the National League to New York. The responsibility for the result is his and his alone."

Chapter 14
The Global League

Following expansion, the major leagues continued in a volatile mode. The new franchises were initially so talentless (the 1962 New York Mets in particular) that enthusiasm for another round cooled considerably. However, such transplants as Milwaukee and Kansas City also developed into less than rousing successes and were again uprooted, the Braves to Atlanta in 1966, the Athletics to Oakland in 1968.

The A's move to California left Kansas City without a major league team and generated increased political pressure for expansion, particularly from United States Senator Stuart Symington, who threatened legislative remedies. As a result, when permission for the shift was granted in October 1967, the American League also voted to expand "as soon as practicable, and no later than 1971."

Such a time frame did little to mollify the irate Kansas City interests. On the floor of the Senate, Symington would go so far as to term A's owner Charley Finley "one of the most disreputable characters ever to enter the American sports scene." He exploded when he heard the news of the A.L.'s expansion schedule and promised renewed legislation.

As a result, the American League voted to expand, to admit Kansas City and Seattle by 1969. By December, the National League had reluctantly also agreed to expand by 1969.

Walter J. Dilbeck, Vietnam, and the Global League

Against this background, an obscure Midwestern businessman named Walter J. Dilbeck, Jr., launched a scheme for a far-flung major league which would not only add to big league ranks but would also serve some great ideological purpose.

Dilbeck was the personification of the small-town self-promoter. Born the son of an army major at Fort Riley, Kansas, in 1915, he grew up in Evansville, Indiana. His first job was for Swift & Co., where he started as a "cellar boy" and soon was tabbed for the meat-packing firm's management development program.

In 1943, Dilbeck was drafted by the United States Army and saw service in the European theatre with the 63rd Infantry Division. In April 1945 at Buschhof, Germany, he slew 68 Germans virtually single-handedly, winning the Distinguished Service Cross and four Purple Hearts.

To say the least, he was quite proud of his wartime accomplishments. "He is not inclined to let you forget it," sarcastically noted one weary *Sporting News* correspondent.

"After the war," Dilbeck once observed, "I returned to Chicago. I worked again for Swift, then branched into real estate, buying and selling tracts and making a good deal of money. I've been in real estate and different businesses ever since then."

Besides his business dealings, he became active in Evansville community affairs, even running for mayor. "Walter did just about everything at one time or another," says Evansville newspaperman Tom Tuley.

In the mid-1960s Dilbeck travelled to war-torn Vietnam as a Pentagon-sponsored "observer-writer" for four newspapers. Improbably, he returned with the idea for the Global League, a circuit that in his mind would leap from hemisphere to hemisphere.

"The people of Asia believe Americans to be a race of soft, decadent people," contended Dilbeck. "I think my idea will change that feeling, as well as help mitigate the Communist trend in all of Asia.

". . . I was in Vietnam in the front lines, being fired at. I saw how the people of that country really love the American GI, the guy who's done so much for them. I want all of Asia—and all of everywhere—to know just how good Americans can be."

However, this was not the only version of his inspiration that the promoter put out. According to his accounts, he had unsuccessfully dickered with Finley for sale of the Kansas City A's. "I decided there was a need for a third major league," he informed the Evansville *Courier*, "when I couldn't buy a major league franchise for 10 million dollars. . . .

"Mr. [Branch] Rickey was better-prepared with his baseball background to organize a third major league than I am, but the country wasn't ready for one then. I think it is ready now when I can't get a franchise for twice its value."

To initiate his enterprise, Dilbeck called together representatives from Milwaukee, Dallas, New York, Seattle, Indianapolis, St. Paul, Denver, Memphis, Miami, Atlanta and St. Louis for an October 19–20, 1966, organizational session. Many of these cities were quite puzzling choices as they already had major league franchises. As for the others, Dilbeck touted new stadiums in Memphis, Seattle and Dallas, new municipal ownership of Perry Field in Indianapolis and lucrative attendance figures in Denver as supportive of his scheme.

Residents from 13 cities arrived for the meeting at Evansville's Hotel McCurdy. Fifty persons—half of whom were locals—attended to organize what Dilbeck was then calling the "All-American League."

Out-of-town guests included John R. Wells, William Warren and Max B. Schumacher of the Indianapolis Sports Commission; Don Walker, secretary of the Portland club of the Pacific Coast League; Lincoln Hackim of Akron, Ohio, president of the American Amateur Baseball Congress; Mr. and Mrs. Raymond Fernandes Narral of San Juan, Puerto Rico; Malcolm Gross and Gilbert Adler of New York; Sydney M. Eisenberg, Milwaukee trial lawyer; Victor J. Tedesco of St. Paul; Harold Rankin of Cincinnati; Charles A. Esser, assistant city manager of Phoenix, Arizona, along with Jack Schwartz and Robert Wagner of that city; Frederick Fober of Chicago; and Ramon Felix and Vincente Corea of Manila.

Dilbeck was laying it on thick for his audience, promoting his circuit as a great moral revolution. Beyond that, he indicated there would be no problem in finding playing talent. In fact, he contended that "Right now . . . there are only 20 players or so in each league who would even be good enough to play in our league."

He further claimed the aura of international competition would carry the day for his circuit, holding by way of example that a game featuring Tokyo at St. Paul would outdraw a Yankees–Twins game "By about 10 to 1."

First to arrive for the gathering was Don Walker of Portland. "Anything that can further the interests of baseball is a positive program," Walker piously commented. "I agree with Mr. Dilbeck that we need a canon of ethics and that's one reason I was so interested in being here. What impresses me of Mr. Dilbeck's dream is that it amounts to a spiritual revolution by placing the emphasis on the sportsmanship qualities of the game."

Little was accomplished, however, save for a "Declaration of Intent." Its Preamble read:

> This League is hereby created to bring organized baseball to the people of the world so they can enjoy international sportsmanship, mutual respect, and the friendly rivalry which will encourage understanding, brotherhood, and goodwill.

Only eight men – Dilbeck, Adler, Gross, Schwartz, Wagner, Narral, Corea and Eisenberg – signed it.

Dilbeck projected that he would begin operations in 1968 with 12 American teams divided into two six-team divisions. Each franchise would possess two farm clubs. Division winners would meet in a "real world series." After the first few years franchises in Tokyo, Puerto Rico, Manila and Honolulu were "feasible."

At the session was at least one individual who would be reporting back to Organized Baseball. Lincoln Hackim, president of the American Amateur Baseball Congress, publicly mouthed assurances to the gathering that talent was available to stock a new league and that expansion was a necessity.

Privately he termed Dilbeck and Milwaukee attorney Sydney M. Eisenberg "naive" regarding the operation of Organized Ball. Eisenberg, he said, had a "chip on his shoulder," presumably because of the recent transfer of the Braves from Milwaukee.

"Mr. Dilbeck," observed Hackim, "has no past association with baseball, other than that of a sponsor of amateur teams [he supposedly had put $25,000 into 'Dilbeck's Riflemen,' a local Stan Musial League team]. While he appears to be sincere, he is obviously quite naive. . . . A film of his war exploits is being made by Warner Brothers. Conceivably, Mr. Dilbeck is using whatever publicity he can obtain to give his name exposure prior to the completion and release of the movie, since reference to the movie was made throughout the meeting."

Others were equally unimpressed. "My candid opinion is Dilbeck will have to get more solid associates in other cities before his dream becomes a reality," thought the Evansville *Courier*. "Some of the representatives here impressed me as fugitives from the cruel facts of life in the professional sports sphere. They couldn't have been further in the blue yonder with their views if smoking marijuana."

Said one attendee from Long Island: "Sure, we could support baseball, but our plans have to be contingent on others. A league couldn't operate with just a couple of teams. We need at least ten, and whether or not we can go depends very much on how many others can."

A reporter from St. Paul expressed more puzzlement than enthusiasm: "We already have a baseball team, but the idea sounds good, and we're curious."

Also in attendance was the Philippine consul from Chicago, who admitted rather sheepishly, "In my country basketball is really the national sport."

More Meetings

In November the league convened again, this time in Chicago. The first order of business was to name Dilbeck chairman of the board. Also elected was a "provisional board" consisting of Robert Wagner; Sydney M. Eisenberg; Raymond F. Narral; Vicente Correa; Malcolm Gross; Jerome F. Berman of Chicago; Leren J. Cassina of London, Ontario; Ray A. Johnston of Dallas; John Beck of San Diego (producer of the projected Dilbeck war film); and Kenji Nakane of Tokyo.

Probably the only individual on that list with baseball experience was Ray Johnston. Starting as a hot dog vendor at Navin Field, Johnston eventually ran concessions there and also at Boston's Braves Field. He went on to operate clubs at Toledo, Indianapolis and Dallas. Out of baseball, he ran the "Universal Travel Service" in Dallas. Johnston was described by official G.L. handouts as "most valuable" to Dilbeck.

A third session, hosted by Robert Wagner and Jack Schwartz, took place at Phoenix's Del Webb Town House in February 1967. Here, some concrete progress was made. Five cities posted a $50,000 bond, and Dilbeck boasted that "the Global League is on its way." There was a disquieting catch, however: each club's money could be "withdrawn" at any time.

At the session Dilbeck outlined his philosophy, often in rather garbled syntax:

> It'll [the Global League] be a shot in the arm to the game that has not kept pace with the patronage progress made by football and basketball. Baseball has lagged because it has been controlled too long by the two major leagues. They have choked the minor leagues to death and confined the sport to 17 cities in a nation of over 200 million people. Don't tell me there isn't room for another major league or two in North America with upwards of 50 cities major in everything but baseball.
>
> If baseball is to continue as a leading spectator sport, it must expand and offer its product to more people in more cities. Civic pride is not dead. Neither is baseball enthusiasm. It's just dormant in many cities.
>
> There are enough AAA and AA players to stock four major leagues. Ninety percent of the major leaguers today could be replaced by a Triple A or Double A player without any fan or scout detecting a decline in efficiency. Many players reach the majors on a manager's whim, others are regulated [sic] to the minors. Many of major league potential quit the game after a few years because they weren't given a chance to play major league ball. The Willie Mays [sic] and Sandy Koufaxs [sic] are few and far between.
>
> We will be the first, not second or third, as the baseball attraction in every city we operate. I realize we wouldn't be No. 1 in a city at the start if we bucked an established club there our first year. We want to pioneer major league baseball in populated areas blacked out by the monarchical monopolists controlling baseball today.

American Cities Begin to Enlist

In February 1967 Dilbeck arranged for four parks to be ready for the 1968 season—in Milwaukee, Jersey City, Omaha and Dallas. "Concrete and steel are among the most essential ingredients in the formation of the league," Dilbeck announced, "and I'm greatly encouraged by receiving permission . . . to use the parks mentioned. I have two more parks lined up but can't announce them right now. I will have twelve adequate parks when the organizational meeting is held in June."

Dilbeck's big catch was Milwaukee's County Stadium. The Global League was given a "90-day option," although the locality reserved the right to nullify the deal if it was granted either an expansion team or an established big league franchise. Dilbeck informed authorities that initially the Global League would operate the Milwaukee club, but that local investors would eventually have the opportunity to purchase the franchise.

In Omaha a three-year lease on 17,500-seat Rosenblatt Stadium ("a wonderful ballpark") was obtained. In Jersey City, 24,000-seat Roosevelt Stadium, home of the Brooklyn Dodgers in 15 games during 1956–57, was leased. "We are interested," enthused Mayor Jimmy Whelan. "We want a team." In Dallas the huge Cotton Bowl would be utilized.

"Build the Global League with stickers, men with fortitude to take a bad bounce or two and keep pitching," advised Hall of Famer Edd Roush (who had played semipro ball with Dilbeck's father). "In a year or two, you'll have a good television contract and have it made. Television keeps the other two leagues going. . . . You can stock your league. Get a few name players, some AA and AAA players, a TV contract and you're safe at home with a winning score."

"We plan for this to be the third major league in not too many years," explained Dilbeck. "We're here to compete with Organized Baseball."

Noticeably missing from Dilbeck's plans were such obvious choices as Montreal or New Orleans. That Dilbeck was reaching down into such cities as Omaha so soon in the game was an ominous sign.

In fact the league did not start in 1968, and by July 9, 1968, Dilbeck was flying down to Houston for the All-Star break to try to cut a deal for an expansion major league franchise for Louisville. When he, along with representatives of such cities as Dallas–Fort Worth, Jersey City and Milwaukee, was rebuffed, he immediately reverted to his third-league theme, pledging to get it under way by 1969.

The Global League and Organized Baseball

In October 1967 Dilbeck, being unable to easily defeat Organized Baseball – or even get started at this point – bought his way *into* Organized Baseball.

Toronto had been a member of the International League for 78 years, but over the past four years it had lost an estimated $500,000. During 1967 it drew only 113,098 fans and went on the auction block. Dilbeck bought the club from owner Bob Hunter for $65,000, shifting it to Louisville, a city which had formerly enjoyed American Association baseball. Dilbeck leased Louisville's Fairgrounds Park for $17,000 and obtained a working agreement with Washington. He also bought the Rock Hill Club in the Class A Western Carolinas League and expressed interest in obtaining a Southern League franchise.

He was not giving up his big league dreams, however. "We've got the Triple-A club now," he boasted. "The majors are next. . . . As far as I'm concerned the idea of a Global League will never be dead."

In September 1968 the Global League, to clarify its rather hazy objectives, took out the following ad in the *Sporting News:*

JUST A MEMO

Please do not confuse the purpose of the Global League, we in the Global League own stock in major league teams and own outright clubs in the National Association of Professional Baseball Clubs.

The operators of the United States clubs in the Global League just do not agree with the operation of professional baseball in the majors or minors either.

For instance, we do not agree with the "draft" of citizens, we consider that the principal of compunction in matters that rightfully lie in the field of human volition is repugnant to the idea of individual worth and freedom of choice. The Global League does not want any player that is connected with Organized Baseball and mark this well, the Global League is not to be called an "outlaw" league without the danger of severe financial damages being claimed. And sued for by the damaged parties. We have very tender feelings.

GLOBAL BASEBALL LEAGUE   JACK CORBETT, Executive V-P

Corbett, former owner of the El Paso Texans of the old Class C Arizona-Texas League, had long been a rebel. On learning that he could not sign players remaining in Mexico following settlement of the Mexican League war, he sued Organized Baseball for $300,000 in damages for being denied access to them. His case and that of two other disgruntled individuals formed an unsuccessful challenge *(Toolson v. The New York Yankees)* to baseball's legal status which eventually reached the U.S. Supreme Court in November 1953.

The Japanese Connection

In early October 1968, Dilbeck held a press conference in Louisville. He announced there would be four clubs in Japan—Tokyo, Nagoya, Osaka and Yokahama—as well as in Louisville and Jersey City in the States. No Mexican or Latin American clubs were mentioned, although he claimed applications from Mexico City and Oakland had been rejected. Noticeably missing were the Milwaukee, Omaha and Dallas franchises; no explanation for their disappearance was provided.

What Dilbeck was promoting at this juncture, though, were geisha girls, who would provide fifth-inning entertainment for fans. Dilbeck also promised other Japanese flourishes. "We've got to capture the youngsters' imagination," he contended. "I feel the impact and color of football are lacking from baseball." In charge of enlisting Japanese talent for the circuit was George Yoshinaga, editor of the *Kashu-Mainichi*, a Los Angeles–based paper for Japanese-Americans.

Ironically, despite this influx of Japanese culture and talent, Dilbeck announced no games would be played in Japan in 1969. Finances were tight, and contests would be scheduled only in the States, in Louisville, Jersey City—or in Kansas City, Houston, Los Angeles, Chicago or San Francisco. In fact, they could occur anywhere a stadium with a 15,000-seat capacity could be found.

The season, Dilbeck stated, would begin in June and culminate in a "World Series" in Louisville sometime around Labor Day.

Big Names Begin to Appear

Attending this press conference was recently fired White Sox manager Eddie Stanky, who verified that he had been negotiating with Dilbeck over the possibility of his managing the Louisville franchise, tentatively called the "Sluggers."

"I have not made an agreement with Mr. Dilbeck," Stanky noted, "but I am not laughing at the Global League. Where I was in New York and saw Mr. Dilbeck was working with Commissioner [William D.] Eckert, I thought the whole thing sounded very good.

"The main thing I'm interested in is that the Global League has some association with Organized Ball, that there will be no raiding of players, that it will not be at Organized Ball's throat and vice versa."

While Stanky procrastinated, a major personality came on board. On October 22, 1968, 70-year-old former Commissioner A. B. "Happy" Chandler was named Global League commissioner at $4,000 per month. Even this brought no stability. In just a couple of weeks, the G.L. roster had now switched to include Louisville, Jersey City, an unnamed West Coast city and just three Japanese teams.

In early November the league signed its first player: Arnold Davis, a black 21-year-old right-handed pitcher from Evansville.

A big catch came aboard the following month—future Hall of Famer Johnny Mize, who was signed to manage one of the G.L. franchises. Mize pondered bringing in some other "names."

"We're thinking of Roy Campanella for the manager in Jersey City," said the "Big Cat." "He's been wanting to get back into baseball, and he would make a fine manager.

"I've been talking to Enos Slaughter, Allie Reynolds and Bob Turley. It could be a very interesting thing."

Eventually Mize would be named manager of the New Orleans franchise, and Slaughter would be designated as his coach—although there never would be a team in New Orleans.

Later that month retired National League umpire Jocko Conlan was signed to be supervisor of Global League arbiters. He would be replaced in February by retired American League ump Bill McKinley. "This provides an opportunity to stay in the game," said the 58-year-old McKinley, who indicated that he would not only supervise the G.L. staff but also ump a few games himself.

Dilbeck continued to court Eddie Stanky. "We had originally offered Stanky $250,000 for four years," bragged Dilbeck, "but that was just to manage the Louisville club. Now we want him to be vice president of the league, in charge of player procurement. His salary offer has gone up $75,000 a year for a four-year contract."

Stanky, who had two years left on his Chicago contract, professed little interest in Dilbeck's offer: "My only plans for the future are possibly to coach college baseball in Florida."

"No problem," responded an unfazed Dilbeck. "All Stanky has to do is straighten out that little problem with the Chicago club, and he'll be with us."

At about the same time Dilbeck was failing to communicate with several Organized Baseball figures.

First, he promised that a franchise was "95 percent set" for Tampa, Florida, and that former minor league player and manager Malcolm "Bunny" Mick, "an aide to Gov. Claude Kirk, has made his application for the franchise, and, as far as I'm concerned, he's got it."

Mick denied any such thing ("That's not saying I wouldn't like to, or don't plan to, but I sure haven't yet"). Mick contended that his only involvement with the Global League was that he had negotiated with Dilbeck for rental of a seven-diamond training complex in Daytona Beach, Florida. Mick's brother, Mitchell, was owner of the Tampa Tarpons of the Class A Florida State League.

News of a possible Tampa franchise infuriated Florida State League President George McDonald, who threatened to "fight [Dilbeck] in every way I can" if FSL territory were invaded.

Such hostility did not faze Dilbeck, who further announced "agreements" with the National Association, the Pacific Coast League, the International League and the Texas League. In return for not raiding their rosters, Dilbeck stated, "they've promised to let me use any ballpark I want to when the home team is away. With, of course, the permission of the park owner."

Every party to Dilbeck's "agreements" denied knowledge of them, some vehemently.

Nonetheless, there was some inkling of "co-operation" with Dilbeck. "Sure, we're going to let him use our parks—although we have not told him that," admitted one anonymous league president to the *Sporting News*. "But why not collect a little extra rent on nights when the park would otherwise be empty? We feel this whole idea has to be a horrendous flop. We're sure not afraid of any competition from him."

An undaunted Dilbeck, having failed to nail down solid franchises, now moved on to the new phase: player recruitment. On February 8, 1969, an ad appeared in the *Sporting News* announcing "TRYOUT CAMPS for the exciting new GLOBAL LEAGUE." They would be held in Long Beach, California; Bryan, Texas; Mobile, Alabama; Baton Rouge, Louisiana; and Jacksonville, Florida. The sessions were to be under the "personal supervision" of former major league pitcher and pitching coach Gordon Jones with the assistance of ex-hurler Stu Miller. Featured in the ad were photographs of Johnny Mize and Enos Slaughter.

Jones and Dilbeck gave out conflicting data regarding players under contract. "I haven't looked at all the contracts, but my men tell me that they've signed quite a few major leaguers," said Dilbeck, adding that Caracas had 12 players assigned to it and San Juan "some." He did not specify how these players had been obtained.

Jones, however, declared, "We have only nine players under contract now and our goal is 50 by March 1. . . . None [of the players the G.L. would sign] would be under contract to teams in Organized Ball."

The Global League Goes After Major Leaguers

Besides tryouts, the Global League also reportedly made sizable—but unsuccessful—offers to established stars. In March, Angels shortstop Jim Fregosi admitted to reporters that he had been offered $500,000 plus a 2.5 percent interest in the Global League to sign a four-year contract.

"It's not easy to reject security for life," reported Fregosi, "but I felt I was part of the Angels or rather that the Angels were part of me. The organization has been very good to me in every respect. It's been eight years and it's like a family."

Other stars supposedly received similar offers. Pitchers Jim Bunning, Don Drysdale, Juan Marichal, Joel Horlen and Jim Maloney; third basemen Brooks Robinson and Ron Santo; second baseman Bill Mazeroski; and outfielder Roberto Clemente were all targeted by Dilbeck.

"I'd say yes," said a player present at the players' session with G.L. representatives. "All of us but Marichal were at the meeting. I don't know about Juan. Drysdale was to be the recruiter to contact the players. There was some fantastic money talked about . . . and it's still there, we hope."

"And you could get the money any way you wanted," added another. "It was a lump sum or spread out over 'X' years."

"I'd definitely consider it if it came up again," admitted Bunning.

The basic offer was the same tendered to Fregosi. Supposedly in back of the whole deal—and thus of the Global League itself—was mysterious billionaire Howard Hughes and his planned Hughes Sports Network. The Philadelphia *Bulletin* reported that the Global League was "Hughes' new league" and theorized that Hughes would lure away enough stars to force a merger with the established leagues, much as the upstart American Football League had.

"Mr. Hughes has the resources," the *Bulletin* quoted Hughes Sports Network President Dick Bailey as saying. "All we need is the product. You'll hear from us."

When the story hit the streets—and was reprinted in the *Sporting News*—the Hughes Sports Network denied everything, branding the tale "ridiculous."

"The article is full of untruths," Bailey charged. "We have never discussed a proposal of any kind or entertained any ideas of working with the Global League."

He did admit to meeting with a group of unidentified big leaguers: "I was asked to see them and I consented. They asked me what I thought about the chances of the new league succeeding. I told them that it was a ridiculous scheme and was doomed to failure.

"They never got around to discussing television. I stopped them by telling them we had no interest in the league."

At about the same time, the Washington *Post* reported that offers *had* been made to the players in question but had come not from the Hughes group but from the Global League itself. It further stated that Dilbeck and Chandler had attempted to negotiate a $6,000,000 broadcast contract with HSN but were rejected.

It was yet another bizarre episode in the Global's League soon-to-be-concluded history.

The Season Begins—and Ends

The time had finally come for Dilbeck to put up or shut up. Behind the scenes, Dilbeck had assembled what passed for rosters and schedules. When the 1969 season began, six franchises were announced, "representing" Puerto Rico, two Japanese cities, the Dominican Republic, New York and Los Angeles. A year before, no games had been scheduled to be played in Japan by this supposed "Global" League; now none were to be played in the United States. Its scope of operations was restricted to backwaters in Central and South America.

There was some evidence that Dilbeck was hurting for funds. In April he attempted to sell the Louisville Colonels to Indianapolis investor Tom Redmond, owner of the Las Vegas Cowboys of the Continental Football League. The club was in financial straits even though it had drawn quite well in 1968 (243,987 fans, the highest figure in the circuit). Redmond and his Bankers Acceptance Corporation had been providing financing for the Global League. The International League, however, refused to let the deal go through.

The entire Global League scheme collapsed on May 22 when a Caracas hotel stopped extending credit for meals and threatened to evict the 88 Global League players quartered there unless their $12,000 bill was paid. Dilbeck, who had been in Caracas, had conveniently headed for Houston the week before.

"We've only been playing three weeks, we don't even have team nicknames and already we're in trouble," complained James Purcell, who was manager of the New York team. "My boys have to eat."

Expenses had been piling up for years but had really started accumulating once play began. The Japanese personnel Dilbeck signed had been brought over at a cost of $27,500. He had 125 players training at Daytona Beach. They weren't paid salaries for the training period but were provided with room and board and $15 per week miscellaneous expense money. Dilbeck hoped the cash flow would reverse itself once the season opened, but crowds were sparse.

"The Global League was the most-mixed-up affair I've ever seen," admitted Jack Corbett once the fiasco was over. "Dilbeck is quite a man and I really like him, but he had no setup and talked a good game.

"He was trying to get a couple of teams in Mexico City and I made a trip there for him. But I eventually discovered that all this wasn't for me and I got out. He still owes me about $1,500 in expense money and $7,500 in salary. Believe me, it was an Alice in Wonderland deal."

It was no wonder that few paid to see Dilbeck's rattletrap circuit. The playing talent was hardly impressive. "Terrible," said one ex-big leaguer regarding Global talent. "Most of the talent was Class A at best and some of it was worse. There were a few good players, but they were hardly pros when we had them."

"It is hard to describe the confusion that existed when we arrived in the Caribbean," explained G.L. manager Johnny Mize. "The men Dilbeck sent to Central America must have been on vacations. They didn't do much, if anything, for the league. They painted a great picture for Dilbeck and kept wiring him for more money. I think he deserved better than that, because he really put his heart in this thing."

Not everyone was so kind. "I was conned," complained Stu Miller, who abandoned the project almost upon joining it.

The first sign of trouble came when the Puerto Rican squad left for home after failing to be paid. Tokyo Dragons paychecks then bounced. So did checks to the Hotel El Conde, where the team was staying. A bill of $20,000 had been run up. The Dragons tried to leave the country but were evicted from the plane when it was discovered the check for the tickets also bounced. Then things really got bad. Players were forced to sell their personal belongings to survive. On July 4 a judge ordered these hapless players not to leave the country. They turned to the Japanese consul general for help and were given shelter—all 25 to just one room—and were allowed to take meals at the embassy for the next two months. Finally, money came in from the Global League's new owners to enable them to fly back to Indiana. Once there they endeavored to secure their back pay from Dilbeck, but as their visas were expiring they were forced to return home to Japan.

American-born players sought help from the U.S. Embassy, as not only the Hotel El Conde but four other Caracas hostelries had cut off meals to stranded G.L. personnel.

"One of the teams was calling us long-distance," recalls the Evansville *Courier*'s Tom Tuley, "because we were the only ones who would accept their collect calls."

Outfielder Ron Manders (a five-year veteran of the Indians farm system who was had only advanced to the Class A California League by 1967), was one of the players signed by Dilbeck. He complained he lost 20 pounds in Venezuela from lack of food. He further stated he was paid for only 3½ days and that whatever profits there were went to the Venezuelans. When he "escaped" from South America, he signed with Tampa of the Florida State League.

A similar experience greeted Tokyo Dragons catcher Masaji Ishizuka. After training for three weeks in Florida, his team embarked for Caracas, where it took seven of eleven contests against teams representing New York, Caracas and Los Angeles.

"We went down to Santo Domingo," recalled Enos Slaughter in July 1990, "never played a game. They say you should never go into Santo Domingo without a round-trip fare. Dilbeck sent us in on one-way tickets. They were having a revolution. The walls were covered with 'Yanqui Go Home!' We didn't go out of our hotel room for two weeks.

"Then we went down to Venezuela—paid our own air fares and hotel bills.

"Dilbeck finally came down. He had $55,000 in cash in a cardboard box. He gave me and Mize $1,500 [each] and some of the players $1,000.

"He had the guts to call us after we got back. The American players and the Japanese teams played around Indianapolis after we got out of Venezuela. I don't know if the [Japanese] ever got home....

"[Dilbeck] still owes me money. Mize was getting $25,000 to manage. I was getting $22,500. I actually was paid only about $3,000."

The Baptist Foundation of America Comes to the "Rescue"

Partway into this calamitous season, the Global League revealed it had a new owner: the Baptist Foundation of America.

In July 1969 Dilbeck announced that this organization had purchased the Global League along with a lake and 110 acres of western Kentucky lake property ("Reel-em-in Lake") for $3,860,000. The Kentucky holdings amounted to $1.1 million of the purchase price.

The BFA was a Los Angeles–based not-for-profit foundation with noble-sounding purposes. It was reputedly "born to assist worthy institutions in their struggles to meet the challenge of our times, born to do good for all men . . . a monument to faith in God and to freedom and courage of the human spirit." It was set to provide hospitals, retirement homes and youth programs for believers, and produced a youth-oriented television program in California.

Enos Slaughter (left), photographed with author David Pietrusza, was among the baseball people stung by Walter J. Dilbeck's Global League scheme.

The Foundation, which had first been seen in Evansville when it attempted to buy or lease the now-bankrupt McCurdy Hotel, was supposedly impressed by the Global League's training rules, which banned smoking and drinking and mandated a rigorous exercise program and a 10:30 bedtime. "Anything that promotes good clean minds and bodies," commented the BFA's president, the Rev. T. Sherron Jackson, "is all to the good for the country." Jackson also liked the "opportunity [that the league provided] for more young men to participate in baseball around the world."

He thought that baseball exerted a wholesome influence on its participants: "I can't imagine too many good ballplayers coming from Haight-Ashbury or off of some sections of Sunset Boulevard." That anyone would be interested in buying Dilbeck's shattered dream was odd, but as a front-page story in the July 1, 1970, *Wall Street Journal* revealed, that was only the tip of the iceberg.

The article, the result of a five-month staff investigation, revealed a bizarre pattern of BFA financial manipulations.

Moreover, *Journal* reporters were not the only ones probing the group. The California Attorney General's Office, the Securities and Exchange Commission, the Justice Department, the Post Office Department and local authorities were also taking a hard look at the Baptist Foundation of America.

Despite the fact that the BFA claimed assets of $20 million, little of its mission had been advanced. There were no retirement homes, no hospitals, only a tangled financial web.

Typical of its dealings was a plan to buy a California inn in exchange for notes backed by 52,739 acres of land in Cumberland County, Tennessee, valued at $1,054,000. The local assessor could not even find the parcel, which was odd since it would have covered one-seventh of the county.

Another asset was California mining property which the BFA carried on its books at a value of $7.5 million, a figure which did not jibe with its assessed valuation of $1,600. The mine's last producing year was 1966, when it yielded 13 tons of antimony—valued at $17,000.

Another deal involving BFA notes concerned Datacorp Service Corporation, a New Jersey–based firm controlled by one Seymour Pollack, who had already been convicted in a California loan scandal. Also involved with Datacorp was a reputed New York Mafia figure, Salvatore Badajamente.

Many of the BFA's questionable transactions involved a shadowy promoter named Nat Rosenberg, who already had a record of several arrests and at least one conviction for passing rubber checks. In 1969 both Rosenberg and the BFA were enjoined by a Baltimore federal court from further violating the securities law.

The *Wall Street Journal* grilled Jackson as to why he continued dealing with such a suspicious character as Rosenberg. "To tell you the truth," Jackson responded, "Rosenberg kept promising to convert to Christianity, so I stayed with him for a time hoping he would do it."

The Global League's sale had actually occurred on January 12, 1969, in East St. Louis, Illinois. Outwardly there was no change whatsoever. Dilbeck remained as Global League president. In fact, the entire transaction remained secret. Why it was not made public until July—after the circuit had basically collapsed—was never revealed.

All this did little to aid Dilbeck. In April 1969 his Rock Hill franchise in the Western Carolinas League was forfeited to the league and transferred to Statesville. The following month, his Louisville Colonels were locked out of their ballpark due to lack of a lease. Despite the fact the Colonels had led the International League in attendance and other less-popular franchises that were profitable, Louisville was reportedly $161,000 in debt. The I.L. declared the franchise forfeit and transferred it to William A. Gardner, nephew of Boston's Tom Yawkey. "The organization wasn't functioning," charged International League President George Sisler, Jr., "and by that I mean people working in the front office hadn't been paid for three months." In June 1969 the IRS began seizing the property of Dilbeck's Louisville Colonels Baseball Club, Inc. In July Dilbeck was back in the news, suing Gardner for use of the Colonels uniforms. Gardner retorted that he had paid Dilbeck's overdue dry cleaning bills to get the uniforms in the first place. Dilbeck did, however, retain his Columbus, Georgia, team in the Class AA Southern League.

Dilbeck was experiencing disasters on other fronts. The Global League was evicted from its Evansville offices in early 1970. And not surprisingly, Walter Dilbeck found there was no market whatsoever for the $3.8 million in BFA notes he now held. To remedy the situation he exchanged $3 million worth of them back to the BFA for 147,000 shares of Standard Computer & Pictures Corporation, reputedly valued at $10 each.

"We figured," explained Dilbeck, "that $1.5 million in letter stock is much better than $3 million in BFA notes, seeing as we couldn't get a dime on them."

The only problem was that the $10-per-share price tag was based on a promise to buy it back by Standard Computer's parent company, Computerealty, and both Standard Computer and Computerealty had been charged by the SEC in December 1969 with violations of registration and antifraud statutes.

Shortly after the *Wall Street Journal* article hit the streets, the Reverend Jackson was indicted by a San Joaquin (California) County Grand Jury in regard to a $1,500,000 deal with Avco Thrift Corporation. He was charged with grand theft, passing bad checks (including one for $50,000) and attempting to bribe a loan officer. Bail was set at $25,000 but later reduced to $5,000.

By December, Federal Judge A. Andrew Haak was enjoining Jackson from selling off any of the Foundation's assets and had named a receiver to oversee the BFA's tangled fiscal woes.

It was the end of one of the most bizarre episodes in baseball history, but it was not the end of Dilbeck.

The Continuing Saga of Walter J. Dilbeck

By 1975 Dilbeck was back in the national news again, this time as the business partner of disgraced former–Vice President Spiro T. Agnew.

Dilbeck had not known Agnew before his fall, but once Spiro had hit the skids he attracted Dilbeck's interest. "When Ted Agnew resigned from the vice presidency," Dilbeck's friend, producer John Beck, recalled, "Walter called me and said, 'You know, we ought to get Agnew into our business. He knows a lot of these right-wing bankers. He could be of some help getting us financing.'"

Dilbeck has dabbled in politics previously. He claimed to have donated $140,000 to California Governor Ronald Reagan's abortive 1968 presidential campaign and $200,000 to Hubert Humphrey's failed 1972 bid for the White House. Additionally, he had contributed $140,000 to Indiana Democratic Senator Vance Hartke. It was Dilbeck who introduced a land speculator named Walter T. Duncan to Hartke, who was serving as Humphrey's campaign manager. Duncan ended up giving $300,000 to Humphrey despite a myriad of financial woes.

Beck thought the Agnew idea a good one and approached comedian Milton Berle, reportedly a good friend of Agnew's. Berle arranged for Beck and Dilbeck to meet Agnew at a Palm Springs party thrown by Frank Sinatra for Jack Benny's 80th birthday.

Agnew joined forces with Dilbeck for a reputed four-year contract of $100,000 per annum, "plus one-third of the profits the first year, and half the profits of the other three." Soon the papers were filled with news of deals involving foreign investors and coal mines and 1,600-acre Kentucky resorts.

Dilbeck showed little interest in the ethical tangles that led to Agnew's disgrace. "What he did when he was in office—that's American politics," Dilbeck explained. "I believe the squealers should have gotten more than the guy they squealed on. After all, Agnew never went to trial. . . ."

There was even renewed talk of Dilbeck's film biography, still to be produced by John Beck and now called *OK, Private Dilbeck*. Doing the screenplay was Charles "Blackie" O'Neal, father of Ryan O'Neal. "I think Stuart Whitman or Burt Reynolds or Jeff Bridges or one of those actors is going to play me as a young man," mused Dilbeck.

Yet by February 1975, Agnew was severing his relationship with the former Global League owner. Agnew wrote Dilbeck that "it is virtually impossible for us to be successful because your desire for publicity has violated the confidentiality of many negotiations in progress and shocked our clients.

"In the beginning I thought the problem was your inexperience with news media. But now I must conclude that your exaggerations and outright misstatements of facts were a calculated scheme to promote your image at the expense of my integrity."

Agnew also alleged that Dilbeck was behind on his quarterly salary payments.

Dilbeck had formerly bragged of Agnew's ties to the Arab world, but he now charged that the former veep's "apparent preoccupation with Arab governments is distasteful and unsatisfactory because of my long-standing association with many Jewish people and interests in this country."

The next year Dilbeck hit bottom. The IRS charged him with filing false income tax statements from 1968 to 1972. His five-bedroom, 35-acre Henderson, Kentucky, home was sold at auction, but the liens were so high the sale fell through.

On December 1, 1976, in a plea bargain, Dilbeck pled guilty to filing false tax statements for 1969. He faced three years in prison and a $5,000 fine. In February 1977 the 58-year-old investor was sentenced in U.S. Federal Court to 60 days in the Vanderburgh County, Indiana, jail.

"It's a nice jail, a good jail," Dilbeck sanguinely informed reporters from his cell. "The inmates are friendly and everyone's treated me fairly. There's no problems."

Further, he alleged that he had no shortage of deals in the offing, that many prominent businessmen ("including one of the largest companies in this area") were approaching him while he was incarcerated.

"Every time you guys give me a headline and write a story about me," he chided the media, "it just helps me make money. Print that."

Asked if anyone had insulted him while he was behind bars, Dilbeck replied somewhat pathetically. "People never do that to my face. They always wait until my back is turned."

And what has since become of the Global League founder?

Epilogue

Walter Dilbeck remains in Evansville. "I don't want to use the word 'shady,'" says one observer of the local scene, "but he's very secretive." In the early 1980s he again proposed starting a new league, and by the end of the decade he was once more talking of a movie about his life – this time the subject would be his challenge to Organized Baseball.

Talk of new circuits has continued since the laughable experience of the 1969 Global League. In 1974 a Sean M. Downey, Jr., announced the launching of the World Baseball Association, with teams in Birmingham, Columbus, Jersey City, Memphis, Mexico City and Tampa–St. Petersburg.

That was simple enough, but then plans got increasingly complex. By January 1975 it was announced the league would feature 32 cities, including Taipei, Taiwan. Innovations included five designated hitters per club, plus a designated pinch runner and an orange baseball. Speed in all its many facets was encouraged. A steal of home after the sixth inning – you see that every day – would count for *two* runs. Intentional walks would be automatic. Only three balls would be needed to draw a walk.

It was different, and it never got off the ground.

In November 1984 a North American Baseball League was announced, with prospective franchises in Brooklyn, Buffalo, Denver, Indianapolis, Mexico City, Miami, New Orleans, Tampa, Vancouver and Washington.

In 1989 rumors were flowing freely concerning formation of yet another third major league, reportedly planning on seizing the opportunity of a lapsing Major League Players Association contract. Thought to be involved were prominent sports agent Richard Moss (whose clientele included Jack Morris and Fernando Valenzuela) and New York attorney David LeFevre, former minority owner in the Houston Astros. Hall of Famer Bob Gibson and management consultant Douglas Nelson were also rumored to be part of the organization.

"All the conditions are there to start a new league," commented former Players Association head Marvin Miller. "There's people with money and the interest to get into baseball. There's the availability of players, because in their stupidity to conspire against free agency, the owners cut back on the length of contracts. Now, most players are on one year contracts. And they could be

319

available if a strike is called next year. Lastly, there are meaningful TV rights as a prospect."

Eventually, the new league was named "The Baseball League," and in August 1989 the name of billionaire developer Donald Trump entered the scene. He was to have a team in northern New Jersey. Also thought to be involved was racetrack owner Edward DeBartolo, Sr., an unsuccessful one-time bidder for the White Sox, who would place a club either in San Jose or New Orleans. Meshulam Riklis, a friend of Trump and the husband of actress Pia Zadora (then–vice president of the Pacific Coast League's Portland Beavers), was rumored to be backing the Los Angeles franchise.

Other possible league cities were said to include Denver, Miami, Portland, Vancouver and Washington.

"I see it as a very viable league," Trump told the New York *Times.* "Otherwise I wouldn't do it. We'll have a long-term contract with a major television network or a number of major networks."

Franchises were to go for $5 million each, and it was hinted a 154-game schedule would begin in April 1990, featuring a three-tiered playoff system in September. Six of the eight teams would be eligible for the playoffs. All revenues except for ticket sales, concession rights and stadium advertising would be shared equally between franchises. In other words, there would be no disparity in local broadcasting contracts, as evidenced by George Steinbrenner's recent $500 million pact with MSG Cable.

The league predicted its progress in some detail, forecasting average per-team attendance at 800,000 in its first year of operations (1990) and 1.5 million per club by 1994. Losses were projected for the first two seasons, a break-even scenario for the third and profits in the third ($500,000 per club) and fourth ($4.5 million) years.

Player development would be totally centralized, and only prospects of "high-quality potential" would be signed. Talent would not be farmed out to traditional minor league clubs but would trained at one centralized location. The "Baseball League" contended this would cut such costs by 90 percent. In August 1989 rumors flew that the new circuit was actively going after Louisiana State University prospect Ben McDonald.

Also to be centralized were the front offices of all clubs. Savings of $2 million per team were projected. It appeared that the new circuit would be a rebirth of an old concept—syndicate baseball.

However, the scheme soon began to unravel. Organized Baseball made record deals with CBS and ESPN, and those options evaporated for "The Baseball League." Nonetheless, talks continued with NBC, ABC and various cable outlets. ABC admitted to not "discouraging" contact. HBO's Seth Abraham liked the idea of networks' bankrolling a new league and having a part of it, rather than contracting for broadcasting rights. "It's cheaper to own than to rent," he pithily observed.

Hurting the new circuit was the slow-motion expansion plan of the National League. Two new N.L. franchises would not be announced until summer 1991, and the most viable groups were more inclined to pursue a franchise in an established league, rather than to go after a possible will-o-the-wisp. "That new league is a mystery," said Buffalo multi-millionaire Bob Rich. "We want to be in the bigs."

News of the loop faded from the scene, although in May 1990, Dick Moss surfaced and revealed that Donald Trump was no longer involved and that Trump's money had been returned the preceding November ("That's good for the group. You know his history"). Moss claimed the circuit was still feasible, however, stating, "There is something going on in the organizational stage. Down the road, in a month or two, I expect an announcement."

In 1990 some thought an Oregon lumber baron named Bruce Engel was stockpiling players (at Erie in the NY–Penn League) for a "Baseball League" franchise in Portland. He had even secured the lease on Portland's Civic Stadium for the 1992 season.

To be continued . . . maybe.

Appendices

National Association, 1871–75

1871 standings

CLUB	MANAGER	G	W	L	PCT.
Philadelphia Athletics	Dick McBride	29	22	7	.759
Chicago White Stockings	Jimmy Wood	29	20	9	.690
Boston Red Stockings	Harry Wright	33	22	10	.688
Washington Olympics	Nick Young	33	16	15	.516
Troy Haymakers	Wm. Craver/Lip Pike	31	15	15	.500
New York Mutuals	Bob Ferguson	35	17	18	.486
Cleveland Forest City	Charlie Pabor	29	10	19	.345
Fort Wayne Kekiongas	H. Deane/Wm. Lennon	28	7	21	.250
Rockford Forest City	Scott Hastings	27	6	21	.222

1871 league leaders

AT-BATS – Ross Barnes, Boston, 172
RUNS – Barnes, 66
HITS – Levi Meyerle, Philadelphia, 65
BATTING AVERAGE – Meyerle, .492
WINS – Albert G. Spalding, Boston, and James Dickson "Dick" McBride, Philadelphia, 20
WON-LOST PCT. – McBride, .800
GAMES PITCHED – Reinders A. "Rynie" Wolters, New York, 32

1872 standings

CLUB	G	W	L	PCT.
Boston Red Stockings	48	39	8	.830
Philadelphia Athletics	47	30	14	.682
Baltimore Lord Baltimores	57	34	19	.642
New York Mutuals	56	34	20	.630
Troy Haymakers	25	15	10	.600
Cleveland Forest City	21	6	15	.286

CLUB	G	W	L	PCT.
Brooklyn Atlantics	35	8	27	.229
Washington Olympics	9	2	7	.222
Middletown Mansfields	24	5	19	.208
Brooklyn Eckfords	29	3	26	.103
Washington Nationals	11	0	11	.000

1873 standings

CLUB	G	W	L	PCT.
Boston Red Stockings	60	43	16	.729
Philadelphia White Stockings	53	36	17	.679
Baltimore Lord Baltimores	56	33	22	.600
Philadelphia Athletics	52	28	23	.549
New York Mutuals	53	29	24	.547
Brooklyn Atlantics	55	17	37	.315
Washington Nationals	39	8	31	.205
Elizabeth Resolutes	23	2	21	.087
Baltimore Marylands	5	0	5	.000

1874 standings

CLUB	G	W	L	PCT.
Boston Red Stockings	71	52	18	.743
New York Mutuals	65	42	23	.646
Philadelphia Athletics	55	33	23	.689
Philadelphia White Stockings	58	29	29	.500
Chicago White Stockings	59	28	31	.475
Brooklyn Atlantics	56	22	33	.400
Hartford Dark Blues	54	17	37	.315
Baltimore Lord Baltimores	47	9	38	.191

1875 standings

CLUB	G	W	L	PCT.
Boston Red Stockings	82	71	8	.899
Philadelphia Athletics	77	53	20	.726
Hartford Dark Blues	86	54	28	.659
St. Louis Brown Stockings	72	39	29	.574
Philadelphia White Stockings	70	37	31	.544
Chicago White Stockings	69	30	37	.448
New York Mutuals	71	30	38	.441
St. Louis Red Stockings	18	4	14	.222
New Haven Elm Citys	47	7	40	.149
Washington Nationals	27	4	23	.148
Philadelphia Centennials	14	2	12	.143
Keokuk Westerns	13	1	12	.077
Brooklyn Atlantics	44	2	42	.045

National League, 1876–80

1876 standings

CLUB	G	W	L	PCT.	GB
Chicago White Stockings	66	52	14	.788	–
St. Louis Brown Stockings	64	45	19	.703	6
Hartford Dark Blues	69	47	21	.691	6
Boston Red Stockings	70	39	31	.557	15
Louisville Grays	69	30	36	.455	22
New York Mutuals	57	21	35	.375	26
Philadelphia Athletics	60	14	45	.237	34½
Cincinnati Red Stockings	65	9	56	.138	42½

1876 league leaders

RUNS – Ross Barnes, Chicago, 126
HITS – Barnes, Chicago, 138
DOUBLES – Paul A. Hines, Chicago; Barnes, Chicago; Dick Higham, Hartford, 21
TRIPLES – Barnes, Chicago, 14
HOME RUNS – George Hall, Philadelphia, 5
TOTAL BASES – Barnes, Chicago, 190
RUNS BATTED IN – James "Deacon" White, Chicago, 60
BASES ON BALLS – Barnes, Chicago, 20
BATTING AVERAGE – Barnes, Chicago, .429
ON BASE PERCENTAGE – Barnes, Chicago, .462
SLUGGING AVERAGE – Barnes, Chicago, .590
WINS – Albert G. Spalding, Chicago, 47
WON-LOST PCT. – Spalding, Chicago, .797
GAMES PITCHED – James Devlin, Louisville, 68
COMPLETE GAMES – Devlin, Louisville, 66
SHUTOUTS – George Bradley, St. Louis, 16
SAVES – Jack Manning, Boston, 5
INNINGS PITCHED – Devlin, Louisville, 622
STRIKEOUTS – Devlin, Louisville, 122
ERA – Bradley, St. Louis, 1.23

1877 standings

CLUB	G	W	L	PCT.	GB
Boston Red Stockings	61	42	18	.700	–
Louisville Grays	61	35	25	.583	7
Hartford Dark Blues	60	31	27	.534	10
St. Louis Brown Stockings	60	28	32	.467	14
Chicago White Stockings	60	28	33	.441	15½
Cincinnati Red Stockings	58	15	42	.263	25½

1878 standings

CLUB	W	L	PCT.	GB
Boston Red Stockings	41	19	.683	–
Cincinnati Red Stockings	37	23	.617	4
Providence Grays	33	27	.550	8
Chicago White Stockings	30	30	.500	11
Indianapolis Blues	24	36	.400	17
Milwaukee Grays	15	45	.250	26

1879 standings

CLUB	W	L	PCT.	GB
Providence Grays	59	25	.702	–
Boston Red Stockings	54	30	.643	5
Buffalo Bisons	46	32	.590	10
Chicago White Stockings	46	33	.582	10½
Cincinnati Red Stockings	43	37	.538	14
Syracuse Stars	22	48	.314	30
Cleveland Blues	27	55	.329	31
Troy Trojans	19	56	.253	35½

1880 standings

CLUB	W	L	PCT.	GB
Chicago White Stockings	67	17	.798	–
Providence Grays	52	32	.619	15
Cleveland Blues	47	37	.560	20
Troy Trojans	41	42	.494	25½
Worcester Ruby Legs	40	43	.482	26½
Boston Red Stockings	40	44	.476	27
Buffalo Bisons	24	58	.293	42
Cincinnati Red Stockings	21	59	.263	44

International League, 1877–80

1877 standings

CLUB	W	L	T	PCT.
Tecumsehs	14	4	2	.778
Allegheny	13	6	0	.684
Rochester	10	8	0	.556
Manchester	9	10	0	.474
Buckeyes	9	11	2	.450
Maple Leafs	4	12	0	.250
Live Oaks	1	9	0	.100

1878 standings

CLUB	W	L
Buffalo	27	10
Syracuse	26	10
Utica	23	14
Manchester	20	18
Lowell	15	20
Springfield	9	25

(Clubs not finishing season)

Tecumseh	23	13
Rochester	20	15
Hornell	9	12
Worcester	9	26
Binghamton	6	6
Hartford	2	10
Allegheny	1	11

1879 standings

CLUB	W	L
Albany	27	13
Holyoke	23	16
Nationals	23	18
Worcester	19	23
New Bedford	12	30

(Clubs not finishing season)

Springfield	16	14
Manchester	7	8
Rochester	6	9
Utica	3	5

1880 standings

CLUB	W	L
Nationals	27	12
Rochester	9	15
Albany	7	16

American Association, 1882–91

1882 standings

CLUB	G	W	L	PCT.	GB
Cincinnati	80	55	25	.688	–
Philadelphia	75	41	34	.547	11½

CLUB	G	W	L	PCT.	GB
Louisville	80	42	38	.525	13
Pittsburgh	79	39	39	.500	15
St. Louis	80	37	43	.463	18
Baltimore	74	19	54	.260	32½

1882 league leaders

RUNS – Ed Swartwood, Pittsburgh, 86
HITS – Warren "Hick" Carpenter, Cincinnati, 120
DOUBLES – Swartwood, Pittsburgh; Michael R. Mansell, Pittsburgh, 18
TRIPLES – Mansell, Pittsburgh, 16
HOME RUNS – Oscar Walker, St. Louis, 7
TOTAL BASES – Swartwood, Pittsburgh, 162
BASES ON BALLS – Jack Gleason, St. Louis, 27
BATTING AVERAGE – Pete Browning, Louisville, .378
ON-BASE PERCENTAGE – Browning, Louisville, .430
SLUGGING AVERAGE – Browning, Louisville, .510
WINS – Will "Whoop-La" White, Cincinnati, 40
WON-LOST PCT. – White, Cincinnati, .769
GAMES PITCHED – Tony Mullane, Louisville, 55
COMPLETE GAMES – White, Cincinnati, 52
SHUTOUTS – White, Cincinnati, 8
SAVES – Edward L. Fusselback, St. Louis, 1
INNINGS PITCHED – White, Cincinnati, 480
STRIKEOUTS – Mullane, Louisville, 170
ERA – John F. "Denny" Driscoll, Pittsburgh, 1.21

1883 standings

CLUB	G	W	L	PCT.	GB
Philadelphia	98	66	32	.673	–
St. Louis	98	65	33	.663	1
Cincinnati	98	61	37	.622	5
New York	97	54	42	.563	11
Louisville	98	52	45	.536	13½
Columbus	97	32	65	.330	33½
Pittsburgh	98	31	67	.316	35
Baltimore	96	28	68	.292	37

1884 standings

CLUB	G	W	L	PCT.	GB
New York	112	75	32	.701	–
Columbus	110	69	39	.639	6½
Louisville	110	68	40	.630	7½
St. Louis	110	67	40	.626	8

CLUB	G	W	L	PCT.	GB
Cincinnati	112	68	41	.624	8
Baltimore	108	63	43	.594	11½
Philadelphia	108	61	46	.570	14
Toledo	110	46	58	.442	27½
Richmond	46	12	30	.286	30½
Brooklyn	109	40	64	.385	33½
Washington	63	12	51	.190	41
Pittsburgh	110	30	78	.278	45½
Indianapolis	110	29	78	.271	46

1885 standings

CLUB	G	W	L	PCT.	GB
St. Louis	112	79	33	.705	–
Cincinnati	112	63	49	.563	16
Pittsburgh	111	56	55	.505	22½
Philadelphia	113	55	57	.491	24
Brooklyn	112	53	59	.473	26
Louisville	112	53	59	.473	26
New York	108	44	64	.407	33
Baltimore	110	41	63	.376	36½

1886 standings

CLUB	G	W	L	PCT.	GB
St. Louis	139	93	46	.699	–
Pittsburgh	140	80	57	.584	12
Brooklyn	141	76	61	.555	16
Louisville	138	66	70	.485	25½
Cincinnati	141	65	73	.471	27½
Philadelphia	139	63	72	.467	28
New York	137	53	82	.393	38
Baltimore	139	48	83	.366	41

1887 standings

CLUB	G	W	L	PCT.	GB
St. Louis	138	95	40	.704	–
Cincinnati	136	81	54	.600	14
Baltimore	141	77	58	.570	18
Louisville	139	76	60	.559	19½
Philadelphia	137	64	69	.481	30
Brooklyn	138	60	74	.448	34½
New York	138	44	89	.331	50
Cleveland	133	39	92	.298	54

1888 standings

CLUB	G	W	L	PCT.	GB
St. Louis	137	92	43	.681	–
Brooklyn	143	88	52	.629	6½
Philadelphia	136	81	52	.609	10
Cincinnati	137	80	54	.597	11½
Baltimore	137	57	80	.416	36
Cleveland	135	50	82	.379	40½
Louisville	139	48	87	.356	44
Kansas City	132	43	89	.326	47½

1889 standings

CLUB	G	W	L	PCT.	GB
Brooklyn	140	93	44	.679	–
St. Louis	141	90	45	.667	2
Philadelphia	138	75	58	.564	16
Cincinnati	141	76	63	.547	18
Baltimore	139	70	65	.519	22
Columbus	140	60	78	.435	33½
Kansas City	139	55	82	.401	38
Louisville	140	27	111	.196	66½

1890 standings

CLUB	G	W	L	PCT.	GB
Louisville	136	88	44	.667	–
Columbus	140	79	55	.590	10
St. Louis	139	78	58	.574	12
Toledo	134	68	64	.515	20
Rochester	133	63	63	.500	22
Syracuse	128	55	72	.433	30½
Philadelphia	136	54	78	.409	34
Brooklyn/ Baltimore	134	41	92	.308	47½

1891 standings

CLUB	G	W	L	PCT.	GB
Boston	139	93	42	.689	–
St. Louis	139	85	51	.625	8½
Baltimore	139	71	64	.526	22
Philadelphia	143	73	66	.525	22
Cincinnati/ Milwaukee	138	64	72	.471	29½
Columbus	138	61	76	.445	33

CLUB	G	W	L	PCT.	GB
Louisville	139	54	83	.394	40
Washington	139	44	91	.326	49

Union Association, 1884

Players of note signed by the Union Association from National League and American Association ranks and their 1883 records:

PLAYER	1883 TEAM	GAMES	AVG.
Charles Briody	Cleveland (NL)	40	.234
Dick Burns	Detroit (NL)	37	.186
Sam Crane	New York (AA)	96	.235
Pat Burns – Not in majors – with Baltimore (AA) in 1884			
Lew Dickerson	Pittsburgh (AA)	85	.248
Fred Dunlap	Cleveland (NL)	93	.326
Ed Fusselback – In minors in 1883 – with St. Louis Browns, 1882			
Jack Glasscock	Cleveland (NL)	96	.287
Jack Gleason	St. L.–Louisville (AA)	93	.290
Emil Gross	Philadelphia (NL)	57	.307
Bill Harbidge	Philadelphia (NL)	73	.221
Levi Meyerle – Out of baseball since 1880			
Tom O'Brien	Baltimore (AA)	33	.268
Yank Robinson – In Northwest League – with Detroit in 1882			
George Shaffer	Buffalo (NL)	95	.292
Bill Taylor	Pittsburgh (AA)	83	.260

PITCHER	1883 TEAM	GAMES	W-L
Jersey Bakeley	Philadelphia (AA)	8	5-3
Tommy Bond – Out of baseball in 1883 with sore arm			
George Bradley	Philadelphia (AA)	26	16-7
Larry Corcoran	Chicago (NL)	56	34-20
Ed Cushman	Buffalo (NL)	7	3-3
Hugh Daily	Cleveland (NL)	45	23-19
Charlie Hodnett	St. Louis (AA)	4	2-2
Jim McCormick	Cleveland (NL)	43	28-12
Tony Mullane	St. Louis (AA)	53	35-15
Dupee Shaw	Detroit (NL)	26	10-15
Charles Sweeney	Providence (NL)	20	7-7
William Sweeney – With Athletics in 1882			

Standings

CLUB	MANAGER	W	L	PCT.	GB
St. Louis Maroons	Ted Sullivan	94	19	.832	–
	Fred C. Dunlap				

CLUB	MANAGER	W	L	PCT.	GB
Cincinnati Outlaw Reds	Dan O'Leary	69	36	.657	21
	Sam Crane				
Baltimore Unions	Bill Henderson	58	47	.552	32
Boston Unions	Tim Murnane	58	51	.532	34
Milwaukee Grays	Tom Loftus	8	4	.667	35½
St. Paul White Caps	A. M. Thompson	2	6	.250	39½
Chicago Unions/	Ed Hengle	41	50	.451	42
Pittsburgh Stogies	Joe Ellick				
	Joe Battin				
Altoona Unions	Edwin R. Curtis	6	19	.240	44
Wilmington Quicksteps	Joe Simmons	2	16	.111	44½
Washington Nationals	Mike Scanlon	47	65	.420	46½
Philadelphia Keystones	Fergy Malone	21	46	.313	50
Kansas City Unions	Harry Wheeler	16	63	.203	61
	Matt Porter				
	Ted Sullivan				

League leaders

RUNS — Fred Dunlap, St. Louis, 160
HITS — Dunlap, St. Louis, 185
DOUBLES — George Shaffer, St. Louis, 40
TRIPLES — Dick Burns, Cincinnati, 12
HOME RUNS — Dunlap, St. Louis, 13
TOTAL BASES — Dunlap, St. Louis, 279
BASES ON BALLS — Yank Robinson, Baltimore, 37
BATTING AVERAGE — Dunlap, St. Louis, .412
WINS — Bill Sweeney, Baltimore, 40
WON-LOST PCT. — Jim McCormick, Cincinnati, .875
GAMES PITCHED — Sweeney, Baltimore, 62
COMPLETE GAMES — Sweeney, Baltimore, 58
SHUTOUTS — McCormick, Cincinnati, 7
INNINGS PITCHED — Sweeney, Baltimore, 538
ERA — McCormick, Cincinnati, 1.54

Club-versus-club records (as given in
Spalding's Official Base Ball Guide **for 1885):**

	Alt.	Blt.	Bos.	C./P.	Cin.	Key.	Nat.	St.L.	K.C.	Wil.	Mil.	St.P.	WON
Altoona	—	1	1	0	0	1	3	0	0	0	0	0	6
Baltimore	3	—	10	6	3	10	12	1	10	1	0	0	56
Boston	1	6	—	4	5	8	12	8	8	4	2	0	58
Chi./Pitts.	0	6	8	—	6	3	4	1	12	0	0	0	40
Cincinnati	3	11	11	8	—	8	10	2	10	2	0	3	68
Keystone	3	2	3	5	0	—	4	0	4	0	0	0	21
National	1	4	4	8	6	8	—	3	8	4	1	0	47

	Alt.	Blt.	Bos.	C./P.	Cin.	Key.	Nat.	St.L.	K.C.	Wil.	Mil.	St.P.	WON
St. Louis	8	13	8	11	14	8	13	–	10	4	0	2	91
Kan. City	0	2	4	3	0	0	4	0	–	0	0	1	14
Wilmington	0	0	0	0	1	0	1	0	0	–	0	0	2
Milwaukee	0	3	2	0	0	0	3	0	0	0	–	0	8
St. Paul	0	0	0	0	0	0	0	1	1	0	0	–	2
LOST	19	48	51	45	35	46	66	16	63	15	3	6	413

Players' National League, 1890

Standing committees

Committee on Playing Rules—B. F. Hilt, Julian Hart, William Ewing, John M. Ward and N. Fred Pfeffer.

Schedule Committee (drawn by lot)—Brooklyn, Chicago, Cleveland, Buffalo and Philadelphia.

Committee on Ball—Hilt, Hart, Ewing, Ward and Pfeffer.

Law Committee—J. M. Vanderslice, Hart, Ward.

Printing and Supplies Committee—Albert L. Johnson, Moses Shire and G. E. Andrews.

Finance Committee—Johnson, Ward and John Addison.

Opening day lineups

PITTSBURGH	CHICAGO
Hanlon, cf	Latham, 3b
Visner, rf	Duffy, cf
Carroll, c	O'Neill, rf
Beckley, 1b	Comiskey, 1b
Fields, lf	Pfeffer, 2b
Kuehne, 3b	Farrell, rf
Corcoran, ss	Bastian, ss
Galvin, p	King, p

NEW YORK	PHILADELPHIA
Richardson, 2b	Griffin, lf
Gore, cf	Shindle, ss
Connor, 1b	Fogarty, cf
O'Rourke, lf	Wood, rf
Ewing, c	Pickett, 2b
Slattery, rf	Mulvey, 3b
Hatfield, ss	Farrar, 1b
Whitney, 3b	Buffinton, p
Keefe, p	Cross, c

BOSTON	BROOKLYN
Richardson, lf	Seery, lf
Stovey, rf	Bierbauer, 2b
Kelly, c	Andrews, cf
Nash, 3b	Ward, ss
Brouthers, 1b	Orr, 1b
Quinn, 2b	McGeachy, rf
Johnson, cf	Joyce, 3b
Irwin, ss	Daily, c
Kilroy, p	Van Haltren, p

BUFFALO	CLEVELAND
Irwin, 3b	Stricker, 2b
Hoy, cf	Delahanty, ss
Rowe, ss	Browning, lf
Wise, 2b	Twitchell, rf
Carney, 1b	Tebeau, 3b
Beecher, lf	Larkin, 1b
Rainey, rf	McAleer, cf
Mack, c	Gruber, p
Haddock, p	Brennan, c

Standings

CLUB	MANAGER	W	L	PCT.	GB
Boston Red Stockings	Mike "King" Kelly	81	48	.628	–
Brooklyn Wonders	John M. Ward	76	56	.576	6½
New York Giants	Wm. "Buck" Ewing	74	57	.565	8
Chicago Pirates	Charles Comiskey	75	62	.547	10
Philadelphia Quakers	James G. Fogarty	68	63	.519	14
	Chas. G. Buffinton				
Pittsburgh Burghers	Ned Hanlon	60	68	.469	20½
Cleveland Infants	Ted Larkin	55	75	.423	26½
	Oliver "Patsy" Tebeau				
Buffalo Bisons	Jack Rowe	36	96	.273	46½
	Jayson S. Faatz				
	Jack Rowe				

League leaders

RUNS—Hugh Duffy, Chicago, 161
HITS—Duffy, Chicago, 191
DOUBLES—Pete Browning, Cleveland, 40
TRIPLES—Joseph Visner, Pittsburgh; Jake Beckley, Pittsburgh, 22
HOME RUNS—Roger Connor, New York, 13
TOTAL BASES—William Shindle, Philadelphia, 281
RUNS BATTED IN—Arthur "Hardy" Richardson, Boston, 143

BASES ON BALLS—William "Scrappy" Joyce, Brooklyn, 123
BATTING AVERAGE—Browning, Cleveland, .373
ON-BASE PERCENTAGE—Dan Brouthers, Boston, .466
SLUGGING PERCENTAGE—Connor, New York, .541
STOLEN BASES—Harry Stovey, Boston, 97
WINS—Marcus "Fido" Baldwin, Chicago, 34
WON-LOST PCT.—William Daley, Boston, .720
GAMES PITCHED—Baldwin, Chicago, 59
COMPLETE GAMES—Baldwin, Chicago, 54
SHUTOUTS—Charles F. "Silver" King, Chicago, 4
SAVES—George Hemming, Cleveland-Brooklyn, 3; Henry F. O'Day, New York, 3
INNINGS PITCHED—Baldwin, Chicago, 501
STRIKEOUTS—Baldwin, Chicago, 211
ERA—King, Chicago, 2.69

Western League, 1894–99

1894 standings

	W	L	PCT.
Sioux City Huskers	74	50	.597
Toledo Swamp Angels	66	55	.545
Kansas City Blues	68	58	.540
Minneapolis Millers	63	61	.508
Grand Rapids Rustlers	61	65	.484
Indianapolis Hoosiers	60	66	.476
Detroit Creams	56	69	.448
Milwaukee Brewers	50	74	.403

1895 standings

	W	L	PCT.
Indianapolis Hoosiers	78	43	.645
St. Paul Saints	74	50	.597
Kansas City Blues	73	52	.584
Minneapolis Millers	64	59	.520
Detroits	59	66	.472
Milwaukee Brewers	57	67	.460
Toledo Swamp Angels/ Terre Haute Hottentots*	52	72	.419
Grand Rapids Gold Bugs	38	86	.306

*Franchise shifted in July

1896 standings

	W	L	PCT.
Minneapolis Millers	89	47	.654
Indianapolis Hoosiers	78	54	.591
Detroit Wolverines	80	59	.576
St. Paul Saints	74	63	.540
Kansas City Blues	69	66	.511
Milwaukee Brewers	62	78	.443
Columbus Senators	52	88	.371
Grand Rapids Yellow Jackets	45	94	.324

1897 standings

	W	L	PCT.
Indianapolis Hoosiers	98	37	.726
Columbus Senators	89	47	.654
St. Paul Saints	86	51	.628
Milwaukee Brewers	85	51	.625
Detroit Wolverines	70	66	.515
Minneapolis Millers	43	95	.312
Kansas City Blues	40	99	.288
Grand Rapids Bobs	35	100	.259

1898 standings

	W	L	PCT.
Kansas City Blues	89	51	.636
Indianapolis Hoosiers	84	50	.627
Milwaukee Brewers	82	57	.590
St. Paul Saints	81	58	.583
Columbus Senators	73	60	.549
Detroit Wolverines	50	89	.360
Minneapolis Millers	48	92	.343
Omaha Babes/	43	93	.316
St. Joseph Rough Riders*			

*Franchise shifted in July

1899 standings

	W	L	PCT.
Indianapolis Hoosiers	75	47	.615
Minneapolis Millers	76	50	.603
Detroit Tigers	64	60	.516
Columbus Senators/Grand Rapids	63	62	.504
St. Paul Saints	57	69	.452
Milwaukee Brewers	55	68	.447

	W	L	PCT.
Kansas City Blues	53	70	.431
Buffalo Bisons	53	70	.431

American League, 1900–02

1900 standings

CLUB	W	L	PCT.
Chicago White Stockings	82	53	.607
Milwaukee Brewers	79	58	.577
Indianapolis Hoosiers	71	64	.526
Detroit Tigers	71	67	.514
Kansas City Blues	69	70	.496
Cleveland Spiders	63	73	.463
Buffalo Bisons	61	78	.439
Minneapolis Millers	53	86	.381

1901 standings

CLUB	W	L	PCT.	GB
Chicago White Stockings	83	53	.610	–
Boston Puritans	79	57	.581	4
Detroit Tigers	74	61	.548	8½
Philadelphia Athletics	74	62	.544	9
Baltimore Orioles	68	65	.511	13½
Washington Senators	61	73	.455	21
Cleveland Bluebirds/Bronchos	55	82	.401	28½
Milwaukee Brewers	48	89	.350	35½

League leaders

RUNS–Napoleon "Larry" Lajoie, Philadelphia, 145
HITS–Lajoie, Philadelphia, 232
DOUBLES–Lajoie, Philadelphia, 48
TRIPLES–James T. Williams, Baltimore; William Keister, Baltimore, 21
HOME RUNS–Lajoie, Philadelphia, 14
TOTAL BASES–Lajoie, Philadelphia, 350
RUNS BATTED IN–Lajoie, Philadelphia, 125
BASES ON BALLS–William E. "Dummy" Hoy, Chicago, 86
BATTING AVERAGE–Lajoie, Philadelphia, .426
ON-BASE PERCENTAGE–Lajoie, Philadelphia, .451
SLUGGING PERCENTAGE–Lajoie, Philadelphia, .643

1901 league leaders

WINS–Denton True "Cy" Young, Boston, 33
WON-LOST PCT.–Clark C. Griffith, Chicago, .744

GAMES PITCHED – Joseph J. "Iron Man" McGinnity, Baltimore, 48
COMPLETE GAMES – McGinnity, Baltimore, 39
SHUTOUTS – Young, Boston; Griffith, Chicago, 5
SAVES – William L. "Chick" Hoffer, Cleveland, 3
INNINGS PITCHED – McGinnity, Baltimore, 382
STRIKEOUTS – Young, Boston, 158
ERA – Young, Boston, 1.63

1902 standings

CLUB	MANAGER	W	L	PCT.	GB
Philadelphia Athletics	C. Mack	83	53	.610	–
St. Louis Browns	J. McAleer	78	58	.574	5
Boston Puritans	J. Collins	77	60	.562	6½
Chicago White Stockings	C. Griffith	74	60	.552	8
Cleveland Bronchos/Naps	Wm. Armour	69	67	.507	14
Washington Senators	Tom Loftus	61	75	.449	22
Detroit Tigers	F. Dwyer	52	83	.385	30½
Baltimore Orioles	J. McGraw/ W. Robinson	50	88	.362	34

1902 league leaders

RUNS – Paul "Topsy" Hartsel, Philadelphia; David Fultz, Philadelphia, 109
HITS – Charles T. "Piano Legs" Hickman, Boston-Cleveland, 193
DOUBLES – Ed Delahanty, Washington; Harry Davis, Philadelphia, 43
TRIPLES – James T. Williams, Baltimore, 21
HOME RUNS – Ralph "Socks" Seybold, Philadelphia, 16
TOTAL BASES – Hickman, Boston-Cleveland, 289
RUNS BATTED IN – John F. "Buck" Freeman, Boston, 121
BASES ON BALLS – Hartsel, Philadelphia, 87
BATTING AVERAGE – Delahanty, Washington, .376
ON-BASE PERCENTAGE – Delahanty, Washington, .449
SLUGGING PERCENTAGE – Delahanty, Washington, .590
WINS – Denton True "Cy" Young, Boston, 32
WON-LOST PCT. – William H. "Strawberry Bill" Bernhard, Philadelphia-Cleveland, .783
GAMES PITCHED – Young, Boston, 45
COMPLETE GAMES – Young, Boston, 41
SHUTOUTS – Addie Joss, Cleveland, 5
SAVES – John J. "Red" Powell, St. Louis, 2
INNINGS PITCHED – Young, Boston, 385
STRIKEOUTS – George Edward "Rube" Waddell, Philadelphia, 210
ERA – Edward T. Siever, Detroit, 1.91

United States League, 1912–13

Rosters of the various franchises announced in May 1912

CLEVELAND—C. Hobert, 2b; Roy Kirby, ss; Jerry Freeman, 1b; Joe Delahanty, cf; Pelter, rf; George Ort, rf; William Britton, 3b; Green, c; Clay Blanke, p; Rube Walters, p; Compton, p; Bill Rafferty, p; Doc Moyer, p.

CINCINNATI—Fred Mollenkamp, 1b; James Burton, 3b; Lutz, 3b; Dieman, ss; Ollie Chapman, lf; Winter, cf; Fred Badel, rf; Dennis Hicks, c; Lee Dashner, p; Kline, p.

CHICAGO—Crowley, 3b; Schall, 2b; Johnson, ss; Walters, 1b; Stanley, lf; Louis Gertenrich, rf; Lynch, cf; Ed McDonough, c; Daly, c; Bugs Raymond, p; Hamilton, p; Parker, p; Tom McGuire, p; Gardner, p.

NEW YORK—Zollen, cf; Boney, 3b; Tierney, lf; Joe Wall, 1b; Griffin, rf; Hynes, 2b; Foyer, ss; Frank Bruggy, c; Walton, c; Peterson, p; Pfiester, p; Waco, p.

PITTSBURGH—Warren, 2b; Duff, ss; Callahan, cf; Brown, rf; Stine, lf; Miller, 1b; Fowler, 3b; Gove, c; Hughes, c; Piper, p; Johns, p; Curley, p; Hamilton, p; Deacon Phillippe, p.

READING—Dysert, rf; Frank Sheckard, cf; Charlie Malay, lf; Artie Brouthers, 2b; Sabrie, 1b; Himes, 1b; Heine Dieters, 3b; Manning, ss; Edgar Porte, c; Sam Fletcher, p; Guy Milliman, p; Jack Cronin, p; Jackson, p.

RICHMOND—Prout, 2b; Hoffman, 3b; O'Hare, lf; Socks Seybold, rf; Hexmus McFarland, cf; Bohannon, 1b; Bert Blue, c; Newnham, ss; Taylor, p; Grover, p.

WASHINGTON—Fallon, lf; Gus Dundon, 2b; Adler, 3b; George Browne, rf; Dowling, cf; Geary, ss; Farricker, 1b; Born, c; Tobin, c; Trainor, p; Bennett, p; Frank Owen, p; Big Jeff Pfeffer, p; Trenton, p.

1912 standings (source: Frank V. Phelps)

CLUB	MANAGER	W	L	T	PCT.	GB
Pittsburgh	Deacon Phillippe	27	17	0	.614	–
Richmond	Duke Landgraf	21	14	0	.600	1½
Chicago	Burt Keeley	17	15	1	.531	4
Cincinnati	Jimmy Barton	14	13	1	.519	4½
Reading	Leo Groom	12	12	2	.500	5
Washington	George Browne	6	8	1	.429	6
Cleveland	Jack O'Connor	8	13	0	.381	7½
New York	William Jordan	2	15	1	.118	11½

1912 team-versus-team records (source: Frank V. Phelps)

	Pgh.	Rch.	Chi.	Cin.	Rdg.	Wsh.	Clv.	N.Y.	WINS
Pittsburgh	x	2	7	2	5	–	8	3	27
Richmond	7	x	1	3	1	4	–	5	21
Chicago	4	3	x	5	2	–	3	–	17
Cincinnati	5	2	2	x	2	1	2	–	14
Reading	–	4	1	–	x	3	–	4	12

	Pgh.	Rch.	Chi.	Cin.	Rdg.	Wsh.	Clv.	N.Y.	WINS
Washington	–	2	–	–	1	x	–	3	6
Cleveland	1	–	4	3	–	–	x	–	8
New York	–	1	–	–	1	–	–	x	2
LOSSES	17	14	15	13	12	8	13	15	

1913 standings

CLUB	MANAGER	W	L	PCT.
Baltimore	Charles Babb	2	0	1.000
Brooklyn	Leo Groom	1	0	1.000
Philadelphia	Elmer Essler	1	1	.500
Reading	David Driscoll	1	1	.500
New York	?	1	1	.500
Newark	Jos. P. O'Neill	1	1	.500
Washington	?	0	1	.000
Lynchburg	Hugh McKinnon	0	2	.000

Federal League, 1913–15

1913 standings

CLUB	MANAGER	W	L	PCT.
Indianapolis	Bill Phillips	75	45	.625
Cleveland	Cy Young	63	54	.538
St. Louis	Jack O'Connor	59	59	.500
Chicago	Burt Keeley	57	62	.479
Cov./Kan. City	Sam Leever	53	65	.449
Pittsburgh	Deacon Phillippe	49	71	.408

1914 standings

CLUB	MANAGER	W	L	PCT.	GB
Indianapolis	Bill Phillips	88	65	.575	–
Chicago	Joe Tinker	87	67	.565	1½
Baltimore	Otto Knabe	84	70	.545	4½
Buffalo	Larry Schlafly	80	71	.530	7
Brooklyn	Bill Bradley	77	77	.500	11½
Kansas City	George Stovall	67	84	.444	20
Pittsburgh	Doc Gessler/Rebel Oakes	64	86	.427	22½
St. Louis	Mordecai Brown/Fielder Jones	62	89	.411	25

1914 league leaders

RUNS–Benjamin M. Kauff, Indianapolis, 120
HITS–Kauff, Indianapolis, 211

DOUBLES—Kauff, Indianapolis, 44
TRIPLES—Louis R. "Steve" Evans, Brooklyn; James J. Esmond, Indianapolis, 15
HOME RUNS—Edward H. "Dutch" Zwilling, Chicago; William J. "Duke" Kenworthy, Kansas City, 15
TOTAL BASES—Kauff, Indianapolis, 305
RUNS BATTED IN—Frank "Pot" LaPorte, Indianapolis, 107
BASES ON BALLS—Albert Wickland, Chicago, 81
BATTING AVERAGE—Kauff, Indianapolis, .370
ON-BASE PERCENTAGE—Kauff, Indianapolis, .440
SLUGGING AVERAGE—Evans, Brooklyn, .556
STOLEN BASES—Kauff, Indianapolis, 75
WINS—Claude Hendrix, Chicago, 29
WON-LOST PCT.—Russell W. Ford, Buffalo, .778
GAMES PITCHED—Hendrix, Chicago; Frederick P. "Cy" Falkenberg, Indianapolis, 49
COMPLETE GAMES—Hendrix, Chicago, 34
SHUTOUTS—Falkenberg, Indianapolis, 9
SAVES—Ford, Buffalo, 6
INNINGS PITCHED—Falkenberg, Indianapolis, 377
STRIKEOUTS—Falkenberg, Indianapolis, 236
ERA—Hendrix, Chicago, 1.69

1915 standings

CLUB	MANAGER	W	L	PCT.	GB
Chicago	Joe Tinker	86	66	.566	–
St. Louis	Fielder Jones	87	67	.565	–
Pittsburgh	Rebel Oakes	86	67	.562	½
Kansas City	George Stovall	81	72	.529	5½
Newark	Bill Phillips/Bill McKechnie	80	72	.526	6
Buffalo	L. Schlafly/W. Blair/H. Lord	74	78	.487	12
Brooklyn	Lee Magee/John Ganzel	70	82	.461	16
Baltimore	Otto Knabe	47	107	.305	40

1915 league leaders

RUNS—William B. "Babe" Borton, St. Louis, 97
HITS—John T. "Jack" Tobin, St. Louis, 184
DOUBLES—Louis R. "Steve" Evans, Brooklyn-Baltimore, 34
TRIPLES—Leslie Mann, Chicago, 19
HOME RUNS—Harold H. Chase, Buffalo, 17
TOTAL BASES—Edward J. Konetchy, Pittsburgh, 278
RUNS BATTED IN—Edward H. "Dutch" Zwilling, Chicago, 94
BASES ON BALLS—Borton, St. Louis, 92
BATTING AVERAGE—Benjamin M. Kauff, Brooklyn, .342
ON-BASE PERCENTAGE—Kauff, Brooklyn, .440
SLUGGING AVERAGE—Kauff, Brooklyn, .509

STOLEN BASES – Kauff, Brooklyn, 55
WINS – George "Slats" McConnell, Chicago, 25
WON-LOST PCT. – McConnell, Chicago, .714
GAMES PITCHED – David W. Davenport, St. Louis, 55
COMPLETE GAMES – Davenport, St. Louis, 30
SHUTOUTS – Davenport, St. Louis, 10
SAVES – Hugh C. Bedient, Buffalo, 10
INNINGS PITCHED – Davenport, St. Louis, 393
STRIKEOUTS – Davenport, St. Louis, 229
ERA – E. Victor Moseley, Newark, 1.91

Mexican League, 1946

Standings

CLUB	NICKNAME	W	L	PCT.	GB
Tampico	Alijadores	56	41	.577	–
Mexico City	Reds	55	42	.567	1
Puebla	Angeles	52	46	.531	4½
Torreon	Union Laguna	50	47	.515	6
Monterrey	Industriales	48	49	.495	8
Nuevo Laredo	Tecolotes	48	50	.490	8½
Vera Cruz	Blues	41	57	.418	15½

League leaders

HITS – Napoleon Reyes, Puebla, 140
DOUBLES – Roberto Ortiz, Mexico City, 28
TRIPLES – George Hausmann, Torreon, 15
HOME RUNS – Ortiz, Mexico City, 25
RUNS BATTED IN – Ortiz, Mexico City, 108
STOLEN BASES – Agustin Bejerano, Nuevo Laredo, 47
BATTING AVERAGE – Claro Duany, Monterrey, .375
SLUGGING AVERAGE – Ortiz, Mexico City, .657
WINS – Agapito Mayor, Nuevo Laredo; Sal Maglie, Puebla, 20
WON-LOST PCT. – Martin Dihigo, Torreon, .733
STRIKEOUTS – Booker McDaniels, San Luis Potosi, 171
ERA – Max Lanier, Vera Cruz, 1.94

Bibliography

Periodicals

The Albany *Daily Evening Times*
The Buffalo *Evening News*
The Chicago *Daily Tribune*
The Evansville *Courier*
The Evansville *Press*
The New York *Clipper*
The New York *Times*
Sporting Life
The Sporting News
USA Today

Books

Alexander, Charles C. *John McGraw*. Viking, New York, 1988.
Allen, Lee. *Cooperstown Corner: Columns from the Sporting News*. Society for American Baseball Research, Cleveland, 1990.
_____. *The National League Story*. Hill and Wang, New York, 1961.
_____. *100 Years of Baseball*. Bartholomew House, New York, 1950.
Appel, Martin, and Burt Goldblatt. *Baseball's Best*. McGraw-Hill, New York, 1980.
Axelson, G. W. *"Commy."* Reilly & Lee, Chicago, 1919.
Bartlett, Arthur. *Baseball and Mr. Spalding*. Farrar, Straus and Young, New York, 1951.
A Baseball Century: The First 100 Years of the National League. Macmillan, New York, 1976.
Bavasi, Buzzie, with John Strege. *Off the Record*. Contemporary Books, Chicago, 1987.
Béisbol Liga Mexicana. *Quien es Quien en El Béisbol Liga Mexicana 1989*. Mexico D.F., Mexico, 1989.
Benson, Michael D. *Ballparks of North America*. McFarland, Jefferson, N.C., 1989.
Brashler, William. *Josh Gibson: A Life in the Negro Leagues*. Harper & Row, New York, 1978.
Breslin, Jimmy. *Can't Anybody Here Play This Game?* Viking, New York, 1963.
Campanella, Roy. *It's Good to Be Alive*. Little, Brown, Boston, 1959.

343

Bibliography

Chandler, Albert B. "Happy," with Vance Trimble. *Heroes, Plain Folks, and Skunks.* Bonus Books, Chicago, 1989.

Church, Seymour R. *Baseball: The History, Statistics and Romance of the American National Game.* The Pyne Press, Princeton, N.J., 1974 (reprint).

Creamer, Robert W. *Babe: The Legend Comes to Life.* Simon & Schuster, New York, 1974.

Dellinger, H. L. *The Kansas City Unions: A History of Kansas City's First Major League Team.* Two Rivers Press, Kansas City, Mo., 1977.

Dickey, Glenn. *The History of American League Baseball.* Stein and Day, New York, 1980.

_____. *The History of National League Baseball.* Stein and Day, New York, 1979.

Durso, Joseph. *The Days of Mr. McGraw.* Prentice-Hall, Englewood Cliffs, N.J., 1969.

Eckhouse, Morris (ed.). *Baseball in Cleveland.* Society for American Baseball Research, Cleveland, 1990.

Fitzgerald, Ed (ed.). *The American League.* Grosset & Dunlap, New York, 1955.

Frommer, Harvey. *Primitive Baseball.* Atheneum, New York, 1988.

Gorman, Tom, with Jerome Holtzman. *Three and Two!* Charles Scribners' Sons, New York, 1979.

Graham, Frank. *McGraw of the Giants.* G. P. Putnam's Sons, New York, 1944.

_____. *The New York Giants.* G. P. Putnam's Sons, New York, 1952.

_____. *The New York Yankees.* G. P. Putnam's Sons, New York, 1943.

Hershberger, Chuck. *Sports Hall of Oblivion.* Self-published, Pleasant Ridge, Mich., 1985.

Holway, John B. *Blackball Stars.* Meckler, Westport, Conn., 1988.

_____. *Voices from the Great Black Baseball Leagues.* Dodd, Mead, New York, 1975.

Honig, Donald. *Baseball: When the Grass Was Real.* Coward, McCann, Geoghegan, New York, 1975.

James, Bill. *The Baseball Book 1990.* Villard, New York, 1990.

_____. *The Bill James Historical Baseball Abstract.* Villard, New York, 1986.

Kaese, Harold. *The Boston Braves.* G. P. Putnam's Sons, New York, 1948.

Kahn, James M. *The Umpire Story.* G. P. Putnam's Sons, New York, 1953.

Leitner, Irving A. *Baseball: Diamond in the Rough.* Criterion, New York, 1972.

Levine, Peter. *A. G. Spalding and the Rise of Baseball.* Oxford University Press, New York, 1985.

Lewis, Franklin. *The Cleveland Indians.* G. P. Putnam's Sons, New York, 1949.

Lieb, Fred. *The Baseball Story.* G. P. Putnam's Sons, New York, 1950.

_____. *The Boston Red Sox.* G. P. Putnam's Sons, New York, 1947.

_____. *Connie Mack: The Grand Old Man of Baseball.* G. P. Putnam's Sons, New York, 1945.

_____. *The Detroit Tigers.* G. P. Putnam's Sons, New York, 1945.

_____. *The St. Louis Cardinals.* G. P. Putnam's Sons, New York, 1945.

Lowenfish, Lee, and Tony Lupien. *The Imperfect Diamond.* Stein and Day, New York, 1980.

Lowry, Phil (ed.). *Green Cathedrals.* Society for American Baseball Research, Cooperstown, N.Y., 1986.

McGraw, Blanche, with Arthur Mann. *The Real McGraw*. David McKay, New York, 1953.

Mack, Connie. *My 66 Years in the Big Leagues*. John C. Winston, Philadelphia, 1950.

Moreland, George L. *Balldom*. Balldom, New York, 1914.

Morse, Jacob. *Sphere and Ash: History of Baseball*. J. F. Spofford, Boston, 1888 (Reprinted by Camden House, Columbia, S.C., 1984).

Names, Larry D. *Bury My Heart at Wrigley Field: The History of the Chicago Cubs: When the Cubs Were the White Sox*. Sportsbook Publishing, Neshkoro, Wisc., 1990.

National League. *Seventy-Fifth Anniversary of the National League*. Privately Printed, New York, 1951.

Okkonen, Marc. *The Federal League of 1914–15*. Society for American Baseball Research, Garrett Park, Md., 1989.

Orem, Preston D. *Baseball 1845–1881*. Self-published, Altadena, Calif., 1961.

_____. *Baseball 1882*. Self-published, Altadena, Calif., 1966.

_____. *Baseball 1884*. Self-published, Altadena, Calif., 1967.

Overfield, Joseph M. *100 Seasons of Buffalo Baseball*. Partners Press, Kenmore, N.Y., 1985.

Peterson, Robert. *Only the Ball Was White*. McGraw-Hill, New York, 1970.

Pietrusza, David. *Baseball's Canadian-American League: A History of Its Inception, Franchises, Participants, Locales, Statistics, Demise and Legacy, 1936–1951*. McFarland, Jefferson, N.C., 1990.

Polner, Murray. *Branch Rickey*. Atheneum, New York, 1982.

Puff, Richard (ed.). *The Empire State of Baseball*. Society for American Baseball Research, Garrett Park, Md., 1989.

Reddick, David B., and Kim M. Rogers. *The Magic of Indians' Baseball 1887–1987*. Indians, Indianapolis, 1988.

Reiss, Steven A. *Touching Base: Professional Baseball and American Culture in the Progressive Era*. Greenwood Press, Westport, Conn., 1980.

Rice, Damon. *Seasons Past*. Praeger, New York, 1976.

Richter, Francis. *A Brief History of Baseball*. Philadelphia, Sporting Life, 1909.

Rogosin, Donn. *Invisible Men: Life in Baseball's Negro Leagues*. Atheneum, New York, 1983.

Schacht, Al. *Clowning Through Baseball*. A. S. Barnes, New York, 1941.

_____. *My Own Particular Screwball*. Doubleday, Garden City, 1955.

Seymour, Harold. *Baseball: The Early Years*. Oxford University Press, New York, 1960.

_____. *Baseball: The Golden Years*. Oxford University Press, New York, 1971.

_____. *Baseball: The People's Game*. Oxford University Press, New York, 1990.

Smith, Ken. *Baseball's Hall of Fame*. Grosset and Dunlap, New York, 1962.

Smith, Robert. *Baseball*. Simon & Schuster, New York, 1970.

_____. *Illustrated History of Baseball*. Grosset and Dunlap, New York, 1973.

Spink, Albert H. *The National Sport*. National Game, New York, 1910.

Spink, J. G. Taylor. *Judge Landis and Twenty-Five Years of Baseball*. Thomas Y. Crowell, New York, 1947.

Thorn, John (ed.). *Days of Greatness: Providence Baseball 1875–1885*. Society for American Baseball Research, Cooperstown, N.Y., 1984.

_____ (ed.). *The National Pastime*. Warner Books, New York, 1987.

_____, and Pete Palmer (eds.). *Total Baseball.* Warner Books, New York, 1989.

Tiemann, Robert, and Mark Rucker (eds.). *Nineteenth Century Stars.* Society for American Baseball Research, Kansas City, Mo., 1989.

Vecsey, George. *Joy in Mudville.* McCall, New York, 1970.

Voigt, David Quentin. *America Through Baseball.* Nelson-Hall, Chicago, 1976.

_____. *American Baseball: From Gentleman's Sport to the Commissioner System.* University of Oklahoma, Norman, Okla., 1966.

_____. *American Baseball: From the Commissioners to Continental Expansion.* University of Oklahoma, Norman, Okla., 1970.

_____. *American Baseball: From Postwar Expansion to the Electronic Age.* Penn State, University Park, Pa., 1983.

Williams, Ted. *My Turn at Bat.* Simon and Schuster, New York, 1969.

Wright, Craig R., and Tom House. *The Diamond Appraised.* Simon & Schuster, New York, 1989.

Guides

Beadle's Dime Base-Ball Player
DeWitt's Base Ball Guide
Reach Official Base Ball Guide
Spalding's Official Base Ball Guide
Spink (Sporting News) Official Baseball Guide

Magazine Articles

Brace, George. "3 Major Leagues?: A Players' Strike Once Made It a Reality." *Oldtyme Baseball News,* Winter 1990, p. 4.

Coen, Ed. "Early Big Time Teams Left Milwaukee Bitter." *Baseball Research Journal,* 1985, pp. 10–12.

Drebinger, John. "The Mexican War Ends." *Baseball Magazine,* August 1949, pp. 291–293.

Egenriether, Richard. "Chris Von der Ahe: Baseball's Pioneering Huckster." *Baseball Research Journal,* 1989, pp. 27–31.

Johnston, W. Lloyd. "1877 Duel Put Syracuse on the Map." *Baseball Research Journal,* 1984, p. 44.

Johnson, Walter. "Why I Signed with the Federals." *Baseball Magazine,* April 1915, pp. 53–62.

Kush, Raymond D. "The Building of Wrigley Field." *Baseball Research Journal,* 1981, pp. 10–15.

Lane, F. C. "Is There Room for a New League?" *Baseball Magazine,* November 1914, pp. 43–52.

Overfield, Joseph M. "Buffalo and the Baseball Revolt." *Niagara Frontier,* Autumn 1956, pp. 74–80.

_____. "Minor League Team in New York." *Baseball Digest,* February 1958, pp. 41–44.

_____. "Professional Baseball in Buffalo—How It Began." *Niagara Frontier*, Spring 1954, pp. 29–35.

Rothe, Emil H. "Was the Federal League a Major League?" *Baseball Research Journal*, 1981, pp. 1–9.

Shearer, Lloyd. "Spiro Agnew—He's Becoming a Millionaire in Real Estate." *Parade*, January 19, 1973, pp. 4–5.

Simons, Herb. "CONTINENTAL—or just plain CON?" *Baseball Digest*, October-November 1959, pp. 67–70.

_____. "The Continental League—A Four Month Pipe Dream!" *Baseball Digest*, October-November 1959, pp. 71–74.

Terrell, Roy. "'The Damnedest Mess Baseball Has Ever Seen.'" *Sports Illustrated*, December 19, 1960, pp. 16–19.

_____. "3rd League Cities Pin Hopes on This Man." *Sports Illustrated*, July 20, 1959, pp. 30–32.

Thornley, Strew. "The St. Paul Unions: Minnesota's First Fling in the Majors." *Baseball Research Journal*, 1985, pp. 71–75.

Topp, Richard. "Manager Merry Go Round: The Saga of Chris Von der Ahe." *Oldtyme Baseball News*, Winter 1990, p. 15.

Wagner, Bill. "The League That Never Was." *Baseball Research Journal*, Number 16, pp. 18–21.

Unpublished Article

Kavanagh, Jack. "In the Federal League's Shadow."

Index

349

Houston Colt .45's (National League) 299
Houston Sports Association 284
Howe, George W. 87
Howell, Harry 163
Howsam, Bob 295
Hoy, William E. "Dummy" 113, 167, 334, 337
Hughes (player) 339
Hughes, Howard 310
Hughes, Jim 134
Hughes, Sammy T. 261
Hughes Sports Network 310, 311
Hulbert, William Ambrose ix, xiii, 23–26, 27, 28, 30, 31, 37–39, 43, 50, 52, 60, 63, 64, 66, 72–74, 171
Hulen, Judge Ruben M. 266
Hulswitt, Rudy 182
Humphrey, Hubert H. 316, 317
Hunter, Bob 306
Hurley, Richard 2
Hussey, Amos 197, 201
Hutchinson, "Wild Bill" 115
Hynecke, Rudolph 175
Hynes (player) 203, 339

I

Indiana State League 119
Indianapolis (Columbian League) 209
Indianapolis (Continental League) 289
Indianapolis (Continental League 1921) 254–256
Indianapolis (Global League) 303–304
Indianapolis (League Alliance) 50
Indianapolis (North American Baseball League) 319
Indianapolis (Players' League) 107
Indianapolis Blues (American Association) 84, 92

Indianapolis Blues (National League) 40, 326
Indianapolis Club 37, 47
Indianapolis Hoosiers (American League) 150, 155, 337
Indianapolis Hoosiers (Federal League) 212, 214, 221, 226, 227, 240–242, 254, 340, 341
Indianapolis Hoosiers (National League) 54, 100, 103, 112, 117
Indianapolis Hoosiers (Western League) 145, 148, 217, 335, 336
Indianapolis Indians (American Association) 84, 87, 92, 329
Indianapolis Indians (American Association– minors) 217, 243, 254
Indianapolis Sports Commission 303
Interborough Rapid Transit 168, 176
Internal Revenue Service 317
International Association 43, 47–61, 67, 326, 327
International League 119, 191, 282, 286, 297, 298, 300, 306, 309, 311, 315
Inter-State Association 80
Interstate League 119
Ireland 16
Iron & Oil Association 81
Irvington club 4
Irwin, Arthur A. "Doc" 113, 123, 156, 334
Irwin, John 137, 334
Isbell, Frank 146, 167
Ishizuka, Masagi 313
Ivanhoes (semipros) 280
Irvin, Monte 259–261
Irvington Club 4

J

J. G. Sohn & Co. 67
Jacklitsch, Fred 229, 230

Jackson (player) 339
Jackson, James "Projector" 81
Jackson, Rev. T. Sherron 313, 315, 316
Jacobs, Charles 292, 299
Jacobs, Louis 292, 299
Jacobs, Marvin 292, 299
Jacobson, Merwin "Jake" 238
James, Bill 21
James Everhard's Celebrated Lager Beer 111
Janesville (League Alliance) 50
Janis, Robert 266
Janney, Stuart S. 250
Jeffries, Jim 184
Jennings, Hughie 134, 140, 162, 185, 245
Jersey City (Global League) 305, 307, 308
Jersey City (International Association) 59
Jersey City (World Baseball Association) 319
Jersey City–Newark (Continental League) 288
Johns (player) 339
Johns Hopkins University 152
Johnson (player) 334
Johnson (player) 339
Johnson, Albert L. 105, 109, 121–125, 127, 128, 130, 333
Johnson, Andrew 12
Johnson, Arnold 289
Johnson, Byron Bancroft "Ban" ix, xiii, 132, 144–153, 155–157, 159–161, 163, 167, 170, 174–183, 186, 198, 199, 200, 204, 205, 225, 243, 248, 279
Johnson, "Chief" 221, 226, 229, 231
Johnson, Dave xi
Johnson, Sen. Edwin Carl 282, 285–288
Johnson, Ernie 200
Johnson, Frederick A. 276, 277
Johnson, Jack 184

364 Index

Vila, Joe 176, 177
Virginia League 201, 206
Visner, Joseph P. 333
Voigt, David Quentin 120
Voiselle, Bill 263
Voltz, William H. 99
Von der Ahe, Chris 63,
 65–70, 80, 81, 97, 111,
 112, 122, 127, 131, 135,
 136, 221
Vonderhorst, Harry 65,
 67, 86, 122, 132, 134

W

Waco (player) 339
Waddell, Rube 146, 174,
 338
Wainwright Brewing Co.
 82
Wagner, Bill 347
Wagner, Honus 174, 187,
 189
Wagner, J. Earl 109, 124,
 125, 128
Wagner, Johanna 116
Wagner, Robert 303–305
Wagner, Mayor Robert F.
 279, 280
Wagner brothers 118, 121,
 123
Wainwright, Ellis 82
Waite, L. C. 48
Waitt, Charles C. 65
Waldorf-Astoria (NYC) 248
Walker, Don 303
Walker, Fred "Dixie" 265
Walker, Fred "Mysterious"
 226
Walker, G. Herbert 283
Walker, Oscar 328
Walker, William 217, 239
Wall, Joe "Gummy" 198,
 200, 202–204, 339
Wall Street Journal 314–
 316
Wallace, "Bobby" 134,
 157, 165, 174
Wallace, Judge William P.
 116
Walsh (player) 229, 230
Walsh, David xi
Walsh, Jimmy 233

Walters (player) 339
Walters, Rube 339
Walton (player) 339
Wakefield, Dick 198
Wakefield, Howard 198
War Memorial Stadium
 (Buffalo) 292
Ward, George 219, 221–
 223, 234–236, 239,
 242, 244, 247, 248
Ward, John Montgomery
 xiv, 55, 56, 99, 100,
 102–105, 107, 109, 111–
 113, 116, 121–124, 173,
 182, 221, 239, 333,
 334
Ward, Robert S. 219,
 221–223, 234–236,
 239, 242, 244, 247,
 248
Ward, William S. 236
Waring (player) 212
Warner (player) 60
Warner Bros. 304
Warren, William 303,
 339
Warwick Hotel (NYC) 289
Washington (American As-
 sociation 1894) 129
Washington (Daniel
 Fletcher's League) 190
Washington (Eastern
 Championship Associa-
 tion) 62
Washington (Federal
 League) 212, 221
Washington (North Ameri-
 can Baseball League)
 319
Washington (Player's
 League) 107
Washington (United States
 League) 197, 198, 200–
 202, 205, 339, 340
Washington Nationals (In-
 ternational Association)
 2, 4, 12, 21, 327
Washington Nationals (Na-
 tional Association) 7,
 323, 324
Washington Nationals (Na-
 tional Baseball Associa-
 tion) 56, 58, 59, 60, 62
Washington Nationals

(Union Association) 82,
 83, 89, 95, 96, 332,
 333
Washington Olympics (Na-
 tional Association) 4, 6,
 7, 10, 12, 21, 324
Washington Park (Brook-
 lyn) 219, 224, 225,
 248, 255, 256
Washington *Post* 152,
 234, 311
Washington Redskins
 (NFL) 280
Washington Senators
 (American Association)
 84, 87, 128, 134, 329,
 331
Washington Senators
 (American League) 130,
 151, 153, 161, 167, 168,
 175, 178, 180, 198,
 200, 227, 234, 238,
 240, 247, 264, 285,
 290, 299, 306, 338
Washington Senators (Na-
 tional League) 100, 112,
 115, 128, 148, 154
Waterman, Fred 2
Watkins, Billy 150, 217
Watkins, Harvey 169
Weddell House (Cleveland)
 109
Weeghman, Charles 216,
 217, 220, 221, 223,
 225, 233, 234, 239,
 244, 248, 250, 251
Weeghman Park (Chicago)
 223, 231, 248
Weiss, George M. 287,
 290
Welch, "Smiling Mickey"
 99
Wells, John R. 303
Wells, Willie 259, 261
Welles, Della 69
Werden, Perry 96
West Side Park (Chicago)
 250
Western Association 136,
 166
Western Carolinas League
 293, 306, 315
Western Federal League
 212